GOVERNMENTS UNDER STRESS

COLIN CAMPBELL

Governments under stress

Political executives
and key bureaucrats in
Washington, London,
and Ottawa

UNIVERSITY OF TORONTO PRESS

Toronto Buffalo London

©University of Toronto Press 1983
Toronto Buffalo London
Printed in Canada

ISBN 0-8020-5622-9

Canadian Cataloguing in Publication Data

Campbell, Colin, 1943–
    Governments under stress

    Includes index.
    ISBN 0-8020-5622-9

    1. Presidents – United States – Decision making.
    2. United States – Politics and government – Decision making.
    3. Prime ministers – Great Britain – Decision making.
    4. Great Britain – Politics and government – Decision making.
    5. Prime ministers – Canada – Decision making.
    6. Canada – Politics and government – Decision making.
    I. Title.

JF1525.D4C35   351.007′25   c82-095353-9

To the memory of

Joseph John Nelligan
William Patrick Nelligan
Nora Elizabeth Smith
Margaret Catherine Armstrong

Contents

Acknowledgments

At long last this four-year project has come to a close. I owe a great deal to many people whose generosity made this book possible. First, there is George J. Szablowski, my colleague at York University, Toronto, with whom I wrote *The Superbureaucrats*. I have learned so much from him and had such fun along the way that I cannot read a page of this book without thinking of his contribution to our field of inquiry.

Gail Lyons deserves special mention. She joined the project in 1979 as senior research assistant and stayed with it for two years. In addition to managing a research staff which numbered seven people during the summer of 1980, she worked virtually as a collaborator on the verification of transcripts, development of the codebook, coding, and data analysis. She became totally conversant in every aspect of the study. I tried out many ideas with her, she offered several of her own, and, generally, she contributed greatly to this book.

Other research assistants worked on this project as if it were their own: Robin Esco, Margaret Evans, Lucinda Flavelle, Bruce McLeod, Donald Naulls, and Mark Sudnick.

Two hundred and sixty-five officials made the project possible through giving their time and insights. For many, arrival of yet another academic at their doorstep must have evoked the same response that the Red Cross Bloodmobile strikes in me when it rolls up to York University. Yet they all proved themselves most gracious and generous.

This project took me to two foreign capitals where I was an unknown quantity. Richard Rose and William Plowden helped introduce co-operative people in Whitehall and gave me tips on how to interview there. Several top officials in Ottawa wrote their opposite numbers in London in an effort to help me with access. Several journalists, Peter Hennessy, William Keegan, and Adrian Hamilton, provided a number of short courses on Whitehall that gave an excellent view of the inside. Nearly everyone in governmental studies at the Brookings Institution in Washington, DC, contributed in a similar fashion while I was a guest scholar in the program. However, I must single out Joel Aberbach, now of the University of Michigan, who shares many common research concerns and took a very strong interest in this project.

Approximately twenty scholars, practitioners, and journalists criticized all or part of the first draft of this book. Some of the scholars contributed anonymously through University of Toronto Press. I can thank Bert Rockman, Richard Chapman, Michael Lee, Robert Presthus, and Richard Stubbing. The government officials who read the manuscript gave as unstintingly then as when I interviewed them. Both Peter Hennessy and William Keegan offered detailed comments. Finally, Virgil Duff of University of Toronto Press provided me, for the third time, with all the help a writer could ever hope for from his editor. He was joined by John Parry, whose copy-editing has eliminated many stylistic infelicities. The deficiencies remaining in this final version belong entirely to me.

The Faculty of Arts Word Processing Unit, and not Toronto winters, has kept me at York. Under the cheerful guidance of Doris Rippington, the staff completed drafts so quickly and well that they greatly expedited production of the book. I owe special thanks to Patricia Humenyk, who spent days transcribing segments of interview tapes with accents and background noise that had bewildered everyone else. Caroline Gee of Gee's Management arranged transcription of the London interviews; Geri Laithwaite in London did this work exceedingly well. Jean Levin and Beverly Nadel, directors of The Work Place in Washington, provided transcribers for the Washington interviews and a great deal of help with correspondence. At York, three secretaries in the Department of Political Science, Phyllis Feldman, Doreen Muttart, and Sara Costantini, produced preliminary drafts of the manuscript from my very poor typing.

The Social Sciences and Humanities Research Council of Canada provided almost all the funding for this project. However, Michael A. Fahey, SJ, generously arranged for emergency assistance from the Loyola Jesuits' University Fund which permitted a last-minute trip to London in order to take into account recent changes under Prime Minister Margaret Thatcher.

A final word of thanks goes to my Jesuit colleagues at Bellarmine Residence in Toronto, Farm Street Church Residence in London, and

Carroll House in Washington. Many have taken a keen interest in the project and have offered their unfailing support.

A great deal of sadness can occur in four years. Since I lost both my father and mother by the time I was twenty-five, my aunts and uncles have tended to view me as one of their own. During the period in which this book was produced, my mother's four brothers and sisters died. I therefore dedicate this book to their memory.

GOVERNMENTS UNDER STRESS

1

Executive leadership and central agencies

The title of this book stems from two facts of life surrounding the operation of central agencies in advanced liberal democracies. First, these organizations have operated under extreme stress in the past decade. The decline of the world economy has perhaps contributed most to these pressures. However, crises of faith in liberal democracy, among leaders and citizens alike, have deepened the sense of malaise. Second, central agencies house those units of government most consistently in the line of fire when political executives struggle with their difficult economic and political environments. As we will see, these departments, agencies, and offices perform the functions essential to co-ordination and control of bureaucracy throughout government.[1]

This study limits itself to central agencies in three countries, the United States, the United Kingdom, and Canada. The fact that these are all northern Atlantic democracies with common institutional roots facilitates a comparative approach. As well, the three countries have placed considerable stock in central agencies as institutional means for improving the ability of political executives to come to terms with these difficult times. Yet many fascinating points of contrast present themselves in this three-nation study. The United States operates according to the presidential-congressional system of government while the United Kingdom and Canada follow a cabinet-parliamentary model. We will find that the United Kingdom and Canada differ considerably in the ways they follow their model. As well, the United Kingdom maintains unitary structures for meshing national and regional interests while the United States and Canada operate federal systems. Yet, the Canadian provinces have become much more effective than the American states in protecting areas of autonomous jurisdiction and bringing regional concerns to bear on federal policies.

THE ISSUE OF EXECUTIVE LEADERSHIP

The growth of central agencies and the consolidation of executive authority appear to be inextricably linked. This phenomenon has given rise, in each of the three countries, to recurrent concerns that improved central-agency resources will concentrate power in the hands of the chief executive or an inner circle of the cabinet. While we should consider carefully the evidence supporting such assertions, one must also caution against alarmist views of increased resources which would deny the executive leadership the capacity required to give direction to government.

In Canada and the United Kingdom, prime ministers who attempt to upgrade the machinery and staffs responsible for central co-ordination and control often encounter the criticism that they have taken on 'presidential' trappings.[2] Some observers fear that improving central agencies jeopardizes the principles of individual ministerial responsibility for what goes on in departments and collective responsibility for what is decided by the cabinet.[3] But concentration of power certainly was not noticeable in Washington during this project's 1979 interviews with officials in Jimmy Carter's administration. Indeed, Carter laboured under the shadow of Watergate-induced fear of 'imperialization' of the presidency. Were things so bad in the aftermath of Watergate and in face of the energy crisis, inflation, and global instability that even presidents had lost control? Or did Jimmy Carter simply prove particularly adept at bringing home the inherent limitations of the US presidency?

We will find that fears of concentrated executive power intimate only crudely a more profound phenomenon that has shown itself in several liberal democracies. Specifically, chief decision-makers and cabinets require elaborate machinery and large staffs devoted to co-ordination and control just to get on with the job of governing. Canadians, for instance, have accused Pierre Elliott Trudeau of turning the federal government into a virtual presidential system. Many of the changes he has introduced, however, find their origins in the statutory and conventional authority of the Canadian prime minister.[4] Further, they follow in many respects the principles of advanced management sciences,[5] and thus owe a debt to modern techniques which, though highly developed in the United States, are applied regardless of national boundaries. Fears of presidential power, thus, simply reflect a tendency among Canadians and, sometimes, Britons to label aspects of contemporary society that they do not like 'American.'

To make the point even more strongly, our Canadian and British respondents often exaggerated the resources available to presidents while understating the machinery and staffs available to their respective prime ministers. In both countries, however, the cabinet decides all important matters through a hierarchical process of committee review. Here prime ministers always stand at the apex by virtue of their chairmanship of the crucial committees and the cabinet itself. Almost invariably, officials in Britain and Canada will assert: 'We are a very lean shop here, certainly nothing like what is available in Washington.'

Such statements distort reality. In the UK Cabinet Office, for instance, some 48 senior career officials run secretariats for the cabinet and interdepartmental committees and provide briefing material for the prime minister. Another 5 career officials working in two rooms right next to the prime minister in 10 Downing Street operate an intelligence system geared to assuring that she keeps her hands on the most important levers in Whitehall. A further 18 senior professionals, seconded from government and the private sector, advise the cabinet and the prime minister on issues that require longer-term analysis than the Cabinet Office has time to coax from departments. In Canada, comparable machinery exceeds that available in the United Kingdom. The Privy Council Office (PCO) and the Federal-Provincial Relations Office (FPRO) together house 58 senior officials. They track and co-ordinate cabinet decision-making and serve as the prime minister's advisers on the full range of policy matters.

British and Canadian officials base their claims of relative leanness on the distinction that most advisers to the cabinet and to the prime minister are career officials rather than political appointees. They conjure up the image of immense capabilities on the part of the staffs of the White House and the Executive Office of the President to safeguard the expressly partisan interests of the president in various policy sectors. This impression belies close scrutiny. For instance, under Carter the Domestic Policy Staff (DPS), with some twenty-six appointees, most youngish and new to government, if not to Washington, gave the president only a weak sister to the British and Canadian secretariats. This applied even when DPS worked on the president's agenda, which it did not always do. The staff frequently felt pressures from strong ties outside the administration.

The Canadian and British perspectives do then raise an important issue for the analysis of the role of central agencies in facilitating executive leadership. Conventional wisdom notwithstanding, evidence suggests that the first-among-equals of liberal-democratic chief executives, i.e. the president, often does not adequately staff and organize central agency machinery, especially on domestic policy. Presidents tend to get appointees too inexperienced, inexpert, and poorly disciplined to staff functions that require seasoned professionals and tight organizations. Although only one of many factors, Jimmy Carter's failure to recognize such pitfalls early in his administration contributed greatly to his problems in domestic policy. He underestimated just how far behind other systems the United States had fallen both in its machinery for co-ordinating interdepartmental decision-making and in selecting personal staff responsible for policy advice.

The section that follows focuses on the issues raised by the Carter administration. If we ask why Carter failed to staff and organize his advisory system adequately, we must develop the question further by examining the factors that influence how presidents and prime ministers view their central agencies. Certainly, most of us have engaged in morning-after-the-election discussions of how a defeated chief executive could have done a better job. Statements such as 'Trudeau listens too much to the bureaucrats,' 'Joe Clark was overwhelmed by the Ottawa mandarins,' 'The "Iron Lady" will most certainly lose if she does not sack the monetarists,' and 'Jimmy Carter depended too much on the Georgians' all touch on central-agency issues. Such statements enjoy a wide currency – at bus-stops in Calgary, pubs in Yorkshire, and factories in Toledo, as well as in the corridors of power in Ottawa, London, and Washington or the faculty lounges of McGill, Oxford, and Berkeley. In a sense, this book appeals to the latent chief executive in many of us by asking, 'If you were president or prime minister, how would you try to get it "right" from the start?'

INFLUENCES ON CHIEF EXECUTIVES' STYLES

Students of executive leadership attempting to bring themselves up to date on influences on style face a bewildering array of conceptual frameworks. This section pulls together many key contributions from various frameworks. In assessing influences on chief executives' choice of one or another style for their administration or government, one must look at six factors: *secular trends* in the political environment that appear as if they will persist far into the future; *metacycles*, or trends that will probably sustain themselves at least through more than one administration or government but not indefinitely; *term-cycles*, or phases that occur during terms or periods of office and relate for the most part to the legislative and electoral calendars; the *partisan situation* of chief executives; *ex officio factors*, including the support given to chief executives and the institutional resources at their disposal; and the chief executives' *personalities*.

Secular Trends
These factors transcend political time-limits. Several such trends that are identified in the literature readily apply to the three systems. Each political environment has changed in several important respects over the past two decades. The roles of our three governments have so expanded that popular expectations for goods and services have been radically transformed. However, inflation and resource problems persist and intensify despite efforts to control them. These conditions focus more and more attention on the need for restraint in public spending. In foreign policy, the bipolar nature of global politics appears to have disintegrated to the point where middle and minor powers may assert themselves much more than in the first decades after the Second World War. The United Kingdom lost early on from this transition and the United States now finds it necessary to make radical adjustments. Canada, however, could benefit from the transition. Richard E. Neustadt described the US experience well when he noted that changes in the US political environment have significantly reduced the president's power and, ironically, added profoundly to his workload: 'These ... developments – and these are not alone – confront a President with other chief executives, public and private, abroad and at home, each of whom presides over a governmental system of his own.'[6]

Centrifugal forces in each of our systems have accompanied changes in the political environment. Norman C. Thomas has employed the term *subgovernments* to convey the degree to which centrifugal forces in the United States incubate relations among interest groups, departments and agencies, and congressional committees as they work out policy agreements. Under the subgovernment system, American presidents find it much more difficult than chief decision-makers in other systems to introduce and deliver substantial policy changes.[7] Stephen J. Wayne carries this view further by asserting that due to overload in the White House, departments and agencies have increased their ability to work on their own agendas.[8] Neustadt, in fact, raises considerable alarm by suggesting, in reflections made during the Carter administration, that the American system has atomized. Congressional factions fail more than before to deliver votes in support of the president; fractiousness in departments and agencies increases; interest groups proliferate and institutionalize; and, generally, staffs expand everywhere in Washington.[9]

Meanwhile, in Westminster, formerly the paragon of the disciplined, two-party system, factionalism has struck with a vengeance in both major parties. In fact, disunity in the Labour party has helped spawn the Social Democratic party which, through its alliance with the Liberals, stands a good chance of capturing the centre. Both the two-party system and discipline have proved much more resilient in Canada, but this fact contributes to the widespread belief that Ottawa does not listen to regional voices. Interminable conflicts between the federal and provincial governments over powers and authority frequently bear all the marks of a political system that might well come apart at the seams.

One option presents itself to chief executives overwhelmed by changes in the political environment and centrifugal forces in government. They can attempt to shoot the gap on the basis of personal appeal and sheer determination. Such attempts appear, in fact, to dovetail with the contemporary expectations for chief executives in our three systems. The mood harbours two secular trends. First, a Cincinnatus complex operates behind the initial enthusiasm for leaders such as Jimmy Carter, Ronald Reagan, Margaret Thatcher, Pierre Elliott Trudeau, and Joe Clark. Cincinnatus (born ca 519 BC) was thought by Romans of his time to be a model of the life of virtue and simplicity. Tradition has it that he was twice called from the humble circumstances of his farm to serve as dictator. People believed that a common, ordinary, decent citizen with the innate wisdom of a farmer could bring order to the surrounding chaos. Thomas E. Cronin points out the degree to which Carter's image as a gifted farmer-turned-governor appealed to voters.[10] The fact that many of these voters now seem to have turned to Ronald Reagan, a former 'B' movie star and governor of California, totally lacking in experience in Washington, suggests that the tendency has maintained its secular upswing in the United States.

In Britain, the hierarchical nature of Westminster careers prevented individuals without long tenure in Parliament from becoming prime minister. However, the last two prime ministers have played up their 'ordinary' backgrounds. James Callaghan, the son of an Irish immigrant, a petty officer during the Second World War, and a former civil-service union bureaucrat, found himself often billed simply as 'Jim.' Margaret Thatcher, raised in a staunchly middle-class home, and a chemistry graduate turned barrister, upholds the values and traditions of 'middle-England' in the most pristine form imaginable. Unlike Britain, Canada has through most of this century almost systematically pursued prime ministers with relatively little experience in Parliament. Pierre Trudeau, an expert on constitutional law teaching at the University of Montreal and enjoying a sizeable inherited fortune, came to Ottawa, at the age of forty-five, more as the philosopher king than a Cincinnatus. Although he had never previously held public office, he became prime minister, on the crest of 'Trudeaumania,' in four years. Joe Clark hailed from High River, Alberta, where his family published a newspaper. A political operative with a checkered academic background, Clark became leader of his party less than four years after first winning election to Parliament and became prime minister at the age of forty.

Cronin looks at another side to popular expectations for chief executives. In addition to having a touch of Cincinnatus, they must be able to muster an uncommon performance once in power. The idea of a peanut farmer-cum-engineer titillated Carter audiences during the 1976 campaign. Here was a man both soft and hard, with both pastoral instincts and a grasp of rational order in the world. Relatedly, Nelson W. Polsby touches on the perceived need for chief executives with a rational grasp of complex reality.[11] In this respect, Trudeau ceaselessly wrestles with Olympian issues. Immediately following the 1980 election, these included the constitution, North-South relations, and the Canadianization of the economy. His reputation for rationalization of machinery of government has reached legendary proportions, at least in Canada. All this contributes to the aura of mystery surrounding Trudeau. Though many despise him, most Canadians believe he is the only person capable of 'running' the country. Margaret Thatcher provides an English-garden variety of Pierre Trudeau. Rather than steeping herself in Renaissance majesty, she fences with crises by invoking, through rapid-fire appeals, middle-class propriety. Thus, she deflects further news of failures in her monetarist economics with sermons on the importance of Britons learning to live within their means.

Metacycles
In discussing cycles, one distinction from secular trends comes immediately to mind. With cyclical views, when downtrends appear to have proved pessimists to be right, optimists will be looking for signs of an upswing. When upswings lend credibility to optimists, pessimists will point to indications of a downswing. Whatever their inclinations, chief executives must pay attention to two types of cycles, metacycles and term-cycles.

Metacycles operate independently of terms or periods of office. The apparent breakdown of the Phillips curve, the inverse relation between inflation and unemployment, in advanced industrial nations brings home the distinction between metacycles and term-cycles. Now that high unemployment and high inflation coexist to the degree they do, chief executives cannot so readily as before manipulate the economy to produce the optimal circumstances for re-election. Thus, Jimmy Carter found himself with a 'balanced' budget and no tax cuts in an election year. Pierre Elliott Trudeau faced, in 1978, astounding survey data indicating clearly that his government *would not* gain re-election without convincing expenditure cuts. As Margaret Thatcher's government draws closer to an election it still finds that it cannot afford within its monetarist terms of reference the spending spree that would ease the burden of its policies long enough to assure its popularity. Put another way, the world-wide economic cycle has swung into prolonged stagflation that has essentially swamped the conventional machinery available to chief executives for coping with swings during the final year of their term or Parliament.

It is difficult to track the influences of metacycles on US presidents as they are limited to two terms and only one president since the war, Dwight D. Eisenhower, has enjoyed a full eight years in office. Similarly, instability in the British electorate has meant that no twentieth-century prime minister has held office for more than nine consecutive years. Pierre Trudeau's long period in office has alerted observers to the influences of metacycles on Canadian chief decision-makers. In fact, Trudeau owes much of his survival to an uncanny ability to adjust his style to major swings in the political environment.[12] Notwithstanding US presidents' short periods in office, Arthur M. Schlesinger sr detected tidal shifts in Americans' expectations for the chief executive between limited and expansive government during the period 1765 to 1947.[13] Cronin charts the movements up to the present swing, beginning in 1973, characterized by public retrenchment from the explosion of government after the war.[14]

Term-cycles

In the United States these influences have attracted much more scholarly attention than metacycles. Cronin, for instance, points up the inevitability of slippage in a president's popularity by noting that the longer he is in office the less he is liked.[15] Polsby seems to suggest that presidents should anticipate such slippage at the outset.[16] For instance, Richard Nixon initially used his cabinet appointments to strengthen ties with various constituencies. Once he had built the coalitions necessary for re-election, he switched to an appointments strategy that would contribute to his centralization of power in the White House. Jimmy Carter might now regret not taking a similar tack when making his first cabinet appointments.

Authors such as Stephen Hess and John H. Kessel have developed the study of term-cycles into a fine art.[17] During the first term, presidents must face the following phases: the honeymoon, which allows them to generate comprehensive plans for the term; a period of decompression, which brings home the difficulty of learning tasks and working with the bureaucracy and Congress; a period of paring, which provides the now-experienced aides an opportunity to focus on the few issues that will win them points with the electorate; and the re-election campaign, which, if the president faces an uphill battle, can focus most creative thinking in the administration on political survival. Hess and Kessel part ways slightly in their views of cycles in the second presidential term. Hess stresses the degree to which the cycle of the first term repeats itself, although he notes as well the lame duck phenomenon brought on by the two-term limit.[18] Kessel, in contrast, stresses the creative possibilities faced by a president elected for a second term who enjoys strong majorities in both houses of Congress.[19] However, scholarly opinion suggests that second terms start off less expansively than first terms. I.M. Destler, who highlights the extent to which presidents play to historians,[20] finds that they lose interest in consideration of options during the first term and, by the second term, doggedly pursue goals which, if achieved, will improve their standing in posterity.

Presidents and their aides need not always map out strategies specifically designed for riding out term-cycles. For instance, at the time of the Washington interviews for this study, Carter's senior advisers thought it innovative enough to have worked out the annual legislative program. Yet, judging from the remarks of one respondent, career officials in Office of Management and Budget (OMB) view their work during particular administrations very much in relation to term-cycles:

We operate on what I call the 'rule of four.' The first year of an administration is a year of thinking, and planning, and doing broad-gauged studies. We do a big interagency look which involves all the players who are critical – that's Defense, State, and the NSC staff. From a defense standpoint, we look at what the threats are and are apt to be, where our current capabilities are and what are the areas of emphasis that we will push – that the administration should push. A whole series of options is prepared and you usually try to get guidance from the president in the form of a decision document. So, the first year is his opportunity to shift from whatever his predecessor did. The second year is less so. Third year? By then they're heavily impregnated with their own decisions unless outside events caused a massive change (actually, right now there is a kind of a move toward that with the Middle-East blowup ...). And the fourth year? Nothing happens because it's the election campaign.

With respect to the United Kingdom and Canada, we should note that the uncertain length of governments in parliamentary systems strains the term-cycle concept somewhat. In a modest way, the fact that a majority government may seize an opportune time for an election months, even years, before the end of its mandate gives it a strategic weapon not available to us administrations. From the outset, minority governments must eschew bold initiatives that might sufficiently raise the hackles of voters to encourage the opposition parties to precipitate an election. Certainly, Joe Clark walked into such a trap in 1979 with his 'short-term-pain-for-long-term-gain' budget. Be that as it may, Pierre Trudeau has made, at least since 1974, clear efforts at the beginning of his mandates to map out strategies for phases of his governments. One finds less conscious planning for term-cycles in Britain. However, a recent book on the British economic-policy process by William Keegan and R. Pennant-Rea traces convincingly the interrelationship between where a government is in its mandate and how it handles various economic crises.[21]

The Partisan Situation
The partisan situation of chief executives concerns most essentially the obstacles they face to their taking positions at variance with the expectations of legislatures, the bureaucracy, and their own party. Here Americans habitually idealize conditions under the parliamentary model, at least as found in the United Kingdom and Canada. In the latter countries, the majorities in the legislative branch are often of the same party as the prime minister, career bureaucrats are supposed to serve political masters faithfully regardless of the party in power, and tightly organized national machines should provide both an endless stream of acculturated recruits for positions and links to the thinking of the party rank and file. All of these conditions, the conventional wisdom suggests, add up to much greater potential for programmatic rationality in the efforts of prime ministers than is possible for presidents.

The reality falls far short of the idealized version. Recent articles by Leon D. Epstein and John E. Schwarz bring home the degree to which party discipline has declined in the British House of Commons.[22] There, as we have noted, factionalism has re-established itself. Both the government and opposition parties must expect back-bench revolts that force withdrawal from key policy positions or, worse, embarrassing defeats in votes. For example, on 19 May 1980 Margaret Thatcher's government withdrew retroactive application of sanctions against Iran when Conservative whips found that as many as 100 of their back-benchers were prepared to vote against the government on the provision. When US officials wondered out loud what type of British government could fail to deliver on a key international agreement, Lord Carrington, then the foreign secretary, directed a mini-course on British politics to Secretary of State Edmund Muskie: any British government relies on Parliament for its support.[23] Similarly, both the neutrality of the career public service and the election-manifesto policy intentions of parties in the United Kingdom fall considerably short of American perceptions. Studies by Richard Rose and by Hugh Heclo and Aaron Wildavsky have documented very well Whitehall's deftness at diverting ministers from bold measures so as to maintain the status quo.[24] Rose studied as well the programmatic achievements of two governments, Labour 1964–70 and Conservative 1970–4.[25] He found neither was able to remain faithful to the platform upon which it ran.

In Canada, although discipline remains exceptionally strong in all three national parties, frequent minority governments and the necessity of provincial assent to an increasing proportion of federal initiatives severely constrain the ability of the federal government to pursue long-term goals.[26] Further, as Joe Clark discovered, Liberal control of the government for most of this century has politicized the bureaucracy. This fact makes a sham, particularly at the highest levels, of the principle of a non-partisan public service in which advancement is based on seniority and merit. Finally, the links between party manifestos and rank-and-file policy views, for what they were, have all but atrophied. For instance, during the 1980 election campaign, a group of forty Liberals worked in secret to pound out a platform which Trudeau kept under lock and key (there was only one copy) and barely used. Adding insult to injury, he insisted upon a national policy conference in early July 1980 which most of the party, especially members of the Quebec caucus who had the 22 May referendum on sovereignty-association to fight, thought would be a travesty given the inadequate time in which to prepare. The party faithful, largely oblivious of the near-revolt in the Quebec caucus, dutifully trekked off to Winnipeg to provide a cast of thousands before which Trudeau could plug his ideas on constitutional reform.

The British and Canadian experiences suggest then that Americans could look more realistically at the partisan situation of the presidency if they better appreciated the obstacles and shortcomings of prime ministerial power. However, it is important to add that presidents can meet different fates within the band of what is realistic. For instance, Neustadt's observations about atomization of the system[27] seem to apply doubly to

Carter's relations with Congress. He and too many of his staff were too new to Washington. With respect to the career public service, Richard Nathan presents very convincingly the case that Richard Nixon allowed the White House counterbureaucracy and, eventually, the administrative presidency to develop as they did because he wanted counterweights to a 'liberal' public service that refused to participate in reversing Johnson's Great Society.[28] Finally, Neustadt's observations about the exceptional amount of internecine warfare among aides during Carter's transition period raises serious questions about the partisan position of any Cincinnatus.[29] A Cincinnatus will build his campaign around a core group almost totally lacking in standing in the national party organization and experience in Washington. No matter how effective at mobilizing the party for victory at the polls, the core group will find, once it gets to Washington, that at best it is a rump movement in the party establishment. Further, it will soon lose its sense of direction. As institutional and partisan pressures begin to bear down, it will discover that no matter how cohesive it was during the campaign it has no sense of how to operate as a team in Washington.

Ex officio

These factors influencing chief executive style divide into two types, use of symbols and institutional resources. In the United States the former frequently have religious overtones. For instance, Ronald Reagan's moment of silent prayer during his acceptance of the Republican party nomination suggests that he perceived himself having a mission to become president. At least, he wished to evoke religious sentiments along these lines. Interestingly, both British and Canadian prime ministers rarely display religious sentiment. Perhaps they leave this to the monarch. However, Margaret Thatcher recited the prayer of St Francis of Assisi on the steps of No. 10 as she took charge of her new government in 1979. The use of such symbols evokes more than religious sentiment. It taps as well both the statutory and conventional proportions of chief executives' jobs and the élite and popular perceptions of the type of individual required to do them.

Presidents, largely because of their stronger constitutional authority over foreign affairs, traditionally have emphasized this policy sector more than domestic affairs.[30] Stephen Hess observes that before Franklin Delano Roosevelt Americans expected relatively modest involvement of the president in domestic policy.[31] Roosevelt started the process whereby presidents have increasingly engaged themselves in domestic affairs, through efforts either to advance the welfare state or to reverse it. Both Hess and Richard Rose acknowledge the degree to which involvement on the domestic side has seduced presidents into thinking of themselves as the chief managers of the federal government.[32] Neustadt adds a pessimistic note at this point. He argues that the sheer weight of current presidential responsibilities might be too much for one person to handle.[33]

Both Hess and Rose lend a perspective to presidential overload that offers a way out for incumbents. They recommend that presidents focus their attention only on actions with the greatest political significance.[34] People expect presidential involvement in crucial matters concerning national sovereignty. They also look for cues in his key policy statements, namely the budget, the state of the union message, and his responses to critical events which call for him to propose legislation. But following the tack suggested by Hess and Rose introduces other pitfalls to the presidency. As Polsby suggests, the president often finds himself in a plebiscitary frame of mind.[35] That is, he can resort to appeals directed to the electorate when he cannot resolve conflicts within Washington policy subgovernments. In this regard, Cronin comments that presidents can improve their image by wrestling with crises which place the country in a severe predicament.[36] But a president who cries 'wolf' too many times will lose credibility.

Neustadt cautions that presidents cannot deliberately deceive the people into thinking there is a crisis when there is not.[37] One wonders about this. For instance, much of the public must have seen Jimmy Carter's modulation of his response to the Iranian hostage crisis as an effort to obscure problems at home. Others must have viewed the tactic as legitimate. A sizeable proportion of the electorate sees presidential politics as a card game. Under this view, the hostage incident became for a time a lucky hand. It opened the way for Carter to bluff his way through the Democratic party primaries. Thus, crises can help a president in two ways. They provide him an opportunity to appear presidential to those thirsting for the excitement of a severe threat; they also widen the band of manoeuvrability within which he can manipulate issues to focus the public's attention where he would rather have it.

In a sense, the ability of prime ministers to use symbols compares unfavourably to that of presidents. Most fundamentally, neither the British nor Canadian prime minister serves as head of state. On the positive side, this relieves them of many ceremonial duties performed by the monarch (who is represented in Canada by the governor-general). On the negative side, neither prime minister enjoys the 'halo effect' that comes with being a head of state. Expressions such as 'dignity of office' too often appear anachronistic for the political leaders who draw the most fury when running the House of Commons gauntlet. Apart from not being heads of state, the British and Canadian prime ministers neither claim the title 'commander-in-chief' nor head nations with the prominence the United States enjoys in world affairs. Thus, they find it more difficult to enhance their images by modulating their handling of military and foreign affairs.

Having registered the customary disclaimers, one must allow for large grey areas in these distinctions. For instance, some prime ministers have proven adept at associating themselves with ceremonial roles in ways which suggest near head-of-state status. Certainly, Margaret Thatcher often exudes 'royal jelly' both in the way in which she dresses and in her condescension. Despite his disdain for lesser ceremonies, Pierre Elliott Trudeau both sets up national galas and takes centre stage in these more than any prime minister in this century. Trudeau also has benefited greatly from the fact that, despite resentment at home, he has attained standing among world-class statesmen. This point is not lost entirely on Canadians. Both British and Canadian prime ministers belong to the exclusive group of western leaders who attend the annual economic summits. For Canadian prime ministers this has become a particularly cherished perquisite since it was obtained over strenuous French objections. Currently, Trudeau's initiatives towards greater dialogue between rich and poor nations leading to the October 1981 Cancun conference underline for Canadians his exceptional status in the world community.

Prime ministers use language to evoke patriotic responses by couching domestic issues in national security terms. Jimmy Carter's characterization of the energy crisis as the moral equivalent of war demonstrates how presidents use the same device. Both British and Canadian prime ministers preside over political systems that often require little encouragement before lapsing into near-hysteria over domestic concerns. Thus, Margaret Thatcher continues to justify her monetarist policies in terms of national survival. Chapter 4 addresses the degree to which Trudeau and his top advisers viewed the constitutional crisis as a national security issue. Although it did not sell in Chicoutimi, Quebec, or Medicine Hat, Alberta, the approach struck a chord at the Legion Hall in Barrie, Ontario, or, for that matter, among students at York University in Downsview.

Institutional resources comprise the second category of ex officio influences on a chief executive's style. Stephen Wayne chronicles various stages in the development of institutional machinery and staffs available to us presidents since Roosevelt.[38] There have been ebbs and flows, with Roosevelt building up the White House, Truman and Eisenhower regularizing functions, Kennedy reinstituting Roosevelt's emphasis on personnel over structure, Johnson creating his domestic policy staff in an attempt to bring the same degree of rigour to the domestic side as existed in foreign affairs, and Richard Nixon attempting to institute a supercabinet system. Wayne sees, however, a clear development toward routinization of the presidential advisory system in response to centrifugal forces elsewhere in the policy arena.

Correspondingly, both Richard Rose and Peter Self have worked out some boundaries within which the gradual enhancement of resources available to chief executives must stay for it to have best results.[39] Larger staffs increase the capacity of chief executives to influence operational departments. But a law of diminishing returns sets in when their staffs become so large that key advisers find their direct and personal contact with the chief executives and one another severely limited. However, the sheer weight of work eventually forces undesirable increases in staff. Here clear lines of organization can introduce economies of time and effort which can help restore personal contacts. Unfortunately, they also cut down on the amount of diversity and criticism in the system. They make for a relatively harmonious but unimaginative administration in which a chief executive accepts non-creativity in most policy sectors. He must to a degree close off the bureaucratic aspects of his job and discipline himself and his aides to keep an eye only on the most crucial issues.

Earlier, this chapter mentioned in passing the tendency among British and Canadian central agents to underestimate the resources available to the prime minister and the cabinet in relation to those serving presidents. Subsequent chapters will treat this issue at much greater length. On the side of the British and Canadians, their central agencies operate much more than their counterparts in the United States in ways that support the cabinet's collective decision-making as well as the chief executive. In addition, prime ministers in both countries face relatively severe constraints on appointing partisan advisers to government positions. However, some British and Canadian central agencies maintain staff resources that would make their US counterparts envious. Further, some prime ministers, through intelligence, force of personality, length of time in office, or some combination of these, prove adept at getting what they want from central agency career officials.

Keeping in mind these caveats, an examination of the actual resources in American, British, and Canadian central agencies will help clear away some of the confusion in discussions of the institutional supports available to chief executives in the three countries. First, the agencies in this study include only those that take or share the leading role in one of three broad categories of control and co-ordination functions: development of strategic plans for the government/administration and assuring that decisions adhere to these, development and integration of economic and fiscal policies, and allocation and management of human and physical resources. This list of functions fails to make explicit mention of two central-agency activities also given special attention in Colin Campbell and George Szablowski's *The Superbureaucrats*. The first of these, recruitment and management of senior personnel, will receive detailed consideration in chapter 10 of this book as a subfunction of allocation and management of human resources. The second, management of intergovernmental affairs, receives less attention in this study than in *The Superbureaucrats*. The United States has just begun to develop many of the types of institutions designed to co-ordinate the conduct of federal-state relations with which Canadians now have considerable experience. In the United Kingdom, of course, the unitary nature of the system precludes discussion of intergovernmental affairs.

Table 1.1 includes all the key central agencies in each of the three countries. In the United States, these include the Executive Office of the President, the Treasury Department, and the Office of Personnel Management. In turn, the Executive Office of the President takes in the White House Office, the Office of the Vice-President, the Council of Economic Advisers, the Council on Environmental Quality, the Policy Development Office, the National Security Council, the Office of Administration, the Office of Management and Budget, the Office of Science and Technology, and the Office of the United States Trade Representative. In the United Kingdom, agencies covering similar roles included No. 10 (the Prime Minister's Office), the Cabinet Office, Her Majesty's (HM) Treasury, and the Civil Service Department. The latter agency was split in November 1981, with one-half of its functions going to the Cabinet Office, under the Management and Personnel Office, and the other to the Treasury. A fifth agency, the Central Policy Review Staff, operates within the Cabinet Office. In Canada, comparable agencies include the Prime Minister's Office, the Privy Council Office, the Federal-Provincial Relations Office, the ministries of state for Economic and Regional Development and for Social Development; the Department of Finance; the Treasury Board Secretariat; and the Office of the Comptroller General.

For all but one case, Table 1.1 lists resources covering only the policy, as opposed to operational, activities of the various departments. For instance, the figures for the British Civil Service Department exclude allocations to the Civil Service Catering Organization, the Civil Service College, the Central Computer and Telecommunications Agency, and the Recruitment Group. The US Office of Personnel Management provides the exception here. The breakdown of figures for that agency did not adequately differentiate policy and operational units.

TABLE 1.1
Estimated senior staffing, total staffing, and expenditure for fiscal year 1981–2

Country and agency	Senior executives	Total staff	Budget (in country's currency): millions
United States			
The Executive Office of the President			
White House Office	37	393	22.3
Office of the Vice-President	7	25	1.6
Council of Economic Advisers	6	36	2.3
Council of Environmental Quality	5	32	3.7
Policy Development Office (DPS under Carter)	10	42	3.0
National Security Council	13	68	4.0
Office of Administration	3	154	13.4
Office of Management and Budget	108	676	40.1
Office of Science and Technology	8	32	3.2
Office of US Trade Representative	22	135	10.0
Treasury Department (Office of the Secretary)	78	939	37.3
Office of Personnel Management	85	6,202	129.5
United Kingdom			
No. 10	11	69	*
Cabinet Office			
Secretariats	48	331	10.3
Central Policy Review Staff	18	33	†
HM Treasury	141	1,029	12.8
Civil Service Department‡	263	2,012	16.4
Canada			
Privy Council Office (including PMO and FPRO)	58	525	28.3
Ministry of State for Economic and Regional Development	21	108	5.5
Ministry of State for Social Development	16	65	3.8
Treasury Board Secretariat	65	825	41.0
Office of the Comptroller General	26	196	9.7
Department of Finance	35	568	26.7

SOURCES: *Estimates for the Fiscal Year Ending March 31, 1982* (Hull, Quebec, 1981); *Budget of the United States Government, Fiscal Year 1982* (Washington, DC, 1981); Committee on Post Office and Civil Service, House of Representatives *Policy and Supporting Positions,* (Washington, DC, 1980); *Supply Estimates 1981–82* (London 1981); correspondence from Manpower 1, United Kingdom Civil Service Department, 1981
*Expenditure estimate part of CSD
†Part of Secretariats
‡Split in November 1981

The resources listed for each agency include senior staff, total staff, and total expenditures. The financial resources appear in the currencies of the respective countries. The senior executive category varies considerably in the three countries. In the United States, it takes in members of the senior executive service, who earn from $54,755 to $58,500, and sub-cabinet executive-level appointees, who make between $57,500 and $60,662. In Britain, it covers principals, whose salaries start at £11,372, to super-permanent secretaries, who make £35,845 (figures exclude additional allowances for working in London). In Canada, it includes executive-level appointees, who begin at $43,300, and deputy ministers, who may reach $93,000. Notwithstanding the sizeable discrepancies in remuneration, the various groups in Table 1.1 all enjoy senior-executive status in their respective countries.

In viewing the data in Table 1.1 we find some startling evidence that suggests that the United States provides relatively lean resources to its central agencies. All the units under the Executive Office of the President, except the Council of Economic Advisers, the Office of Management and Budget, and the Office of the United States Trade Representative, focus their efforts in some way on developing the administration's overall strategies and assuring that major decisions adhere to these. However, the White House Office and the Office of the Vice President operate essentially as switchboards, taking care of the president's and the vice president's political affairs and liaison with cabinet secretaries, Congress, states, the press and media, and outside interests and attentive publics. They contain virtually no capability for independent analysis either of the merits of various priorities or of specific policy proposals. The Office of Administration operates at a relatively low technical level by providing services, largely clerical, to the rest of the Executive Office of the President. The Council on Environmental Quality (CEQ) and the Office of Science and Technology (OST) do, indeed, conduct independent assessments of policy proposals before the president. The work of both agencies centres on relatively narrow issues and does not link up directly with specific cabinet-level committees. However, some heads of these offices have developed especially good relations with presidents which contribute to their agency's profile. This leaves us with the National Security Council (NSC) and the Policy Development Office (OPD). The former maintains a long-standing tradition of independent assessment related to specific cabinet-level deliberations; the latter, under Reagan, has attempted to develop along the same lines.

Taking simply NSC and OPD, we find 110 staff, including 23 senior officials, with resources amounting to $7 million. If we add to these CEQ and OST, the figures increase to 174 staff, including 36 senior executives, with resources of $13.9 million. No matter how we view them, the US offices with policy-assessment roles do not compare well with similar units in the United Kingdom and Canada. The British Cabinet Office claims a complement of 331, 48 of whom are senior executives, while the Central Policy Review Staff operates with 33 members, 18 of whom hold senior positions. Together the agencies spend £10.3 million. Canada, whose budget and population remain around one-tenth those of the United States, assigns 525 staff to the Prime Minister's Office, the Privy Council Office, and the Federal-Provincial Relations Office. Of these, fully 58 belong to the senior ranks. The agencies spend a total of $28.3 million. Although the Americans clearly outstrip the British and the Canadians in the resources allocated to the chief executive's partisan and liaison activities, they trail the others in support of independent policy processing relating to the priorities that the chief executive and/or the cabinet set out for the administration or government.

Turning to development and integration of economic and fiscal policies, the three US central agencies operating mainly in this field (the Office of Management and Budget plays a part, but the central thrust of its work is expenditure control) include the Treasury Department, the Council of Economic Advisers, and the Office of the United States Trade Representative. These agencies operate with combined staffs of 1,110, 106 of whom are senior officials, and budgets totalling $49.6 million. The British Treasury, which handles most of the comparable functions to the US agencies *plus* expenditure review, kept on 1,029 officials, 141 of whom were senior, and spent around £12.8 million before it adopted its share of former Civil Service Department units. Thus, the Canadian agency provides the leanest operation here. The Department of Finance keeps a complement of 568, with only 35 working in senior positions. However it does manage to spend $26.7 million.

Finally, with respect to allocation and management of human and fiscal resources, two US agencies occupy this area. The first, the Office of Management and Budget (OMB), dominates the field through its role in expenditure review and development of management policy. OMB maintains a total staff of 676, 108 of whom are senior, and spends about $40.1 million. The Office of Personnel Management (OPM) was a result of Jimmy Carter's attempt to bring personnel policy, especially that affecting senior officials, under closer presidential guidance. It maintains a number of operational functions performed previously by the now defunct Civil Service Commission. Thus it keeps on a massive staff – 6,202 – and spends $129.5 million. However, consistent with the fact that many of its units do not develop policy, OPM boasts only 85 senior officials.

We saw above that the resources available in HM Treasury must stretch further than those in US agencies working on economic and fiscal policies. The British department takes responsibility for expenditure review as well as for the other functions. Until 1981, the Civil Service Department, with 2,012 staff (263 senior officials) and a budget of £16.4 million for policy units, eased the Treasury's burden by assuming a delegated responsibility for both management and personnel policy. A new agency, the Management and Personnel Office, and former CSD units that moved to the Treasury now watch over the policy areas. The Canadians devote by far the greatest resources to allocation and management of human and physical resources. The four central agencies operating in this field, namely the ministries of state for Economic and Regional Development and for Social Development, the Treasury Board Secretariat, and the Office of the Comptroller General, together take in 1,194 staff, 128 of whom are senior, and spend $109.5 million. One should add here the fact that these figures do not include those for the Department of Supply and Services and the Public Service Commission, both of which handle many of the operational functions for which the Treasury Board Secretariat develops policies.

This brief overview has underlined the importance of fleshing out the institutional resources of our chief executives. To be sure, US presidents command much greater in-house capabilities for partisan and liaison work than do prime ministers. However, the nature of the US system, given the strength of Congress and interest groups, more open government, and a more egalitarian society, exposes the president to many more assaults from outside the executive-bureaucratic community. In contrast, the relatively lavish resources found in British and Canadian central agencies suggest that executive leaders and top bureaucrats in neither system leave much to chance. In some respects, their central-agency functions appear to receive more adequate institutional support than do those of US presidents.

Personality
James David Barber has analysed the relationship between personality and chief executives' style.[40] His work has focused on US presidents. Barber's four personality types, active-positive, active-negative, passive-positive, and passive-negative, have gained such common usage that they even prompted Jimmy Carter to confide to Barber that he hoped he would be an active-positive president.[41] It is precisely this type of sentiment that tips us off to a weakness in Barber's conceptual framework. Its bias towards the active-positive, the president immersed in his work and enjoying every minute of it, fails to recognize that precious few of us avoid burning out if we work at a frantic pace at the same job for more

than two years. The issue's relevance seems particularly pressing when the options for positive action appear much more limited today than in the 1960s. Neustadt's caveat that presidents must be ambitious without being *driven* bears restating here.[42] Beware of the man who wants desperately to be active-positive. He will fill his calendar with 'face-to-face' en- counters, like Johnson,[43] bury himself in a mound of paper, like Nixon,[44] or succumb to both failings simultaneously like Carter, by wanting to personally approve virtually everything (including the White House tennis schedule); insisting upon discussion of details, even with relatively low-level career officials; and preserving gas-station-backroom access for all the 'good ol' boys' from Georgia.

A TYPOLOGY OF LEADERSHIP STYLES

The above sets up a number of guideposts for a detailed treatment of the relationship between executive leadership and the roles of central agencies in the United States, Britain, and Canada. Secular trends, metacycles, term-cycles, the partisan position of a chief executive, ex officio factors, and personalities all work their effects on the size, shape, and adequacy of central agencies.

By keeping in mind the various influences on executive leadership, we may now develop profiles of how they coalesce. How do the factors come together in such a way that a chief executive pursues a particular style of leadership which, in addition to setting the tone for his/her administration or government, brings about changes in the resources, organization, and operation of central agencies? Here we start with the assumption that chief executives may assess the various determinants of their style and decide upon a management plan that will provide the best possible results for their administration or government. The choices fall between two intersecting continua (see Figure 1.1).[45] The first continuum concerns the degree to which the chief executive wishes to foster 'countervaillance' in the advisory system by having policy management responsibilities shared by two or more units or, in contrast, decides to limit conflict by dividing policy management responsibilities into highly differentiated bureaus with sole sign-off (approval) power. The second continuum concerns the extent to which the chief executive draws policy decisions into central agencies in order to effect greater control over the bureaucracy or, on the contrary, chooses to keep 'routine' and 'technical' questions outside central agencies.

With such a paradigm, four styles emerge: 1) broker politics, whereby many key policy decisions are made in the periphery, but through negotiations, between units with competing expertise and authority in a

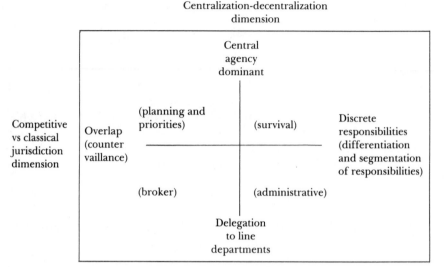

Figure 1.1
The administrative styles of chief executives relate to the degree to which they will draw functions into central agencies and allow competition between units.

policy sector, which are tracked and managed by central agencies; 2) administrative politics, whereby decisions largely occur in the periphery so that single departments and agencies obtain near hegemony over segments of policy management; 3) the planning-and-priorities style, whereby the chief executives attempt to maximize the accomplishments of their administration or government by challenging units to come up with imaginative and cross-cutting policy alternatives while, at the same time, expecting central agencies to bring these alternatives together in a comprehensive strategy; 4) the politics of survival, whereby an administration or government, usually under severe stress from the political environment – possibly accompanied by internal chaos – will attempt to gain control by sharply reducing the number of countervailing units and bringing many matters previously decided in the periphery to the centre.

THE PLAN FOR THIS BOOK

The three parts that follow immediately will focus, respectively, on central agencies' actual performance of functions related to 1) the setting of priorities and assuring that major decisions adhere to these, 2) the development and integration of economic and fiscal policies, and 3) the allocation and management of human and physical resources. Each of these chapters will outline the resources, structures, and roles of the central agencies involved in these functions. In cases where more than one central agency operates within a functional area, the treatment will give special attention to conflict resolution between competing institutional interests. As well, each part will emphasize the effects of the styles of various chief executives on central agencies.

Interviews with central agents in the three countries form the basis for this study. These lasted ninety minutes, on average, and took in a total of 265 officials. Appendix I provides a detailed explanation of methodological considerations connected to the interviews. The interview material provides a wealth of insights upon which to base descriptions of central agencies and assessments of their effectiveness. However, part IV takes us beyond reporting the responses of central agents to analysis of structured interviews. Researchers connected with the central agency project have coded respondents' answers to each question. This process made the material amenable to computer analysis. Thus, part IV analyses quantitatively a number of issues connected with the types of people who run central agencies. It will focus on cross-national differences concerning officials: 1) the relative emphasis given to various central agency roles, 2) awareness of executive-bureaucratic networks and perceptions of formal and informal links to these, 3) accessibility and openness to legislators, officials of other governments, interest groups, and attentive publics, 4) views of accountability, and career paths and orientations, and 5) socio-demographic backgrounds. Further, the US sample includes sizeable numbers of both appointees and career officials. This fact permits us to examine differences in US respondents which appear to relate to the 'track' they followed before assuming their positions.

Each part in this book provides a comprehensive treatment of its topic together with detailed summaries and conclusions. A final chapter outlines how central agencies could be improved or reformed. Along the way, it will examine recommendations that appear to have merits across the board, in specific countries and under the various circumstances in which political executives find themselves.

PART ONE

Arranging priorities and making decisions

Introduction

This series of chapters focuses on the most important of central agency functions. Chief decision-makers must map out strategies. Early on these will amount to more or less detailed plans of what they hope to accomplish during their mandate. As time goes on, the desire for a renewal of the mandate will inevitably divert chief decision-makers' attention from cherished long-term goals to the short-term accomplishments thought necessary for re-election. Whether long- or short-term, strategies must guide day-to-day decisions. Whether the administration desires to deliver a comprehensive legislative program or simply tackle those issues that must be satisfactorily resolved to maintain or increase voters' support, chief decision-makers have to make substantive choices that advance their strategy.

2

The American presidency and obstacles to strategic planning

With respect to executive authority, the reader should keep in mind that the United States departs from the two other countries in one crucial respect: the president shoulders responsibility individually for the executive decisions of his administration. Thus, when American scholars and practitioners employ the term *cabinet government* to describe their system they usually mean something diametrically opposed to what it implies in the other systems. In the United States, the term denotes the belief that individual cabinet secretaries strive to keep from the president's in-tray issues that could just as easily be resolved within departments.

On the face of it, any new president may call upon resources far beyond those provided to chief decision-makers in the United Kingdom and Canada. In fact, one finds it difficult to describe the constellation of offices dedicated to various corners of presidential activity without turning the exercise into a litany. We can, however, divide the numerous offices into functional categories. Since the interviews upon which this study is based occurred in 1979, the current discussion will focus on how Jimmy Carter set up his White House. However, a section will treat briefly how Ronald Reagan has organized his White House.

The president, as a partisan leader, must ensure that his handling of policy issues fits voters' perceptions of what he must do if they are to support him or his party in the next election. Thus, presidents will always bring on board top aides who will constantly keep in focus the partisan implications of the administration's policies. Under Jimmy Carter, for instance, Hamilton Jordan assumed the title assistant to the president. The bland nomenclature concealed the fact that Jordan put a political-strategy gloss on virtually every key decision. Carter formalized Jordan's role when he declared him chief of staff during the summer of 1979. Jordan, of course, left the White House in the spring of 1980 to devote his efforts exclusively to the president's re-election campaign. In many respects, the move simply reflected the fact that the president's future depended at that stage more on what happened in the campaign than in the White House.

Other key partisan affairs offices under Carter included those of the assistants for political affairs and personnel and for communications and the press secretary. Carter used the office of political affairs and personnel as both a lightning-rod to prevent partisan-political brushfires in the Democrats' organization and as a clearing-house for matters relating to political appointments. After the summer of 1979, the officials responsible for the former function gradually moved from the White House payroll to the official re-election and Democratic party machinery. Tim Kraft, for three years assistant to the president for political affairs and personnel, led this move.

On the personnel side of the office, after initial placement of top administration appointees, Carter had hoped to avoid over-involvement in personnel issues – above all the type of witch-hunt directed by Richard Nixon against disloyal appointees in his administration.[1] However, by the spring of 1979, Carter's aides convinced him that many appointees had proved to be either unreliable or incompetent. Carter thus set the wheels in motion for his own purge. Kraft's deputy, Joel McCleary, led a secret evaluation of the performance of existing appointees. Meanwhile Arnold Miller, a professional 'head hunter,' began to search for replacements. The two projects came together in summer 1979, when Carter eased out a number of administration officials, including four cabinet secretaries.

Under Carter, two offices – press secretary and assistant to the president for communications – carved up the important work involving the president's image in the media. The former office, under Jody Powell, attended to daily press needs. The latter gave Gerald M. Rafshoon, Carter's advertising executive from Georgia, overall responsibility for assuring that the president was stressing the issues that would win him the continued support of the electorate. Significantly, Carter disbanded the communications group in the summer of 1979, and Rafshoon and his top deputy, Greg Schneiders, joined the presidential re-election machine.

In another realm – personal legal affairs – the office of counsel to the president, John Dean's old position under Richard Nixon, maintained much of the prominence it first obtained in the wake of Watergate. Increasingly as a matter of course, the president faces situations in which he must have highly competent legal advice. Under Carter, a staff of five attorneys served the president's requirements for counsel.

None of the offices so far discussed had the resources to take the lead either in strategic planning of the administration's policy program or in assuring that major decisions are consistent with it. However, offices designed primarily to tend to the partisan and personal affairs of chief decision-makers continually wield significant influence over advisory machinery more closely linked to the policy process per se. Thus, under Carter, Hamilton Jordan often had the last word on policy matters and even took the lead in some issues (for instance, the Strategic Arms Limitation Treaty – SALT); Tim Kraft's shop obviously played an important role, through its mid-term personnel inventory, in assuring that appointees were toeing the administration's line; Powell and Rafshoon both played crucial roles in setting agenda and even involved their offices in task forces formulating policy programs; and the work of the counsels to the president spilled increasingly over to assessments of the legal implications of policy proposals, particularly in the justice field.

The next cluster of offices in the White House shouldered the brunt of policy development. Within the cluster, under Carter, the assistants to the president for domestic affairs and policy and for national security affairs divided the policy world into the two fields. Carter's assistant on the domestic side, Stuart E. Eizenstat, headed a group of thirty appointees, housed in the Domestic Policy Staff, who managed various policy sectors. Most of these were youngish, exceptionally bright individuals with relatively little experience in Washington. Eizenstat had looked to young political activists who helped with Carter's campaign when setting up DPS. Thus he overlooked many experienced hands from the vast pool of older operatives who already had spent considerable time as appointees in previous Democratic administrations, on congressional staffs, or in the numerous law firms, think tanks, and advocacy institutions that have a Democratic tinge. As if this tack did not pose enough danger for the effective operation of the domestic advisory secretariat, Eizenstat indulged his high-flyers further by giving them very great latitude in deciding which policy issues they would follow. For instance, the staff divided nominally into associate and assistant directors. Yet the senior designation, associate director, did not in fact identify umbrella units under which assistants worked. Titles became more a function of how much pay and status were required to entice individuals to the White House than an indication of a chain of command.

Zbigniew Brzezinski inherited a much more institutionalized secretariat when he became assistant to the president for national security affairs.

Of course he also assumed an office that traditionally provides much more profile than that of the principal adviser on the domestic side. Under Carter, the National Security Council (NSC) staff operated essentially as a cabinet-level secretariat, that is, it served a highly routinized system of cabinet-level committees. NSC work occurred under two labels. First, policy review committees, usually chaired by the department most affected by an issue, treated broad policy matters such as relations between the Arab nations and Israel, the operation of the Agency for International Development, or detailed reassessments of relations with specific countries. Second, special co-ordinating committees focused on much more specialized issues such as management of specific crises (in which case Brzezinski would chair), intelligence activities, and the SALT negotiations. Carter's NSC staff generally brought to their work much more experience in Washington – in the armed services, and in government and private think tanks – than did members of DPS. Also, the organization delineated functions very sharply by having officials assume specific regional, subject-matter, and strategic responsibilities.

Several other offices serve the president in ways that *link* the White House's policy interests with virtually every segment of the political arena. Most important of these are Congressional Liaison, the Office of the Vice-President, and the Secretary to the Cabinet and Assistant to the President for Intergovernmental Affairs.

Frank B. Moore, legislative relations aide to Carter while he was governor of Georgia, managed the sizeable establishment (fourteen professionals) that tried to shepherd the president's legislative program through Congress. The unit became notorious for its ineffectiveness. At mid-term, under the direction of Les Francis and James M. Copeland, it developed stronger ties with the policy gestation process to assure that congressional obstacles were given better consideration by those formulating the president's legislative program. Thus, through Francis, Congressional Liaison began to participate heavily in the annual setting of priorities whereby departments learn which of their proposals will receive most favourable treatment from the White House. Copeland, meanwhile, tracked the elaborate network of administration task forces working on policy and legislation to ensure that policy development adhered to the president's legislative timetable and that draft bills anticipated difficulties in Congress. The Office of the Vice-President won its prominence in policy formulation by virtue of an exceptional responsibility given to Vice-President Walter F. Mondale by Carter. Each year, Mondale took the lead in setting out the legislative priorities for the administration. The role involved very close liaison with the White House and the president.

But at the end of the process, the vice-president assumed responsibility for developing the administration's annual legislative program and informing department secretaries where their proposals stood in the queue. An assistant to the vice-president, Gail Harrison, actually led the staff side of the exercise. She worked with the congressional liaison office and with Eizenstat's and Brzezinski's people.

The cabinet and intergovernmental affairs unit belonged in the cluster of policy-related offices by virtue of the latter part of its title: the cabinet secretariat proper took little of the unit's time. Under Carter, and for that matter most of his recent predecessors, the cabinet rarely engages in the type of collective decision-making that necessitates circulation of cabinet documents and the recording, interpretation, and monitoring of decisions. Carter, however, departed from previous practice by attaching the intergovernmental affairs responsibility to the cabinet secretariat. As in many other federal systems, government departments in the United States increasingly use special offices to work out the state and local implications of their programs. By bringing an intergovernmental affairs function to the White House, Carter gave added weight to this trend. However, the office engaged in relatively modest exercises such as development of urban and rural policy papers. Its 'fire-fighting' role attained greater importance. For instance, the office could give presidential attention to jurisdictional conflicts that arose during such crises as the nuclear accident at Three Mile Island.

A number of Carter White House units reflected the importance of special-interest politics in the United States. In fact, if the presidential advisory system deserves at all its reputation for lavish staffing, offices involved in public liaison contribute the most to this image. The most important units in this sector are the Office of the Assistant to the President for Public Liaison, the Office of the Special Representative for Trade Relations, the Office of Science and Technology, and the Council on Environmental Quality.

By the middle of the Carter term, Public Liaison concentrated its efforts in advising administration task forces about the concessions necessary to gain public support for legislation and trying to sell policy positions to group representatives. In chapter 5 I will have more to say about the trade relations office. Its functions concern primarily economic policy. The Office of Science and Technology served primarily general policy development in the White House where major scientific and technological matters were at stake. The Council on Environmental Quality under Carter became, in the eyes of many career officials who thought it was an irritant, an advocacy institute for environmentalists. Several other units followed even narrower specialties within the development of policy. These included offices for consumer affairs, reorganization (with responsibility for selling restructuring of government departments to client groups), and health issues.

Offices such as the appointments secretary and the staff secretary which concerned themselves essentially with scheduling and the flow of paper have been left out of this treatment. In addition, I will examine the Office of Management and Budget and the Council of Economic Advisers in chapters that concern more directly their roles. We turn now to a consideration of how Carter used the resources available to him. This examination, based mostly on the perspectives of his senior appointees and career officials, will provide an insight into how the presidential advisory system actually operated.

JIMMY CARTER

At the outset, we should put ourselves in Carter's shoes and assess his situation after the 1976 election. With respect to secular trends, all of the factors in the political environment that indicated severe stress on the presidency and atomization in Washington were present at the time. Metacycles that appeared as if they would last throughout Carter's 1977–81 term included especially gloomy economic prospects and the spectre of the taxpayer revolt in California that resulted in approval of Proposition 13. These two factors left little manoeuvrability, as acknowledged by Carter's quest for a balanced budget. Cycles within terms are perennial. Carter would have to take special note of the need to build coalitions through his appointments and to pare his agenda by the second summer so as to have delivered something tangible by the third. In fact, he failed to take either tack.

As a moderate Democrat, Carter could expect reasonably harmonious relations with the bureaucracy so long as his efforts to balance the budget and to reorganize departments and agencies did not disrupt their world too much. However his unfamiliarity with Washington, coupled with the atomization in US politics, made it highly unlikely that ambitious and comprehensive legislation could be pushed through Congress during the first term. To add to his problems, Carter's core group of campaign advisers were not appropriate for Washington. If he had not been able to recruit top figures in the Democrats' advisory subculture during the campaign, he would certainly have to during the transition period.[2] Carter should have realized that the immense growth in managerial tasks of the presidency, and the concomitant bureaucratization of the advisory system, introduced an inertia that works its effect no matter how much an incumbent wants change. Carter was too optimistic about how his personality would be able to cope with the stress of office.

Given this assessment of Carter's situation when he took office, we can arrive, through a process of elimination, at what would have been the best possible style for him. All the determinants discussed above suggest that the time was not ripe for Carter to adopt a planning-and-priorities style. But things were not bad enough, at least not at the outset, to justify immediate acceptance of the politics of survival. The choice then was between broker and administrative politics. The latter might have contributed to Carter's re-election prospects. He would probably have made fewer mistakes. However it would not allow for the type of imagination that he wanted to bring to his administration. The circumstances would force him to choose broker politics.

Carter's Plan: Spokes in a Wheel
Strangely enough, even after interviews with 132 administration officials one still has difficulty fleshing out Carter's plan for organizing his advisory system. Within the lengthy interview transcripts, one finds little explicit reference to planning before the inauguration. This observation dovetails with Richard E. Neustadt's to the effect that the Carter people found very great difficulty switching from campaign to administration roles[3] and Stephen J. Wayne's that they virtually occupied the White House without changing it.[4] The assumption of the administration seems in large part to have involved initial chaos and ultimate reversion to original campaign fiefdoms, with the qualification that Zbigniew Brzezinski and Stuart Eizenstat now belonged to the inner circle. As one strategically located respondent put it: 'At first, there was a tremendous amount of conflict over questions such as who should be going to what meetings, who should be seeing this, what should be going directly to the president, what should be handled by the NSC staff or the DPS. ... There are now a lot of things which occur more or less automatically. But, the process largely derives from the way responsibilities were divided during the campaign.'

The absence of a clear design for the advisory system left ample room for good, but unrealistic, intentions to fill the empty space. Thus, several respondents described the advisory system in terms of what they wanted to avoid; sentiment prevailed over design. Wayne gives us an insight into this. A cabinet approach to policy-making would provide department and agency heads with direct access to the president and more individual discretion in running their organizations; DPS aides would act as 'honest' brokers, assuring that a wide range of alternatives was available to the president, rather than as advocates for specific positions; the president would serve as his own chief of staff to avoid concentration of power in the hands of any one aide.[5]

Too much sentiment obscured several facts of organizational life. Secretaries and agency heads will not decide matters on their own if they can run off to the president at will. Thus, the Office of the Secretary to the Cabinet soon took, as one of its major tasks, the control of access to the president by secretaries and agency heads. Career officials find it difficult enough to be neutral brokers. The idea that political appointees have either the knowledge of the system or the detachment from their own causes to fill such roles seems exceedingly naive. Administration organizers threw caution to the wind, even avoiding, as much as possible, hierarchial assignments. In fact, newly arrived staff members were given excessive latitude in staking out their own turf. For instance, one assistant director in DPS listed as her interests 'neighborhood commission, community development, city planning, Indian housing, ethnic housing, housing counseling, historic preservation, architecture, business strip revitalization, industrial conservation, lending institution practices (redlining, greenline and reinvestment strategies), Small Business Administration, housing for handicapped'; she was astounded to find that her 'interests' ended up in directories as part of her formal job description. Finally, Carter did not in the end serve as his own chief of staff. Rather, the Georgians did. At the time of the interviews, Hamilton Jordan, Jody Powell, Gerald Rafshoon, Frank Moore, and, to a lesser degree, Stuart Eizenstat jointly controlled the direct channels of advice that enabled them to promote or head off others' input to the president. One true believer in the spokes-in-a-wheel system gave away its actual operation in a frank description: 'The president is the hub of a wheel and around the wheel there are probably – there is the cabinet – but there are probably in addition to that 13 people with direct access to the president, who have, therefore, control of spokes from the rim to the hub ... to get something done, you've got to control more than one spoke. On civil service reform... we had to do some strange things such as get Hamilton Jordan's old college roommate – Jay Beck – excited about the project so that we could get in to see Hamilton.' In the end, whom you knew counted at least as much as your ability to work the multiple points of access.

The Illusion of Broker Politics
The spokes-in-a-wheel view of Carter's advisory system perpetuated the illusion that broker politics prevailed. Most respondents at least gave lip

service to the notion that options were fully explored, if need be by the president personally. Paradoxically, every effort was to be made to keep issues as far outside the White House or the Oval Office itself as possible. Belief in the principle of countervaillance hung in large part on the Carter administration's desire to be the antithesis of Nixon's: 'Even this so-called Georgian mafia is more myth than reality ... Certainly, it's nothing like one reads about the Nixon White House with all the back-stabbing and things like that.' True believers based such assertions on procedures such as circulation of materials. And, as is common among advisers dedicated to any great man, the sanguine also attributed exceptional powers to the boss: 'I don't think you can say there is an inner circle. The president reads a hell of a lot of stuff.'

Several other respondents highlighted the importance of there not being, at the time of the interviews, a chief of staff in the White House. One of these, a deputy to a key adviser, even left his interviewer with the impression that the White House was run like a commune: 'It has taken the White House staff some time to learn to live with the fact there is no chief of staff. So, what we do now is informally have frequent deputies' lunches, and other groups, where we meet and just kind of coordinate ourselves in a collegial body. Nobody serves as chairman.'

The principle of countervaillance in Carter's administration correspond-ed with the president's training in administration received under Admiral Hyman Rickover: 'I have discussed this with him and his feeling, which I share, because we came from a common background – both having been trained initially by Rickover – is that he doesn't know how to do a job well without looking at the details because it's the details that make up the whole.' When the president wanted details, he got details. Career officials in OMB, who normally interact with the president only on ceremonial sessions, found themselves sitting opposite Carter in mammoth review sessions (one went from 3 to 11 p.m.), fielding questions about the intricacies of the budget. The pervasive interest of the president comes across best in the experience of an OMB GS-16 who, despite the fact he was three rungs down in the career hierarchy, gained access to the president because he knew more about one area of policy than anyone else in the Executive Office of the President (I, interviewer; R, re-spondent):

I: Have you been to meetings with the president?

R: I have had an opportunity to have the president say he didn't like to disagree with people but he disagreed with me.

I: Did you reciprocate?

R: No, I decided that the discussion was over and I stopped pressing the point I had been trying to make.

Despite Carter's absorption in details, some key Carter staff knew full well how the broker model could be operated to keep the president from trivia. One DPS respondent even drew very clear boundaries within which, he believed, the staff should work. These fit roughly the process-management role of a more conventional policy secretariat. He believed he could focus his attention only on the big issues. At the time, these were health insurance and the containment of hospital costs. Both demanded disproportionate attention because they involved huge sums of money. Everyone concerned with inflation, the White House, the Council of Economic Advisers, OMB, Alfred Kahn (the president's top adviser on inflation), and Treasury, had a stake. Under such circumstances, our DPS respondent ensured that all relevant departments and agencies became involved to the necessary degree. But he could not stop there. He also had to 'prod' departments. As the gestation process dragged on he reminded key departments of the president's interest and got them working in the direction he wanted things to go. He tried then to hold off advocacy to final stages of the process. When asked whether his role involved 'riding shotgun' for the department, our respondent added: 'Well I think that that has been probably one of our roles, to sort of keep the economic agencies somewhat in line. Now, they have had a big impact on the president's decision along the way not to go for a fully comprehensive plan but to go for a less-than-comprehensive plan. Certainly that was the result of the economics people's input. But, as we got closer and closer to a plan there is no question that we probably played the decisive role of holding off the economics people and saying that for a variety of social, political and other reasons we were nevertheless going to have a quite substantial plan.' In sum, the respondent offers a textbook description of the role of broker whereby lapses from neutrality occur only when the president has decided to move and a workable and legitimate deal has been struck.

The Obsessive-Compulsive Reality
The illusion of broker politics notwithstanding, several respondents gave clear evidence that the principle of countervaillance and the resolve of the administration to leave details to departments had not even remotely succeeded. Carter's trusted Georgians still had the final word on key matters. Hamilton Jordan enjoyed the greatest amount of influence. Even two key NSC staff members who had worked on the Middle East

settlement noted that they worked closely with Jordan, especially in assessing the political impact of various options. Jordan, as we note above, also took the chair for the White House's SALT II task force. A senior White House staff member provided a picture of the situation before Jordan relinquished some of his responsibilities in 1978. His office had become a cluttered clearing-house for just about every issue: 'Hamilton Jordan had been primarily responsible for any and everything political, whether it was a state chairman requesting a picture to liaison with the Democratic National Committee and political things all over the country; and he also was responsible for the personnel office. And there were always the dozen and one other crises that would occupy his daily attention.' Jody Powell, Frank Moore, Gerald Rafshoon, and Stuart Eizenstat likewise found their timetables cluttered with tasks that only the most trusted could perform.

Another respondent pointed up a basic inconsistency in Carter's style that was leading to disaffection among appointees who did not have the access that the Georgians did. On the one hand, officials knew that the president was reading their material; on the other, they knew that what they wrote could be undermined in private sessions of the Georgians: 'We're constantly writing stuff – huge things, because that's what he wants. But those around him believe in an oral tradition. So there is a strange truncation of the process whereby we write these huge things and the president is supposed to be deliberating on the basis of them but what really counts is what the Georgians say to him.'

This respondent probably would have found surprising the observations of one senior Georgian that indicate that compartmentalization of the advisory system had spread to the inner circle: 'The people important to a subject do important work on it. They make the recommendations to the president. Stu [Eizenstat] chairs an energy task force. I don't think Hamilton's [Jordan] ever been to a meeting or ever will go to a meeting or ever heard a report ... Hamilton chairs a SALT task force. I sit on both those task forces. And I doubt that Stu has ever been invited, would ever go, would ever need to go. He doesn't want to go. All he knows about SALT is what he reads in the paper ... This is the way Carter has always operated and it's the way his staff operates.'

By mid-May 1979 the collapse of Carter's popularity had the Georgians working jointly on one thing, the president's political future. One disgruntled respondent underlined the importance of this effort: 'Right now every day, the president and Frank Moore, Jody [Powell], Ham, Stu and Rafshoon meet exclusive of everybody else and discuss the week's events or the day's events. That's an innovation. It didn't use to happen ... It's more the people who are managing the president's political future ...

It excludes a lot of people with the same title. These are the ones who are totally and completely secure in their jobs, unchallengeable, and therefore above pettiness in many respects. But they, also, are not all that interested in inviting outside opinion.'

The breakdown of countervaillance stemmed from the Georgians' special access to the president and the fragmentary method of dealing with issues, and also from a failure on the part of Eizenstat to give DPS adequate leadership. Several DPS members registered concern about its operation. As already noted, policy clusters headed by associate directors were essentially nominal. Most matters were reported directly to Bert Carp, the deputy director, who channelled memoranda to Eizenstat. The relative autonomy of staffs brought about excessive competition. They tended to hoard information in the belief that an individual's strength and position came from what he knew that others did not. All this led one respondent to wonder out loud about Eizenstat: 'The thing that worries me, and I wonder about the people at the very top, is, it would seem to me, that when you hire staff, you must have a concept of what you want to achieve. I wonder if Eizenstat feels that he's been successful in the team that he's put together ... I wonder if he has a vision other than just focusing on problems.'

Finally, the collapse of countervaillance related very strongly to the personalities involved – the president's and the Georgians'. Several respondents volunteered the observation that Carter is a shy, retiring individual. He did not, as one respondent found, encourage spontaneity in the Oval Office: 'We had lunch with him. It was awkward. Eventually, I was the one who asked a question and talked a little bit about popularity and the trade-off between international and domestic issues and sort of opened the door to more controversial subjects. I came out of a very heavily Democratic party background in the Midwest. I'm used to going into meetings, and slugging it out with people and ending up friends in the end. That wasn't the atmosphere in which to do that.' An OMB official, much more sanguine about sessions with Carter, gives us an important clue about Carter's attitude toward interactions on the budget with those outside his most intimate circle: 'In doing the briefings that the associate directors do, we will generally ... he likes to use these view graphs on the screen. Throw a view graph up that will say here's the issue, here's the description of the issue, here are the alternatives and, if we know, we will reflect how the staff and the departments have voted on issues, and then we will make our observations about what we think is relevant and then just point around to Brzezinski, to Hamilton [Jordan] – whoever wants to make a comment.' Obviously, Carter sought in such sessions more to replace paper exchanges than to initiate dialogue. As suggested above by a top aide, he was back on the submarine mulling over problems in the electrical system or the reactor.

Carter's compulsiveness focused on the budget review, which became his principal vehicle for probing the inner workings of programs. Of course, the president rationalized the depth of his involvement on the basis of the importance of a balanced budget to his 1976 campaign. Previous presidents, although perhaps as interested as Carter in cutting deficits, limited themselves mostly to declarations of targets. Kennedy, for instance, relied on cabinet secretaries, as indicated by his relations with Robert McNamara, to administer actual cuts. Nixon one year boasted that he had spent twenty minutes reviewing the entire budget.

Some career officials saw Carter's involvement in budgetary detail to be beneficial. One noted that his interest in the relation between economic development and employment programs during one review session gave a major project a much-needed shot in the arm. But others had reservations. One indicated that the president always wanted more details than even the career people had at their fingertips: 'When we went to do urban policy, I was presenting it to the president. He raised a number of issues at the time and it was clear that we just didn't have the kind of background that he seemed to be looking for.'

Carter aides were easily the most overworked respondents encountered during the project. In fact, their apparent state of physical and mental exhaustion, coupled with Carter's constant delving into details, suggests that as president he became a taskmaster. The strains appeared especially in areas of DPS where advisory work was insufficiently related to the budget or management to attract OMB's attention and, therefore, staff assistance. Two appointees, one working on justice matters and the other on deregulation, gave a sense of work to be done with no staffing:

One of their bills is the FBI charter. Because it is a major formulation of what you believe about investigative agencies and individual rights, my job is making sure that what gets down here from Justice and what we ultimately bless is something that we fully understand. I can't emphasize that enough because I just found that issue is a zoo.

The worst part of this job is the following: I've gotten very deep into trucking, not just how politically you put this package together but what is a private carrier and how is it regulated and how should we change that? I'm actually helping draft that legislation. I'm working to the most detailed part. The trouble is, I'm the only one here, in the White House, who works on that. I can't do the basic trucking work. What you need is a large staff of people ... The responses that I get from the agencies are very uneven ... So a lot of the time I find that I have to do a lot of the work myself.

On to Armageddon

This treatment of strategic planning and substantive decision-making under Jimmy Carter underlines the degree to which his presidency drifted from broker politics to excessive involvement with detail. This process occurred as a result of defects in both the president's personality and his advisory system. The latter failed the Carter administration because it combined the two critical flaws: an intricate system of countervaillance overtaxed the president to the point where memoranda and meetings became highly ritualized, and the cadre of Georgians anticipated too much of what the advisory system fed into the Oval Office, thereby intensifying the ritualistic dimension of the advisory system.

By the late spring of 1979, Carter and his most intimate aides had concluded that the advisory system had collapsed under its own weight. Tim Kraft had assumed responsibility for a highly confidential appraisal of administration appointees. A few weeks later, Hamilton Jordan revealed a major White House shake-up was being planned.[6] The Carter administration was shifting to survival politics. However, the new style did not become official until after a decent period of augury at Camp David. Finally, on 15 July, the president returned to Washington with Hamilton Jordan elevated to chief of staff and a major purge of 'disloyal' appointees under way. By 20 July, four cabinet secretaries had left the administration. The first phase of survival politics had come into effect. Carter consciously abandoned the rhetoric of cabinet government; the administration had 'drawn the wagons in a circle.' As one DPS aide noted, 'From now on, the Cabinet will have to clear everything with the White House.'[7]

The first phase of survival politics assumes that one last effort to close ranks will save an administration. Yet much of Carter's pursuit of this strategy only emphasized its cosmetic significance. Hamilton Jordan simply would not bring the necessary rigour to his new job to have the title mean anything in practice. Alonzo McDonald, who now served as White House staff director – helping Jordan with 'process management' – eventually struck White House staffers as pompous, and he reportedly became an object of derision.[8] Hedley Donovan, brought in from Time Inc allegedly to buttress the administration's links with the eastern establishment, failed to break into Carter's clutch of Georgians. He resigned in August 1980.[9] In the end, Jimmy Carter found himself just as isolated and mired in detail as before Camp David.[10]

The candidacy of Senator Edward Kennedy, the Iranian hostage incident, the Soviet invasion of Afghanistan, the recession, and the 'Billygate' scandal surrounding Carter's brother gradually pushed the administration into the second and most desperate phase of survival politics, the channelling of staff resources towards the re-election campaign. By the summer of 1980, twenty-five top aides had left the White House to join the campaign for re-election.[11] Included were Hamilton Jordan and his deputy, Les Francis; Tim Kraft and his deputy, Joel McCleary; Gerald Rafshoon and his deputy, Greg Schneiders; and Eliot R. Cutler. The latter, although assigned to OMB, had co-ordinated the administration's energy policy. By leaving only Jack Watson, Jody Powell, Frank Moore, and Stuart Eizenstat to mind the house, Carter essentially conceded defeat in the first phase of survival politics – regaining control of the administration. His presidency regressed one step further into apparent chaos.

RONALD REAGAN[12]

At the time of writing it is too early to provide a detailed assessment of how Ronald Reagan has organized his advisory system for strategic planning and decision-making. However, we can look briefly at his approach to key issues centring around the operation of his White House office, the Executive Office of the President, and the cabinet. These include his principal policy objectives, his appointments, the hierarchical structure within the White House, efforts to enhance collective decision-making within the cabinet, and provision of staff support to cabinet committees.

Reagan appears to have chosen administrative politics as his style. In comparison to Carter, he conveys a nonchalance about the details of government that has provoked some commentators to question whether he has applied himself adequately to his job. Yet his first year in office found success – particularly with tax cuts and the budget – that brought howls from many observers about the demise of Congress. Although the honeymoon has finally expired, we still must give Reagan full credit for exploiting his landslide election victory and the Republican majority in the Senate. Reagan's antipathy to the welfare state preordained that he would not adopt the planning-and-priorities style. He could best tackle his key commitments, namely tax cuts to stimulate the economy and a vast increase in defence expenditure, by cutting back and eliminating social programs. His strategy called for harsh enforcement of severe cuts that, campaign rhetoric aside, would not leave room for assessment of which programs were effective and efficient. The point was to strike while the iron was hot.

So far, Reagan has received the highest marks for his appointments, at the cabinet and sub-cabinet levels, in various departments.[13] The new administration took special pains to ensure that appointees agreed philosophically with the president's objectives regarding the economy and the role of the state and would remain loyal even under the influence of 'natives' in far-flung departments. The person who perhaps best fulfilled these requirements, David Stockman, became the exemplar of Reagan's approach. As director of the Office of Management and Budget, Stockman gave short shrift to career officials' scenarios for the administration's alterations to Jimmy Carter's last budget.[14] He even forced a reworking of OMB's assumptions about the performance of the economy. He convinced the president of the potential severity of budget deficits if he failed to cut to the bone in several sectors. He then embarked on a series of bilateral discussions with cabinet secretaries that impressed them with the need for dramatic action before their officials had a chance to safeguard their favourite projects.

Stockman's success affected the operation of both the White House and the cabinet. The budget commitments so thoroughly ran the administration's policy agenda that the White House found relatively little to mediate and enforce. Thus, during its first year it largely centred its policy role on 'implementation,' that is, ensuring that the essential elements of the administration's economic program came across adequately to Congress, interest groups, and the public.

To say that the White House ran relatively smoothly in the first year does not suggest that it failed to generate controversies. Clearly former secretary of state Alexander Haig deeply resented the involvement of both the vice-president and the assistant to the president for national security in international affairs. The latter, Richard V. Allen, left the administration under a cloud of scandal. He was followed by Reagan's assistant for policy development, who apparently failed adequately to manage the successor to Carter's Domestic Policy Staff, namely the Policy Development Office (OPD).

Reagan can thank three men for keeping his White House on an even keel despite the more obvious difficulties, including the assassination attempt. Edward Meese, the counsellor to the president, claims a cabinet-level post and shoulders responsibility for cabinet administration and for development of policy on both domestic issues and national security. James A. Baker III, the chief of staff, guides all units responsible for political and communication functions, including personnel, congressional relations, communications, the counsel to the president, political affairs, intergovernmental affairs, the press secretary, public liaison, the staff secretary, and the speechwriters. Michael K. Deaver, assistant to the president and deputy chief of staff, rules over the day-to-day details of the White House – advance work for trips, scheduling, special support services, and the first lady's office. Meese brings to his work comparable experience with Reagan while the latter served as governor of California; Baker, who was an under-secretary of commerce in the Ford administration and joined the Reagan campaign through George Bush, keeps the White House running smoothly and provides vital links to the Washington establishment of the Republican Party; Deaver's relatively mundane responsibilities conceal the fact that he has enjoyed long-standing friendship with the president and has access to the forums where major decisions are made in the White House.

The Reagan scheme skirts neatly the conundrum of whether a president should provide equal access for all his advisers or channel communication through a chief of staff. He has added a layer to Carter's spokes-in-a-wheel format by having offices that work on policy development, politics, and communication report to chiefs who, in turn, have equal access to the president. The system appears to avoid the dangers of truncation so endemic to the Carter administration. Although special access stems from personal trust, each of the members of the White House triumvirate has assumed responsibilities that largely justify direct and continual contact with the president. As well, their equal status and constant interaction heighten their mutual attentiveness to concerns emerging from disparate White House units.

Although Reagan has ensconced himself in administrative politics, he has not neglected development of machinery for collective decision-making by cabinet secretaries. In fact, some of his transition advisers, principally Meese and Caspar W. Weinberger, currently the defence secretary, pressed for a highly structured cabinet-committee system that would greatly increase the use of collegial decision-making in the US executive. Other members of the transition team, most notably Baker, believed that over-emphasis on cabinet structures, especially designation of committee chairmen as superministers, would work to the detriment of the central theme of the administration's organizational plan – that cabinet secretaries should take control of and run departments. A workable compromise emerged with the creation of cabinet councils covering – in addition to national security – economic affairs, commerce and trade, food and agriculture, human resources, natural resources and environment, and, recently, legal policy.

Theoretically, the president chairs formal sessions of these councils. Cabinet-level planning sessions, headed by the chairman *pro tem* assigned to each council, provide a line of defence against issues that need not go to the president and prepare those that should. In practice, cabinet councils have worked unevenly. The National Security Council, of course, benefits from historical precedent in maintaining its relatively institutionalized committee system. The Council on Economic Affairs builds as well on previous, albeit less well developed, committees in the Ford and Carter administrations. Indeed, among the councils on the domestic side, it has maintained by far the highest level of activity, with meetings almost twice weekly. In addition, it has continued a triumvirate arrangement whereby its key members, the secretary of the treasury, the director of the Office of Management and Budget, and the chairman of the Council of Economic Advisers, meet weekly for breakfast. However, other aspects of the councils' operations have proved sporadic. For instance, the president, having chaired only six meetings of councils on the domestic side in his first five months of office, appears not to have involved himself vitally in these groups. In the same period, the councils on food and agriculture and on human resources each met only three times. As well, advocates of stronger collective decision-making in policy sectors have resented the fact that secretaries most vitally involved with issues must deal ultimately with another committee, the legislative strategy group. This body, consisting of Baker and his top aides, David Stockman, Secretary of the Treasury Donald Regan, Meese, and Edwin L. Harper (the new assistant to the president for policy development), considers the feasibility of key decisions.

Despite Reagan's modest advancement of cabinet machinery designed to enhance collective decision-making, his administration failed to provide adequate staff support for these efforts. Indeed, the relatively mediocre appointees to key positions in the National Security Council, largely the product of Richard Allen's poor selections, undermined the effectiveness of the NSC committee system during the administration's first year. On the domestic side, the Office of Policy Development, apart from labouring under similar difficulties to those of the NSC staff related to the quality of personnel, worked with about half the professional staff available in Carter's Domestic Policy Staff. Ironically, OPD took on much more structured tasks than did DPS. Its special assistants to the president serve as secretaries for cabinet councils and chair the staff secretariats, consisting of sub-cabinet representatives from member departments, which prepare issues for review by councils.

Of course, the administration has become painfully aware of the inadequacies of the NSC staff and OPD. It has replaced Richard Allen and Martin Anderson with William P. Clark and Edwin L. Harper, respectively. The former, an object of derision when he proved himself woefully unknowledgeable about international affairs during Senate hearings into his appointment as deputy secretary of state, should benefit greatly from his friendship with Reagan. He enjoys direct access to the president, which was denied Allen. Harper, whose first assignment in the administration was deputy director of OMB, gained widespread recognition in the White House even before assuming his current post.

In addition to these changes, the administration has purged a number of staff in the two secretariats and placed them both under the scrutiny of in-house assessments of their effectiveness. Reagan and his advisers might well view such steps as essential management moves in administrative politics. However, their ability to make these mid-course corrections drives home the fact that they have demonstrated a much more astute respect for the importance of staff organization than did the Carter administration.

CONCLUSION

This discussion of the setting of priorities and the making of decisions in the White House and the Executive Office started with the fact that executive authority in the United States resides in a single person, the president. When Americans employ the term *cabinet government*, they usually refer in fact to the amount of discretion that secretaries exercise while administering their departments. Further, the president's power of appointment permeates the White House and most of the Executive Office of the President. The Office of Management and Budget provides the closest exception to this rule. However, even this agency now allows for political appointees in its three uppermost layers.

The centralization of executive authority in the hands of the president and his power of appointment can produce less than satisfactory results. A strong case appears to be emerging for greater use of collective decision-making by US cabinets. The National Security Council and its many committees take their origin in the view that secretaries, operating collectively, can relieve the president of some of his burdens. Many respondents in the Carter administration believed that presidents should apply the concept to domestic policy sectors, especially economics. We have seen that Ronald Reagan's efforts toward this goal have not yielded the desired results. Relatedly, presidents have failed to get the full benefit of the power of appointment. Too much of the White House and the Executive Office of the President centres its activities on 'switchboard' functions linked to the president's partisan political activities. Especially in their view of the domestic policy secretariats, presidents have proved too reluctant to apply rigour to organizational charts and too timorous about appointing to policy staffs experts who readily command respect in Washington.

Presidents differ considerably in the way they come to terms with their excessive workload, the lack of clarity in the nature of cabinet government, and difficulties with getting the most out of their power of appointment. The terms *broker politics, administrative politics, priorities and planning,* and *survival politics* have proved useful in discussing the styles adopted by presidents for organizing and running their advisory systems. As applied to Carter's view of the role of the White House and the Executive Office of the President, we found the style he chose – broker politics – would have met the circumstances under which he assumed the presidency. His relatively heavy agenda – especially his objective of a balanced budget – coupled with hard times suggested that he would have to leave many important issues to be worked out by cabinet secretaries and structure his policy shops so that they would strain out the 'gnats' from his decision memos. Carter, in large part because of his penchant for detail, failed to follow these tacks. Indeed, a severe incongruity developed between the operation of Carter's cabinet and advisory system and what the administration was attempting to do. As if the president had decided upon administrative politics, structures functioned loosely. Yet Carter behaved increasingly as if he personally could shoulder the burden of a priorities-and-planning workload. Ronald Reagan, facing more adverse times and committing himself to severe policies, chose administrative politics from the outset. However, he has recognized systemic defects that suggest the need for enhancement of collective decision-making. To date, the commitment to administrative politics eclipses somewhat the apparent desire to improve the capabilities for cabinet-level decision-making.

3

British cabinet government and restrained strategic planning

In contrast to the situation in the United States, Britain has both a highly developed machinery for assisting the cabinet and its committees in mapping out strategy and reaching decisions and resources available to the prime minister for determining the course of the government and making policy. Especially in the cases of the Cabinet Office and the Central Policy Review Staff, officials live a double life that requires that they service ministers both collectively and individually. In the latter instance, officials must brief the chairmen of cabinet and its committees. Since the prime minister by convention chairs both the cabinet and many of its key committees, officials in the Cabinet Office and the Central Policy Review Staff often find themselves briefing the prime minister directly.

No. 10

One institution serves the prime minister almost exclusively. Formally titled Prime Minister's Office, the unit is more widely known as No. 10. The unit's staff of some seventy crams itself into the famous house on Downing Street that spawned its nickname. Many British respondents made much of the fact that No. 10 falls far short of the White House both in size and accommodation. They overstate the reality. In Washington, the most vital segment of the presidential staff uses quarters in the West Wing of the White House that are almost as cramped for space. In Ottawa, most of the Prime Minister's Office squeezes into tight accommodation, prized for its proximity to the prime minister, in the west end of a large building, the Langevin Block, which houses much of the Privy Council Office. Hence, in looking at No. 10 one should remember that much of its compactness relates to a tendency among staffers who must be close to the chief decision-maker and one another to bunch up in the nooks and crannies of hopelessly congested facilities.

Prime ministers need not organize No. 10 in the same way as their predecessors. However, some positions seem to stand the test of time. These include the private secretaries, a political adviser, a policy adviser, a press secretary, a secretary for government appointments, a member of the House of Commons who serves as parliamentary private secretary, and a personal or constituency secretary. Margaret Thatcher deviated from this pattern slightly by appointing a chief of staff and, in October 1980, a personal economic adviser. As we will see, the former of the new titles bears only nominally on what its incumbent actually does.

The private secretaries occupy the nerve centre of No. 10, known as the 'private office.' They also fulfil, more than any other staff, our expectation that key officials will tolerate nearly insufferable accommodation just to maintain proximity to the chief decision-maker and each other. All the private secretaries come on secondment, for roughly two years, from career positions in government departments. A deputy secretary heads up the private office. In an operational department, deputy secretaries would normally ensconce themselves in splendid offices with large desks, lounge chairs, and sofas, for informal meetings, and a large table, for more serious work sessions. In No. 10, the deputy secretary and four other private secretaries, together with the personal assistant to the prime minister and a duty clerk, fit into two small rooms immediately adjacent to the prime minister's. The deputy secretary sees everything that goes to the prime minister from Whitehall. Three of his colleagues in the private office cover specific areas of governmental activity. One, from the Foreign and Commonwealth Office, watches overseas affairs; another, from Treasury, handles the economy and industry; another, usually from an operational department on the domestic affairs side, concentrates on social policy. One remaining private secretary works on the prime minister's business in Parliament, including briefings for her semi-weekly appearances during question period in the House of Commons. A personal assistant rules over management of the prime minister's schedule.

The members of the private office perform a threefold function within their domains. First and foremost, they gather intelligence for the prime minister on what is happening in government departments. The private secretaries come from the cream of high-flying career officials. A stint in No. 10 marks them further as prospective mandarins. Thus they can plug into networks in and between departments to a degree unparalleled by personal staff to chief decision-makers in Washington and Ottawa. Here we should note as well that private secretaries draw upon their own expertise derived from direct involvement, before coming to No. 10, in many of the policy matters on which they keep a watching brief for the prime minister. The private office also covers all cabinet committee meetings chaired by the prime minister and all meetings of officials organized by the Cabinet Office where the prime minister's interests are at stake. The working conditions of the private office assure, as well, that intelligence teased out by individual private secretaries becomes community property: 'Since we all live, work, in two very overcrowded offices, not because we don't deserve better accommodation ... then in the course of the day one thing after another will be the subject of discussion between us as to whether we should get some more advice on this, what's going on on that, what do we think about thus.'

Second, the private office puts briefs from several different government sources into a comprehensive package. The prime minister relies heavily on such briefs to get to the bottom of issues without losing herself in a mound of papers. We can assume that, on crucial matters, the prime minister will find in her folder briefs from two or three cabinet ministers, a co-ordinated brief from the Cabinet Office with perhaps further advice from the Central Policy Review Staff, and notes from her political advisers inside No. 10. One member of the private office takes off from this point to give us an idea of what he must do to make the material of greater use to the prime minister: 'Now someone has to tell the prime minister that this is what you have got, and suggest to her the sequence in which she should read these in order to make sense of them, to draw together the salient points that they are making – hopefully they are all moving in some kind of direction – bring out the points of conflict and so lead the prime minister to the point where she is able, without having herself to write an essay, to give specific directions as to what she wants done on the issues that are now before her.'

Third, the private secretaries work to assure that the prime minister's positions and decisions on various matters that come to No. 10 are communicated to operational departments. A great deal of this role involves more than circulation of information. As one respondent was quick to note, letters to departments often raise as many questions as they resolve. Thus, the private office must constantly be prepared to interpret the prime minister's mind when elaborations are requested.

We should raise here the issue of whether private secretaries can serve both the prime minister and their careers at the same time. Neither of the other systems studied has non-partisan career officials working as personal staff to the chief decision-maker. In fact, private office civil servants normally manifest a natural immunity to partisan politics. However, partisan politics is the operative term here. Appointees in No. 10 leave the visitor with the impression that it is just as likely that the prime minister becomes enamoured of the private office culture as private secretaries are to become political in a partisan sense. One political appointee underlined the degree to which the ethos of the private office permeates No. 10. He asserted that even his political colleagues, let alone the prime minister, begin to behave as the civil servants do: 'We're so secretive here ... Outsiders when they come to No. 10 are not secretive by nature, especially academics or journalists, or people who've operated in politics. The natural thing for them to do is to tell other people what they're doing and discuss it. But you find that that's not the way things are done here. If you tell one of your colleagues something you shouldn't have, then you're much less likely to be told something by one of the established civil servants next time ... And it's not only from the civil servants. It's from the prime minister himself. Both the prime ministers I've worked for had wanted things to be kept very, very secret.'

We return to the matter of the relationship in No. 10 between the partisan appointees and the career civil servants when we look specifically at the differences in the operation of planning and decision-making under Callaghan and Thatcher. Thus, I will reserve discussion of the roles of the political staff until a later point in this treatment of the British system.

Three No. 10 positions remain to be discussed: the secretary for appointments, the parliamentary private secretary, and the press secretary. The secretary for appointments, a career civil servant, belongs to the private office and reports to the principal private secretary. He manages the process whereby the prime minister exercises a key prerogative, recommending to the queen names of recipients of numerous government appointments and honours. The prerogative provides the prime minister with opportunities to reward service to her party as well as fill vacancies in appointive positions and honour those who have served the United Kingdom in a special way.[1]

The parliamentary private secretary, always a member of Parliament, usually occupies the prime minister's office at nearby Westminster Palace, where the houses of Parliament are located. Normally, MPs who wish to have messages conveyed to the prime minister or want to have meetings with her would approach the parliamentary private secretary. Of course, the especially well connected might find it useful to communicate with the prime minister through someone actually working in No. 10.

Finally in No. 10, we find in the person of the press secretary a career civil servant who, unlike his opposite numbers in the other countries, wields influence over public and media relations that encompasses the entire government information service. Each of the press secretaries under Callaghan and Thatcher, respectively Tom McCaffrey and Bernard Ingham, has brought to his work many years' experience as an information officer in Whitehall departments. In addition, the press secretaries can command access to both the prime minister and Whitehall co-ordinative machinery that far exceeds their civil service grade, under-secretary (two rungs down from the top of the career ladder). The press secretary must keep constant contact with the prime minister to assure that her views are adequately communicated. Some press secretaries, depending on the preferences of the prime minister, have even enjoyed the privilege of formalized meeting times.[2] Joe Haines, a political appointee who served as Harold Wilson's press secretary at No. 10 during two Parliaments, joined the private secretaries each morning to discuss with the prime minister the events of the forthcoming day; Tom McCaffrey, perhaps somewhat more privileged, met privately each morning with Callaghan to provide a briefing on issues that were important in the media. The astute press secretary soon learns how to use these precious meetings with the prime minister to cross over the line between information officer and policy adviser.

The press secretary does not operate a one-man show. He has, in addition to two senior deputies, six other professionals to aid him in his work. The other side to his role, co-ordinating the rest of the Whitehall information machinery, keeps much of the staff busy. Under Callaghan, an assistant press secretary serviced a weekly meeting of Whitehall directors of information that was chaired jointly by Tom McCaffrey and a parliamentary secretary in the Privy Council Office, William Price, MP. The assistant personally chaired a weekly meeting of Whitehall officials responsible for day-to-day relations with the press and with ad hoc groups concerned with specific issues. The latter groups included the frequent meetings of press officers from departments involved in selling Callaghan's various incomes policies. Through such bodies, No. 10 exercises a degree of influence on departmental media relations that would make press secretaries to chief decision-makers in our other countries envious. The No. 10 press secretaries find ample mechanisms to ensure that departments are disseminating essentially the same story. They also work for the release of documents at times that will provide the most possible exposure for stories that will help the government's image and the least possible coverage for matters that will hurt it. The office exercises clearance power, on behalf of the prime minister, over ministerial statements and media engagements.

It appears that the Whitehall information machinery has tightened up somewhat under Thatcher. She has elevated the status of the information function by placing it under the care of a member of the cabinet: first Angus Maude (now Sir Angus), then the paymaster general, and later successive house leaders, Francis Pym and John Biffen. Further, Bernard Ingham, the current press secretary, has become more intimately involved in the Whitehall side of the press secretary job than his predecessor. He has headed up special committees on thorny issues. For instance, he steered a group studying ways to improve the public view of Britain's relations with the European Economic Community.[3] These enhanced responsibilities towards Whitehall suggest the seriousness that Thatcher ascribes to media relations.

THE CABINET OFFICE

Next door to No. 10, and with its entrance in Whitehall, stands the least obtrusive of government buildings along the street that is the British public servant's most sought-after location. Yet the building at 70 Whitehall contains the nerve centre of British bureaucracy. Entering the building, the inside of which looks very much like a functional 1960s university structure, one can see a lengthy passage to a relatively untouched segment of the old Treasury Building dating back to 1737. While walking towards the older wing with the inevitable escort who has been sent to the front entrance to fetch them, visitors will certainly be asked if they have been in the 'cockpit' before. Eyebrows rise if one answers 'yes' to this question. The cockpit, after all, splendidly furnished and further adorned with artefacts, houses the secretary of the cabinet and his top colleagues in the Cabinet Office. The cockpit prizes its private doorway to No. 10. Only the secretary of the cabinet keeps a personal key to the door. Other officials must rely on copies kept in the secretary of the cabinet's private office.

One could not quarrel with assertions that the Cabinet Office is busy. However, one cannot accept that, given its function, it is small.[4] In Carter's Domestic Policy Staff and the National Security Council staff, we found, all told, some 110 staff members, including secretaries and clerks. Further, the DPS officials came largely from outside government. Their inexperience raised very serious questions about their usefulness in helping the president co-ordinate departmental views on issues and reach decisions that would reflect the priorities of his legislative program. The somewhat truncated hierarchies of both DPS and the NSC staff provided few high branches. Thus, most officials covered their responsibilities with no assistance from other professional staff.

The Cabinet Office, not including the Central Policy Review Staff and the Central Statistical Office, housed in 1981 a permanent secretary (Sir Robert Armstrong, the current secretary of the cabinet), three deputy secretaries, five under-secretaries, and ten assistant secretaries. The British *Civil Service Yearbook* no longer lists staff below this level in Cabinet Office – strangely, it does for others. However, the 1973 yearbook named thirty-two principals and nine military officers – the latter all naval captains and commanders, army colonels, and air force wing commanders. Figures provided by the Civil Service Department suggest that the Cabinet Office's 1981 complement included twenty-seven principals and six military officers. This brings the entire senior staff to fifty-two.

Add the eighteen officials at the Central Policy Review Staff and our figure rises to seventy. This amount of senior staffing clearly outstrips the comparable complement in the United States. It bears restating, however, that the British officials represent the cream of their breed, largely taken on secondment from high-flying or accomplished careers elsewhere in Whitehall. Their US counterparts, although exceedingly bright young professionals, often bring to their jobs no previous experience in bureaucracy.

Contrary to official positions, the serious observer does not find that the Cabinet Office essentially performs mechanical tasks for the cabinet and its committees.[5] One respondent from the Cabinet Office put two emphatic glosses on such roles that place them in a balanced perspective. The first elaboration admitted that its work goes beyond mere mechanics of cabinet decision-making. Despite maintaining that it does not take policy positions of its own, the respondent made it clear that the Cabinet Office does intervene when departmental squabbling has derailed a decision process: 'We don't try to integrate ministers' stances, obviously. One will very often see a ministerial paper and say, "Well, has this been shown to the Treasury?" ... that sort of thing. However, we don't try and co-ordinate ministers. At the official level, very often, we are playing a role here. I mean, one of the things I think we are very emphatic on is that the Cabinet Office doesn't and oughtn't sort of develop its own policies.... But, there very often is a role for us to do, knocking departmental heads together.'

Another respondent went further to suggest the frequent occurrence of what he termed *wet-towel exercises*. These involve the Cabinet Office in initiating the gestation of policy ideas by 'having a preliminary meeting with probably no bit of paper at all, or only a few suggestions on my part as chairman as to what further work was required. And then, you know, commissioning papers and starting pretty well from scratch. That's much more of an effort, that one. It requires a greater input from the chairman and from the secretariat.' Indeed, one official offered a clear account of the Cabinet Office setting its heart on a specific course of action. Here the Cabinet Office role went so far as to exclude other departments with natural interests in the issue from interdepartmental discussions: 'I have been feeling that they have a role here. But, the trouble is at the moment that we're doing things that I'm sure they wouldn't approve of and so we don't consult them.'

We must take care not to inflate the Cabinet Office's actual function. One official gave us a very good profile of its involvement in co-ordination. The description points to a number of pitfalls while not trying to sell the secretariat short. First, the respondent acknowledges that Cabinet Office views inevitably develop on key issues. Its cumulative understanding of the matter never approximates, however, the orthodoxies that constrain other departments, the Treasury included: 'The Treasury ... is more or less the classical Whitehall department where advice is embodied in folklore. That is, the Treasury actually has its own line on different subjects independent of its ministers, almost, however constitutional that might be ... Advice, in the first instance at least, will almost 80 – 90 per cent consist of folklore: "Our line on flexible exchange rates is this and here it is." ... [Cabinet Office involvement in these cases is] pretty superficial. You mainly have to deal with "The brief has to be up by then, the meetings, the what did they decide for heavens sake."' Also, no matter how clear their mandate, secretaries do not always find that they can break deadlocks. These develop from intractable positions taken by departments the interests of which are threatened: 'I find that problems are dealt with for years in the bowels of some wretched department. It doesn't consult and behaves in the most abysmal way. Then it surfaces and people object. Then, instead of the next stage being to resolve, that never happens. People consider the whole question all over again when that stage is reached and, no matter how urgent it is, they go right back to the beginning and see if co-ordination is possible.'

The official, however, does admit to a positional advantage of the Cabinet Office officials over their opposite numbers, derived largely from their responsibilities towards cabinet and interdepartmental committees: '[In cabinet committees] it's the tradition that the secretariat just listens and then does all the speaking after the meeting trying to clear up everything of the big mess that was left. [In interdepartmental committees] ... generally, the rule is that Cabinet Office must not speak unless they provide the chairman, then they do practically all the speaking.!'

The second gloss on officially sanctioned descriptions of the Cabinet Office's role concerns its very heavy commitment to the prime minister. This, of course, stems from her position in the cabinet and her chairmanship of several key committees. Any major issue that commands her attention will warrant a brief from the Cabinet Office. One senior official explained in detail how the Cabinet Office's commitment to the prime minister naturally takes a disproportionate amount of its time.

Notwithstanding his eagerness to stake a claim for the Cabinet Office's special obligations towards the prime minister, the respondent labours the point that the secretariat serves another master as well, namely the cabinet. The respondent has fixed on the fact that the Australians maintain a single central agency, the Department of the Prime Minister and Cabinet, to perform functions parallel to those of No. 10 and the Cabinet Office: 'In this country ... we haven't got a prime minister's department. In theory, the Cabinet Office serves all ministers; in practice, it serves the prime minister a good deal more than anyone else. But he hasn't got a department to serve him. He has, at No. 10, very efficient private secretaries who can deal with his daily life and his mail and that sort of thing. But, they, when they want advice, almost always look here. I mean I don't want to pretend we are a prime minister's department under another name, because we're not. We haven't got that position yet, and the prime minister isn't the chief executive. He can't overrule his colleagues just like that. He's got to get his consensus in cabinet. But we are the department that services him.'

The passage shows just how ambivalent our respondent's views were toward the constitutional position of the Cabinet Office. Such ambivalence takes much deeper root in confusion over the authority of the prime minister in the cabinet form of government. It harks back to the discussion in chapter 1 of British and Canadian tendencies to equate institutionalization of the prime minister's resources with a drift toward a US-style presidency. Many reputable scholars, however, question whether US presidents can be characterized as exercising authority in the 'monocratic' way suggested by our respondent's comments.[6]

Researchers wishing to plumb the depths of the Cabinet Office face formidable obstacles. Classification under the Official Secrets Act enshrouds its organizational chart in mystery. Respondents warily skirt details with statements such as: 'If you look at the – I'm not serious you should, but if you did look at the structure of our different components in the Cabinet Office.' However, left to their own devices, researchers can parlay interview material into a fairly clear picture of how the Cabinet Office actually operates. They must learn as well to use information from sources such as the *Civil Service Yearbook* and *Who's Who?* They can, with reasonable accuracy, derive the staffing of various secretariats from what they can find about the backgrounds of Cabinet Office staff.

We have already met the secretary of the cabinet. He presides over five secretariats: overseas and defence, economic affairs, home and parliamentary affairs, European affairs, and, finally and most secretively, security and intelligence. Each secretariat serves several cabinet committees operating in its sector. Ministerial committees consist exclusively of members of the government; official committees consist exclusively of civil servants. Among the latter, some work to specific mandates set down by the Cabinet Office secretariats; others 'shadow' ministerial committees by preparatory work for cabinet-level meetings. In sum, Cabinet Office secretariats service cabinet committees and the top official committees in Whitehall. They also take the lead in the more intractable issues that require special guidance from the prime minister or a ministerial panel.

The secretary of the cabinet operates at the apex of the Whitehall deliberation process. He serves as the senior secretary for meetings of the entire cabinet and committees chaired by the prime minister. This work, of course, involves a great deal of direct briefing of the prime minister on the major issues faced by the cabinet. Usually, the secretary of the cabinet will find himself chairing several official committees addressing matters of special concern to the prime minister. For instance, under Callaghan, Lord Hunt headed groups working on economic summits – the secretary of the cabinet takes the lead in preparing the prime minister for these – Northern Ireland, the sterling crisis, and, during our interviews, the dollar crisis.

Lord Hunt was also involved in a formerly secret but now celebrated body.[7] In Britain, conventional wisdom maintains that officials rarely participate in give-and-take sessions with ministers. However, under Callaghan, Lord Hunt, Sir Douglas Wass (permanent secretary of the Treasury), and Sir Kenneth Berrill (head of the Central Policy Review Staff) met regularly with the prime minister, Harold Lever (chancellor of the duchy of Lancaster – a cabinet minister without portfolio who gives policy advice to the prime minister), and the chancellor of the exchequer (the minister in charge of the Treasury). The governor of the Bank of England also joined what became known as the macroeconomic policy group, or simply 'the seminar.'

The secretary of the cabinet usually provides a fair amount of latitude to deputy secretaries heading up units within the Cabinet Office. In fact, briefing materials to cabinet committee chairmen do not go as a matter of course to the secretary. However, he has mechanisms for keeping watch on business flowing through the Cabinet Office. Principal among these is the 'future business' meeting held each Friday morning with his deputy secretaries, the principal private secretary at No. 10, and the head of the Central Policy Review Staff and his deputy. This meeting looks ahead two to three weeks in an effort to set the agenda of the cabinet and its committees. On one level, the process gives officials clear influence over ministers on the setting of priorities. However, the ministers, especially the prime minister, can reject the schedule. More fundamentally, the officials benefit from meeting in one of the few regularized bodies co-ordinating work in No. 10 and the Cabinet Office. During such sessions, they find the time to discuss various cross-currents in cabinet business. Cabinet ministers, in contrast, carry out discussions in a much more formal setting, sticking mostly to the points raised in departmental briefs.

Among the secretariats within the Cabinet Office, the home and parliamentary affairs unit, though the smallest, involves itself more than the others in the only work directly connected to strategic planning. Under Callaghan, the head of the unit served two cabinet committees, future legislation and legislation. The former, composed of ministers who, theoretically, have fewer contending bills than others, prepares the legislative program for each session. This exercise takes final and public form in the queen's speech, the government's legislative program set out at the beginning of each session of Parliament. Under Callaghan, the home secretary chaired the committee. He, of course, heads a department with a very large number of programs on the domestic side involving administration of justice, immigration and nationality, community relations, public safety, and broadcast policy. In effect, then, the home secretary simply brought to his responsibility for the future legislation committee seniority and standing in the cabinet. These qualities allowed him to lead other ministers in the difficult task of taking a broader political view of legislative priorities. The legislation committee, chaired by the leader of the government party in the House of Commons, guided the legislative program through sessions of Parliament. Margaret Thatcher has merged both committees into 'QL,' i.e. the queen's speech and legislation, and assigned the chair to the leader of the House of Commons. The final responsibility of the secretariat centres on the Cabinet's home and social affairs committee. Chaired by the home secretary, this body reviews the legislative proposals and green and white papers of domestic departments. The departments of Health and Social Security, Education and Science, Environment, the Home Office, and the Lord Chancellor's Department, which administers courts and tribunals, provide most of the committee's work.

The economics secretariat, with a deputy secretary, an under-secretary, two assistant secretaries, and four principals, contains considerably more officials than home and parliamentary. The large secretariat serves the key cabinet committee on macroeconomic policy as well as other committees considering specific aspects of economic policy. These, under Callaghan, included industrial policy, wage policy, and energy. Thatcher has established committees for microeconomic affairs, nationalized industries (policy, and finance), and public-sector and public-service pay policy.

Committees in the economics field take on many of the most intractable issues facing the British government. Hence the economics secretariat finds itself leading Cabinet Office official committees, often when other interdepartmental panels have failed to come up with acceptable policies. In addition, it must involve itself with other segments of the Cabinet Office somewhat more than other secretariats. For instance, the long-standing presence of the Central Policy Review Staff in the economics field assures to a degree that it will get involved on the most contentious matters. Also, the European secretariat, because of the importance of the European Economic Community for trade and monetary affairs, must let the economics unit look at much of what it does. The secretariat, finally, enforces the understanding that Treasury be consulted on the financial implications of policy programs.

In the European secretariat, issues in the EEC have tended to bring the Ministry of Agriculture, Fisheries and Food; the Foreign and Common-wealth Office; and the Treasury into policy discussions more than other interested departments such as Trade, Industry, Energy, and Transport. Margaret Thatcher set out early in her government to obtain a reduction in Britain's contribution to the community budget. She finally obtained some success in the summer of 1980 through concessions made to the other countries during renegotiation of the EEC Common Agricultural Policies (CAP). In 1980, the staffing of the European secretariat reflected Thatcher's interests. An official from the Ministry of Agriculture, Fisheries and Food served as deputy secretary, a former diplomat to the EEC as under-secretary, and a Treasury man and a Foreign and Commonwealth Office man experienced in Europe as assistant secretaries. The deputy secretary in the European unit minds the entire secretariat but with a heavy stress on relating directly to ministers and lead officials in departments involved in key issues. For instance, he would accompany the secretary of state for foreign and commonwealth affairs to all major meetings with other ministers from EEC countries. Under both Callaghan and Thatcher, the deputy secretary has chaired the official steering group on Europe.

From the worlds of home and parliamentary affairs, economics, and Europe we cross over to an area of the Cabinet Office in which interviews were denied. However, some information from other sources enables me to sketch this area in broad outline. Starting with the overseas and defence secretariat, we know certainly that this unit, headed in 1982 by Robert Wade-Gery (a deputy secretary seconded from the Foreign and Commonwealth Office) services the overseas and defence (OD) committee of the cabinet. Historical precedent alerts us to the benefits of keeping a watchful eye for the types of exercises the secretariat might assist, with or without the involvement of all members of OD. Peter Hennessy gives us a good example of how to proceed here. Take a defence issue such as replacing the United Kingdom's existing nuclear deterrent, the Polaris missile, with a new one, Trident.[8] We know that Clement Attlee, prime minister in 1947, struck a secret cabinet committee; he wanted to keep the decision to build a British atomic bomb away from some problematic ministers on the overseas and defence committee covering this area. We may expect that similar committees have existed surrounding the Trident decision. After probing, Hennessy found in fact that Callaghan used a committee of four to assess the Trident option. This included, in addition to Callaghan, the chancellor of the exchequer, the secretary of state for defence, and the foreign and commonwealth secretary. Mrs Thatcher has used a group consisting of the same ministers plus the home secretary.

Concerning security and intelligence, any government must co-ordinate and analyse centrally information coming from several sources. In the United Kingdom, the 'intelligence' community involves the various armed forces, the Ministry of Defence, the Foreign and Commonwealth Office, domestic police, and the official intelligence agencies, namely MI5, which handles espionage-related operations in Britain, and MI6, which co-ordinates international surveillance. One respondent was kind enough to give us just a glimpse of the work circumstances in security and intelligence while explaining the fact that the secretariat was the only section of the Cabinet Office with a modern computerized word processor: 'There is one in this building. But it is on the second floor where all sorts of mysterious things happen we do not enquire into but we have our ideas, and they sit and use it all the time and anyway you have got to go through fifteen locked doors [exaggeration, we may assume] to get there ...'

Security and intelligence serves official committees more than cabinet-level ones, even though the prime minister chairs a body, 'Intelligence Group,' that supervises the activities of MI5, MI6, and the government communications headquarters. The official committees centre either upon gathering intelligence or maintaining internal security. On the former side, the Joint Intelligence Committee (JIC), chaired by the senior deputy to the permanent secretary in the Foreign and Commonwealth Office, brings together various elements of intelligence-gathering within the Cabinet Office. Its efforts produce weekly briefs to ministers, one going to all members of the overseas and defence committee and the other circulating still more restrictively only to ministers who 'need to know' especially sensitive intelligence. A recent explanation of its activities in relation to the Falklands crisis provided by the *Economist* offers a detailed look at the inner workings of security and intelligence:

The JIC includes the head of the cabinet office security and intelligence secretariat, Sir Anthony Duff, and the head of the secret intelligence service. It is not part of the foreign office and is quite capable of taking an independent view of foreign office inputs. Yet it is the decisive filter of intelligence information. Early in the week, its subcommittees known as CIGs (current intelligence groups) meet to assess the yield from all sources, open and clandestine, for their area. This first stage of processing the raw material is supervised by Mr. Robin O'Neill, a diplomat on secondment to the cabinet office. The CIG covering Latin America is chaired by Brigadier Adam Gordon and includes officials from the secret intelligence service, the government communications headquarters (the supplier of signals intelligence) and the ministry of defence's intelligence organization.

On Wednesday mornings, the full JIC meets in the cabinet office to pull all the strands together into a 10- or 12-page document known as the 'Red Book' ...

Mrs. Thatcher's inquiry [into the handling of the Falklands crisis including the response to the warning signs of the Argentinian invasion] will be particularly interested in the CIG 'assessment' of Argentine information and intelligence in the eight weeks prior to the invasion. Intelligence sources have been quick to argue that their raw material was far more alarmist than the much blander assessments of it reaching ministers.[9]

THE CENTRAL POLICY REVIEW STAFF

CPRS theoretically makes up for the Cabinet Office's deficiencies in the field of strategic planning. As several respondents put it, the Cabinet Office reveals a bias toward keeping the machinery of government going; CPRS attempts to add enough grit to prevent things from going too smoothly. Initially, CPRS drew a clear mandate from its creator, Edward

Heath's 1970–4 Conservative government, to provide the cabinet with a pool of young, bright, and energetic advisers. Half were career officials and half from outside government. The staff would enable ministers to tackle issues in a more imaginative way. In the long haul, CPRS's support would strengthen collective responsibility by helping the cabinet control the direction of the government, break as much as possible organizational barriers to co-ordination among departments, consider options that would be unthinkable in conventional terms, and look beyond the limited time scales of politicians and bureaucrats.

Under Lord (Victor) Rothschild, CPRS began auspiciously enough. On a few occasions ministers went to Chequers, the British prime minister's country retreat, for entire days to listen to CPRS briefings on the state of the mandate. Heath accomplished his objective in such meetings. He wanted to pull ministers away from departmental briefs. He believed that in many instances departmental briefs so inhibit dialogue within the cabinet that ministers become mere surrogates for officials. Ultimately, however, events turned for the worse and the Heath government found itself no better than others at avoiding engrossment in day-to-day fire-fighting.

Although the Heath government failed to win another mandate, CPRS survived. It faced in its first thirteen years no small amount of derision. Criticism notwithstanding, several factors have contributed to its survival. First, it carries in its terms of reference a mandate to advise the cabinet on priorities. It has traditionally exercised this mandate by linking in a special way to public expenditure review. I will treat this area in greater detail in chapter 8. However, CPRS has always participated in the annual public expenditure survey in which the long-term expenditure plan is worked out. It also joins in in-depth reviews of the effectiveness of specific government programs, formerly called policy analysis and review, and studies of the expenditure and economic implications of new programs that will require heavy funding. Second, especially under Sir Kenneth Berrill, Lord Rothschild's immediate successor, CPRS enjoyed considerable credibility as an alternative source of economic advice to that provided by the Treasury and the Cabinet Office. Third, CPRS benefits, from time to time, from very strong relations with prime ministers. Margaret Thatcher, for example, has discovered in CPRS much of what she lacks in No. 10. She resorts to it when she requires a unit that can provide independent appraisals of policy programs introduced by departments. Mrs Thatcher's appointment of an industrialist, Robin Ibbs, as Berrill's successor indicated the degree to which she perceives CPRS to be a potential ally in her fight to bring Whitehall to toe under her brand of economics. On 1 April 1982, Thatcher replaced Ibbs with John Sparrow, a banker whose advice on financial policy she had sought for a number of years.

CPRS gains access to ministerial deliberations mainly through two channels not available even to the Cabinet Office. First, it can advise ministers directly without integrating its brief with that of the Cabinet Office. CPRS, however, does face continual pressure from the Cabinet Office to integrate briefs to the committee chairman. Independent briefs, however, can be potent weapons. Both departmental and Cabinet Office briefs tend to be the lowest common denominator of positions worked out between entrenched departments. CPRS notes can outshine the others by presenting to ministers appealing options that have been excluded from more conventional briefs. In addition to CPRS's privileged access to ministers through direct briefing, the head of CPRS and his deputy secretary benefit from unrestricted entry to any cabinet committee they wish to cover. Since CPRS has no minister, its top two officials may participate fully in cabinet committees. CPRS's access, thus, exceeds even that of the Cabinet Office and No. 10. Although officials in the latter two attend committee meetings, they usually do not take part in the give and take of exchanges between ministers.

As a Whitehall unit, CPRS operates unconventionally in a number of ways. Officials take great stock in informing one another about their activities. All outgoing correspondence and draft memoranda circulate in the 'float' that automatically crosses the desks of all officials. This mechanism provides in particular an opportunity for officials working in seemingly unrelated areas to make comments on others' briefs when they are able to add a dimension to the issue that has been overlooked or not adequately stated. Officials meet much more frequently in staff session than do their counterparts in the other central agencies. Each Monday morning they gather to assess the events of the past week and make plans for the coming one. This meeting contributes greatly to the co-ordination of CPRS activities as well as to the unit's *esprit de corps*. Also, the staff holds frequent seminars in which members give progress reports on specific CPRS studies.

The staff's unorthodox behaviour extends even to relations with those outside government. CPRS may call upon considerable funds available for consulting either private firms or academics. Further, it finds in its relations with outsiders that, derision by the media notwithstanding, it carries considerable weight. Some officials complained that CPRS finds it too easy to get red-carpet treatment when it approaches corporations for views on issues. In other words, officials find themselves whisked into executive suites when they actually sought only to speak with operational staff.

The CPRS convention whereby staff come both from the career public service and from outside works to assure that the unit forms an amalgam of individuals aware of the art of the possible in Whitehall and those with fresh ideas about the problems faced by the cabinet. Unfortunately, the convention does not operate as effectively as had been hoped. At the time of my interviews, the non-career officials had fallen to simply one-third of the entire staff. More recent appointments have restored the outsiders to around 50 per cent of the CPRS complement. Still, non-career officials face the fact that Whitehall's folkways introduce constraints on behaviour in CPRS that make life somewhat more formal than it could be. One respondent from the outside went so far as to suggest that career officials find it very difficult to learn how to operate in CPRS: 'Some of the bad appointments have been bureaucrats themselves, people who find it hard to adjust to working in a less structured and less hierarchical set-up than they are used to.'

Another respondent, also an outsider, registered somewhat more testily the view that the mores of career officials can have a deadening effect on life in CPRS: 'I don't like to walk into peoples' offices without notice. So I sort of dribble my fingers along the wall or put my head around the doorframe before entering someone's room. I did this recently to a very new recruit from the civil service ... About an hour later, he came to my room and just burst open the door and sat down and quite airily said, "You know of course about the etiquette about knocking on doors? ... You never knock on doors in the civil service. It implies that the occupant is doing something he shouldn't."'

In addition to intramural conflict over mores, CPRS has suffered from serious criticism of its work. Tony Benn, the dissident Labour MP and former cabinet minister, has cited CPRS on a number of occasions. For instance, he has claimed that it attempted to scuttle his efforts to see that the United Kingdom chose its own reactors over American contenders for the next generation of nuclear power. He objected in particular to the fact that Sir Kenneth Berrill took the side of officials in Benn's own ministry, the Department of Energy. His officials, allegedly, had gone behind his back to persuade CPRS to submit an independent brief against him.[10] Benn also questioned the constitutionality of Berrill, an official, being able to present views directly to a cabinet committee.

Benn's interpretation of events seems somewhat questionable. The prime minister, James Callaghan, had condoned CPRS's deeper look when the conflicts between Benn and his officials became apparent. Clearly,

Benn suffered acute embarrassment when CPRS came out on the side of his recalcitrant officials. However, the case does not seem to present constitutional problems. Ministers' collective responsibility encompasses situations where they take the side of operational department officials over that of a particular minister. In fact, at that stage in the Callaghan government, Benn had already pressed his criticisms close to the limit. Most prime ministers would have sacked him.

Another furore arose over CPRS in 1978 when it published the results of its exhaustive study of British representation overseas. CPRS had focused attention on the issue by questioning the effectiveness of overseas representation. The Foreign and Commonwealth Office responded by suggesting that CPRS do an in-depth study of the subject. The final product, a published report that came out some two years after the study had commenced, faced a barrage of criticism from all corners of Whitehall. A subsequent government white paper produced in response to the report neatly skirted any suggestion of fundamental change. In addition, CPRS's lavish expenditure of manpower on the study had already weakened morale in the unit: 'It tied up a very large amount of skilled CPRS manpower which was needed for a variety of other jobs including social policy activities ... on a body of work which couldn't by any sense of the term be said to be related to strategic issues. I mean if you like there were some quite basic strategic questions about the functions and role of the Foreign and Commonwealth Office which can be asked fairly quickly. The business of actually looking at what the Foreign and Commonwealth Office and the BBC Overseas Services do in relation to those questions or to the answers of those questions is very much quite certainly for somebody else to answer. It isn't for the CPRS to go about measuring the telegram traffic. That's a detailed nuts-and-bolts type of job.'

In sum, CPRS has retreated from its original task of providing ministers with an overview of the mandate. It now attempts to assess particularly contentious policy issues in terms of their strategic consequences for the government. As well it attempts to avoid studies that will drag on beyond six or nine months. Long-term studies simply assume too much about what will interest the cabinet at the next bend in the road.

JAMES CALLAGHAN

James Callaghan faced greater constraints on his style of executive leadership than did Jimmy Carter. Callaghan inherited his mandate when Harold Wilson resigned as prime minister and leader of his party in 1976. To understand any British government, we must take stock of the degree to which decaying industrial capacity and fractious unions limit the likelihood of new and imaginative government programs. Even allowing, however, for the perennial economic difficulties Britons faced, Wilson had yielded the prime ministership to Callaghan at the least opportune of times.

At the outset, Callaghan met increasing pressure from the US Treasury for him to seek assistance from the International Monetary Fund (IMF) to save the pound from collapse.[11] The ultimate arrangement with the IMF imposed on the United Kingdom continued and intensified commitments to wage controls and cuts in public expenditure. Under this regime, Callaghan focused a great deal of attention on economic policy. However, pressures bore down on him from the British political environment as well. With three years left in the mandate, he did not have time for comprehensive planning. Yet he could attempt to prove to the public that Labour could manage the economy better than the Conservatives could. Efforts to get unions to limit wage demands formed the keystone of such a policy. Callaghan benefited somewhat from an interventionist stance in the Cabinet Office, the effectiveness of CPRS as a source of independent advice, and the partisan counsel of the policy unit in No. 10. The latter, under the direction of Dr Bernard Donoughue, had been operating for only two years. Further, a trend in cabinet government allowed Callaghan to hold many decisions close to his vest – increasingly, prime ministers reserve some key issues from the entire cabinet until thorny matters have been handled by the ministers whose assent is crucial.

We noted earlier that we would reserve discussion of the political advisers available to prime ministers until we looked at specific governments. Under Callaghan, Bernard Donoughue's policy unit and Tom McNally's small political staff provided partisan advice. At the time of the interviews, the policy unit housed five advisers. Donoughue, a former reader at the London School of Economics, had supervised public opinion polls for the Labour party while it was in opposition. He joined the management team for Wilson's 1974 campaign. In No. 10, he directed the work of four young analysts concentrating on social policy, devolution, economic policy, and wage restraint. The policy unit often challenged conventional wisdom; it tried to maintain the intellectual talent necessary to resist counter-attacks from Whitehall: 'We must be of a stature intellectually and of an expertise that we can take on a departmental representative in a particular area. Our social policy person has to be as good as a senior person in the Department of Health and Social Security; our economist has got to be as good, it so happens that he is better, as any senior person in the Treasury.'

One may legitimately ask whether, creativity and obvious intellectual ability notwithstanding, such a small unit can actually have an effect on the prime minister's decision-making. In the face of the Whitehall machine, the policy unit was an institutional David in a valley of Goliaths. Yet it manifested very considerable resourcefulness. Donoughue himself had nurtured exceptional contacts in Whitehall. He held his post for five years. During that time, he became acquainted with numerous career officials who had served stints in the No. 10 private office, the Cabinet Office, and CPRS. When the officials went back to their home departments to assume more senior posts, Donoughue kept in touch. As well, Donoughue attended cabinet committee and official meetings at will. A gradual accretion of contacts put him on very firm footing in relations with a number of permanent secretaries. Of course, members of the policy unit, as Labour party operatives, developed close contacts with cabinet ministers. They drew, in addition, on intelligence gathered by partisan advisers working for ministers elsewhere in Whitehall. As well, advisers used old university contacts among career officials to get information out of departments which normally would not be forthcoming. Finally, advisers learned in time about certain disenchanted career officials who would provide papers that a department would rather not circulate outside its walls.

Policy unit networks proved useful also for influencing the prime minister and cabinet. Callaghan would view skeptically a single brief from the unit if it was at odds with conventional wisdom being served up by departments and his career advisers. Under such circumstances, the astute member of the unit would realize that he could have an influence on official briefs by subtly suggesting that the prime minister might be thinking along other lines or that No. 10 thought the weight of the evidence pointed in another direction. However, Callaghan would often think unconventionally without prodding: 'The prime minister will specifically ask us to do something ... On economics, for example, he has asked us to take a separate look at the implications of the European Monetary System for British monetary policy ... And he often does that type of thing, and he quite often will do that when he's thinking of something that he doesn't necessarily want outside people to know he's thinking about, not even the Treasury.' In these situations, the unit had to tread very lightly in extracting information or raising other viewpoints for fear of tipping departments off to Callaghan's thinking.

Despite these points in support of the effectiveness of the policy unit, it lived with a number of handicaps. First, its size clearly limited the depth with which it could involve itself in issues and the number of areas that it could cover. Second, it constantly played in the shadow of the private office. The latter, of course, basked in immediate proximity to the prime minister and the insiders' grasp of the Whitehall network. None the less, we will see that the policy unit operated more effectively than a comparable unit, also created in 1974, in the Prime Minister's Office in Canada. The British unit avoided a major pitfall that spelled the eventual demise of the Canadian one: it worked as much as possible on the prime minister's immediate policy decisions and eschewed comprehensive plans for the entire mandate. This tack might not have served the prime minister in the development of strategic plans. However, given the size of the unit, it kept expectations at a realistic level.

Tom McNally, now a Labour MP, served as Callaghan's political adviser. He had two others helping him on a full-time basis and half of another person's time. McNally kept his eyes on all papers going to the prime minister. He watched for undetected ramifications for relations with the electorate generally, a region of the country, or the party. He also maintained close ties with the official Labour party machinery headquartered at Transport House in London. Finally, he managed much of the prime minister's political life by handling his political correspondence and meetings. McNally went through his 'in' box to give us an idea of his workload:

A telegram of thanks from the president of Dominica ... A brief on the National Executive Committee. [The Labour party] has put up a paper putting forward the party's priorities for legislation and this is a brief which draws his attention to the major items in it and what the government is actually proposing in each of the areas ... This is a letter to two MPs on the situation in Iran. Two Labour MPs. Sometimes he will send a straight reply. But sometimes he might say go and explain to them what we are doing and why we are doing it. On the kind of cruder things, that's an opinion poll and a proposal for the next 'party political' [convention] ... An invitation from the Scottish Trade Union Council for him to address their conference. Now, I ring the Scottish regional secretary of the party and say, 'Do you want him up in Inverness next April to speak?' ... That's a list of ministers who have made political speeches ... It is worthwhile because at the beginning of the session he will be giving them a pep talk and he might talk out some improvement in terms of weekend engagements ... That is a typical one from Gavin Davies [the policy unit] on microchips [computers] which I think, for a guy like the boss going into a cabinet committee, gives a good shape of the problems and the possibilities. And, it is the right length, it is mercifully short ... This is a letter from Edmund Dell, the secretary for trade, about textile industries because Reg Underhill, the party's national agent, wrote me saying could we have something candidates in the textile seats could use on the record ... Some of it gets down to my own election, my electricity bill, and my rates and other things ... What will start in about half an hour is that everyone elsewhere in Whitehall will decide that they can get home by 5 p.m. and will clear their desks and it will start rushing into No. 10 ... There's a regional group moaning that they are not loved ...

McNally, as a good political adviser, viewed everything with elections and party organization in mind. It all seems rather partisan. But when a political adviser sets off an alarm his prime minister had better take note. This applies even if the matter concerns finely honed policy outputs from Whitehall.

Callaghan's leadership leaned in the direction of the politics of survival. We have already noted that he tried to minimize general cabinet discussions on the economy and confrontation in the committee on macroeconomic policy. He convened an exclusive seminar on economic policy to which only the absolutely essential players were invited. But, as often happens, Callaghan's politics of survival ultimately misfired. Unfortunately for him, it did so at the most inopportune time – the run-up to the 1979 election.

In the summer of 1978, the Treasury fully expected an October election. As a result, it advised a fairly serious 'phase four' of the government's pay restraint policy. The cabinet mainly opposed continued wage controls but was persuaded that a phase four would make a good plank for an October election. Additionally, the cabinet wanted to avoid at all costs a mandatory ceiling for wage increases. However, the Treasury pressed for a specific level simply because it believed that without a ceiling phase four policy would lack credibility with voters.

No one anticipated a rigid follow-through with the pay policy after the election. In fact, the Treasury had not really prepared itself to assure that phase four was implemented. Under phase three, the Treasury pursued a firm policy of requiring departments and the private sector to follow its guidelines. About the time that Callaghan had tentatively set for calling the election, polls showed the first signs that his government had lost favour with the electorate. Callaghan suddenly got cold feet. To the astonishment of his colleagues, who expected him to break the election news to them, he announced to his cabinet that it was off. Now saddled with a 5 per cent ceiling on pay increases that was both unenforceable and unexpected by the Treasury, Callaghan passed irrevocably into the winter of labour discontent that destroyed public confidence in his party.

MARGARET THATCHER

One of the least endearing qualities of Britian's 'iron lady' is her determination. So far, however, this trait has led to much greater success for Margaret Thatcher than most observers would have predicted. Specifically, she has shepherded her resources in an exceptionally astute way. She has disciplined herself to focus only on the matters that will continue to earn the respect of the electorate for her ability to manage the affairs of the United Kingdom as well as can be expected.

Thatcher's style as prime minister departs to a considerable degree from that of Edward Heath, the Conservative prime minister from 1970 to 1974. Heath tended decidedly towards the planning-and-priorities style of executive leadership. He created the Central Policy Review Staff to serve as an alternative source of advice to that of Whitehall with particular responsibility for keeping the cabinet aware of the direction of the mandate. He also assigned to some ministerial positions and advisory posts a number of Conservatives who had prepared plans for instituting throughout Whitehall improved methods for policy analysis. Before long, Heath's innovators had put in place policy analysis and review. Under the system, the Treasury, with the assistance of the Central Policy Review Staff, would direct departments through comprehensive studies of the effectiveness of programs that required closer scrutiny than routine budgetary review allows for.

One might have expected Thatcher to continue Heath's efforts to improve comprehensive planning and analysis in Whitehall. The Conservative party certainly continues a bias in the direction of priorities and planning. For at least two years before the 1979 election, the shadow cabinet had pretty well settled on the contours of its policies in the next government. Two Conservative think tanks, the Centre for Policy Studies and the Conservative Research Department, provided each shadow minister with a mass of material with which to prepare for the assumption of a portfolio. As well, the think tanks provided the new government with a large pool of potential advisers for ministers.

Thus, those who placed a great deal of emphasis on the density of activity in Conservative preparations for office might have come to the erroneous conclusion that Thatcher would operate essentially as Heath did. In retrospect, Thatcher never really indicated an interest in innovation comparable to that of Heath. The Conservative election manifesto, in fact, contained few commitments to innovative policies. Thatcher and her closest advisers in the shadow cabinet recalled, of course, how bold promises have a way of haunting governments.

Notwithstanding the restraint exercised over the manifesto, however, Thatcher departed from Heath in a more fundamental way. Heath took a passionate interest in the operation of the policy process in Whitehall. When he became prime minister, Heath found a tutor in Sir William Armstrong, (later Lord Armstrong of Sanderstead, died 1980). Armstrong, as permanent secretary of the Civil Service Department and head of the British civil service, won Whitehall acceptance for many of Heath's reforms. He so ingratiated himself with the prime minister that the two became inseparable. Thatcher had come under a different spell even before forming her government. Her mentor, Sir Keith Joseph – secretary of state for industry – instilled in Thatcher an unshakeable trust in monetarist economics. Stated simply, the prime minister believed that control of money supply and government spending will force economies upon industry and the individual that ultimately will revitalize productivity and competitiveness.

Several of our respondents, whom we visited once again to catch up with developments under the new prime minister, pointed out ways in which the decision-making process has changed under Thatcher. Along with a studied detachment from microeconomic issues, she has tolerated much less collective decision-making through formalized cabinet committees. One official put the contrast between Thatcher's attitude toward committees and James Callaghan's rather starkly: 'Under the last administration, we had a committee ... that looked at incomes and this wretched committee used to meet about twice a week and they used to get into the most incredible, mind-blowing detail on whether or not some group out there in the private sector should have so many percentage points and how much was in productivity and how much etc, etc. So you don't have any of that. It is true that the prime minister does have ad hoc meetings with ministers. She often likes to have a small group look at a problem, the ministers directly concerned ... Then ... if this is of any importance, she will take it to cabinet or to a cabinet committee.'

One official put Thatcher's style especially well by saying she operates much as a lawyer (which she is) with the luxury of choosing her clients and focusing at any time on one or two big cases she knows she can win. The same official cited the case of Britain's budget problems with the European Economic Community. Here she became interested in the issue only through her concern for reduction of public expenditure. The Treasury played a key role in the discussions through its natural interest in this and related economic issues; the Foreign and Commonwealth Office entered by virtue of its responsibility for relations with Europe; the Cabinet Office assumed its usual co-ordinating function. Of all the other departments that might conceivably have played a part, only the Ministry of Agriculture, Fisheries and Food (MAFF) gained entry. As our official indicates, the latter, in fact, got into the discussions simply because, in the end, it was making the concessions necessary to negotiate a new deal with Europe: 'In the case of MAFF, we're really rubbing their noses in it and saying "Agree to this" and they come back and say "Well, we can't go that far, we have our own farmers" and "That's really kicking New Zealand in the teeth" and that sort of thing. New Zealand is an interest of the prime minister's. The thing gets modified. But, eventually, they sign on the bottom line.'

By de-emphasizing collective decision-making and staying away from matters that do not bear directly on her macroeconomic policies, the prime minister has pursued administrative politics. Under this style, a chief decision-maker tries to devolve responsibility for day-to-day decisions to individual ministers. As one respondent put it: 'I think there is some sort of shift toward ministers being responsible for their own department and getting on with it.'

Thatcher's approach deviates from recent trends in British cabinet government in two ways. It suggests that ministers, who in the past few decades have increasingly stressed collective decision-making, should spend more time on their departmental business. Here macroeconomics should return to the private domain of the prime minister and the chancellor of the exchequer. Only if other issues impinge on this domain in a serious way do the prime minister and chancellor get involved. According to one observer,[12] a very modest concession to this norm brings two other cabinet ministers, Sir Keith Joseph and Michael Heseltine, into the macroeconomics inner sanctum. And these two gain access only because they are true believers. In her first year, in fact, Thatcher kept the cabinet almost completely out of conflicts over public expenditure and general discussions of the state of the economy.[13]

Thatcher, in a way consistent with her view of collective decision-making, has altered somewhat the advisory system available to the prime minister. Officials in the Cabinet Office and the Central Policy Review Staff find themselves working more to the specific agenda of the prime minister. Further, at the outset, she established an amicable relationship with her private office in No. 10. Thus, her ability to use fully the institutional resources at the disposal of any prime minister has helped her intervene effectively when she chooses to get involved in issues.

On the partisan side of No. 10, Thatcher initially adhered to the view that she could not convincingly preach economy in government if she permitted her political bureaucracy to increase. In addition to allowing only half as many special advisers to ministers as provided under Callaghan (i.e. ten instead of twenty), Thatcher initially eliminated the No. 10 policy unit. Under the new arrangement, two partisan advisers contended for the territory formerly covered by Bernard Donoughue. David Wolfson, former secretary of the shadow cabinet, carried the title 'chief of staff,' but actually exercised no authority over the private office or other partisan appointees, and, indeed, had no staff. He did, however, involve himself heavily in issues that the prime minister followed on the domestic side. He attended cabinet committees at will and maintained strong links with party think tanks. John Hoskyns, a special adviser, worked with a career civil servant in Thatcher's 'Policy Unit.' Due to the interests of the government and his ties to Sir Keith Joseph, Hoskyns's work on strategy largely centred on the Conservatives' economic policies. A political secretary occupied the same room and position as Tom McNally did, maintaining links between No. 10 and the party machine and Conservative MPs. Derek Rayner, who doubled as joint managing director of the retail firm Marks and Spencer, directed a small career unit headed by an under-secretary. Thatcher further concentrated her partisan advisory system along the lines of her interest in macroeconomics by hiring Alan Walters. Walters, a noted British monetarist, commanded an unprecedented salary to compensate for his leaving a senior teaching post at Johns Hopkins University in the United States and a lucrative consultancy with the World Bank. The salary, then estimated at £50,000, exceeded considerably that paid to second permanent secretaries – Walter's rank. The excess came from the Conservatives' Centre for Policy Studies, the think tank set up by Sir Keith Joseph.

CONCLUSION

In comparing British central agencies involved in strategic planning with those in the United States, one must first stress that in Britain the cabinet serves much more effectively as an organ for collective decision-making. Prime ministers consciously strive, especially through wide use of committees, to get ministers to reach agreement over contentious matters even without resorting to the entire cabinet. Highly developed secretariats both manage cabinet committees' agendas and paper flows and provide advice on how to 'knock heads together' and ensure that departments actually carry out what they agree to. As well, these secretariats monitor closely, or even take charge of, committees of officials attempting to iron out conflicts between departments. Prime ministers exert only a limited power of appointment when they first come into office. However, they control both the development of machinery of government and appointments to the most senior public-service positions. The former power enables them, within limits, to leave their mark on the organization of central agencies and departments; the latter ensures that over time they influence considerably the types of individuals appointed to the highest echelons.

Regarding the mix between career civil service advisers and appointees, the British have proven quite innovative. No. 10 provides a small-scale but effective blend of career officials, policy advisers with partisan coloration, and party operatives. CPRS provides eighteen officials who divide evenly between career civil servants and outsiders on secondment. Although the unit often suffers derisory criticism, its special access both to the prime minister and to cabinet committees has often resulted in sober second thoughts that have come in right on target.

The varying styles of prime ministers appear to influence the operation of central agencies at least as much as do those of presidents in the American system. From the very beginning of his relatively brief period in office, James Callaghan found himself in a struggle for political survival. As well, a weakness for rethinking routine advice often found him immersed in details that he should not have gotten into. Under Callaghan No. 10 played an especially important role. The contribution of Bernard Donoughue through the policy unit reflected Callaghan's exceptional reliance on No. 10. Margaret Thatcher has practised a style that contrasts sharply with Callaghan's. Largely contenting herself with an unshakeable commitment to monetarist economics, Thatcher has studiously avoided matters of detail. Her strong emphasis on the need for her ministers to assume greater responsibility for the management of their departments indicates just how determined she is to keep many more decisions away from the cabinet and off her desk. More than most British prime ministers, she has resorted to small groups of ministers operating independently of formalized cabinet committees to settle thorny issues. In the end, her government has worked exceptionally smoothly. Until its upsurge in the wake of the Falkland Islands crisis, its inflexible commitment to monetarism, rather than any administrative incompetence, led to the erosion of its popular support.

4

The Canadian
fascination with
co-ordinative machinery

Among the three countries, Canada manifests the strongest tendency for creating central agencies or units within them. This observation applies especially in the realm of institutions designed to service the prime minister and the cabinet in the task of setting strategic plans and assuring that major decisions are made in accordance with these. In fact, the proliferation of units working in this area will certainly astound non-Canadian readers. In 1968, we would have centred our discussion simply on the Prime Minister's Office (PMO) and the Privy Council Office (PCO). Now we must look as well at three additional institutions, the Federal-Provincial Relations Office and the ministries of state for Economic and Regional Development and for Social Development. We will see, in addition to an abundance of central agencies, a remarkable degree of differentiation of functions even within the five organizations operating in this sector.

THE PRIME MINISTER'S OFFICE

Casual observers have tended to place PMO at the pinnacle of this cluster of agencies. Since many of PMO's seventy-odd staff members are political appointees, it provides an easy target for those asserting that central agencies 'presidentialize' the prime minister's advisory system. Such conclusions miss entirely the fact that the prime minister receives virtually no policy advice from PMO. The popularized description of PMO as a cadre of partisan operatives who mould policy programs grossly distorts the reality. In fact, PMO's contribution to policy, with a few exceptions, has not served even the prime minister's need for a partisan review of the options he faces.

At best, PMO operates as a switchboard. We cannot attribute to it a sustained and significant role in the cabinet's handling of policy and the advice given to ministers on issues. As a switchboard, it simply manages various aspects of the prime minister's day-to-day relations with other ministers, Parliament, his caucus, his extra-parliamentary party organization, and the public. Those with No. 10's role clear in their minds will note that we have excluded relations with bureaucratic departments as a switchboard function in PMO. PMO houses nothing comparable to the private office in No. 10. The prime minister, thus, does not even enjoy the benefit of a small unit staffed by career officials who can, independently of the cabinet secretariats, look into entanglements within the bureaucracy and advise on the ways in which he might intervene to produce the policy outcomes he needs.

A principal secretary heads PMO. He differs from his approximate British counterpart in that he operates as a chief of staff with executive responsibility for the activities of all other PMO officials and their units. Other officials interact directly with the prime minister and take on special assignments from him. They must, however, keep the prinicipal secretary informed of the substance of their involvement with Trudeau. Unlike his British counterpart, the principal secretary normally is an operative of the government party with no experience in the career public service.

Jim Coutts, principal secretary from 1975 to 1981, emphasized PMO's commitment to the switchboard role. Coutts had served Lester B. Pearson (prime minister 1963–8) as appointments secretary until 1966. He then spent a number of years out of politics before surfacing once again as a party operative by accompanying Trudeau throughout the 1974 election campaign. Later, when Trudeau required help selling an anti-inflation package in 1975, Coutts rejoined PMO. He first managed the packaging of the stiff program that violated the Liberals' campaign promise that they would not introduce mandatory wage and price controls. Once this battle was over, he turned his attention toward preparing the prime minister and the party for the next election, which was expected to occur in the spring of 1978.

Bleak electoral prospects beginning in the spring of 1978 delayed the election an entire year. PMO remained in a state of suspended animation until finally Trudeau called an election for one of the last dates left in the mandate. During this lengthy period of anticipation, PMO made one incursion into the policy process that reflected the degree to which the gloomy electoral prospects had riveted its attention on survival at all costs. At an economic summit during the summer of 1978, Helmut Schmidt, the

West German chancellor, convinced Trudeau, allegedly while on a sailing excursion, that dramatic cuts in expenditure by the governments of the major powers would restore public confidence in the Western economies. Seizing this as a panacea for his domestic problems, Trudeau decided to cut $2 billion from the 1978 budget. Jim Coutts, believing that finally Trudeau had come upon the type of decisive action that would revive his electoral support, heartily endorsed Trudeau's decision and personally wrote the prime minister's speech announcing the program. However, the 'sailboat decision,' at best a calculated risk, ultimately led to disastrous results. Trudeau had failed to consult his finance minister and the president of the Treasury Board before deciding upon the cuts program. Both men almost resigned in face of this assault on their portfolios. Further, their departments could not, on such short notice, adequately prepare to sell and implement the package. For weeks following Trudeau's move, confusion and delays resulted in negligible improvement of the Liberals' image among the electorate.

To say that PMO currently operates as a switchboard does not imply that other principal secretaries have not employed other models. During Trudeau's first government (1968–72), Marc Lalonde developed the position of principal secretary into a crucial link for the prime minister into Ottawa's bureaucratic machinery. Lalonde had never belonged to the permanent public service. However, he had held a number of advisory positions in Ottawa. In addition to being exceptionally well attuned to the vagaries of bureaucracy, Lalonde had developed a deep commitment to Trudeau's vision of Quebec's role in federalism. Thus he provided Trudeau with an unusual combination of knowledge of the Ottawa scene and personal commitment.

After the 1972 election, Lalonde became a member of Parliament and immediately assumed a cabinet portfolio. His successor, Martin O'Connell, a defeated member of the previous cabinet, had little time to establish himself as principal secretary before he left PMO to run again for the House of Commons in 1974. One of his innovations, regional desks that attempted to keep PMO up to date on significant political developments in various sections of the country, simply incurred the wrath of Liberal MPs. They believed that the regional desks would short-circuit their representational roles. O'Connell's innovation had simply added to the general mystique that had led many observers to believe that PMO was becoming too powerful.

Trudeau turned next to Jack Austin as principal secretary. Austin had run several years before as a Liberal candidate for the House of Commons and had been defeated. Since 1970, he had filled a career civil service position, deputy minister of Energy, Mines and Resources (EMR). Trudeau, unlike many Canadian prime ministers and certainly their British counterparts, has always taken a keen interest in accelerating the careers of bright young bureaucrats. This concern often results in promotions over the heads of many other officials with greater seniority. Jack Austin had benefited from Trudeau's preference for hand-picked high-flyers.

Strangely, Austin failed to leave his mark as principal secretary. At the outset, he pursued with his assistant principal secretary of policy planning, Mike Kirby, an ambitious scheme for strategic planning. Here PMO would guide the cabinet toward establishing its priorities for the mandate won in 1974 and monitor departments' progress toward meeting the strategic timetable. By the spring of 1975, the entire 'priorities exercise' had foundered. Austin turned his hand to addressing the nation's economic ills. But he soon found it impossible to get the co-operation of the economics departments, especially Finance. When departments and the cabinet finally faced the harsh reality that wage and price controls would have to be adopted, the prime minister turned to Coutts to develop his switchboard.

In addition to principal secretaries, policy advisers in PMO have played significant enough roles in strategic planning and substantive policy decisions to merit some attention here. From 1970 to 1978, Ivan Head, a former law professor at the University of Alberta and now president of Canada's International Development Research Council, helped Trudeau maintain a high level of personal involvement in foreign affairs. Head often acted as Trudeau's surrogate in sensitive discussions with foreign powers. He also kept a watching brief on the activities of the Department of External Affairs.

The question arises as to why Head was not replaced when he resigned from his PMO job after a gruelling eight years' service. Allan Gotlieb, the under-secretary of state for external affairs until 1981, perhaps provides an answer. Gotlieb, one of a charmed circle of career officials whose style and brilliance Trudeau admires,[1] brought a distinctive background to the highest career position in the department. Although originally an External Affairs official, he operated largely as a legal counsel there and had only modest exposure to the diplomatic corps. In 1968, he left External Affairs to assume two successive deputy minister positions in departments on the domestic side. Thus, many External Affairs officials have viewed Gotlieb with suspicion. When he first assumed leadership of their department, they believed he instinctively questioned the conventional wisdom they served up. With Gotlieb's departure from External

Affairs the department went through a major restructuring. As well as taking on two new ministers, it now boasts three deputy ministers, all of whom have been closely associated with the prime minister. None has based his career in External Affairs.

The case of Mike Kirby provides another interesting vignette of PMO involvement in strategic planning and substantive policy decisions. Kirby joined PMO in the wake of the surprising 1974 election victory that won back the majority lost in 1972. Fired up by the fact that a government could recapture a clear mandate in a year that saw the fall of governments throughout western Europe and the resignation of Richard Nixon, Trudeau and the cabinet saw a unique opportunity to leave their mark on the decade. Jack Austin set out to find bright young Liberals who could work in PMO to keep the new mandate 'on track.' He realized that he needed individuals with strong ties to the grass roots of the party. None the less, he sought individuals who also had proven themselves as 'process managers.' Mike Kirby, a political adviser to Premier Gerald Regan of Nova Scotia who had a doctorate in systems theory from Northwestern University and had taught at the University of Chicago, seemed ideal.

Kirby's plan for the PMO policy unit simply bit off more than he and his staff could handle. Three advisers, including Kirby, aided by three assistants were to provide 'organized, comprehensive political advice' to the prime minister on major policy issues.[2] The unit relied as well on Jack Austin, Ivan Head, and Joyce Fairbairn (the legislative assistant) for help covering all cabinet committees. Even allowing for the seconded help, however, the unit could not begin to tackle its proposed role: '1) To assist the prime minister in developing the goals for the government during the mandate; 2) having established the goals, to work for a cabinet plan to fulfil these "within the timeframe which is most politically advantageous to the government"; 3) monitor development and implementation to assure that "the desired goals and objectives [are] achieved by the time the next election is called"; 4) provide continual political assessments of proposals before the cabinet; 5) enable the Liberal party to contribute to major policy developments; 6) obtain for the prime minister responses to government policy announcements; 7) from time to time, have contacts with groups and organizations concerned about a major policy proposal.' To round out its *deus ex machina* syndrome, the plans for the policy unit made it clear that it would focus only on medium- and long-term issues that would genuinely affect the course of the mandate.

As we have already seen, the priorities exercise, whereby the cabinet was to establish its goals and have departments plan their programs accordingly, foundered in a sea of bureaucratic inertia. Officials in operational departments simply rewrote their pet projects to say, as one respondent put it, 'This is how our existing programs and proposals fit your plan for the next four years.' Meanwhile, the simultaneous rise of inflation and unemployment began to drive home the harsher reality that the Liberals would not be able to afford new programs even if they could agree on priorities. In the spring of 1975 pressure built on the Department of Finance to reverse its insistence on voluntary wage and price restraint. Finally, after an August poll indicated voters placed the blame for Canada's economic woes squarely on Trudeau, the PMO policy unit took the initiative and worked quietly with PCO to bring individual ministers around to accepting the Anti-Inflation Program.

The small group involved in what amounted to a coup against the supremacy of the Department of Finance in the field of economic policy included Ian Stewart, who worked in PCO as assistant secretary to the cabinet committee on economic policy. It sprung its plan on the entire cabinet when it met at Meach Lake, a government retreat north of Ottawa in the province of Quebec. A 1974 meeting at Meach Lake had spawned the priorities exercise. Now, a year later, the cabinet scrapped the whole program and threw its support behind the latest brainchild of PMO and PCO. In the aftermath, John Turner, minister of finance, resigned his post and left politics. As for the policy unit, it gradually realized that, by abandoning the priorities exercise, it had denied its stated raison d'être.

Jim Coutts had little patience with the policy unit. When Mike Kirby left PMO the next summer, Coutts shifted policy advisers to communications tasks such as managing correspondence and taking care of partisan and organizational problems in various regions of the country. Thus, PCO became the real winner in the episode. Ian Stewart became Trudeau's alter ego for economics. He rose to a newly created senior position in PCO, economic adviser, and began to fulfil the role in his policy field that Ivan Head did in foreign affairs. As well, PCO no longer had to worry about PMO crowding its role in strategic planning and the making of major decisions. One PMO official conveyed well the degree to which Mike Kirby's grandiose plan had failed: 'We are just a valve at the junction of the bureaucratic and the political. We add a little of the political ingredient when it appears that it has been overlooked.' A PCO official half-regretted the demise of the short-lived policy role for PMO: 'PMO used to play a strong role in long-term planning because Kirby wanted to. Now we have to plead for the PMO guys to do something with us. They have become short-term tacticians. They're mainly concerned about polls and the next election.'

THE PRIVY COUNCIL OFFICE

PCO, Canada's equivalent to Britain's Cabinet Office, maintains virtual control of policy advice to the prime minister. Beginning in 1978, however, it has yielded some of its responsibility for managing cabinet business and providing briefs to committee chairmen to two new secretariats, the ministries of state for Economic and Regional Development and for Social Development. As well, it has allowed External Affairs to assume considerable co-ordinative responsibilities toward the foreign and defence policy committee of the cabinet. The man who until recently presided over PCO in his capacity as clerk of the Privy Council and secretary to the cabinet, Michael Pitfield, almost warrants a chapter of his own. Pitfield has maintained for many years a close friendship with Trudeau. He worked with Trudeau in the Cité libre movement in Montreal in the late 1950s before either moved to Ottawa. The movement published a journal advocating a rationalist-functionalist approach to political problems in Canada. It repudiated French-Canadian nationalism and called for concerted efforts to achieve social and economic goals.

Pitfield's friendship with Trudeau has always occasioned complaints that he rose too quickly to the clerk-secretary post. However, observers must weigh other important facts surrounding Pitfield's career. For instance, he came to Ottawa as a Progressive Conservative political appointee. Once he joined the career public service, he rose to the position of assistant secretary in PCO by 1966, fully two years before Trudeau became prime minister. Considering Pitfield was only twenty-nine years old at the time, his promotion established him as a high-flyer par excellence. He became clerk-secretary at the age of thirty-seven.

Notwithstanding more benign interpretations, the fall of the Trudeau government in May 1979, and its resurrection in February 1980, tipped the scales toward the conclusion that the Trudeau-Pitfield friendship had short-circuited the distance that previously existed between the prime minister and a clerk-secretary. Prime Minister Clark fired Pitfield because he was too partisan. When Trudeau restored him to clerk-secretary after his return to power, he confirmed definitively the politicization of Canada's top bureaucratic post. This assertion makes a direct assault on the enduring myth that Canada has a merit-based civil service in which advancement occurs on the grounds of achievement and seniority. Pitfield himself has suffered from the myth more than anyone. Geoffrey Simpson, in a recent book, recounts how dumfounded Pitfield was when Clark fired him on the grounds that he was too strongly identified with the Liberals:

The meeting was important because Clark's first act as Prime Minister was to sack Michael Pitfield ... Pitfield knew from Clark's speeches that his fate was probably sealed if the Conservatives took power, but he retained a glimmer of hope that he could stay if he demonstrated his loyalty during the transition period. Pitfield flew to Jasper [Alberta], where Clark and his advisers retreated after the election, to brief the new Prime Minister on the transition of power, but the thoroughness of his presentations could not erase his past friendship and loyalty to Trudeau. His own appointment had politicized the clerk's job, and Pitfield suffered the inevitable consequences when Clark asked for his resignation during a two-hour meeting at Jasper. A week later, Pitfield discharged his last responsibility as clerk of the Privy Council, swearing in the new Conservative Cabinet like a prisoner cleaning the rifles of his firing squad. The next day, Pitfield broke down in tears when he bade farewell to his colleagues in the Privy Council [Office].[3]

Michael Pitfield occupied the most strategic position in the federal public service. Along with the principal secretary, the prime minister's press secretary from PMO, and the deputy secretaries to the cabinet for plans and for operations, the clerk routinely joins meetings with the prime minister held first thing each morning. This gathering plans each day and gets up to date on matters that require special attention from PMO and PCO. In these sessions and throughout the rest of the day, the clerk becomes the equivalent of the British principal private secretary and secretary of the cabinet rolled into one. He places himself at the prime minister's beck and call for gathering intelligence on what is happening within the bureaucracy toward solution of key issues. He also proffers advice on how to handle an impasse or to head off a department's attempt to force an issue. All the while, he monitors the collective decision-making process of the cabinet.

Much of this work involves being at the prime minister's side in cabinet meetings and committees. The latter include three standing committees, priorities and planning (essentially the executive committee of the cabinet), public service, and security and intelligence. However, the clerk's monitoring of collective decisions extends as well to his chairing meetings of deputy ministers that 'shadow' cabinet committees. Under special circumstances, he will participate in committees of deputy ministers set up by the prime minister to address especially sensitive co-ordination. During the economic crisis of 1975, Pitfield chaired a committee called DM-10, which planned the implementation of the Anti-Inflation Program. Ultimately this committee became an even more élite group: DM-5, which managed the termination of the program.

Since 1980, the clerk has chaired a committee that Ottawa mandarins refer to as the 'gang of eight.' Initially, the group consisted of Pitfield's associate secretary (a post since abolished), the deputy heads of all remaining central agencies but PMO, and the under-secretary of state for external affairs. It met regularly to co-ordinate the transition between the Clark and Trudeau governments and the restructuring of central agency functions. The continued existence of the group, now known officially as the senior co-ordination committee, suggests that the inner circle of deputy ministers has formalized as never before. One senior official has raised publicly the question of whether the co-ordination committee defeats the original purpose of central agencies. In the 1960s, the official suggests, Ottawa was weaning itself from the dominance of a few mandarins whose machinations in informal gatherings could easily nullify the best efforts of cabinet ministers to take courses of action at variance with the conventional wisdom in the bureaucracy. Our official suggests that the co-ordination committee threatens to be an institutionalized version of the previous mandarinate: 'Although this can only be purely speculative, what may be emerging, then, is a new "mandarin" group consisting of the deputy heads of central agencies. Whether they will achieve the pre-eminence of the old mandarinate and whether they will succeed in better integrating the disparate activities of modern government remain open questions.'[4]

In looking at PCO rosters in the *Government of Canada Telephone Directory*, one finds stability over time. For instance, despite two changes of government and considerable reorganization of central agencies, thirty-six of the eighty-six professional staff listed in December 1977 remain in the 1980 directory for the same month. Further, nine of these have taken on formal titles for the first time or received promotions. Such figures fly in the face of published policy on staffing PCO. Critics had maintained that it would become a corps of élite bureaucrats who avoid getting their hands dirty in operational departments. In response, Gordon Robertson, the clerk-secretary before Pitfield, has publicly asserted:[5] 'There are virtually no officers making a career within the Privy Council Office ... The term of appointment is purposely kept short: three to five years with personnel on loan from all departments. Vigour and integrity are maintained, but an élite with any sense of separateness or difference is not permitted to form. Privy Council Office service is part of broader career development.'

In practice, PCO's gradual accretion of senior posts has provided many officials with the luxury of advancing their careers while staying close to the centre of power. Gordon Smith has beaten all rivals at this game. In 1972, he joined PCO as an officer in the machinery of government unit. He took the unit over as director in 1974. By 1977, he became a senior assistant secretary for machinery of government with responsibility for two units, government organization and senior personnel. Created specifically for Smith, the new designation now enjoys widespread use in other departments wishing to treat unseemly bulges in their senior ranks. In 1978, Smith took over the entire plans division of PCO with the rank of deputy secretary. He went to External Affairs during the Clark government. When the Liberals regained power he returned to PCO to claim another brand new rank, associate secretary to the cabinet. Thus, in eight years he progressed from an officer to deputy minister. In 1981, he became the deputy head of the Ministry of State for Social Development.

PCO contains eleven secretariats. Two of these, emergency planning and labour relations, perform essentially the same functions as the civil contingencies unit of the British Cabinet Office. That is, they staff cabinet committees responding to major domestic disruptions brought on either by disasters, threats of terrorism, or labour disputes. Two others, legislation and house planning and office of the legal adviser, assist the cabinet's legislation and house planning committee. The former secretariat helps work out the legislative program for each session of Parliament and advises on tactical matters; the latter, actually housed in the Department of Justice, serves as counsel on drafting of government legislation. An orders-in-council unit assists a standing committee of the cabinet that reviews all appointments and regulations that appear as acts of the governor-general-in-council (i.e. the governor-general with the cabinet). A communications secretariat advises the cabinet's communications committee. In addition to taking the lead in development of two recent bills that addressed the issue of freedom of information, the secretariat monitors departments' provision of information. It now requires from departments plans for publicity that must accompany all proposals submitted to the cabinet. In 1976, a few officers in the machinery-of-government unit covered this area along with fulfilling other assignments relating to government organization. Finally, the secretariats for government organization and for senior personnel serve, respectively, the senior co-ordination committee, when it considers machinery of government, and the committee of senior officials, when it reviews both senior appointments and personnel policy. The clerk-secretary chairs both bodies. Both the organization and senior personnel units support the public service committee of the cabinet, which is chaired by the prime minister.

The remaining secretariats work with cabinet committees involved either in the development of strategic plans for the government or in making policy within specific sectors of government programs. Since the advisory system has expanded recently with the creation of the ministries of state for Economic and Regional Development and for Social Development, grey areas abound on this side of PCO. The two ministries of state evolved from the 'expenditure envelope' system instituted under the Clark government. Here, as well as reviewing policy proposals in these sectors, cabinet committees manage the resources allocated to eight general areas of government activity. Michael Pitfield envisioned the system as ultimately including a ministry of state that would service the foreign and defence policy committee in the management of its 'envelopes.' External Affairs, which often considers itself a central agency, successfully fought off this move. We will look at the two existing ministries of state in much greater detail in chapter 8, where I examine the allocation and management of budgets. Meanwhile, the reader may keep in mind the fact that the ministries of state influence to a considerable degree policy decisions by cabinet committees by virtue of their advisory role regarding priorities within expenditure envelopes.

Two PCO secretariats maintain especially strong reporting links to the clerk-secretary. The first of these supports the cabinet committee on priorities and planning. In the United Kingdom, only twenty-two of the fifty-five senior ministers in the government sit in the cabinet. In Canada, all thirty-six ministers belong to the cabinet. The gradual recognition of the fact that a cabinet with thirty-six members is unwieldy has resulted in the priorities and planning committee effectively operating as the executive committee of the cabinet. In fact, Joe Clark employed the title 'inner Cabinet' for this body and rarely consulted the entire cabinet. Although Trudeau still meets with his cabinet each week, priorities and planning sets out the strategic plan for the government's period in office, adjusts it when changes are called for, and vets all major policy proposals. Also, it arranges spending priorities for the annual budget. In fact, the committee recently obtained new leverage over expenditure priorities by virtue of its control over the allocations made to specific envelopes. The second secretariat reporting directly to the clerk houses some eight professionals who perform various analytic tasks for the cabinet's committee on security and intelligence which, like priorities and planning, is chaired by the prime minister. As its name suggests, the committee reviews information originating from armed forces security divisions, External Affairs, and the Royal Canadian Mounted Police on matters of domestic and foreign security.

The four remaining secretariats of PCO operate under the scrutiny of a deputy secretary to the cabinet for operations. Each of these supports one of the subject-matter cabinet committees that divide government programs into four fields. These are economic and regional development, social development, foreign and defence policy, and government operations.

When the expenditure envelope system and the two ministries of state first emerged in 1979, considerable speculation centred on whether the role of PCO as a cabinet secretariat was being challenged. Joe Clark's embracing these changes fuelled the speculation. He had long expressed serious reservations about the dominance exercised by PCO over policy advice to the prime minister and cabinet committees. Contrary to this speculation, we now know that PCO actually spawned the ministry of state concept and the envelope system. In fact, PCO emerged winner, over the Treasury Board Secretariat (TBS), of a struggle for power that had been raging for several years.

TBS had locked horns with PCO on innumerable occasions when the former maintained funds were not available for programs that the latter had advised the cabinet to accept. Earlier in 1976, TBS officials thought that they had consolidated their position by gaining access to all cabinet documents with major expenditure implications as soon as they entered the cabinet committee system. Previously, TBS received such documents only after they had cleared the relevant committees and were slated for the cabinet, often within a few days. The apparent victory was deceptive. The new envelope system has transferred clearance of proposals with expenditure implications from the Treasury Board, the cabinet committee that TBS supports, to the subject-matter committees. The fact that PCO secretariats serve these committees assures it much more proximate access to expenditure decisions than that enjoyed by TBS.

With respect to the modus operandi of PCO, it works very much like the Cabinet Office in Whitehall with the exception that its relatively large secretariats enable it to engage itself much more in interdepartmental deliberations on proposals. PCO occupies a great deal of its time simply processing cabinet business and assuring that ministers are adequately briefed on issues before them. Further, it must from time to time force an issue when a consensus developed over a course of action is resisted by some recalcitrants. In Whitehall, the home and parliamentary secretariat, with some four professionals, covers roughly the same turf as the priorities and planning, social affairs, and legislation and house planning secretariats do in Canada with no fewer than twenty professionals. We see then one example of the immensely greater staff resources available to PCO. Such staffing enables the secretariats to follow the gestation of policy proposals from the earliest stages. In fact, practice dictates that wise departments involve officials from PCO secretariats as soon as they realize that proposals will ultimately reach the cabinet or its committees. Thus, PCO officials, much more than their counterparts in Britain, sit on and chair interdepartmental panels preparing major initiatives for cabinet consideration.

One finds less in Canada than in Britain the view that officials in cabinet secretariats merely attempt to keep the decision process moving along nicely without developing stances of their own. Canadian respondents frankly expressed the fact that their attitudes toward a proposal can influence its prospects. Such attitudes derive to a degree from whether the department has behaved as operational departments must if they want to accomplish what they set out to do without experiencing embarrassing reversals:

If the process goes well, my input is minimal. I simply have to assure that meetings and briefs are properly arranged, that accurate minutes of the cabinet committee proceedings are kept and that the sense of what happened is adequately conveyed. I also have responsibilities for making sure that cabinet decisions are actually followed. Many times, however, the co-ordination between departments is inadequate or the department decides to shoot the gap without first sounding me out to see where the committee is on an issue. It really is up to the department. If they are up front with everyone then I simply become a combination referee–traffic cop. If, however, they play their hand close to their vest, my role will become somewhat more active. I will have to decide whether I should join in some effort to pull the proposal out of the fire or become involved with those who are trying to head it off at the pass. My decision will be based on my view of what will sell in the cabinet committee and, ultimately, the entire cabinet, and, therefore, is worth spending time on.

Another official told how one can follow personal agenda items through to ultimate approval by waiting for the opportune break. I will simply paraphrase the official's comments:

When Trudeau came back, I was very much concerned that we continue to follow a policy first established by Clark. I discussed this with Michael Pitfield who, having just come from a year at Harvard, had himself a favourable attitude toward the policy. However, he urged me to get it approved by Trudeau as soon as possible because he [Pitfield] might change his mind. I got the matter on my committee agenda as soon as I could. The ministers batted it around for quite some time and finally came out in favour of continuing the policy. My chairman asked me, 'Well, where do we go from here?' I suggested that we write the prime minister since really it was up to him. So, I drafted a letter and the chairman signed it and sent it to the prime minister. Of course, PMO didn't know what to do with the letter so they sent it to me for comment. I sent back a glowing approval. Next thing I knew, the prime minister announced continuation of the policy in response to a question put to him in the House.

THE FEDERAL-PROVINCIAL RELATIONS OFFICE

Turning to the Federal-Provincial Relations Office (FPRO), we should note at the outset that it appears to have achieved its status as an autonomous central agency largely by virtue of a personnel problem faced by Prime Minister Trudeau in 1975. If Trudeau was to replace Michael Pitfield's predecessor, Gordon Robertson, where was he going to put Robertson? At the time, Robertson loomed as the virtual dean of the career public service. Trudeau's answer came in the shape of splitting off the federal-provincial relations secretariat from PCO and appointing Robertson secretary of the cabinet for federal-provincial relations. This move reduced somewhat the power Pitfield was to inherit. Robertson retained responsibility for advising the prime minister on top senior civil service appointments until he retired in 1979. But the arrangement cushioned Robertson's departure from the clerk-secretary job. It also kept close to Trudeau an individual with an encyclopaedic grasp of the Canadian public service and personal experience in federal-provincial negotiations covering two decades. Personalities aside, an additional fact places in doubt the need for FPRO as a separate central agency. Until 1977, it supported a distinct committee of the cabinet. In that year Trudeau, responding to the threat to Confederation brought on by the Parti québécois victory in November 1976, so focused the attention of priorities and planning on national unity that ultimately he abolished the Federal-Provincial Relations Committee on the grounds that it was redundant.

One might have reasonably expected the prime minister at that point to reintegrate FPRO with PCO, especially since Robertson was close to retirement. Instead, FPRO experienced an unparalleled aggrandizement. For three years, another deputy-minister-level official besides Robertson worked in FPRO providing advice to the prime minister on reform of the constitution. Also, an assistant-deputy-minister-level official along with several professionals co-ordinated the government's response to the Parti québécois plans for a referendum on separation. Under this official, a newly created Canadian Unity Information Office prepared an advertising campaign against Quebec separatism.

PIERRE ELLIOTT TRUDEAU

In previous chapters, we have looked, while examining central agencies working within the area of strategic planning and substantive decision-making, at the styles preferred by the chief decision-makers in power during the course of our study. We have noted that the chief decision-makers may follow one of four styles, namely broker politics, administrative politics, planning and priorities, or the politics of survival. We will now see, in the next few pages, that Trudeau has resorted to each of these styles at one or other point of the four governments he has formed since 1968.

Trudeau's first government, 1968–72, saw for the most part broker politics. Here the cabinet entered a new phase of collective decision-making as the committee system as we know it today emerged. The co-ordinative machinery, along with creation of several new departments, began to break down the fiefdoms of ministers, along with deputy heads, in operational portfolios. For instance, the Department of Industry, Trade and Commerce was learning to live with competitors in its traditional turf. These included Regional and Economic Expansion, Consumer and Corporate Affairs, Science and Technology, and Communications. More important, Trudeau gave considerable emphasis to the view that countervailing central agencies should vie for his and ministers' ears. As noted above, Marc Lalonde presided over an energetic PMO that began to proffer its own views on policy issues. Meanwhile, PCO and TBS, in addition to competing between themselves, began to challenge the Department of Finance's ability to consistently focus cabinet attention mainly on the economic implications of policy proposals.[6] The age of priorities and planning had not dawned. However, departments were engaging increasingly in collective deliberations, and the prime minister and cabinet more often faced conflicting policy proposals.

In 1972, the Liberals failed to win a majority in an election that focused, more than Trudeau would have wished, on deficiencies in his stewardship. The way in which he defended use of the War Measures Act in 1970 betrayed to much of the electorate unacceptable arrogance. His failure to fulfil popular expectations that he could resolve conflicts between the federal and provincial governments on the constitution further disillusioned voters. Controversies surrounding several Liberal policy initiatives and the criticism of many observers that Trudeau was appropriating too much power through creation of new agencies and expansion of old ones made a minority government an attractive option. Many voters who had not repudiated Trudeau wished at least that he would tone down his experimental and machinery-oriented government.

The voters got what they appeared to want from the election of 1972. PMO yielded almost completely to PCO's policy advice. No new central agencies emerged to provide different slants on the burning issues of the day. Further, departmental fiefdoms had a last hurrah. Gerard Pelletier, Jean Marchand, John Turner, 'Bud' Drury, Otto Lang, and Mitchell Sharp proved especially adept at parlaying strong popular images, identification with regions of the country, and significant portfolios into very forceful cabinet presences. The 1972–4 government produced little by way of innovation. However, it generated public confidence that the flamboyant leadership qualities of Trudeau had been harnessed sufficiently to allow reinstatement of the Liberals as the country's trustee party.

Especially since the 1974 campaign centred largely on whether the country required mandatory wage and price controls – with the Liberals taking the negative position – the electorate did not expect Trudeau and his government to embark on the ambitious priorities and planning exercise discussed above. Suffice at this point for us to note that this exercise fully merited its name. The government attempted a comprehensive exercise whereby ministers established collective priorities. It then began to review specific policy proposals from the perspective of how well they met the priorities and where, in the legislative program for the entire mandate, their insertion would reap the best electoral return. Under this regimen, PMO, PCO, Finance, and TBS worked out both the 'scenarios' for the mandate and the departmental proposals that best suited the broad objectives. In time, events and the natural recalcitrance of departments conspired to neutralize the exercise. The former provided unforeseen items, especially poor economic performance and the separatist government in Quebec, that defied expectations. The latter inundated central agencies and the cabinet with mounds of paper largely responding to the exercise only on the cosmetic level.

The collapse of the priorities exercise in 1976 set the stage for a much gloomier prime ministerial style during the rest of the mandate. In the first place, too many key cabinet ministers were leaving the government. By the election of 1979, all the ministers mentioned above as Liberal barons, with the exception of Otto Lang, had resigned along with Donald MacDonald (who had replaced Turner as minister of finance), James Richardson (a key link to Liberals in the West), and André Ouellet and Francis Fox (two especially talented young ministers from Quebec, both of whom left under clouds of scandal). The Liberal team was falling apart.

More and more it appeared to the public that Trudeau was surrounding himself with weak personalities who would do his bidding.

Trudeau turned more to bureaucrats than to ministers for help in bailing out his foundering mandate. We have already discussed at length his increasing reliance on Michael Pitfield, whose career advancement already owed a great deal to his friendship with the prime minister. The groups of trusted mandarins, DM-10 and DM-5, also emerged in this period. It is important to remember in this context that officials in Canada, unlike their British counterparts, enjoy considerable access to cabinet committees. Thus, well-positioned officials gain almost as much exposure to the prime minister as do cabinet ministers.

Trudeau did not stop at relying heavily on the counsel of officials. He began to construe political problems from the bureaucratic perspective – he increasingly sought institutional solutions to his most intractable problems. The creation of FPRO, of the Office of the Comptroller General from part of TBS, and of the ministries of state for Economic and Regional Development and for Social Development, all between 1975 and 1979, marks perhaps the most furtive expansion of central agencies the world has yet experienced. However Trudeau saw these new creations in an entirely different light from that of the 1968 surge in central-agency growth. Rather than attempting to increase countervaillance in his advisory system, he attempted to harness it by giving the new institutions specialized mandates. As well, he provided a density of resources in the centre that made it all that much more possible for central agents to vie with officials in operational departments for a say in matters of detail. The decline of public confidence in his government and the loss of so many ministers had forced Trudeau into survival politics. He found trustworthy allies among the best and the brightest of the public service. However, he soon became their captive. He succumbed almost entirely to the assurance with which they preached the 'good news' that his political problems could be solved by creation of additional central agencies.

JOE CLARK

Clark proved to be a bitter disappointment to those who placed great stock in his election promises. Before his victory on 22 May 1979, Clark sounded like a Canadian counterpart to the 'iron lady' who had just become prime minister in the United Kingdom. Rumblings from the Tory camp seemed to signal radical reform of executive leadership in Canada: the cabinet would be reorganized into a two-tier system; the size of the Prime Minister's Office would be sharply reduced; a mercifully swift purge of senior officials strongly identified with Trudeau would assure that the bureaucracy would place itself at the disposal of the Conservatives; aggrandizement of the bureaucracy would cease; and the public service would be cut by 20 per cent. Some pundits and scholars viewed these signals with scepticism. Would a two-tier cabinet really differ from Trudeau's arrangement whereby the priorities and planning committee essentially operated as an inner cabinet? Would not Clark actually have to increase the size of PMO if he wished to exercise greater control over the career public service? How could Clark dismiss significant numbers of senior bureaucrats when this clear departure from conventional practice would simply antagonize the remaining officials whose co-operation he would desperately require? Finally, how could anyone cut the public service by 20 per cent?

Once in office, Joe Clark failed effectively to pursue most of these goals and many others. More important, his failure to call Parliament into session until 9 October, almost five months after the election, squandered the new government's honeymoon entitlement. By August, Clark's top advisers already had found a clear softening of public support, derived largely from his failure to get the legislative machinery in motion for delivering at least some of his platform. Although Clark lacked sufficient seats for a majority government, he would have benefited greatly from calling Parliament into a short session immediately after the election. He might then have at least introduced an interim budget and some legislation that appeared to address some of the more tractable machinery-of-government issues such as freedom of information and reform of Parliament.

In the end, Clark brought to Ottawa only one new deputy minister, Grant Reuber, whom he coaxed into relinquishing his job as vice-president of the Bank of Montreal in order to become deputy minister of finance. Michael Pitfield had preordained his successor, Marcel Massé – a former opposite number in the government of New Brunswick with well-known Progressive Conservative connections – by naming him deputy secretary to the cabinet only months before the election. Even the effort to fill overtly political appointments in various commissions, Crown corporations, and courts sputtered on without leaving a dent before the fall of the government on 13 December. In fact, the first large batch of such appointments to emerge from an arduous examination of some 5,000 applications and recommendations still awaited the prime minister's approval the day that Clark requested the dissolution of Parliament. Clark, thus, had not even indulged effectively in the lowest form of prime ministerial initiative, that is, the distribution of patronage positions.

If he had stayed in office, Clark would have followed faithfully the style of administrative politics chronicled in these synopses. Clark fell into an administrative-politics trap at the outset by heeding the advice of a team of business consultants from Toronto that recommended a wholesale revamping of the cabinet. Although this advice had little substantive impact on the reforms Clark made, its unstinting commitment to institutional engineering served as a catalyst when an antidote was required. As we have seen, Michael Pitfield already had got into full swing an ambitious restructuring of cabinet decision-making and central agencies. Clark took on these plans uncritically. They appeared to correspond perfectly with the advice he was receiving from his consultants.

Clark's miscalculation resulted in an overburdening of his cabinet. Ministers found themselves straddling two difficult tasks at once, learning their portfolios and orienting themselves to the Byzantine vagaries of a system which, even at this writing, leaves many practitioners reeling in a sea of confusing acronyms. David MacDonald, who took on two major portfolios for Clark – secretary of state and minister of communications – as well as chairing the social development committee, has publicly faulted Clark for getting the cabinet in this hopeless bind. MacDonald notes that the twofold burden tied ministers to their desks throughout the summer of 1979. While buried under mounds of paper, they found little or no time to keep in touch with MPs and the party faithful, let alone constituents and the mood of the country.

TRUDEAU AS PHOENIX

We would be indulging excessively in speculation if we settled now on a definitive classification for Trudeau's fourth government beginning after the election on 18 February 1980. At the outset, we must remember that Michael Pitfield returned to the clerk-secretary position. Just as Trudeau won a new lease on life, Pitfield came back somewhat refreshed from his time at Harvard. Early on, he was quoted as saying that he wanted to run a much more open shop that would provide a freer exchange of ideas within PCO and greater receptivness to the views of outsiders.

Pitfield planned to limit the agenda for Trudeau's mandate. Assuming that Trudeau would retire in two or three years, the cabinet faced a fairly narrow 'window' for legislative programs. Trudeau would focus his immediate efforts first on beating the Parti québécois in the May 1980 referendum on the separation of Quebec. Having won this, he would work to fulfil his intention of reforming the constitution so that it better reflected the aspirations of Quebec. Reform of the constitution included, of course, the process of patriation whereby the British Parliament would no longer serve as custodian of Canada's constitutional statute, the British North America Act. Also, Trudeau would face the difficult task of devising an energy policy that would satisfy the regional claims of Alberta, British Columbia, and Saskatchewan, which are energy-rich, and Newfoundland, Nova Scotia, and Prince Edward Island, which hope for major discoveries of offshore oil and gas. However, the tone of the campaign and indications in the early days of the government both suggested that Trudeau would use administrative politics. It even appeared as if PCO had quietly conceded much of its role to the ministries of state for Economic and Regional Development and for Social Development. The government's decision to continue the reorganization process at least suggested that many of the most hotly contested battles in the cabinet would centre on issues relating to structure.

Notwithstanding early indications, the Trudeau government in fact has reverted to the survival politics that characterized the last year of the 1974 government. In September 1980 it failed to win provincial support for patriation of the constitution with insertion of a 'peoples' package' of rights. The provinces based their refusal on the federal government's unwillingness to provide powers and institutions that would improve their position vis-à-vis the federal government. The Trudeau government decided subsequently to force a constitutional package through the Canadian and British parliaments before the eight dissenting provinces could obtain court judgments on the legality of the move. A leaked cabinet document provides a chillingly matter-of-fact statement of the survival-at-all-costs syndrome. The document, drafted by Mike Kirby, sets the federal strategy in a frame of extreme urgency: 'This may be a once-in-a-lifetime opportunity to effect comprehensive constitutional change (and perhaps unblock the process), and, as such, should not be lost.'[7]

The reader might find it difficult to fathom why that particular moment was a once-in-a-lifetime chance. The claim takes on meaning only when we consider that Trudeau had attained the age of sixty-one, after twelve years of sporadically attempting patriation and reform. Urgency directly stemming from Trudeau's desire to retire from politics with honour brought about the federal move. Thus, the government would try to push the patriation package, warts and all, through both parliaments. As the Kirby memo argued: 'Obviously, the foregoing suggests that while unilateral action can legally be accomplished, it involves the risk of prolonged dispute through the courts and the possibility of adverse judicial comment that could undermine the political legitimacy, though not the legal validity, of the patriation package ... There would be a strong strategic advantage in having the joint resolution [the package] passed and the UK legislation enacted before a Canadian court had occasion to pronounce on the validity of the measure and the procedure employed to achieve it. This would suggest the desirability of swift passage of the resolution and UK legislation.'[8]

Ministers reviewed the Kirby memo during a priorities session at Lake Louise, Alberta, in August 1980. The session took place just before the provincial premiers met with the prime minister to negotiate a constitutional package. The document gave only lip service to the hope that the federal-provincial negotiations, which had gone on between the governments throughout the summer, would end with agreement. Over half the report detailed strategic options should the negotiations fail.

The Kirby memo stampeded ministers into choosing a unilateral package even before the premiers and the prime minister gave the ill-fated first round of negotiations a decent burial. It also failed to report the findings of government polls that indicated that Canadians overwhelmingly believed unilateral enactment of the 'peoples' package' would violate constitutional convention. As it turned out, rearguard actions by the federal Conservatives and eight provinces forced reference of the new constitution to the Supreme Court of Canada. In September 1981, the latter ruled that the federal government's unilateral action, while observing the strict letter of the law, violated constitutional convention. This forced Trudeau back to the bargaining table. An accord reached with all provinces but Quebec in November 1981 set the stage for patriation in April 1982.

The remaining priorities submitted to the cabinet in late August contribute to the impression of a government geared to the ever-narrowing 'window' of its prime minister. On 28 October 1980 the government submitted a budget that focused largely on an energy policy designed to reduce the powers of energy-rich provinces over their own resources and increase Canadian ownership of the petroleum industry. The first prong of the policy derived from Trudeau's conviction that provinces are too strong; the latter from his relatively recent interest in economic nationalism. The cabinet yielded to – next in order of importance – the prime minister's desire to spend a large portion of his time fostering North-South dialogue, relations between the 'have' and the 'have-not' nations. The fact that the 1981 economic summit of the top seven industrial nations in the free world, which Trudeau chaired, was supposed to focus on North-South dialogue only partially explained

Trudeau's engagement in the issue. He viewed the summit as an opportunity to drive home his long-standing belief that wealthy nations should do more for poor ones.

The cabinet put two important domestic policies, industrial strategy and income redistribution, in a holding pattern. The former, another result of Trudeau's recent interest in economic nationalism, had to await settlement of the energy issue. Income redistribution still stands no better chance of serious attention during this mandate than it did when it received similar acknowledgment by earlier Trudeau cabinets. The Liberals' track record on income redistribution is at best mixed. The exceedingly poor prospects for economic growth suggest that the government will not embrace policies that would, even in the best of times, increase the tax burden on middle- and upper-class voters.

In sum, the 1980 Trudeau mandate bears the mark of a man attempting to wrap up his personal agenda before leaving politics. Whereas initial speculation led some to hope for a more open advisory system, the officials closest to Trudeau have reverted to their old ways. One member of PCO described things in no uncertain terms: 'I am trying to say that things are actually worse than they were. We just got used to opening up the way in which we worked. Massé had changed the atmosphere completely. When Pitfield came back, he promised solemnly in a staff meeting that Harvard had changed him, that we would continue to operate in a different way. Within two weeks it was back to the old PCO. No one shares information with the next guy. Everyone lives in mortal dread of a call from Pitfield's office to come up and explain what you have been doing on this or that.'

CONCLUSION

As readers have probably noted, Canada's recent development of central agencies helping the prime minister and cabinet in formulating and adhering to strategies has followed closely the preferences of one man, Pierre Elliott Trudeau. His lengthy career as prime minister has resulted in his adopting each of my four leadership styles at one time or another. None the less some features have endured all the way from 1968 to the present. Trudeau's profound commitment to development of government machinery that will provide more 'rational' policy decisions has dovetailed with the experimental attitudes toward bureaucratic organization of many of his most trusted advisers. Trudeau's governments have often responded to specific crises by instituting or expanding central agencies. Although his first priorities-and-planning exercise ended in failure, the model has held considerable sway since 1974. Thus, even the latter phase of his style, survival politics, has followed the schedule set out in 1974 whereby the cabinet assesses each autumn the state of the mandate and outlines priorities for the coming legislative year. Finally, Trudeau's interest in institutional reform has combined with his strong control over senior career public service positions to reshape essentially the bureaucracy. The departments and agencies of the government of Canada and the key individuals who operate them reflect the preferences of one man to a degree usually attained only in one-party régimes. Certainly, not even the power of appointment of American presidents affords the type of latitude provided by Trudeau's long years in office.

PART TWO

Co-ordinating economic and fiscal policy

Introduction

No matter what chief decision-makers come up with by way of strategic plans and substantive policies, they must constantly keep in sight the potential impact of their actions on the performance of the economy. Only threats to national survival concentrate their minds as readily as downturns in economic performance. However, when elections are far off, leaders enjoy the luxury of ignoring some economic distress. They bank then on the belief that the economy will straighten itself out by election time. Margaret Thatcher and Pierre Elliott Trudeau provide good examples here. Early in her mandate, Thatcher ignored high unemployment and sharply curtailed the government's social programs. She assumed that by the next general election the economy would take a sharp turn for the better. In 1980, Trudeau believed his government could cushion a lack of confidence in the economy intensified by uncertainty over the future of Canadian federalism. He had hoped that national unity issues would fade into the background by the next election.

While considering the economy, chief decision-makers will give varying degrees of attention to budgetary plans, including taxation and spending. They will want to ensure that these correspond to their goals for economy. Here some dramatic cases come to mind. Trudeau, in the summer of 1978, personally ordered $2 billion cut from the expenditure budget. Helmut Schmidt had convinced him that only radical decreases in expenditures would get the major economic powers off the treacherous wage-price spiral. Jimmy Carter believed that inflation fuelled by public expenditure was destroying public confidence in the economy. He thus set as his main economic goal a balanced budget by 1980. Even though he spent perhaps more of his time working on the details of expenditure budgets than any other president, he undershot his objective by billions.

Chief decision-makers also involve themselves in control of many levers that directly affect segments of the economy. They will engage in the setting of foreign exchange and domestic borrowing rates, distribution of tax burdens and spending to specific sectors of the economy, development of trade policy, and regulation of financial institutions (banks, etc) and equity markets (security firms). To this list of direct levers, we must add government's management of its own financial affairs. The very means by which governments collect, borrow, deposit, and disperse funds can greatly affect the operation of segments of the marketplace.

Four important themes will suggest themselves as we undertake this examination of the role of central agencies in co-ordinating economic and fiscal policies. First, the three systems differ considerably in the degree to which they have had units responsible for these fields in central agencies. While the most vital policy units invariably operate out of central agencies, those responsible for less crucial policy issues and implementation often reside in separate departments and agencies. Second, units actually housed in central agencies do not experience the same amount of countervailing activity. The British Treasury faces relatively little competition from other central agencies; Canada's Department of Finance has seen its near-monopoly eroded considerably over the past two decades; and the US Department of the Treasury has undergone a crisis of authority owing largely to a lack of clarity in the boundaries between the secretary's and the president's responsibilities in this realm. Third, although cabinet-level committees in all three systems provide forums in which interdepartmental disputes may be worked out, these bodies do not all enjoy the same authority. As we have seen before, Americans have difficulty delegating to collective decision-making bodies authority that is exclusively the president's. In the two other systems, cabinet committees working on economic and fiscal policies might encounter serious constraints if the cabinet, senior committees, and/or the prime minister consistently rework interdepartmental agreements. Fourth, the institutionalization of departmental and co-ordinative functions can make economic agencies and decision processes more resistant to the 'dysfunctional' aspect of the styles of chief executives. For instance, we will see that the US Treasury's image among foreign observers suffered greatly during the Carter administration. Under an administration that proved decidedly deficient in policy co-ordination, it appeared that Treasury itself was in disarray. In similar circumstances in the United Kingdom, we might expect that, even if the prime minister demonstrated poor leadership, the concentration of economic levers in HM Treasury and the department's highly institutionalized co-ordinative machinery should prevent the world from concluding that its positions should not be taken seriously.

5

The diffuse machinery of American economic policy

We find in the United States a strong preference for placing units involved in economic and fiscal policies in central agencies. The organizational chart of the Department of the Treasury reflects this tendency. Apart from acting as one of the major players in development of administration policies within these fields, it serves as a 'holding company' for agencies responsible for the operational side of US government finances and the enforcement of tax, tariff, and financial policies. The roles of the Office of the US Trade Representative and the now-defunct Council on Wage and Price Stability provide particularly good evidence of the US proclivity for bringing directly under central agencies functions that would not receive similar profile in Britain or Canada. In both cases, housing these agencies in the Executive Office of the President served to give their activities legitimacy through association with the president. However, such tacks can simply add to the general clutter of central agencies fighting over the same territory. In this respect, the Office of the US Trade Representative has operated reasonably well. Its mandate from Congress to take the lead in trade negotiations, along with the eminence of the most of the individuals who have headed it, has buttressed its proximity to the president. The Council of Wage and Price Stability, in contrast, began to wither on the vine when wage and price controls lost their statutory base. It died when Ronald Reagan deemed its role superfluous.

The fact that no US central agency enjoys dominance in economic and fiscal policy emerges as the characteristic that most sharply distinguishes the American system from the others. To be sure, Treasury keeps under its wing the sharp ends of most taxation, customs, and financial instruments. This makes it by far the biggest of the contending central agencies located along Pennsylvania Avenue. By the same token, it maintains the largest capability for both macro- and microeconomic analysis. However, it does not house some vital instruments. Most crucial here, the Office of Management and Budget rules authoritatively over administration policies concerning public expenditure. Also within the Executive Office of the President, the Council of Economic Advisers (CEA) normally assumes the lead in forecasting. In this regard, the roles of Treasury and OMB in forecasting contribute only partially to the need for a body such as CEA to develop a common administration policy for the president. In addition, operational departments (such as Commerce and Labor) and the Federal Reserve produce forecasts. These often intensify the difficulty of arriving at mutually agreed-on views of how the economy is performing, what the future holds, and what policies will contribute most to achievement of the administration's principal targets.

I will examine briefly the roles of the Domestic Policy Staff and its successor, the Office of Policy Development, and of the National Security Council regarding co-ordination of the administration's positions on major economic issues. Although the United States maintains the most diffuse economic-policy network, it has yet to develop sufficiently specialized secretariats for monitoring and reconciling diverse views of cabinet-level officials on essential elements of economic policy. Our look at the involvement of DPS and OPM, and of NSC, in this field will give a view of the state of this art in the United States.

THE EXECUTIVE OFFICE OF THE PRESIDENT

We visited this cluster of offices when we examined the institutional machinery available for determining strategic plans and making major decisions. In 1979, six offices within EOP played particularly significant roles in integration of economic and fiscal policy. These included the Domestic Policy Staff, the National Security Council staff, the Council of Economic Advisers, the Office of Management and Budget, the Council on Wage and Price Stability, and the Office of the US Trade Representative.

The Domestic Policy Staff (DPS) and the National Security Council (NSC)
Both DPS and NSC under Jimmy Carter involved themselves in overall assessments of the state of the economy. DPS gained access to macro-economic policy by virtue of its membership on the Economic Policy Group (EPG). The steering group of this body met weekly for breakfast in

the treasury secretary's dining room. Stuart E. Eizenstat, the assistant to the president for domestic affairs and policy, attended these sessions on a regular basis. As well, he assigned two DPS officials to economic policy. These represented DPS at meetings of EPG members. DPS, in fact, chaired some EPG work groups on the economy. At the time of the interviews for this study, Eizenstat chaired an EPG subgroup preparing the president's strategy for responding to the energy crisis during the spring of 1979. Eizenstat also had become heavily involved with the 1978 tax reform package, implementation of US agreements made in the Multilateral Trade Negotiations (MTN), and plans to fight inflation. Eizenstat engaged himself personally in these areas for two reasons. First, the president's interests were vitally involved. Second, the attention of a senior adviser in the White House might help get compromises out of contending bureaucratic interests and package these so that they might be accepted by Congress. Although Eizenstat's interventions paid off on MTN and energy policy, they yielded little in tax reform and the fight against inflation.

The NSC staff serves as a secretariat for NSC committees considering various policy issues that arise in foreign affairs, defence, and intelligence. Often heads of the principal economic agencies will sit on NSC committees. As well, their deputies will participate on work groups set up in the NSC system. Thus, NSC committees often vet papers written in part or whole by agencies with lead roles in various segments of economic decision-making. More vitally, NSC has assumed the lead in preparing the president for summits with the top Western economic powers. At the time of the interviews, only one NSC official, Henry Owen, staffed this briefing role. Owen's influence, however, penetrated several corners of the economics bureaucracy. Officials working elsewhere on energy, inflation, monetary affairs, and trade often mentioned him as a key player in the policy apparatus.

Treasury officials took a jaundiced view of DPS and NSC efforts to co-ordinate resolution of some key economic matters. Many respondents found that DPS and NSC involvement often left them out of the play at critical times. Deliberations would focus on political considerations which pre-empted contributions from career people in Treasury: 'I happen to have been a kind of co-ordinator in the Treasury for the last summit meetings ... which didn't mean much because we never knew what was going on. The bosses never told us anything.' One official asserted that the degree of DPS involvement in tax policy under Carter exceeded the normal watching brief of White House policy units. He attributed this heightened activity to Carter's penchant for immersing himself in details: 'DPS did take a tremendous interest in the '78 tax reform programs. I think that that is fairly unusual. I don't think it was true in prior administrations to anywhere near that extent. But, I think that's probably a symptom of the fact that the president, certainly at the beginning, was in up to his ears in every decision. Some people say that is still a problem.'

Under such circumstances, W. Michael Blumenthal, the secretary of the treasury, found it hard fully to exert his authority as the chief economic spokesman of the president. At the time of the interviews it appeared as though Blumenthal had freed himself from the shackles on his authority. The respondent believed DPS under Eizenstat had overextended itself: 'The White House was playing a larger role in general economic policies than it was capable of handling. There was no confidence in our policies ... Since November 1 when it became clear that Blumenthal was made the chief economic spokesman, all the flak from the White House and all the people who were trying to play too strong a hand in economic policies, this all died off ... Eizenstat, for example, was the guy at the White House who tried to play a major role. His name doesn't come up so much anymore in this area.' Of course, the perceived victory was illusory. Blumenthal resigned his post in July 1979.

Criticisms of the effectiveness of interventions by DPS and NSC notwithstanding, future presidents will find they must tighten management of the economic policy process. Currently, too many central agencies share the key leadership responsibilities in the field. Presidents can defer to the traditional pre-eminence of Treasury. However, they will do so at the expense of less countervaillance. One of our respondents believed he saw a way out of the conundrum. He held that the economic policy process should be formalized. Here a secretariat in the Executive Office of the President would co-ordinate decision-making much the same way as NSC does its fields:

The issue ... has almost always been: how do you emulate the National Security Council process on the domestic side? ... It seems to me that that is where we have really fallen down ... Nobody is in charge, you have [Robert S.] Strauss [then US trade representative], Blumenthal, and [G. William] Miller [then chairman of the Federal Reserve System] all saying different things. Charlie Schultze [then chairman of the Council of Economic Advisers] is saying something else ... You don't have people saying: 'Mr President, inflation is a real problem. We don't know how much of it is a problem of structural imbalances in the economy. We would like to know, "What can you do about structural unemployment or reducing sectoral sources of inflation?" Let's do a study. Here are eight issues that ought to be addressed at a minimum ... It ought to be conducted jointly with the following departments.' A report with options will be back by a prearranged date.

The decision memo will go to the president saying: 'Here are the things you can do about it, if anything.' This is the way, for better or worse, you do it in the foreign affairs area.

Our respondent, of course, has described a process that would follow roughly the practice of cabinet decision-making in Canada and Britain as well as that within the NSC system.

The Council of Economic Advisers (CEA)

The reader might wonder whether CEA operates in economic policy much the way NSC does on its side. In fact, CEA gives most of its attention to bringing together disparate analytic approaches to economic problems. The staff comes mainly from academe, and its members do not plan careers in government. Process management simply would go beyond the ken of most and change the tenor of their work relationships: 'We would not want to change the character of the CEA from a very small group of economists working very informally, in a very flexible way ... What we do here is serve as staff economists for a year or at the most, two years. And then we go back to our prior positions. Because we do that, we are able to get top-quality people, the very best in the country.'

In 1979 CEA housed three members of the council, ten senior economists, two staff economists, six junior economists, and a special assistant. In large part, what individuals work on depends on their expertise and interests. However, CEA heads up the interagency forecasting group. This body includes the departments of Commerce and of Labor as well as the principal economics central agencies – CEA, OMB, and Treasury. However, the latter three often huddle privately in a troika to resolve the more difficult problems raised during forecasting exercises. Essentially, the forecasting group assesses how the economy is going to perform under a common set of fiscal and monetary assumptions. The entire process helps determine the annual fiscal framework that will serve as the basis for the president's budget: 'The budgetary policy decision will be one that evolves out of the forecast. We start with a preliminary assumption about fiscal policy. Typically, we will test several different fiscal policies with the base projections that we have made for the performance of the economy. Then we will present those to our principals, the members of the steering committee of EPG. They in turn will present a set of alternatives to the president. But the fiscal policy recommendations ultimately will come out of the forecast.'

CEA often melds economic views from participants in the forecasting group (who do not necessarily arrive at the same conclusions) into a useful projection of the economy. The forecasting group, at the time of the interviews, employed four different models, one each from CEA, OMB, Treasury, and Commerce. CEA led in the task of stripping these models down to their common elements in order to extrapolate the agreed forecast. Lately the stripping process has yielded poor results. The various forecasts have simply differed too widely.

With its role in forecasting as its base, CEA moves into virtually every major policy discussion that relates to the economy. First, as one official explained, CEA makes its views known on a host of domestic issues with implications for the economy: 'We have an input on almost every individual policy decision of any major significance for the economy. If the Department of Labor wants to increase outlays for public service employment by a billion dollars, we will weigh in on that. We will send a memo to OMB ... This "weigh-in" will be done at the staff level first. If we don't come to an agreement there, we will write a memo to the president.'

Second, CEA plays an important role in international economic policy. For instance, Charles L. Schultze, the head of CEA during the interviews, chaired the economic policy committee of the Organization for Economic Co-operation and Development. Through this position Schultze, to the chagrin of at least one Treasury official, was strengthening CEA's role as 'an important co-ordinator in the White House' on the international side. One respondent noted, in fact, that CEA had cracked into a private preserve of Treasury and the Federal Reserve in October 1978. Through Schultze's leadership, it played a key role in developing the emergency package to defend the dollar from foreign exchange pressures: 'We had Charlie signed on quite early ... He, I know, talked to people in Treasury and the Fed ... As the program itself took shape, my reading was that CEA views on how to put it together were strongly influential in terms of the final package.' On the microside of international economic policy, CEA advises on the implications of all major initiatives concerning trade policy. For instance, it vetted the major agreements that resulted from the Multilaterial Trade Negotiations.

Finally, CEA has participated in reviews of regulatory policy. It gained entry to this area largely through the interest of two successive members of the council, William D. Nordhaus and George Eads. Their efforts brought to the review process concern for the macroeconomic implications of reforms. CEA also has effectively pressed development of better procedures for assessing the costs of existing and projected regulations.

The Office of Management and Budget (OMB)
As we have seen, OMB participated under Carter both in the EPG steering committee's reviews of the administration's economic policies and in the troika's forecasting exercises. OMB's assistant director for

economic policy headed a small group of macroeconomists who advised the OMB director on issues before the steering committee. Virtually every major initiative in economic policy affects the budget either through spending programs or tax measures. The small office on economic policy acknowledged the fact that OMB must effectively communicate to makers of macroeconomic policy the implications of their decisions for expenditures. As well, the in-house macroeconomics unit recognized the internal OMB need to maintain, in budget review sessions, respect for the importance of expenditure restraint in the control of inflation. In the troika exercise, a budget review division serves as the keeper of the numbers. The unit houses five large branches. Three of these link directly into forecasting: the budget preparation branch, which maintains the detailed budget data base; the resource systems branch, which monitors accounting systems for dollars and personnel; and the fiscal analysis branch, which assembles data on the performance of the economy.

All this might strike the reader as simply technical servicing of EPG and troika deliberations. We will see in the next chapter how these functions provide an important backdrop to OMB's interest in restraint of expenditure. By virtue of OMB's access to EPG and the troika, officials – from director down to examiners – working with agencies on budget issues find themselves able to invoke authoritatively the macroeconomic limits to the fiscal framework.

The Council on Wage and Price Stability (CWPS)

CWPS emerged in 1974 as part of the Nixon administration's lifting of mandatory wage and price controls. CWPS began to supply data on prices and wages in various sectors of the economy to the administration's discussions of inflation. Unlike CEA, it acquired considerable staff and sought to maintain strong links outside government through 'sectoral' consultation with industry and labour.

During the first two years of the Carter administration, Charles L. Schultze chaired CWPS as well as CEA. A former Brookings Institution colleague of his, Barry Bosworth, directed CWPS. Bosworth obtained access to the meetings of the EPG principals. His involvement at that level upgraded CWPS's public profile in the administration's efforts to curb inflation. As well, CWPS largely co-ordinated the numerous analysis and review groups that were pursuing Carter's interest in regulatory reform.

In the early fall of 1978, inflation rose to an alarming level. Carter believed that he should give the issue still higher profile by appointing a more senior adviser on inflation. He chose Alfred E. Kahn who, as chairman of the Civil Aeronautics Board, had spearheaded deregulation of the airline industry. Kahn found CWPS a useful base for promoting deregulation of industry. For instance, he led a major assault on trucking regulations. As well, he used CWPS reports as springboards for his numerous fire-and-brimstone homilies against inflation.

Despite Kahn's efforts, CWPS became a fifth wheel in deliberations on the economy. It simply lacked the strong links into the budget, fiscal policy, and forecasting that OMB and CEA enjoy. However, the requirement that voluntary wage and price programs derive authority directly from the president preserved CWPS functions from being farmed out of the Executive Office. At the same time, the need for sectoral consultation prevented it from being absorbed by OMB or CEA. Of course, Ronald Reagan disbanded CWPS when he took office on 20 January 1981.

The Office of the US Trade Representative (STR)
STR also owes its existence to the need to attach a policy area directly to the president. In 1962 Congress created STR as a condition upon which it gave the administration authority to pursue the 'Kennedy round' of multilateral trade negotiations. Carter tried to move the negotiation function out of the Executive Office of the President into a proposed department of trade. The reform effort failed and STR remains the lead agency for US trade policy. It operates as a secretariat for delegations abroad and interdepartmental committees at home. At the level of principals, the committee system includes the departments of State, Treasury, Commerce, Agriculture, Labor, Interior, and Defense. CEA and OMB join key committees at lower levels.

During the implementation phase of the Multilateral Trade Negotiations concluded in Geneva in 1979, STR organized twenty-five subcommittees to address the implications of MTN for various industrial sectors. In most cases, it found it could achieve consensus on issues without going to the president for a decision. Here Robert Strauss's standing in Washington helped STR immensely. His close friendship with the president made him an equal among Washington barons. Thus he could intervene effectively when recalcitrant departments would not agree at the deputies' level. Strauss also had the strongest links to Congress of any cabinet secretary. These helped assure that the implementation phase received relatively favourable treatment from Congress.

THE DEPARTMENT OF THE TREASURY

A look at the Treasury organization chart would leave the reader wondering where to begin in considering its role in integration of economic and fiscal policy. The size and complexity of the department mask the fact that it breaks down relatively simply into units that make policy and units that implement policy. Obviously we find grey areas here and there. However, the offices of the assistant secretaries for tax policy, economic policy, domestic finance, international, and legislative affairs fall on the policy side as do the offices of the fiscal assistant secretary and the general counsel. The offices of the commissioner of the Internal Revenue Service, the assistant secretaries for administration and for enforcement and operations, and the comptroller of the currency fall more on the implementation side of our dichotomy. This examination will focus on the offices that concentrate on the Treasury's policy development roles.

Before examining the roles of the policy-oriented offices, we should look briefly at how this side of Treasury is organized. The secretary heads the department and serves as a member of the cabinet. A deputy secretary, a political appointee as well, serves mainly as the secretary's surrogate in matters that he does not have time to cover personally. Thus the deputy secretary's role does not parallel exactly those of deputy heads in our other countries who are career officials. Whereas career deputy heads in the United Kingdom and Canada normally would join in any high-level departmental considerations of policy, the Treasury deputy might find himself only peripherally involved in some policy deliberations.

Two under-secretaries provide an additional reporting layer for some of the offices within Treasury. Two assistant secretaries – for domestic finance and international affairs – and the fiscal assistant secretary report to the under-secretary of monetary affairs. Two other assistant secretaries, for economic and tax policy, report to the under-secretary for tax and economic affairs.

The Office of the Assistant Secretary for International Affairs
During the time of the interviews, Treasury's international affairs office contained six units under deputy assistant secretaries (or equivalent grades). However, traditionally, the office of the deputy assistant secretary for international monetary affairs has worked more closely with the under-secretary for monetary affairs than with the assistant secretary for international affairs. The unit, which in turn houses three offices, advises the under-secretary on strategic questions relating to monetary affairs and relations with other industrial countries. It also keeps him up to date on matters, such as exchange market operations, that require his immediate intervention. The Central Intelligence Agency, the Department of State, and the Council of Economic Advisers all have officials working within the international economic intelligence field. However, the Treasury international affairs office includes about twenty econo-

mists working abroad in ten key countries and three international organizations. Two other units in the international monetary affairs 'deputate,' foreign exchange operations, and international banking and portfolio investment, keep the strong lines of communication with the Federal Reserve System and international banking community necessary for maintaining the stability of the dollar.

The other deputates in international affairs report more to the assistant secretary. They cover trade and investment policy, international economic analysis, commodities and natural resources, developing nations, and Saudi Arabian affairs. Treasury usually enters the trade field in response to situations in which STR or the State Department has taken the lead. Known in the community of departments working in the area as free trade 'freaks,' Treasury officials will look for ways to avoid recourse to protectionist measures at home and abroad. The department's interest in commodities and natural resources brings an economic and financial viewpoint to issues such as energy policy, commodity regulation, law of the sea, and North-South relations, where operational departments take the lead. The deputate on developing nations staffs Treasury relations with multilateral development banks and provides guidance on policy to US executive directors on the boards of these institutions. The banks, of course, rely heavily upon US financing. The unit also houses a development policy office and an office containing desks for developing countries which ensure Treasury can influence policy and provide economic analysis regarding development programs formulated by the Department of State.

The Office of the Fiscal Assistant Secretary
The fiscal assistant secretary, who reports to the under-secretary for monetary affairs, manages the day-to-day financial operations of the government. His work also brings him in constant contact with the assistant secretary for domestic finance. The latter official takes the lead in policy directly affecting public debt management, state and municipal finance, and capital markets. The fiscal assistant secretary's work centres more on the technical side of finances. Two large bureaux – government financial operations and public debt – report to him. As well, three deputates provide him with advice on policy surrounding government financial operations. Seemingly mundane matters, such as development of a new cheque-wrapping system, often occupy the time of officials in one of the deputates, namely planning and research. Yet some operational innovations, though technical, can require considerable finesse to win approval within the executive branch and from Congress. Once

adopted, they can greatly improve the effectiveness of financial operations. Respondents in the office of the assistant fiscal assistant secretary for banking told of an arduous three-year effort to empower Treasury to earn interest on tax deposits in commercial banks. Such matters might on the surface appear excessively mundane to be handled on the policy side of Treasury. In fact, however, they involve difficult issues that concern effective management of very sizeable sums of money.

The Office of the Assistant Secretary for Tax Policy
Taxes, of course, produce most of the revenues of the us federal government. The average American wage-earner has gained a working acquaintance with the Internal Revenue Service (IRS). This agency, however, only collects taxes. The office of the assistant secretary for tax policy shoulders responsibility for advising the secretary of the treasury on the actual contours of the us tax system.

Two deputates, tax analysis and tax legislation, work under the supervision of the assistant secretary.[1] Tax analysis contains approximately thirty-five professional economists. About half of these officials work at producing revenue estimates. The projected revenues of existing tax measures and those of proposed legislation determine in very large part the administration's fiscal framework. In addition, the projections provide data on the distributional effects of taxes – how the tax burdens of specific provisions affect various segments of society. The remaining officials in the tax analysis deputate focus their attention on applied econometrics – numerous long-range studies aimed at improving Treasury's understanding of the implications of the tax law for the economic behaviour of both individuals and corporations.

The tax legislation deputate, with some twenty-five lawyers, attempts to treat deficiencies in existing tax law by putting forth reform measures. In large part, officials in the deputate respond to problems in the administration of tax law discovered by IRS. However, the bulk of lawyers in the unit bring to their work strong personal objectives in the area of tax reform. The officials do not usually enjoy long tenure like their opposite numbers in tax analysis. Thus they tend to have weaker follow-through on long-term projects. However, the lawyers tap considerable experience with the vagaries of existing tax law gathered while working in some of the nation's top law firms. Thus, what the deputate loses because its officials rarely view their work as a long-term career it gains by bringing fresh approaches to the never-ending job of revising tax policy.

Both the tax analysis and tax legislation deputates faced the bitter disappointment during the Carter administration of gearing up for a major tax reform effort only to see it snarled in the congressional labyrinth. Our respondents avowed a keen interest in reforms that would serve the dual purpose of plugging tax loopholes and increasing the proportionate burden of the well off. They also maintained that they keep their eyes peeled for uses of taxes for purposes that should come under the expenditure budgets of operational departments. For instance, they prefer direct grants to stimulate industry over tax deductions and credits. Jimmy Carter introduced a tax reform bill in 1978 that partially addressed reform along the lines sought by Treasury. However, like much of his legislative program, it failed to stir Congress into action.

At the time of our interviews, the tax deputates were simply addressing the ad hoc issues raised by other of Carter's policies. They provided less than enthusiastic follow-through for the president's efforts to introduce real 'wage insurance' as a hedge for workers against the adverse effects of forgoing wage increases. Treasury reservations in this case reflected its traditional concerns about the use of taxation for policy goals other than production of revenue: 'Any scheme in this area has got to be incredibly complicated and not viewed with much enthusiasm, especially by the Internal Revenue Service. It wasn't clear to me that we could make the case that this particular proposal was going to have a major impact in holding back wage increases.'

Later in the spring, the president's energy package began to absorb a vast amount of tax policy's time. One respondent, in fact, resented the fact that energy packages always seemed to be diverting the precious time of assistant secretaries from long-range issues: 'Larry Woodsworth when he was assistant secretary spent practically all of his time on the energy bill. And the access that the staff had to him at the time that we were trying to develop a tax reform proposal that contained the president's '78 tax program was very small. You see he was tied up on the energy proposals. And we are going to have the same thing again. Don Lubick has become for the last month or so an energy lawyer. And we have already spent a lot of time this fall on real wage insurance.'

Notwithstanding their difficulties under Carter, our respondents were pursuing scaled-down efforts at tax reform in less controversial areas. One optimist kept in mind the dry years 1966–8 when Treasury achieved little by way of reform but continued with long-range studies. In 1969 and the early 1970s these projects finally bore fruit. The politicians had taken a sudden interest in tax reform. Treasury responded with a ready-made package of amendments.

Frustration on tax reform notwithstanding, our respondents sensed a growth sector in the administration's increased awareness of the degree to which forgone taxes are equivalent to hidden government expenditures. The principle is fairly straightforward. Every tax break given to accomplish a programmatic goal really deprives the public purse of revenue. If such 'tax expenditures' appeared in departments' budgets, the public would gain a much more accurate view of program costs. However, the new focus on tax expenditures had overloaded the tax policy deputates. As a result, the Treasury view was losing credibility. The department invoked all too often its traditional arguments about preserving the integrity of taxation as a revenue-producing instrument. As the official went on to say, Treasury lacks the staff and expertise to get into detailed programmatic analysis: 'I think that people use the tax system in part as a way of avoiding development of a sensible program. When you have a tax credit for x you can say it in a very simple way. You don't have to develop any of the criteria or anything. Nobody worries as much about spending government money in that way. So we try to demonstrate all that. But we end up with the problem that there are no oil experts here, no housing experts.'

One other option presents itself here. OMB could incorporate tax expenditures more completely into the budget review process. It includes the aggregate tax expenditures figures in the budget. In the spring of 1979, it joined in two pilot projects, one in energy policy and the other in housing, directed toward further integration of budget and tax review exercises. Treasury officials fully realized that such projects would shift an unwelcome burden onto budget officers.

The Office of the Assistant Secretary for Economic Policy
Before Carter's administration, this office had concentrated on analysis of the domestic economy. Daniel Brill, Carter's assistant secretary, assumed his post on the condition that analysis related to international economics also came under his control. This shifting of considerable personnel to secure the appointment of one man eventually worked to the detriment of the smooth operation of the international economic advisory system in Treasury.

Under the Carter administration the domestic analysis side of economic policy fulfilled its traditional role. Here Brill worked effectively as the secretary's leading adviser on the economy. One respondent from the tax policy office highlighted Brill's role in comparison to his own: 'To some extent the responsibility for pure fiscal policy rests more with Dan Brill ... With respect to macroeconomic issues he has probably greater input than me, but I have some input. Once a decision is made to *increase or decrease taxes and how much* it becomes a question of *"which taxes and how?"* – that is the responsibility of the office of tax policy.' By virtue of the secretary of the treasury's chairmanship of the Economic Policy Group, Brill became the lead official in meetings of the EPG deputies' group which met three or four times a week. As one official recounted, good positioning on EPG grew in value over time. Eventually the entire group rarely met, leaving decisions to the steering group.

In comparison to other key participants in EPG, Treasury provided an analytic powerhouse. This is not to say that its analysis was taken uncritically. Even respondents in the office of economic policy recognized deficiences in their techniques. These centred on the adequacy of Treasury models which, they thought, depended excessively on Keynesian assumptions and remained relatively immune to monetarist analysis. As well, respondents in the economic policy deputates on the domestic side increasingly felt the pressure of other members of the EPG steering group who dragged Treasury into political battles: 'The development of the wage-price program ... was quarrelled over in interagency groups for months, thoroughly ventilated in the press, all the details were leaked.'

Such weaknesses did not prevent Treasury from using its analytic edge to get early readings on many developments in the performance of the economy and bring these to bear on major administration stances on fiscal policy. As one respondent told us, the Carter administration's stress on fiscal policy left a particularly good opening when Treasury became convinced that spending was being used too much as a stimulant to the economy: 'Economic policy ... in this government, as you know, is very heavily fiscal policy ... It was part of our feeling, almost a year before anybody else, that the underlying strength of the economy had been underestimated and that we really did not need as much fiscal stimulus as we had been believing all along and, as it turned out, that we didn't really get because of budget underruns. And yet the economy achieved the output and employment goals that had been set.' Good news for Treasury in this instance turned into bad news for Health, Education and Welfare, which was promoting legislation that would greatly increase expenditures in the health field. The office of economic policy played a vital role in quashing the proposed health programs. Thus it fulfilled the pre-eminent role of a treasury department. It veiled its innate social conservatism in the most refined economic argumentation to be found in town: 'I think that we were able to convince the president that our goals concerning health insurance and national health programs were too ambitious in terms of what the economy could afford and we would have to do it in stages. So we did present a view on that which is not necessarily, in fact, our field.'

The deputate covering international economic analysis operated under substantially different circumstances from those of domestic economic policy. As we noted earlier, the office on the international side had, before Carter, reported directly to the assistant secretary for international affairs. Under the arrangement at the time of the interviews, international affairs technically had to clear research requests through the assistant secretary for economic policy. In practice, the various offices under international affairs began to develop internal research staffs. They tended to resort to economic policy only in the larger analytic exercises. One respondent on the international side of economic policy left us with the impression that the arrangement had turned the deputate into a think tank only remotely connected to policy analysis: 'It's a good life in some respects. Because the pressures come upon you only occasionally. There are ebbs and flows. There are certain peaks of activity when you have to do something very fast and very quickly. Usually, it's pretty easily done. But most of the time you're not being bugged. You're left to yourself. If you have something in mind which is of some relevance to the Treasury ... you just sit down and work on a project as if you were a research institute.'

Despite these reflections, we should not dismiss out of hand the concept of in-house research economists working under a different chain of command from the more policy-oriented units of Treasury. The British Treasury has operated a similar structure with considerable success. However, the us Treasury set out on its experiment on the wrong foot by making the changes as a result of pressures from a prospective assistant secretary. The person involved, Daniel Brill, did not help matters by virtually abandoning his interest in the international side once he had taken it into his jurisdiction. When he left Treasury, international economic analysis was transferred back to the assistant secretary for international affairs and, under Reagan, its various parts were reassigned within international affairs.

The Office of the Assistant Secretary for Domestic Finance
Domestic finance serves the dual purpose of safeguarding the arrangements that the United States enters into, either with the private sector or other governments, and integrating the regulatory activities of various agencies concerned with domestic institutions and equity markets.

Many of the office's projects are for the long term. One respondent, for instance, started an effort to consolidate federal agencies' financing of programs. He wanted them to draw upon Treasury securities rather than issuing their own guaranteed securities. It took the official ten years to see the Federal Financing Bank, which instituted his proposal, come into being. Working in the shorter term, the office closely examines the financial arrangements surrounding large government projects. On the capital markets side, the office's deputate reviewed myriad legislative proposals from agencies regulating capital markets. It attempted to resolve conflicts between departments and draft bills that stood a chance of congressional approval.

The entire domestic finance office finds itself constantly struggling with the ingenuity of public borrowers or members of the financial community who have found a new loophole in legislation. One respondent gave us a detailed example that demonstrates pretty well the interlocking responsibilities of the office's deputates against assaults on financial probity:

Some very bright people on Wall Street cooked up a new type of housing bond whereby municipalities can sell tax-exempt bonds, guaranteed indirectly by the Federal National Mortgage Association. It's for purposes of financing single-family housing. What this means is that you or I, as a potential single-family home-buyer, can get financing at tax-exempt rates instead of conventional mortgage rates. We go out and pay 9 or 10 per cent for a mortgage. Here's a way to get it for 7. You can imagine what that does for potential homebuilders and single-family home-owners in a municipality. Suddenly you can literally increase the housing level in your municipality by 20 per cent. You announce that you have $100 million of 7 per cent money available. And the city of Chicago went out and did it. It is estimated that there is $10 billion of such financing in the pipeline. Well, we are against it. It's a basic breach of the time-honoured, for a good reason, federal principle of not having it both ways. You are either tax-exempt or you are federally guaranteed, but you're not both because it creates a security stronger than the federal government's own security. It abuses the basic principle of the tax exemption. It crowds out other borrowers, namely municipalities themselves for their own needs, for whom the whole tax-exempt concept was invented.

THE CARTER ADMINISTRATION

In the previous chapter, we noted that Jimmy Carter started his administration with a firm commitment to the brokerage style of executive leadership. He preferred cabinet government in the American sense of the term – he preferred that secretaries resolve decisions on their own without recourse to the White House. Carter's spokes-in-the-wheel concept of access to the White House dictated, however, that all contesting parties find a forum for their views once an issue percolated through the 'iron gates' and eventually reached the Oval Office.

In chapter 2 I pointed up the degree to which brokerage politics became more myth than reality in the Carter administration. For several reasons, not the least of which were the president's immersion in details and the inexperience of his closest advisers, the administration allowed far too many issues through the 'iron gate' and left the president with unwieldy decision memos. These, rather than simply recommending a decision, all too often presented competing views and left the decision to the president. By the spring of 1979, the administration had fallen so far behind in managing even the issues central to Carter's chances for re-election that it turned to survival politics. This tack involved rationalizing decision-making in the White House and reining in administration appointees in the departments which had gone adrift. Of course, the pressure of the election campaign itself soon eclipsed the efforts directed to survival politics. Given more time, they might have paid off with appreciably better decisions.

The transition of the Carter administration from spokes in a wheel to wagons in a circle provides the backdrop for an appraisal of the former president's handling of economic affairs. Developments in the structure of the Economic Policy Group reflect the inevitability of the process. Successive collapses of the loosely structured decision-making process led to a tightening of the circle. One respondent traced in detail the administration's hit-and-miss approach to structuring its highest economic policy council: 'Technically the economic policy group consists of all economic agencies ... Even more technically the EPG doesn't exist ... It has never been created by an executive order ... It has no legal standing, no budget, no personnel. The EPG ... met only rarely in the early part of the administration. It was very quickly realized that it was an irremedially bulky group ... An executive committee was created ... It too became unwieldy and an informal decision was made in essence to thin down the group still further by creating a steering group ... What you see going on is really a collapse of the policy-making process down to the traditional key actors.'

Earlier in this chapter, I reported that one respondent argued for setting up a parallel organization to the National Security Council staff for handling economic decisions. Short of this level of institutionalization, Carter could have taken a cue from Gerald Ford[2] who had a close friend from Grand Rapids, Bill Seidman, boil down disparate views from elsewhere in the administration into manageable decision memos: 'He knew the field well enough to be able to synthesize the ideas. But I don't think he was a major player. So what you really want to have is someone who's trusted by the president, but really doesn't take a point of view ... understands the arguments but doesn't have arguments of his own.'

Carter added to the disarray by letting Stuart Eizenstat, assistant to the president for domestic affairs and policy, position himself so strategically in the economic policy process. Eizenstat's standing in Washington simply failed to warrant this amount of responsibility. If DPS were to effectively involve itself in steering economic policy, the president should have appointed a director with undisputed credentials.

Whether they believe he should have improved economic policy structures or simply brought into the White House a neutral broker who could have ferreted out competing views and integrated them into manageable decision memos, most respondents registered concern about Carter's endless groping for the right system. No one suffered from the president's indecision more than Michael Blumenthal. Traditionally, the secretary of the treasury serves as chief economic spokesman for the administration. Blumenthal suffered several falls from grace. These made him a prime target for the purge in the summer of 1979. Constant disputes with Eizenstat coupled with Hamilton Jordan's and Jody Powell's hostile distrust made life extremely difficult for Blumenthal.

Several Treasury officials believed the president had dangerously undermined their authority by constantly 'sending Blumenthal to Coventry' yet waiting so long to replace him. One respondent became particularly pointed in his comments. He asserted that the president's attitude toward Blumenthal had materially harmed the international economic position of the United States. He suggested that institutionalizing the traditional role of the treasury secretary as chief economic spokesman would prevent personality clashes with the president from causing so much harm:

The Treasury Department's role is really probably too dependent upon the personal relationship between the president and whoever's secretary. Whether we have a strong or a weak secretary depends upon his relationship with the president, rather than upon the legal mandate of the institution or the staff of the institution ... There is a great deal of sense in institutionalizing the role of the new secretary as the chief economic spokesman. That's very important because the weakness of Blumenthal last year had its implications for the whole monetary system, on the dollar and so forth ... One could argue very logically that, in a world in which we are increasingly interdependent economically – in which most of the other top economic spokesmen are finance ministers who want to consult with and negotiate with their counterparts who have equal authority – the US government is not really geared up to participate in that process.

Such counsel defines a clear limit to which leadership in economic policy can come from the Executive Office of the President rather than from Treasury. International politics might dictate that reforms designed to improve the economic advisory system rely more on process management than on introduction of strong personalities attached to the White House staff.

CONCLUSION

The current situation in the United States begs for more satisfactory institutional solutions. Most Treasury officials argued that both the secretary and the department will work under a handicap so long as they lack a clear designation as the leading agency for economics. The present arrangement, they believe, hampers the department most seriously in international deliberations. These operate under the assumption that any national delegation speaks with one voice. Respondents in the Executive Office of the President usually came up with a different diagnosis. They emphasized the need for improved co-ordination of the advice going to the president. For instance, cabinet-level bodies such as Ford's Economic Policy Board, Carter's Economic Policy Group, and Reagan's Council on Economic Affairs might include only the heads of departments or agencies that have authority over the major elements of economic policy. As well, the committees might operate much more as decision-making organs and less as open-ended seminars on the state of the economy. The latter tend to produce hours of deliberations that too often end in pleas for further analysis and in decision memos to the president that fail to present options and timetables. Officials in the Executive Office often assumed that an economics secretariat would manage the committee's workload and ensure that briefs to the president adequately distilled views of economic issues to leave to him only the most vital decisions.

Jimmy Carter's presidency shows the dangers in a failure to overcome the lack of co-ordination for economic and fiscal policies. Regarding the argument that the treasury secretary should receive a clear mandate to operate as first among equals, Carter first appointed as secretary Michael Blumenthal, an exceptionally strong personality with a very favourable image in Washington. However, Blumenthal soon found that interference and, eventually, hostility from top presidential advisers in the White House made it extremely difficult for him to press his own department's agenda. White House aides eventually won out and Blumenthal left the administration.

Regarding the strengthening of the cabinet-level body responsible for economic and fiscal policies, Carter again failed to act decisively. Only a gradual process of attrition 'shook down' the Economic Policy Group to a steering group that granted access only to the most vital players. Even then, the committee still operated essentially as a seminar. Both the Domestic Policy Staff, through Stuart Eizenstat's role in every policy issue with a major economic component, and the National Security Council Staff, mostly through Henry Owen's responsibility for preparing Carter for economic summits, loomed exceptionally large as foilers of Treasury's claims to dominance. However, only NSC, largely because of the narrower terms of its mandate, contributed consistently to the function of management and integration, as we might expect from an executive secretariat.

6

The conglomerate in British economic policy

In the preceding chapter, the reader might have marvelled at the number of US central agencies (seven) involved in one way or another with economic policy. The reader will be equally astonished to find that HM Treasury contains units comparable to most of those discussed in connection with the United States, *plus* review divisions responsible for the budget of expenditures and for industrial policies. Important co-ordinating functions reside in the Cabinet Office. As well, the prime minister and cabinet call upon some independent economic advice in No. 10 and CPRS. Yet the Treasury contains the lion's share of the units that develop and co-ordinate macroeconomic policy. In addition, it works in the budgeting of expenditure and in industrial policy; in the United States these roles belong, respectively, to the Office of Management and Budget and to the Department of Commerce.

NO. 10, THE CABINET OFFICE, AND THE CENTRAL POLICY REVIEW STAFF

In the previous chapter, I examined in detail the advisory units available to the prime minister and cabinet. These, of course, include the prime minister's personal staff in No. 10, the Cabinet Office, and the Central Policy Review Staff. Since much of the work of these units focuses specifically on economic policy, I will not review the treatment of the roles presented in chapter 2. The evidence suggests, however, that the British system devotes much greater resources to co-ordination of economic policy than does the American.

Since the Heath government, No. 10 has kept on board at least one economic adviser. In fact, a very high-ranking monetarist, Alan Walters, recently joined Margaret Thatcher's No. 10 staff. In the Cabinet Office, the economics and European secretariats, each with eight senior officials, provide the staff support necessary for proper management of collective decisions on economic problems. The secretariats thus parallel closely the units for co-ordination that many US officials wish they had to distil conflicting departmental views into decision memos for the president. Especially under Callaghan, CPRS involved itself heavily with economic policy. Sir Kenneth Berrill, the former head of CPRS, and Richard Ross, his deputy, brought to their work considerable expertise in macroeconomic analysis. Since there is no CPRS minister, these officials also enjoyed the right to attend cabinet committee meetings and press their views in person.

HM TREASURY

The Treasury has maintained its many functions for two reasons. First, experiments in divesting it of some of its powers have failed. The most important of these saw the establishment in 1964 of the Department of Economic Affairs, which was to produce medium-term economic plans. The new department was ultimately disbanded in 1969, largely because it lacked handles on economic power and commanded no special access to the prime minister or cabinet. Since then, the conventional wisdom among officials involved in macroeconomics starts from the premise that their world and microeconomic policy-making form parts of a seamless garment. They do not readily divide into bureaucratic units. We heard this lesson from practically every Treasury official: 'I think the crux of the thing for proper management is that you need to bring together under one hat the policy on expenditure, taxation, and finance. Those are the three parts of a seamless garment. They all run together as economic policy.'

Second, the Treasury's near-monopoly of economic policy can be related to Hugh Heclo and Aaron Wildavsky's well-founded point made in *The Private Government of Public Money*[1] The volume focuses largely on the Treasury's role within review of budgets on public expenditure. However, it discusses this role in light of the pervasive atmosphere of Whitehall's 'village life.' British officials, differences of opinion notwithstanding, work behind a veil of secrecy to develop the necessary consensus for a difficult decision. Secrecy prevents many issues from getting into the public eye at all. In the cabinet and its committees, ministers may introduce political considerations and departmental views with impassioned pleas. At the end of the process, the prime minister states the consensus and that is usually that. Dithering abounds both in the bureaucracy and among ministers. Decisions, however, usually stick. Even if decisions have to pass through Parliament for approval, they normally find acceptance nothing more than an annoying and, sometimes, embarrassing formality. In sum, secrecy, as rooted in the tradition of collective cabinet responsibility, provides a perfect air bubble for an omnibus economic department such as the Treasury.

To say that the Treasury is an omnibus does not suggest that it is monolithic. Keeping various economic disciplines and viewpoints under one roof simply helps to control conflict, it does not eliminate it. In fact, our respondents in the Treasury gave us several glimpses of intramural conflicts. Officials must work out problems arising from disagreements between units covering different sectors of economic management. As well, ideological perspectives often provide another layer to disagreements.

Concerning ideology, the Treasury has had to adjust over the last decade to the gradual shift from Keynesian to monetarist economics. Even under the Labour party, the transition changed the department's emphasis from fiscal policy, centring on spending and taxation, to financial policy, focusing on the supply of money. More fundamentally, Treasury Keynesians found themselves adjusting to both an influx of younger monetarists and the slippage of the reputability of their view even in the universities. Thus, some Treasury discussions stretch on purely for ideological reasons:

We have still got undercurrents of this Keynesian-Friedmanite dilemma. Those are the extremes ... On some of these things it becomes difficult to talk because really quite basic gut feelings about the way the economy works are not consistently shared ... It came perhaps most forcefully to the top a year ago when it just happened to focus on the question of whether the exchange rate should be let go in the interest of stopping an inflow of funds ... It was resolved not by agreement but by one of those kinds of drifts of opinion where you suddenly found that a minority had become a majority and so a decision was taken that way. [The pound was allowed to float up in an effort to keep the British money supply down.] This left a certain amount of unhappiness behind among people who felt it was the wrong decision.

Such ideological restiveness seems to have put an at least partial end to discussions about the lack of countervaillance in Whitehall's economic policy machinery. In fact, one very senior official viewed the need for a competing economic department with the equanimity of an abbot who would prefer not to see his more contemplative monks form another monastery: 'I'm not terribly keen personally on setting up deliberately a countervailing force. That was part of the idea of the Department of Economic Affairs, creating tension and all that kind of thing. But it tends to waste an awful lot of time. If it's institutionalized, sooner or later perhaps one or the other tends to win.'

The Treasury serves six ministers. Two of these, the chancellor of the exchequer and the chief secretary, belong to the cabinet. The other four, the financial secretary, the economic secretary, and ministers of state for the House of Commons and for the House of Lords, ease the burden of the cabinet-level ministers in the department and Parliament. Thus a clear hierarchy of ministers has the chancellor on the top acting as the principal economic minister. The chief secretary shoulders most of the day-to-day decisions concerning public expenditure. He concentrates on developing annual spending guidelines and conducting major bilateral discussions with departments on spending projections. The financial secretary usually enjoys somewhat higher status than his other colleagues at the junior level. The two ministers of state spend a great deal of their time handling tax legislation and other business in Parliament.

On the official side, Treasury organization bears little resemblance to the division of functions among ministers. Sir Douglas Wass, the permanent secretary between 1974 and 1983, presided over a department of just over four thousand officials. A permanent secretary in HM Treasury belongs to a very exclusive club. Along with the secretary of the cabinet, the head of the civil service and permanent secretary of the Civil Service Department, and the permanent under-secretary of state and head of the diplomatic service, he commands special status as a permanent secretary 'plus.' Below him, four second permanent secretaries manage the Treasury sectors. Only a few key ministries list officials of this grade, which stands between permanent secretary and the usual second tier in departments – deputy secretary. Indeed, Treasury ministers also supervise two full permanent secretaries heading departments that operate outside the permanent secretary's purview but report to the chancellor on matters concerning policy. The two departments, the Board of Inland Revenue and HM Customs and Excise, cover roughly the same areas as comparable operational arms of the US Treasury.

The second permanent secretaries manage five subject-area divisions within the Treasury. First, the Public Services Sector takes the lead in developing the spending side of the fiscal framework and controlling expenditure budgeting for most government programs. Second and relatedly, a unit styled 'Pay Group' establishes policies concerning civil-service pay and allowances. Third, the Domestic Economy Sector develops and co-ordinates fiscal and monetary policies, advises the chancellor on industrial policies, and reviews expenditure budgets relating to industry and agriculture. Fourth, the Overseas Finance Sector advises the chancellor on British policy towards the balance of payments, the management of reserves, and international monetary co-operation. It also looks after Treasury interests in foreign aid and relations with the European Economic Community. Fifth, the Chief Economic Adviser's Sector directs Treasury forecasting, co-ordinates the activities of economics units in other Treasury units and heads the professional economics service for the entire British government. For the purpose of this chapter's consideration of the integration of economic and fiscal policy, I consider the functions of only the Domestic Economy Sector's fiscal and monetary policy side, the Overseas Finance Sector, and the Chief Economic Adviser's Sector. The responsibilities of the Public Services Sector, the Pay Group, and the 'industry' side of the Domestic Economy Sector correspond more to the topic of part III, on allocation and management of governmental resources.

THE CENTRAL UNIT

Before discussing the Treasury divisions we should first take note of the Central Unit. We have already examined the relative strength of British machinery for interdepartmental co-ordination of the cabinet's economic policy-making and noted that the Treasury contains most of the advisory units and levers. One might conclude, then, that the department would leave the integration of its stances to the routine interchange between sectors. On the contrary, the Treasury does not exempt itself from the British bureaucracy's ethos of co-ordination. Thus a central unit services the Treasury committees designed to keep channels of communication open among sectors and to assure that all key players are involved in major decisions. By establishing the Central Unit in 1975, Treasury officials recognized the cardinal principle that maintains the cohesiveness of the British public service: 'Think of Britain!' In the words of one respondent, the principle, applied to economic policy, implies much more than mere co-ordination: 'You have to have a view of what the British economy can stand. Ministers left to themselves would do things which would not be consistent with the proper management of the economy.'

Besides stemming in part from a British sense that action must be based on consensus, two other factors make co-ordination especially vital to the operation of the Treasury. First, second permanent secretaries operate with relative autonomy within their sectors. They report directly to the chancellor on the matters they follow: 'For example, [Sir Douglas] Wass wouldn't interfere in the management of a major public expenditure exercise ... There is no doubt who is in charge of that. It is the second permanent secretary for public services. Similarily, when the chancellor is dealing with the European Monetary System negotiations, it is the second permanent secretary for Overseas Finance he deals with, not Wass.' Second, the fact that economic management is an inexact science compounds the obstacles to reconciling ideological perspectives within the department: 'Managing the economy is rather like keeping one's feet on a surfboard. If one is competent and professional one will keep one's feet, even though he might end up on a bit of the beach which he wasn't aiming at ... It's also related to the nature of the waves that hit you ... There can be oil crises or the trade unions getting out of hand, and what can the Treasury do about that? ... Nothing. All we can do is say, "Gosh, this one's going to hit us. How can we possibly adjust to make sure that the thing doesn't get out of control?"'

In fact, ideology and analysis notwithstanding, some respondents noted that the preoccupation of one Treasury generation might well seem anachronistic to the next: 'When I was young the Treasury was defending the pound and went on defending it, in the view of my generation, far too long. This became the accepted view from about 1967 to about 1972. It isn't any more. Last Christmas ... they got all the main forecasting machines in the country to do a rerun of history to see what difference it would have made if they had had a devaluation earlier in the 1960s. They came to the conclusion that had it been done earlier it wouldn't have made all that much difference ...'

The Central Unit consists of two small sections with a total of five senior officials. An under-secretary heads the unit while two other officials serve as secretaries to each of the two all-Treasury co-ordination committees; two economists operate the Treasury briefing division which gathers data on the economy used both in Treasury discussions and in No. 10, the Cabinet Office, and CPRS. The briefing unit provides most of the background material on the economy used by the prime minister in preparation for her bi-weekly appearances during question hour in the House of Commons.

The Policy Co-ordinating Committee (PCC) serviced by the Central Unit attempts to develop a coherent Treasury view on all major economic issues. The five Treasury permanent secretaries attend, along with the seven deputy secretaries who actually oversee the operations of the various groups within the four policy sectors. The committee enters any Treasury exercise, whether cyclical or ad hoc, that requires major trade-offs between sectors. Each year it considers the development of fiscal policy by looking at the total spending requirements of departments, reconciling these with the levels that the economy can tolerate, and relating the aggregate numbers to the desired balance in taxation and borrowing. Independent of this cyclical exercise, it must assess how the Treasury should advise on the direction the country should take at major crossroads in the international economy and respond to crises at home.

At the time of the 1978 interviews, the Treasury was in the throes of advising the government not to join the rest of the European Economic Community in a monetary system (the European Monetary System – EMS) which would limit flotation of the pound to certain points above or below the value of a 'basket' of the European currencies. The Treasury adopted the view that upward pressures on the pound from the US dollar and downward pressure from the German mark could remain too intense for sterling to live within the confines of EMS. Similarly, the Treasury, immediately before the interviews, advised in favour of holding unions to 5 per cent wage increases for the 1978–9 round of pay negotiations. The Labour party's strategy for re-election largely spawned the policy. However, the Treasury's emphasis on pay constraint as a prime instrument against inflation allowed it to overinvest in a policy that ultimately fuelled a union revolt. The ensuing 'winter of discontent' led to numerous wage settlements over 20 per cent.

The Macroeconomic Group (MEG) consists of Treasury under-secretaries (the level below deputy), whose work relates directly to macroeconomic policy. Chaired by the under-secretary who heads the Central Unit, the group typically includes those involved in forecasting, monetary policy on the domestic and foreign sides, taxation, industrial policy, and setting the aggregate figures for public expenditure. The group performs a dual function. On the one hand, it focuses on concerns either raised by PCC or thought to be looming; on the other, it operates as an ongoing seminar aimed at ensuring that under-secretaries involved in macroeconomics develop some common assumptions about the economy: 'It's finding and making sense of the options which come forward to the senior body. It rarely takes an initiative. It's a receiving and refining group ... It pushes stuff up to the PCC which also receives a number of papers about the background of a particular area of policy direct from the relevant division. It's also training people at the under-secretary level to look much wider than their own divisions. They have an instinct to do that. But it gets them used to doing it.'

One respondent gave us an insight into how the Treasury hopes PCC and MEG will further integrate its policies when he discussed the shortcomings of the committees' responses to the EMS proposal in 1978: 'This organization has not worked perfectly with the EMS thing. If we had sufficient foresight and thought that this would be coming forward as an option, we would have taken cognizance of it a month or two before we did. We probably would have organized the flow of options much more clearly for our own ministers and for the European frameworks – the commission and the council and for presentation to the public. We've been reacting rather than taking a clear lead on this. We didn't feed enough to the MEG and then the PCC, largely because we ran out of time.' Essentially, then, the two committees contribute most effectively to Treasury decisions when they draw attention early on to a major issue. Under such circumstances, they provide mechanisms through which the options may be fully developed before outside pressures force the players into a decision.

The Overseas Finance Sector
This sector divides into three groups. The first looks after policy on the exchange rate, reserves, and balance of payments, briefings on the world economy, and relations with international monetary organizations such as the IMF. The second looks after European co-ordination, including the EEC budget, finances, and economic policy. The third includes three divisions that watch out for Treasury interests in foreign aid, commodity policies (especially as related to oil, budgets, and administration of international organizations), and the financing of British exports. This group occupies much of its time on North-South issues – financial relations with developing nations. The group, especially the oil and overseas services division, also takes into consideration the financial implications of trade with South Africa for maintenance of markets in black Africa.

Straddling the Overseas Finance Sector and relating as well to the Domestic Economy Sector, the Finance Economic Unit participates in discussions on monetary policy to ensure that international commitments, overseas financial operations, and domestic monetary targets mesh. For instance, the under-secretary in charge of this unit at the time of our interviews belonged to the group most vitally involved in the EMS decision.

The monetary side of Overseas Finance's work requires very close co-ordination with the Bank of England. Day-to-day discussions centre on the exchange rate and whether the United Kingdom should intervene to maintain the desired value of the pound. Longer-term issues centre on management of the public debt, especially where to borrow in foreign markets. British-style cabinet government does not prevail here. The Treasury and the bank hold monetary policy close to their vests. Ultimately, the big issues command the attention of the chancellor and the governor of the bank, as they will advise the prime minister on major moves. Since the Domestic Economy Sector also maintains strong operational ties to the Bank of England, the permanent secretary often must step into bank-Treasury relations to force agreement when international and domestic goals conflict.

The Treasury's hegemony in international economics notwithstanding, institutional arrangements limit its authority in two notable areas, namely European policy and foreign trade. The European secretariat in the Cabinet Office, mainly because of its size and the previous experience of its officials in the Treasury and operational departments concerned with the EEC, substantially exceeds the normal role in policy formulation taken by a co-ordinative secretariat. Formerly, either the Treasury or the Foreign Office took the lead in bringing departmental views together on economic relations with Europe. On the trade side, the Treasury yields all but the most crucial issues in economic relations to the Department of Trade. Thus, in contrast to the United States, with its trade office in the Treasury and the Executive Office's US Trade Representative, the British system has kept trade policy largely out from under the direct aegis of central agencies.

The Domestic Economy Sector
This large sector consists of five groups. Three of these, Public Enterprises, Industry and Agriculture, and Industrial Policy, develop policy concerning nationalized industries and the relations between public expenditure and private enterprise. The Domestic Economy Unit provides economic advice to the three 'Industry' groups. As noted above, I will examine the industry and public services groups in part III, on allocation and management of resources.

The remaining groups of the Domestic Economic Sector maintain a firm grip on two macroeconomic instruments, taxation and domestic finance. The groups operate under the deputy secretary for public finance. In recent years, the Treasury's handling of this field has served as an example of its organizational adaptability. In chapter 4's treatment of Canadian central agencies operating within the field of strategic planning and major policy decisions, I noted the degree to which alternative organizations arise when existing institutions fail adequately to address an immediate cabinet preoccupation. In chapter 5, I discussed the degree to which the US Treasury has seen its authority over economic policy gravitate piecemeal to other central agencies as successive administrations find it cannot adequately fulfill one or other role.

Admittedly, the British Treasury suffers anguish when governments emphasize macroeconomic instruments which officials believe in only half-heartedly. Yet the implicit realization that it will again have its day in the sun enables the department to swallow its pride and carry on. After all, governments come and go. Public Finance altered its organization to accommodate the Thatcher government. Under Callaghan, it stressed pay policy while keeping a relatively light hand on tax policy and the money supply. Under Thatcher, it dismantled its entire pay policy group, including an under-secretary, two assistant secretaries, and two principals.

Two groups survive in Public Finance, namely Home Finance and Fiscal Policy. The current organization thus reflects the Thatcher government's primary interest in monetary policy and secondary concern for tax policy. The latter emphasis stems from the belief that once tight monetary controls have brought inflation under control, newly affordable tax breaks will move in to improve investment and industrial productivity. As the theory goes, tax measures aimed at the middle- and high-wage earners, rather than at the lower income groups, will stimulate industrial reform instead of inflation-producing demand for consumer goods.

Home Finance has taken on additional staff to handle its current workload. The group includes four divisions. One deals with public and private financial institutions and with government savings and borrowing programs. Another, working closely with the Bank of England, advises on monetary policy, debt sales, and money markets. A third takes responsibility for national savings and government lending to other parts of the public sector. Finally, the accounts division manages and monitors the government's central accounts.

The interplay of monetary policy and government finance requires that Home Finance not ignore any levers. When pursuing tight financial policy, it attempts to keep the lid on both the supply of money and government borrowing. It must co-ordinate with the Bank of England to ensure that interest rates are at levels that will help achieve monetary targets. It will also work with other parts of the Treasury responsible for controlling public expenditure for tax policy. These in-house discussions seek to keep the public sector borrowing requirement (PSBR) low enough to enable the monetary target to be achieved without excessively high interest rates. A tight PSBR performs the important function of indicating to the private sector that government intends to be as abstemious as it expects business and consumers to be. Finally, Home Finance has been concerned with the imposition of the Treasury's most direct check on the money supply, the 'corset.' This device, the supplementary special deposits scheme, has restricted the growth in banks' interest-bearing eligible liabilities.

PSBR and the corset can perform both economic and psychological roles. Sometimes, the latter function forces the Treasury into using both even when technical arguments in their favour are less than compelling. One official told us that in 1978 the Treasury tightened the corset just because it did not want any speculation about what remained in its bag of tricks: '[We made] an appraisal of what was necessary in strict technical terms to ensure that the money supply was brought back under control and it didn't involve the corset ... You have a problem of persuading public opinion to accept that your judgment was right. Therefore, what really forced the corset decision was, first, the determination to make a decision which would succeed and not fail and not even risk failing; and, second, making sure that we did everything and didn't leave anything that anybody could expect you to do next week. So we did the lot, we did fiscal policy, we did the interest rate, and we did the corset.'

The Bank of England, located in the heart of the City (London's banking district), remains staunchly independent. Richard Chapman has chronicled very well relations between the Treasury and the Bank of England when major decisions on interest rates loom.[2] In addition to these intense and high-level discussions during crises, the Treasury and the bank maintain myriad informal links. We noted in chapter 3 that the governor of the bank joined the chancellor, the prime minister, Harold Lever, and a handful of top officials in a macroeconomic group regularly convened by Callaghan. This secret body attempted to broaden discussions between the prime minister and the chancellor on more sensitive issues related to the economy. Independent of such groups, both the chancellor and the permanent secretary maintain weekly contacts with the governor.

Lower down the Treasury hierarchy, officials keep in constant touch with their opposite numbers for the purpose of making operational decisions. The bank, as an independent agency, prefers to avoid formal committees of officials from the Treasury and their own organization. None the less, senior Treasury officials working on the domestic side meet regularly with their counterparts in the bank to assess the general structure of monetary policy.

Treasury's Fiscal Policy Group works somewhat more narrowly than its name would suggest. It safeguards Treasury interests in tax policy as an economic instrument. Compared to tax policy units in the US Treasury, Fiscal Policy operates on an exceptionally thin complement. An under-secretary, two assistant secretaries, a senior economic adviser, three principals, and three executive officers run three divisions. One takes direct taxation; one takes indirect taxation; and one, actually under the deputy chief economic adviser, analyses the implications of various tax policies. These units differ from their US counterparts in another important way. Tax lawyers play no role here. Thus the divisions bring relatively little to discussions of tax reform. Rather, they concentrate on the macro- and microeconomic implications of tax policy. In direct taxation, the Treasury works almost exclusively with the Board of Inland Revenue; regarding indirect taxation, it operates closely with HM Customs and Excise – the department that administers taxes in that field. Treasury policies on indirect taxation must, however, spread the net wider to include the views of the departments of Transport, Environment, and Health and Social Services. These all involve themselves to a degree in indirect taxation.

The Fiscal Policy Committee serves as the principal forum in which officials work out collective views on tax policy. The permanent secretary of the treasury chairs the committee. The chief economic adviser, the chairmen of the Board of Inland Revenue and of Customs and Excise, and deputy secretaries in the respective organizations concerned with tax issues attend the committee. While the Treasury's permanent secretary, Sir Douglas Wass brought considerable experience in the tax field to his leading position on the committee. He often lent his considerable weight to claims from either Inland Revenue or Customs and Excise when he judged that the integrity of the tax system was at issue. In fact, our respondents in the Fiscal Policy Group broadly supported the view that the Treasury should defer to the two tax departments on issues of integrity: 'If taxation doesn't work effectively you are in deep trouble, and by working effectively you mean a system which in a sense commands a degree of acceptance ... It has to be fair, equitable, seen to operate in a particular way which is intended. You can, of course, readily play ducks and drakes with the system if you start imposing a whole set of economic criteria overlaid on each other and adapting this and that piece of the system ... Now this is an area in which Inland Revenue, and Customs and Excise know their stuff. We have to listen to what they say to us.'

As for Treasury ministers, the chancellor takes a strong personal interest in major tax issues directly related to the budget, such as rates of taxation and the levels of personal allowances. There are exceptions to this rule. For instance, Anthony Barber (now a baron), a chancellor under Edward Heath, took a strong interest in administrative matters related to taxation. Normally, the chief secretary maintains delegated responsibility for major changes in the ways in which taxes are to be administered. Under Callaghan, junior ministers followed more detailed administrative matters. I should stress here the fact that Treasury ministers serve essentially as the political authorities for Inland Revenue and for Customs and Excise, as well as for the Treasury itself. Especially through the chief secretary, the tax agencies often find an effective spokesman in the cabinet. The Labour chief secretary at the time of the interviews, Joel Barnett, was an example of this. He headed off an effort by Callaghan to give small businesses concessions beyond what the Treasury and Inland Revenue had agreed to at that point.

That incident pointed up a very important fact about the relations between the Treasury and the revenue departments. Since they operate under the same political authorities as their Treasury counterparts, members of the revenue departments gain entrance to its village community. In other words, Treasury officials will defer to their views and attach themselves to struggles that demand immense expenditure of political capital. Often it is not so much the integrity of taxation that is at stake as Whitehall's convention of seeking consensus and closing ranks once it is found.

The Chief Economic Adviser's Sector
Readers will recall the discussion above of the difficulties the us Treasury has encountered in servicing its policy units with economic advice. In the United Kingdom, the Chief Economic Adviser's Sector goes quite some distance in providing department-wide integration of economic advice and consideration of specific policy options. The sector owes much of its success to the fact that it operates on two tiers. First, the chief economic adviser, a second permanent secretary, oversees two groups headed by under-secretaries that conduct Treasury assessments of various segments of the economy and macroeconomic analyses. The sector thus carries most of the analytic weight for comparable tasks performed jointly by the forecasters in the us Treasury and in the Council of Economic Advisers. Within the Treasury, the sector takes its cues from the monetary and fiscal policies being pursued by the Policy Co-ordinating Committee. Assuming these limits, the sector assesses the consequences if one or other balance is struck within and between the two policy fields. This can then affect the Treasury's view of the balances it should seek.

Outside the Treasury, the sector maintains dialogue with other economic departments, especially the departments of Trade and of Industry, and with the Bank of England. The operational departments find themselves in a disadvantageous position vis-à-vis the Treasury for two reasons. First, the chief economic adviser, as the head of the entire government economic service, enjoys higher visibility than advisers in other departments. Second, the Treasury maintains a much larger staff of economists than do other departments.

The second tier of activity to which the sector also owes much of its success involves the responsibilities of the deputy chief economic adviser. The reader probably noticed, during the discussion of other segments of the Treasury, that several economic advisory units operate between and within sectors. These include the Public Sector Economic Group, the Finance Economic Unit (which bridges the Overseas Finance Sector and the Home Finance side of Domestic Economy), and the Economics of Industrial Expenditure and Economics of Taxation divisions (which serve, respectively, the Home Finance and Fiscal Policy groups). Although all of these units report hierarchically to Treasury officials responsible for specific policy sectors, the deputy chief economic adviser takes responsibility for the advice they give. He also acts as the principal economic adviser to the heads of the three Treasury policy sectors. In this respect, he bears ultimate responsibility for mobilizing economic advice to the three second permanent secretaries involved. When cross-cutting issues call for co-ordination of advice between sectors, he will take the lead in efforts to reach consensus on the economic factors affecting the matter at hand. Thus, the British Treasury seems to have struck a better balance between centralization of economic advice and adequate servicing of policy shops than has its US counterpart. However, it owes its success to the peculiar circumstances of Whitehall. Largely because the Treasury maintains the dominant contingent in the government economic service, the *esprit de corps* of its economists melds with that of the department. This situation produces an atmosphere in which economists relate well to specific policy units while keeping sight of macroeconomic policy as a seamless fabric.

THE CALLAGHAN GOVERNMENT

In a recent book on the economic policy process in the United Kingdom, William Keegan and R. Pennant-Rea stress the effects of cyclical forces on economic policy options and on the relations between ministers and their officials.[3] During the government's first year or so, ministers will follow as faithfully as possible their manifesto commitments. Thus, officials will find it difficult to interest them in employing economic instruments that do not relate to the strategy laid out in the manifesto. We have already seen this process operate in the Treasury. There, officials have responded to the Thatcher government's priorities by upgrading units dealing with monetary policy and eliminating those handling pay policy outside the public sector.

Manifesto solutions are notoriously simplistic. They rely too often on one instrument of economic management when all should be in play. Ultimately, governments recognize that things are no better or have gone completely wrong. They then resort to Treasury wise men. The officials move different fire brigades into action as the crisis intensifies. As Keegan and Pennant-Rea demonstrate, the precarious nature of the British economy simply does not allow for mistakes. Invariably, domestic solutions to the crisis amount to too little too late. Thus governments eventually resort to large-scale international borrowing. Help comes with the condition that the United Kingdom fulfil specific monetary targets. Usually the external assistance restores confidence in the economy and an upswing occurs. At this stage, a Labour government can expect unions, which have accepted wage restraint, to reassert their claims.

James Callaghan took over from Harold Wilson just as the government's crisis period had come to a full boil. At the time of our interviews, he was enjoying a modest upswing in the economy. This improvement intensified union demands to discontinue pay constraint. Callaghan realized that free bargaining would wash away much of the recovery with new inflation. Further, he thought he saw an important opening to a majority government in the election he expected to call in the fall of 1978. Phase four of the constraint program would perhaps convince middle-class voters that a Labour government would, after all, keep wage claims in line. Callaghan ultimately opted for 5 per cent. Then an unexpected downswing of Labour support in polls gave him cold feet about a fall election. The data indicated that he probably would not gain a majority. He scuttled his election plans and embarked on his forced march through the winter of discontent brought on by a clearly unenforceable pay target.

How could a prime minister botch his economic policy so badly? We noted in the preceding chapter that the difficult circumstances under which Callaghan took office severely limited the options throughout his government. Even with the improvement in the economy, conditions still warranted a firm hand. The 1974–9 government saw a period of uncertainty over the economy so intense that Treasury officials clearly viewed their task as more political and psychological than technical: 'We have gone through a particular kind of experience over the last three or four years here when inflation did get out of hand badly. The thrust has been political and psychological, in a sense, rather than economic.' With respect to pay policy, the Treasury had just reached the point where it was prepared to use pay restraint more according to economic than political or psychological criteria. However, it was far from abandoning specific limits: '[Direct] incomes policy ... started as a one-off shock exercise in round one back in '75. Having proved successful with that round, they [Labour] tried it again and then moved into a slightly different idea, not of regarding what had happened as being a once-and-for-all shock exercise but now "Let's try a transition gently into something freer." The present operation is not only a further step in that transition, tightening the thing down further, but – as we made absolutely clear in our white paper – really this government is now persuaded that some permanent framework of a direct attempt to influence the way that leg of the economy goes is part of the scheme of things.' Pressure building to eliminate the pay program congealed the Treasury's resolve. The impending election provided the coat-tails upon which the program could ride. Of course, the department's strategy had it using once again political and psychological warfare. To most informed observers, the Treasury had overdramatized what should have remained a simple exercise to advance further the progress already made in control of wages.

Why did Callaghan buy the Treasury line? Several of our respondents stressed the degree to which Callaghan would take problems to himself and let them be blown out of proportion. During the British deliberations over entrance into the European Monetary System, he plunged the Treasury into confusion. The chancellor, against the Treasury consensus, favoured entrance. Everyone knew that the prime minister would make the ultimate decision. However, the Treasury simply could not figure out which way he was leaning. This uncertainty contributed to the confused way in which the department handled the issue.

On the pay front, Callaghan even allowed his cabinet to work itself into a lather over implementation of existing pay policies. A committee on pay, consisting of the chancellor and the secretaries of state for Prices and Consumer Protection, Employment, and Industry, met more than a hundred times in one year. Concerning tax policy, Callaghan again found it difficult to stay away from details. We have already noted that the chief secretary had to act firmly to stop the prime minister's pressure for greater exemptions to small business. Previously, Treasury officials had to cope with direct pressure from No. 10 concerning tax exemptions to divers working in North Sea oilfields and to forestry interests. In the former case, the Treasury had to accept total tax exemption for the North

Sea divers on the grounds, pressed by No. 10, that the country could not risk a strike by workers so vital to the oil industry.

Callaghan thus manifested a dangerous instinct for meddling. This trait, coupled with the relative urgency of the times, slipped him irrevocably into survival politics. He tended to pursue each issue alone and with considerable commitment of time. A well-placed journalist contrasting Callaghan with Wilson stressed the former's ponderous nature: 'You just cannot predict what he will do. He prefers to take his briefing material home to ponder over things in solitude and then to reach a decision which is as much guided by his political instincts as the advice he has received. On the other hand, you could predict what Wilson was going to do if you knew what his officials were saying. Wilson liked to appear decisive. He loved to be stopped in the hallway and presented with some options and to make a decision on the spot.'

A Treasury official adds another element to a comparison of Wilson and Callaghan. Callaghan would frequently become mesmerized by the long-term implications of what he decided. This weakness derived from a relatively simple patriotism that saw Britain at a crossroads at every turn. As a former Second World War petty officer, Callaghan perhaps saw too much incomprehensible peril in the future: 'Callaghan is much more of the lion than the fox I would say than Wilson. Although I believed Wilson prided himself on being a strategist, funnily enough, I think he was much more likely to do the short-term easy thing. Callaghan quite often takes a longer view – as someone said to me the other day, perhaps because he became prime minister rather at the end of his life. He is not thinking too far ahead about his own future. He is a patriot and takes a long-term view.' Our official thus pointed out why Callaghan foiled his own re-election plans by embracing the Treasury's strategy for a continued pay program. The Treasury interest in maintaining some sort of permanent structure got him thinking of Britain to the detriment of re-election.

THE THATCHER GOVERNMENT

If James Callaghan's weakness was pay policy, Margaret Thatcher manifests a decided penchant for monetary policy. We have already noted that this emphasis has led to the dismantling of Treasury's pay units. As well, the Chief Economic Adviser's Sector experienced a major shake-up in January 1980, when the government replaced the retiring second permanent secretary with an outsider. This unprecedented move put Terry Burns, a thirty-five-year-old monetarist who used to direct the London Business School Centre for Forecasting, into Whitehall's most senior economic advisory post. Burns immediately embarked on a major study of his sector designed to ascertain whether, in the words of one respondent, it 'fits in with his ministers' requirements.' In other words, the remaining Keynesian economists in the Treasury might find their days are numbered.

Thatcher's ministers also changed units within the Treasury not directly involved with macroeconomics. For instance, the Public Services Sector finds itself limited much more than under other governments to simply responding to the financial targets when working out the public expenditure component of the fiscal framework: '[There has been] much more emphasis on the monetary aggregates. That spills through onto expenditure. The principle which sums it all up is that finance determines expenditure rather than expenditure finance ... They start from an objective for the growth of the money supply and regulate everything to that.' The industry groups in the Domestic Economy Sector suffered considerable losses. Ministers believed that if they got the macroeconomics right the micro would take care of itself: 'First, ministers are deliberately standing back from helping lame-duck corporations. Second, they are also standing back from industrial strategy. They haven't got an industrial strategy as such.' Thus, the Treasury temporarily eliminated its division responsible for assistance to industry and the deputy secretary position over the industry groups.

Thatcher ultimately rediscovered Treasury economic instruments which had withered for a time on the vine. We should note, however, that Treasury ministers, headed by Geoffrey Howe, still manifest a deep fervour over monetarism. The comments of one Conservative insider reflect the depth of conviction: 'Monetary policy operates through affecting expectations ... You do so when you have built up a series of conditioning channels. One can always think of it in terms of the Pavlovian process. In Germany, they've had strict monetary targets for some time. They always have had quite an effective system of communicating informally the implications of these to various sectors.' In addition to deep faith in their chosen instruments, Conservative Treasury ministers have shown remarkably clannish behaviour. To the annoyance of their officials, they and three political advisers on their personal staffs have been meeting three times a week, on average, to map out a joint strategy. In the words of our well-placed Conservative: 'We for our part have to be able to impose the political will of the government ... I think if you didn't do it you'd get lousy results in the long run ... It was such an evident necessity. I believe that formal communication structures [through permanent officials] have a very inhibiting influence on people.

They rule out certain kinds of thinking and certain forms of expression ... We felt more than usually the need to run a very tight ship.'

As a result of the private meetings, officials find that they are taking instructions more often directly from Treasury ministers. Further, since no officials attend the meetings, they often must go through the embarrassment of seeking elaboration from one of the political advisers. In the words of one respondent: 'If one is puzzled by an instruction which comes out of a morning meeting, one can ask the special adviser. But even the chancellor's principal private secretary [a career civil servant] is not admitted to these meetings.'

Clearly, Thatcher's exceptionally strong support of monetarism enables Treasury ministers to maintain such determination. Although there was no question that her convictions were at the root of Treasury policies, we found no signs of the involvement in day-to-day matters that Callaghan allowed himself. Thus, she practises what she preaches: within certain limits, rehabilitation of the British economy will come from macroeconomics alone. It is difficult to predict the ultimate results of Thatcher's single-mindedness. Judging from several respondents' observations, however, she long ago ceased to amaze the Treasury with her unflinching tenacity.

CONCLUSION

We have found in the United Kingdom, first, less of a tendency than in the United States to gather units responsible for implementation of economic and fiscal policies directly under the aegis of central agencies. For instance, the Board of Inland Revenue and HM Customs and Excise, the agencies responsible for taxation and tariffs, both report ultimately to the chancellor of the exchequer. However, they largely operate as autonomous departments. Officials at the level of permanent secretary head them; comparatively small units in the Treasury proper advise the chancellor concerning the effects of taxation and tariffs on much broader targets for the performance of the economy.

Second, the Treasury has successfully upheld the view that economic and fiscal policies form part of a seamless garment that must come under a single institutional compass. Unlike the US Treasury it maintains the dominant role in economic forecasting, establishing both the revenue and spending targets of the fiscal framework, shaping international economic relations, and reviewing expenditure budgets. The Treasury's hegemony, however, gives the chancellor close to the maximum number of hats any minister can comfortably wear. Four other Treasury ministers help him fulfil his responsibilities. As well, the five permanent secretaries working within the Treasury give that department more 'brass' than any other in Whitehall.

Outside observers might well conclude that the Treasury's domination of British economic and fiscal policies would soon collapse if it had to operate under the conditions found in the United States. The secrecy fostered by ministerial responsibility and the closely knit village life of Whitehall's officials provide a hermetically sealed environment.

However, this argument takes us only so far. First, the Treasury does not operate as a monolith. It, and not its American and Canadian counterparts, goes to great lengths, through two in-house co-ordination committees and a central secretariat, to integrate internal policies. Their working in a single department, after all, does not obliterate officials' functional and ideological proclivities. Second, the prime minister and cabinet do not accept every pearl of integrated wisdom emanating from the chancellor and his department. Partisan policy advisers in every government since Heath's, if not earlier, have informed the prime minister privately on economics. Career officials with experience in the Treasury work in No. 10, the Cabinet Office, and the Central Policy Review Staff. Certainly they can read between the lines of the department's consensus on matters and probe for views in various units which suggest an alternative course of action. Further, the intricate system of cabinet and official committees surrounding the economics and fiscal policy field grants access to other ministers and departments. The committees provide forums in which those with views at variance with the Treasury's can outline the hazards in their sector of government should a proposed course of action be adopted.

Both Callaghan and Thatcher took a strong personal interest in economic and fiscal policies. However, they have differed considerably in their approaches. Callaghan tended much more than Thatcher to involve himself personally in the details of specific decisions at various crossroads of his economic and fiscal programs. This proved counterproductive in a number of respects. His 1978 pay policy emerged at first as an expedient for a fall election which was never held; his 1979 decision not to enter the European Monetary System took the side of the timid segments of the Treasury against the preferences of his chancellor; and his emphasis on pay policy as an economic instrument led to ministers and officials wasting hours on specific pay settlements.

By way of contrast, Thatcher maintains an appearance of detachment from the details of economic and fiscal policies. Special pleading by ministers and departments regularly meets with the prime minister's reciting formulas of exorcism against what she contemptuously terms 'the Wets.' In order to ensure orthodoxy, she has gone to exceptional lengths to see that both she and Treasury ministers have at their sides committed monetarists. However, as Thatcher's policies appear more and more a too-daring experiment, by half, one must look at the possibility that events will force her into a major salvage operation involving specifics. Her performance to date has seen far too much emphasis on theory for such scant attention to detail. As in chapter 3, we find that what normally makes for a good management style, namely an ability to focus on the most crucial issues, poses the threat of disaster if a chief executive's criteria of importance derive from rigid adherence to macroeconomic policies.

7

The increasingly
crowded field of
Canadian economic policy

Unlike the British Treasury, Canada's Department of Finance does not enjoy hegemony in economic policy. It does not house the principal central agency units responsible for the expenditure budget. The Treasury Board Secretariat and the ministries of state for Economic and Regional Development and for Social Development maintain the integrity of expenditure budgets and control and allocate resources to programs within the government's broadest and most diverse functional categories. In addition, Economic and Regional Development has partially eclipsed Finance's lead responsibility for microeconomic policy; as well, Social Development has recently moved to occupy some of Finance's responsibilities for fiscal relations with provincial and local governments. Although Finance maintains a large interest in tax policy, an autonomous department with its own minister, Revenue Canada, actually administers the tax system. Finally, and most important, the Privy Council Office, sometimes spurred on by officials in the Prime Minister's Office, has seriously challenged Finance's economic policies on several occasions since 1975. Such interventions have gained legitimacy to the point that PCO now views itself as custodian of overall government and prime ministerial priorities within economic policy. It increasingly invokes the principle of collective decision-making to gain entrance to a domain previously characterized by the secret and exclusive advisory role of the minister of finance toward the prime minister.

THE DEPARTMENT OF FINANCE

Notwithstanding the areas where Finance has lost hegemony, the department has hardly suffered evisceration. It still takes the lead in developing macroeconomic policy, including the fiscal framework. From time to time, other departments have encroached upon this role. None, however, has sustained for long challenges to Finance's primacy in these crucial fields. In the US case, I pointed up the degree to which gravitation of key segments of macroeconomic policy to the Executive Office of the President has undermined the authority of the Treasury. The Canadian case contrasts sharply with the US experience. The Department of Finance controls economic forecasting and development of the fiscal framework without interference from the equivalents to the Council of Economic Advisers and the Office of Management and Budget. The Economic Council of Canada is a quasi-autonomous forecasting institute with no direct links to Finance's forecasting exercises, and the Treasury Board Secretariat participates only peripherally in developing the fiscal framework. Thus, Finance stands at a mid-point between the British Treasury, which has effectively safeguarded its prerogatives from cannibalization, and the US Treasury, which has largely failed in attempts to keep the Executive Office of the President from absorbing its functions piecemeal.

Most of the threats to Finance's power have not struck at the heart of macroeconomic policy. The department has lived with separate departments of Customs and of Revenue since 1927. In 1966, the government completed a series of reorganizational moves in response to the Glassco Commission, which focused largely on management of government resources, by transforming Treasury Board staff into an autonomous secretariat. TBS and the Office of the Comptroller General, formally created in 1977, take the lead in general financial management. Here TBS develops and monitors the aggregate expenditure budget; OCG establishes and assesses systems for departmental accounting and evaluation of programs. Both agencies operate under separate deputy ministers who report independently to the president of the Treasury Board.

Economists in operational departments such as Regional and Industrial Expansion, Labour, and Health and Welfare have for many years viewed economic and social development from different perspectives than Finance's. The 1960s and 1970s saw a proliferation of departments specializing in activities with clear implications for the economy. These included Regional Economic Expansion (now defunct); Manpower and Immigration; Consumer and Corporate Affairs; Energy, Mines and Resources; and Environment. In various ways, these departments further crowded Finance's influence on development of various sectors of the economy.

Finally, the creation of the Ministry of State for Economic Development in 1979 (renamed Economic and Regional Development in 1981), followed by approval of the Ministry of State for Social Development in 1980, seriously compromises the traditional veto power exercised by Finance over development issues that raise questions related to the overall performance of the economy. In this respect, the two new secretariats serve as review bodies for the expenditure budget of the government's most costly 'envelopes.' Perhaps more dangerous for Finance, however, is the mandate for co-ordination assumed by the secretariats. For instance, the Ministry of State for Economic and Regional Development draws upon an order in council that clearly assigns it the lead role for ensuring that the bits and pieces of microeconomic policy fit together. It is directed to:

1. Define integrated economic development policy by industrial sector and region, review and concert submissions to the Treasury Board and the Cabinet in light of these, and improve program delivery;
2. Advise the Treasury Board on the allocation of government resources to economic development programs;
3. Lead and coordinate consultation on economic development with the provinces, business, labour, and other public and private organizations;
4. Conduct its own research and policy development.[1]

The Social Development secretariat was given a similar compass with the exception that it did not receive responsibility for outside consultation. However, it recently has stirred alarm in Finance by vying for the leading role in renegotiation of intergovernmental transfer payments. This formerly exclusive preserve of Finance concerns in large part federal funds given to provinces for the maintenance of social programs.

In sum, the period since the mid-1960s, when the minister of finance yielded direct responsibility for developing the expenditure budget to a separate minister assuming the presidency of the Treasury Board, has led to Finance's gradual shedding of involvement in the details of microeconomics. In comparison to developments in Britain, Finance has become a treasury without a public-service sector and industry divisions. However, it enters the field of sectoral economics better armed than the us Treasury, which maintains little presence in economic and social development and only recently gained a capacity for operating, on the policy level, in financial relations with states and local governments.

The Department of Finance contains five branches, namely Tax Policy and Legislation, Federal-Provincial Relations and Social Policy, Economic Programs and Government Finance, Fiscal Policy and Economic Analysis, and International Trade and Finance. Five assistant deputy ministers head these respective branches. An associate deputy minister acts as a surrogate for the deputy minister in interdepartmental matters and issues of co-ordination that cannot be adequately treated by one individual. In relative terms, therefore, Finance labours under a handicap in comparison to the British Treasury. It lacks somewhat the 'brass' necessary to stare down competing officials in other departments.

What Finance lacks in 'brass' it makes up for in 'nerve.' In fact, its officials' confidence in the superiority of their analysis to that of other departments bordered on conceit. At the time of the Canadian interviews – 1976 – many respondents told horror stories of Finance shooting down the economic analyses of operational departments. Judging from many Finance officials' accounts of their roles, one comes to the conclusion that they cultivate their tough-guy image. In the words of one respondent: 'We are the economics powerhouse in Ottawa. Do you think I stay here because I like the pressure and the hours? No, it's because I work in the best economics department in the country, have the type of resources and staff with which I can really do economic analysis, and, above all, have a chance to be in on decisions which have a tremendous impact on the economy. Departments are constantly coming up here with ill-conceived ideas which would either screw up the economy and/or employ an economic instrument, like taxation, for a social or cultural goal. I find it satisfying and exciting to see these policy proposals shot down by our boys purely on the grounds of economics.'

Why do departments still get entangled in discussions with Finance even though many of its direct levers on microeconomic policy have been moved to other central agencies and new operational departments? The simple fact remains that Canada's highly structured machinery for interdepartmental decision-making gives Finance preferential access to every major deliberative body in Ottawa. First, the minister of finance belongs to nine of thirteen standing cabinet committees. Key among these is priorities and planning, which operates as an 'inner cabinet.' Specifically within the field of economic policy, priorities and planning reviews the five-year fiscal framework proposed by Finance. On the basis of the agreed framework, the committee arrives at five-year expenditure guidelines and allocates resources to policy sectors. Meanwhile, the deputy minister of finance has approximately the same strategic position as his minister by virtue of his membership on official bodies paralleling cabinet committees. At the time of the interviews, official committees only loosely shadowed cabinet committees. Deputy ministers would meet to iron out difficulties arising from only the most intractable of deadlocks. Lower-level interdepartmental meetings would develop specific policy initiatives before committees rather than provide a comprehensive review of the entire agenda. However, Trudeau established in 1980 a structured system of deputy-minister-level bodies shadowing standing cabinet committees.

The minister of finance and his deputy concentrate their efforts, respectively, on priorities and planning and its officials' shadow committee, senior co-ordination. In both bodies they draw from much more than the department's economics expertise. Developments in the last two decades notwithstanding, Finance still controls the essential instruments of macroeconomic policy: 'The department is a "Department of Economics" with teeth. That is, it has responsibility for setting the fiscal framework within which the government of Canada must live, drafting the budget [in Canada, this excludes the annual expenditure estimates, which are submitted by the Treasury Board Secretariat], developing tariff and tax policy, and managing a number of financial programs. In these sectors of activity, other departments have to follow our constraints or win our approval for whatever new arrangements they desire.'

In microeconomic policy, the minister and the deputy become directly involved only in major matters. In Britain, either Treasury ministers or permanent secretaries attend meetings at their respective levels, or the department forgoes representation. The Canadian committee system departs from this practice. First, officials accompany ministers to cabinet committees. This rarely occurs in Britain. Second, the accompanying officials need not be the deputy ministers. Many times the director most immediately concerned goes with the minister to committee. Here a director assumes that he has been brought along to whisper in the minister's ear, to assure the departmental line is adhered to, to answer questions directed to him from other ministers, and (once he has accumulated some experience with these forums) to participate when appropriate in the give and take of discussion. Third, and most at variance with British practice, the deputy minister or subordinate colleagues fill in for the minister on cabinet committees he cannot attend. Likewise, Finance officials often sit in for the deputy minister on his committees. The flexible attitude toward committee participation found in Canada thus contributes to the near omnipresence of Finance in decisions not directly related to macroeconomic policy. One respondent even suggested to us that he often represents his minister on a cabinet committee because, after all, he is the one maintaining the position that Finance has taken: 'I'm the one in the department on top of issues which come up before that committee. If I go, it's because Finance has something specific to say about the matter. I'm not there as an observer.

I'm there because I have a viewpoint and something to say.' We can imagine the trepidation struck in the hearts of operational department representatives when the minister of finance's economics tutors appear at the committee table. One Finance official put his department's hard-nosed perspective succinctly: 'Our first requirement is to look at issues that the government is trying to grapple with in as scientific a way as possible. We have to clarify the nature of the problem in economic terms and relate it to the interface with other issues. Since we are advising a minister, we have to be aware of the political implications as well.'

Looking at the track record of one department in conflict with Finance, we can see why anxiety commonly seizes ministers and officials when dealing with the central economics department. Health and Welfare has housed for years economic expertise of its own. Officials there use economics to monitor existing programs and marshal arguments for policy changes. For nearly a decade now, the department has pursued various efforts to establish a guaranteed annual income administered through the tax system. Not even the prime minister's flagging the proposals as priority items by appointing his most trusted Quebec minister, Marc Lalonde, to the Health and Welfare portfolio helped much. At the time of our interviews, Finance respondents boasted about how readily they had headed off a scaled-down version of a guaranteed annual income. At this writing, Health and Welfare continues to suffer acute embarrassment whenever it locks horns with Finance.

During the 1980–1 legislative session, Health and Welfare brought forward to the cabinet a package of reforms for the Canadian pension programs. Monique Begin, the minister, began a series of public speeches designed to sell the proposals. These talks contained what conservative ministers considered an anti-business bias. They believed that Begin was simply antagonizing corporations rather than bringing them along in support of the legislation. The Department of Finance moved in to save the day. It saw to it that its minister assumed from Begin responsibility for shepherding the changes through cabinet and Parliament. Finance may well have shed many of its responsibilities within the microeconomics field. However it normally maintains the muscle necessary to exercise a virtual veto when it deems policy proposals inconsistent with its macroeconomic objectives. It owes this power not just to its expertise in economics. The special status of its minister in the cabinet and the flexibility of access to the cabinet and interdepartmental committees provide a situation whereby no pond is too small to cover if Finance detects that its interests are at stake in government deliberations.

Compared to the elaborate machinery employed in the British Treasury for co-ordination within the department, Finance has revealed relatively little instinct for using formalized means of integrating its policies. A management committee, chaired by the deputy minister, works out the department's principal agenda items and assures that its mandatory exercises, the forecasts, the fiscal framework, and the budget, move along on schedule. Needless to say, individual branches do not operate in a vacuum. The mandatory exercises all assume some degree of participation from each of the five principal units. Finance, however, has not followed the United Kingdom's example and established a central unit responsible for ensuring that problems in co-ordination are isolated and adequately examined by staff.

Fiscal Policy and Economic Analysis
This branch combines functions that in the United Kingdom belong to two separate sectors. It shoulders responsibilities for economic forecasting and developing fiscal policy. With regard to the latter term, Canadian officials take *fiscal policy* to concern the distributional effects of spending and taxation on the operation of various segments of the economy. They also consider under this rubric the implications of the aggregate balance between spending and taxation for the performance of the entire economy.

Of the four divisions in the branch, two, Economic Analysis and Long-Range and Structural Analysis, run Finance's forecasting. The third division assembles the aggregate fiscal policy; the fourth develops policy concerning capital markets. Economic analysis per se, thus, does not enjoy the degree of differentiation found in the British Treasury: it does not merit a branch of its own or its own deputy-minister-level official. The absence of a top-level head provides the clearest contrast with the United Kingdom. In Whitehall, the chief economic adviser, as head of the entire government economic service, weighs in heavily on forecasting being conducted throughout the civil service. His deputy, also more senior than any Department of Finance opposite numbers, co-ordinates the work of economists within the Treasury proper. Until recently, the less formalized Canadian arrangement has not posed particular problems for Finance forecasters. They still benefit greatly from the status of their minister. Further, S.J. Handfield-Jones, until retirement in 1982 assistant deputy minister for fiscal policy and economic analysis, had taken keen interest in forecasting. By virtue of the fact that he had held his post since 1975, Handfield-Jones faced no rivals in the public service in matters concerning the interplay between economic forecasts and the fiscal framework.

Current developments in other departments suggest that Finance experiences considerably more competition in macroeconomic analysis than it did at the time of the interviews. For instance, the Department of Regional and Industrial Expansion elevated economic analysis to a branch function in 1980. The increasingly top-heavy Department of Energy, Mines and Resources (EMR) – its branch heads now command either the title 'associate' or 'senior assistant' deputy minister – claims more and more of a role in economic analysis.

EMR gained entry to macroeconomic analysis as a result of intense controversies since 1973 over the pricing of oil and natural gas. Apart from the broader matter of constitutional reform, this issue has provided the main focus of disputes between the federal government and the provinces. Energy-rich provinces, namely Alberta, Saskatchewan, and British Columbia, have continually pressed for domestic prices closer to the world level and a larger share of tax revenues. The federal government, in contrast, has tried to balance these claims with those of non-producing provinces. These want to protect their consumers and industries from world-level energy prices. Further, the federal government requires revenues from domestic oil to pay subsidies for oil that parts of Quebec and all of the Atlantic provinces must import at the OPEC rate. The trade-offs involved in these conflicting interests now comprise a major portion of the annual budget exercise, including development of the fiscal framework. M.A. Cohen recognized EMR's potential role in macroeconomic analysis when he moved from Finance to become its deputy minister in 1978. Within months, Cohen lured from Finance two of its most senior forecasters. Cohen also created an Economic and Policy Analysis Branch which concentrated much of EMR's economic expertise into one unit. By 1981 this branch had grown into a sub-sector under the leadership of an assistant deputy minister, four directors general, one director, and nine chiefs.

Such an increase in the complement of senior economists in an operational department raises the question of whether Finance can maintain its pre-eminence in macroeconomic analysis. Although trained economists largely staff its other branches, the department's macroeconomic branch houses only an assistant deputy minister, a director general, four directors, and eleven chiefs. However, one division of the branch, Capital Markets, shoulders considerable operational responsibility including liaison with the Bank of Canada, and the management of public debt and policy issues arising from oversight of financial institutions. Thus, in terms of the 'brass' factor so important to the British Treasury economists' domination of macroeconomics, the Canadian counterparts in the Department of Finance find themselves disadvantaged. They benefit from nothing akin to a chief economic adviser perching in the department with all the macroeconomic levers and guiding the careers of all other members of his profession in government.

EMR's new-found access to macroeconomic policy has begun to manifest itself in several ways. The 1980 budgetary exercise reflects its new role. Delays in negotiating a new energy-pricing policy had already prevented the Clark government from producing the 1979 budget, which should have appeared in the spring, until December of that year. The December 1979 budget met defeat in the House of Commons, thereby bringing on the election of February 1980 that restored the Liberals to power. Once back in office, Trudeau met with even stiffer provincial resistance to his pricing proposals than that experienced by Clark. Anticipating a tough battle, Trudeau appointed Marc Lalonde minister of energy, mines and resources. Lalonde took a clear lead in all negotiations with Alberta, the most powerful and fractious of producing provinces. Without an energy policy, Finance waited on the sidelines before finalizing the budget. Negotiations did not produce a settlement. Thus, the federal government moved unilaterally in October. The long-awaited budget dwelt for the most part on the new energy policy. In fact, M.A. Cohen accompanied Finance's deputy minister, Ian Stewart, to the press lock-up in which the budget was explained to the media and did much of the all-day presentation. All of this might be episodic. If and when energy policy becomes less thorny, EMR might revert to a less prominent role. Finance officials have seen interlopers come and go. However, they must be asking themselves by this point whether EMR will ever go.

The International Trade and Finance Branch
This branch has remained reasonably stable since 1976. The Department of External Affairs operates as well in international economics. External Affairs, however, does not provide the same amount of competition to Finance's views in this field as exists in domestic economics. Finance, then, maintains a relatively clear lead in all aspects of international economic policy.

The International Trade and Finance Branch contains four divisions. International Finance has two units. One develops policy concerning relations with international financial organizations such as the International Monetary Fund and the Organization for Economic Co-operation and Development. The other monitors Canada's balance of payments and forecasts international economic performance. International Economic Relations ensures that Finance's interests are safeguarded in international trade and investment, two fields with operational arms largely in other departments or quasi-autonomous agencies. Here Finance differs from the US and British treasuries in one important respect. In the United States, the Office of the US Trade Representative takes the lead in policy development and negotiations; in the United Kingdom, the Treasury yields many of these responsibilities to the Department of Trade. Finance, however, has succeeded in maintaining the upper hand in these matters. For instance, it always contributes the senior official or minister to the Canadian delegation at international panels on trade such as the recent Multilateral Trade Negotiations in Geneva. International Programs focuses largely on policy concerning government trade-development operations. It contains units responsible for export financing, international development, and financial institutions. Finally, Tariffs develops government policies concerning customs duties. In Britain, similar work takes place under the roof of Indirect Tax in the Fiscal Policy group. Notwithstanding the Canadian unit's immediate link to other international policy divisions, it effects a much more pervasive influence on the Customs side of Revenue Canada than the Treasury does on Customs and Excise. Here the level of staffing makes a considerable difference. No fewer than twelve professional-level officials work in Tariffs on policy issues emerging from the government's fiscal plans and problems of administration arising from Revenue Canada.

The Tax Policy and Legislation Branch
This branch at the time of our interviews included units now in Federal-Provincial Relations and Social Policy. We will consider the new branch below. Tax Policy and Legislation bears much more of a resemblance to the Office of the Assistant Secretary for Tax Policy in the US Treasury than to the Fiscal Policy group in Whitehall. It develops tax reform measures as well as policy concerning the role of taxation in the fiscal framework.[2] In fact, the professional complement of some thirty officials working within the Canadian branch comes close to the level of staffing available in the US Treasury. The latter office keeps a roster of around sixty.

While interviewing in the Canadian and US tax units, one will find several officials who know their opposite numbers in the other country. The Americans had developed their interest in Canadian tax law during the 1960s when Finance was drafting legislation for comprehensive law reform. Canadian efforts to make income tax more progressive interested the Americans the most. During the reform effort, several young tax experts joined Finance from the private sector and academe. They introduced a number of imaginative ideas to the reform effort. US

Treasury officials none the less regretted the fact that the reformers saw few of their progressive ideas actually incorporated in the 1971 tax reform bill. As one Treasury official put it: 'The Canadians shot for the moon and ended up in the US!'

Size is not the only characteristic that makes Finance's tax unit much more similar to the American than to the British. In Canada, officials do not work in tax policy unless they have cognate skills. Thus, economists, lawyers, and accountants staff the tax branch. The unit usually finds itself at the centre of budget discussions in the department. The fact that Finance's interest in the budget largely concerns the revenue side of the fiscal framework, leaving expenditure estimates to the Treasury Board and the ministries of state for Economic and Regional Development and for Social Development, puts the Tax Policy and Legislative Branch in a pivotal position for bureaucratic politics surrounding Finance's economic plan. Recent years have heightened its role in relation to macroeconomic policy. We have already discussed the degree to which discussions on energy policy influence the development of the fiscal framework. Many of the proposed solutions turn to the tax system.

The Clark government added to the branch's burden during 1979 by setting its heart on mortgage-interest-rate and property-tax deductibility. This proposal sought to make homeowning more accessible to middle-income groups. Finance dragged its feet throughout Clark's government in an effort to block the proposal. In fact, Finance briefs to the cabinet on the topic dwelt voluminously on the regressive aspects of this type of tax expenditure and the obstacles to effective administration of proposed programs. US Treasury officials indicated one reason why Finance came to the cabinet armed with such well-argued reservations. From the time Clark formed his government, Treasury officials had handled a heavy caseload of Finance counterparts searching for facts and figures that would help shoot down the tax deduction proposals. This illustrates the degree to which Canadian and US officials think alike about taxes. They draw from comparable pools of expertise and share commitments to the same long-term goal, namely, to improve the progressiveness of the tax system. In some instances, this stems from a belief that higher-income groups should carry a proportionately greater share of the tax burden. More practically, it results from officials' desire to reduce revenue losses through deductions.

The Federal-Provincial Relations and Social Policy Branch
This branch has emerged from the one discussed above as an accretion of Canadian federal-provincial relations. As such, it is concerned more with intergovernmental affairs. Its birth owes much to the principle of

countervaillance. Finance originally dominated federal-provincial relations. The splitting off of the Federal-Provincial Relations Office from the Privy Council Office, the emergence of the considerable capability in federal-provincial fiscal relations' in Energy, Mines and Resources, and the creation of the ministries of state for Economic and Regional Development and for Social Development have cumulatively amounted to an exceedingly serious threat to Finance's continued presence in federal-provincial relations. The establishing of the new branch suggests that the department has decided to fight for a continued high profile in the field.

The Economic Programs and Government Finance Branch
This unit relates more to the allocation and management of government resources than to integration of macroeconomic and fiscal policy. Thus, we will discuss it in greater detail in chapter 8. However, we find here another area of Finance's work that has experienced increasing competition from other departments in the last few years. Both the Ministry of State for Economic and Regional Development and the Department of Energy, Mines and Resources have occupied much of the former department's territory.

TRUDEAU, 1968–79

During his first government, 1968–72, Pierre Trudeau followed the principle that the Department of Finance should yield some of its power in economic policy to specialized departments. These latter, he believed, would relate better to the claims of particular sectors of society. Further, Trudeau formalized the cabinet committee system. This move, a two-edged sword, gave Finance preferential access to cabinet committees but also exposed its policies to ever-widening circles of ministers and officials. In particular, the committees on priorities and planning and on economic policy began to vet the department's positions on the fiscal framework. Thus, Trudeau's 1968–72 government significantly opened Finance to countervailing positions on the economy.

None the less, this period escapes characterization as a phase of priorities and planning. Trudeau left J. Edgar Benson, his minister of finance through most of the period, with latitude to promote his department's views in cabinet without too much intervention from PMO or PCO. Trudeau's attitude toward Finance thus corresponded to the broker politics that characterized his first government. Indeed, Trudeau failed to intervene in the most critical matter pressed by Finance during this period. As we have already noted, the department worked from 1966 to 1971 to provide a comprehensive package of tax reforms. Its 1969 white paper, in fact, embraced many of the far-reaching proposals of the 1966 report of the Royal Commission on Tax Reform. But the white paper and the bill based on it faced one of the most intense parliamentary reviews of a legislative initiative in recent years. By the time the tax bill became an act in 1971, many argued that the review had changed it into a regressive measure. The case provides the first instance in which Trudeau's lip service to social democratic ideals collapsed under pressure from the business community. Our respondents who joined the department to assure meaningful reforms stressed the disillusionment they felt over the way Benson and Trudeau had lost sight of the government's commitments.

When Trudeau emerged from the 1972 election with a minority government, he retreated to administrative politics. He appointed John Turner minister of finance. The young MP, whom virtually all the pundits touted as Trudeau's heir apparent, ran Finance as a fiefdom. As the darling of Canada's business community, Turner fed into the hands of the department's conservative wing headed by Simon Reisman, the deputy minister, and Bill Hood, the associate deputy minister. This segment effectively resisted growing pressure later in the mandate for wage-and-price restraint. It argued that such controls entailed excessive state intervention in the marketplace.

By the election of 1974, the government still had not acted decisively to address mounting inflation and unemployment. Robert Stanfield, the leader of the Progressive Conservative party, chose as the centrepiece of his campaign a clear commitment to mandatory wage-and-price controls. His decisiveness backfired. Trudeau turned the issue to his advantage with incisive ridicule both of the Tory leader and of the key plank in his platform. The election produced a solid majority government for the Liberals. Trudeau and his ministers set out on their bold priorities exercise, which we have already treated in detail in chapter 4.

Notwithstanding the government's bravado about leaving its mark on the 1970s, 'stagflation' began to eat away, at a voracious rate, public support for the Liberals. Richard Gwyn follows this period closely in a recent book on Trudeau.[3] In January 1975, Trudeau came across John Kenneth Galbraith's *Economics and the Public Purpose*. The work justifies mandatory wage-and-price controls on the grounds that the free market no longer operates effectively to restrain inflation. Coincidentally, Ian Stewart, a former economist at Cornell University responsible for developing many of the Bank of Canada's forecasting models, worked as an assistant secretary for economic policy in the Privy Council Office to promote the same view. Like water dripping on a stone, his memos brought about an awakening of Trudeau's interest in economics.

By the spring of 1975, stagflation reached the point where Finance began to dust off contingency plans for mandatory controls. But neither the department nor the cabinet could muster the resolve necessary actually to institute a program. By late summer alarming slippage in Liberal support in the polls convinced Mike Kirby and Michel Rochon, two aides in the Prime Minister's Office, that they should act on their own to move ministers toward adoption of a program. The two found a strong ally in Ian Stewart. PMO and PCO forced Finance to support mandatory controls. In the mean time, John Turner resigned from the cabinet. Trudeau eventually announced his Anti-Inflation Program on 13 October.

During the remainder of the 1974–9 government, Trudeau involved himself increasingly in macroeconomic policy. Donald MacDonald, another pretender to the leadership with strong ties in the business community, took over Finance from Turner only to resign and leave politics in 1977. He particularly objected to Trudeau's keeping controls after they had outlived their effectiveness. The prime minister's political advisers found continuance of the program contributed significantly to a resurgence of support for the Liberals. Yet Jean Chrétien, MacDonald's successor and the first French-Canadian to hold the Finance portfolio, suffered the greatest humiliation of all the finance ministers at the hands of Trudeau's involvement in macroeconomic policy. Trudeau sprung on Chrétien his summer of 1978 decision to cut spending by $2 billion. Jim Coutts, the principal secretary in PMO, and Michael Pitfield, the head of PCO, had worked out the program with no consultation with Finance. Chrétien almost resigned over the incident. Further, both he and the President of the Treasury Board, Robert Andras, found it virtually impossible to administer the program effectively. Neither of their departments had geared up for massive cuts.

The confusion surrounding the cuts ultimately led in the late fall of 1978 to another initiative that further undermined Finance's position in economic policy. In addition to cutting $2 billion, the program sought to free $300 million for economic development programs. This move started a stampede for the only 'new money' in town. Meanwhile, the Department of Industry, Trade and Commerce (now Regional and Industrial Expansion) had failed adequately to manage tripartite con-sultations between business, labour, and government on post–Anti-Inflation Program mechanisms. Gordon Smith, long Pitfield's most trusted machinery-of-government confidant, designed a new organization to get both the economic development and consultative programs on track. The government created a Board of Economic Development Ministers to handle the various claims on the $200 million and to take over the faltering consultative process. A new central agency, the Ministry of State for Economic Development, provided staff support to the new cabinet committee. These bodies eventually became the cabinet's economic and regional development committee and the ministry of state by the same name. The reform placed in serious question the Treasury Board's authority in control of expenditure. It appeared also to wrest from Finance much of its conventional leading role in advising ministers on the economic implications of industrial and regional development programs. Finance, once again, saw its authority brushed aside by the short-term exigencies of a government now locked irrevocably in a fight for its electoral life.

THE CLARK GOVERNMENT

We have already noted the emphasis given by the Clark government to resolving disputes over energy pricing and taxation and to instituting mortgage-interest and property-tax deductions for homeowners. The Clark government had not expected that it would have to pursue these goals in an economic environment that increasingly reduced manoeuvrability. The farther the government got into the fall of 1979 the clearer it was that rising interest rates were undercutting its efforts to provide tangible relief for hard-pressed middle-income families. Clark's election campaign had centred largely on middle-class appeal. The strategy had paid off in the form of a minority government. Real progress in the government's first year would permit it to obtain a majority in an election tentatively scheduled for June 1980.

Clark waited five months to call Parliament into session. He believed his ministers needed the summer of 1979 to learn their portfolios. As the theory went, ministers, once in command of the substance of their departments, would get much more out of their career officials and perform more confidently during question period in the House of Commons and the Senate. The strategy failed. Bureaucrats soon recovered from the jolt of a new government. The absence of parliamentary activity for five months left the public with the impression that the Conservatives were a 'do-nothing' government.

Within this setting, Finance provided more than its share of grief for the government. Early on, it became apparent to Clark that the department's new deputy minister, Bill Hood, would not co-operate in the development of the deductibility program for homeowners. Jim Gillies, a professor of administrative studies at York University and former MP, joined the Prime Minister's Office soon after the election to serve as Clark's personal economic adviser. Gillies recruited Grant Reuber, a vice-president of the Bank of Montreal, to take over from Hood. Notwithstanding this dramatic move, the department continued to serve up briefs that dwelt on the obstacles to the deductibility scheme. In time, even the minister, John Crosbie, began to oppose the program. At one point, the department even resorted to a technical excuse. The deadline had passed for the program to be incorporated in the 1979 tax forms.

Clark eventually intervened to force the program on Finance and on Crosbie. But the department did not stop there. It went on to draft a stringent budget that essentially washed away any gains homeowners would realize from the deductibility scheme. This included increases of other taxes – mainly for gas and fuel oil. The budget, of course, led to the government's defeat on 13 December 1979. Finance proved itself most immune to political initiatives that deviated sharply from its economic viewpoints.

TRUDEAU'S FOURTH GOVERNMENT

We have already discussed above the degree to which Finance during Trudeau's current government continues to grapple with competition in its traditional areas of authority. It has worked closely with the Department of Energy, Mines and Resources (EMR) in drafting three budgets. Meanwhile, the ministries of state for Economic and Regional Development and for Social Development have continued to pressure Finance in microeconomic policy and financial relations with the provinces. However, the Privy Council Office has not kept on an economic adviser with sufficient stature consistently to challenge the view of Finance on macroeconomic policy. Instead, Ian Stewart, the first PCO official to seriously challenge Finance, served as deputy minister of the department. As one PCO official put the arrangement: 'Why would the prime minister need a senior economic adviser here when he has Ian over at Finance?' Initially, Trudeau appointed his most senior cabinet colleague, Allan MacEachen, as minister of finance. However, as increased economic woes pressed in on the government, he became involved again in economic policy. In the fall of 1982 MacEachen and Stewart stepped aside in favour of Marc Lalonde and M.A. Cohen, who moved from EMR. The shuffle gave Trudeau two like-minded surrogates to implement a combined mandatory and voluntary wage-and-price policy initiated in the summer.

CONCLUSION

Since the early 1960s three trends have become particularly pronounced in Canada's machinery for economic and fiscal policies. First, departments designed to deliver policies within specific fields have proliferated at an unprecedented rate. Second, two of the departments set up essentially to deliver programs, namely Energy, Mines and Resources and Industrial and Regional Expansion, have developed capacities for economic analysis rivalling those of the Department of Finance. Third, Finance has seen the Privy Council Office gradually expand its influence on the fiscal framework and spending guidelines, and the Treasury Board Secretariat (1966) and the ministries of state for Economic and Regional Development (1978) and for Social Development (1979) take over entirely its former responsibility for review of expenditure.

Normally, so many assaults on the territory of what used to be a comprehensive, traditional economic department would suggest that it had approached a nadir from which it would not recover. Two features of Finance's current situation suggest that, in fact, it remains a healthy department. First, unlike the US Treasury, it still dominates forecasting, fiscal policy, and international economics. Second, its ministers still enjoy standing in cabinet whereby they belong to cabinet committees covering every major policy field.

Pierre Trudeau clearly has left his mark on the current system. The proliferation of both operational departments and central agencies in economics and fiscal policy reflects his fascination with institutional reforms. Trudeau's attention gravitates much more readily to constitutional issues than to others. However, when he intervenes in economic and fiscal policies he does so with a vengeance. His imposition of wage-and-price controls in 1975 brought to a precipitous end months of dithering in the Department of Finance. His 1978 stringency exercise introduced major cuts without his minister of finance being consulted. In both instances, Finance lost institutionally.

PART THREE

Allocation and management of resources

Introduction

This part deviates from the format of the two preceding ones. Rather than looking at the umbrella function, allocation and management of resources, as a 'seamless garment,' the part breaks it down into three components. Within these, however, we will move country by country – just as in parts I and II. Why treat the material this way? Simply, the elements of the umbrella function divide clearly into three activities, namely review and approval of expenditure budgets, improvement of the efficiency and effectiveness of government, and management of personnel.

Fads sweep over this terrain with lightning speed. Like memorable storms, each has a name. This is the land of planning programming and budgeting systems, public expenditure survey, policy analysis and review, management by objectives, zero-based budgeting, cash limits and expenditure envelopes. However, as the saying goes, 'We have not here a lasting city.' Often, by the time the techniques win adoption by other countries, they have already fallen into disfavour in their own land.

The high priests of this sector of government activity show less patience with their gods than do their colleagues in economic policy. One does not find here the enduring commitments of Keynesians and Friedmanites. In fact, allocation and management really only produce demigods. Usually, economic policy determines the limits within which the function is performed. Various techniques emerge for better allocation and management within given constraints. Few stand the test of time. Too often, they fail appreciably to improve allocation and management. This fact leaves many openings for the next guru with a 'better idea.' Yet the previous fads rarely dissipate entirely. Instead, they usually accumulate like layers on a coral reef.

In addition to the vulnerability of this sector of activity to fads, allocation and management can mean different things in our various countries. In each, central agencies clearly give highest profile to review and approval of expenditure budgets. However, they differ considerably in the emphasis on other subfunctions. Canadians have maintained over the past decade a keen interest in direction by central agencies of effectiveness evaluation that finds no parallel in the other countries. Also, Ottawa has experimented much more with various institutional reforms designed to sharpen review of expenditure budgets. Americans tend to compartmentalize the various subfunctions. Thus, the divisions of the Office of Management and Budget concerned with efficiency perennially find it difficult to attract the attention of expenditure review divisions. Until 1979, personnel management took place largely in an independent agency, the Civil Service Commission. Thus, apart from setting staff levels, central agencies wielded very little sway over departments' management of personnel. Senior personnel management suffered especially from an absence of central planning and guidance. The British, in contrast, have long seen both efficiency and personnel management as principal concerns for central agencies. Before creation of the Civil Service Department in 1968, both functions received attention within HM Treasury. The British, as well, have long given very strong central guidance to the selection and training of senior executives. In the more detailed discussions that follow, we will find a number of opportunities to dwell on the reasons why our three countries have given varying priorities to the subfunctions.

Finally, we should keep a weather eye open for the influence of various administrations and governments on the emphasis given to subfunctions. In Britain, Edward Heath's 1970–4 government invested considerable energy developing new analytic techniques designed to bring greater programmatic rationality to expenditure review.[1] The Wilson and Callaghan governments (1974–9) backed off from Heath's almost experimental interest in innovations. His new techniques had failed to produce the hoped-for miracles and had drawn criticism from those suspicious of rationalistic decision-making. Margaret Thatcher brought to her government a stripped-down Heathian view that focuses more on improvement of management than on the analytic foundation for allocation decisions. In the United States, Richard Nixon enshrined the principle of management by objectives,[2] another way of saying 'government efficiency,' to such a degree that he was accused of establishing the 'administrative Presidency.'[3] Jimmy Carter gave a higher priority to allocation and management of resources than any of the chief decision-makers discussed here. He took the strongest personal interest in review and approval of the expenditure budget. He embarked as well on ambitious projects aimed at reorganizing the bureaucracy and bringing personnel management much closer to the centre. In Canada, Pierre Trudeau remains much more the philosopher king than the managerial chief executive. None the less, he frequently has admitted into his band of courtiers wise men who have come up with a new way to allocate and manage resources.

8

Review and approval of expenditure budgets

THE UNITED STATES

We have already seen that the Office of Management and Budget, along with the Treasury Department and the Council of Economic Advisers, develops the fiscal framework. It shares with the other agencies responsibility for advising the president on the balance between government expenditure and taxation. In the area of review and approval of actual expenditure budgets, OMB takes a very strong leading role in advising the president both about dividing expenditure among departments and about which programs within agencies should receive more or less support or be curtailed.

The director of OMB enjoys cabinet rank. The last three directors, Bert Lance and James McIntyre under Jimmy Carter, and David Stockman under Ronald Reagan, have commanded considerable personal trust from the president. The former two did so both through personal friendship and Carter's intense interest in the budget; Stockman, who is relatively young, owes his importance largely to extraordinary talent and luck. He found himself in the right place just as Reagan was searching for a tough-minded fiscal conservative to head up OMB. Whatever the vagaries of his power base, an OMB director will find himself in the political spotlight. A considerable mystique enshrouds his position. The president invariably views the director as one of his top advisers; Congress will see him as the prime witness for defence of the administration's expenditure plans.

OMB has two divisions: Management and Budget. OMB's involvement with management policy will receive detailed attention in chapter 9. The functions surrounding the examination of budgets operate out of four pairs of divisions. The first of these contains International Affairs and National Security; the second, Health and Income Maintenance and Labor, Veterans, and Education; the third, Commerce, Transportation, and Housing and Urban Development and Justice, Treasury and General Management; and the fourth, Natural Resources and Energy and Science. A final unit, Budget Review, plays the role of ringmaster vis-à-vis the production of the aggregate budget.

Readers from Britain and Canada who expect OMB to house vastly greater staff than similar central agencies in their countries will be surprised to find that only about 600 professional and clerical employees work there. Of these, less than 200 work as budget examiners. One finds here considerable variation in the attention paid to policy areas. National Security maintains the largest complement with some forty professional budget examiners working in five branches covering separately intelligence and personnel policy as well as each of the three large services. But the relative opulence turns out to be as much apparent as real. For instance, in 1979, only six professional-level officials in the Air Force branch shouldered responsibility for $40 billion in estimates. In the same year, Canada's entire expenditure budget came to only $51 billion (Canadian). Even more leanness shows up in OMB units on the domestic side. The biggest gap between staff size and responsibility existed in the health and income maintenance field. There, in 1979, a division of thirty-five reviewed 45 per cent of the entire US expenditure budget.

A number of factors mitigate the pressure imposed on budget examiners by virtue of their sparse numbers in relation to the sizes of the budgets they review. First, as the reader will recall from our treatment of the British Treasury's role in economic and fiscal policy, 'brass' can compensate for numbers. Organizations with disproportionately high numbers of very senior staff find this an advantage in relations with operational departments. OMB maintains four layers of political appointees, namely the director, the deputy director, the executive associate director, and associate directors. And the highest level of career official heads the budget divisions. OMB officials do not shy away from flaunting their rank. Even career public servants display their standing with somewhat more spacious and better furnished offices than found elsewhere in Washington. Indeed, they and their political masters ensure that visitors keep in mind their host's proximity to the president. The office decorations at the higher levels invariably include US flags and presidential seals. In neither Britain nor Canada do officials resort to such blatant symbols to remind others of authority.

Second, OMB career officials bring to their work the acumen of exceptionally long and stable service. Many have spent most of their government careers in budget review and consider it their profession. Such perceptions contrast sharply with those of British and Canadian officials. These, for the most part, consider their assignments to budget review as temporary. One OMB political appointee, while praising the ability of his two most senior career officials – both of whom had served as budget examiners since the early 1960s – expressed well the advantages of such long-term appointments: 'They know where all the skeletons are buried. They know everything that has been tried in the last twenty years, why it worked, why it didn't work, who likes it on the Hill [Capitol Hill], who doesn't like it on the Hill.'

Third, OMB controls the vital legislative co-ordination functions that contribute immensely to its ability to keep up with departmental activities with expenditure implications. A relatively small unit in OMB, Legislative Reference, has worked since 1939 to fulfil these functions. It limits itself mostly to identifying issues for closer scrutiny in the major policy units elsewhere in OMB and the Executive Office of the President. However, its location in OMB gives the budget side a critical strategic advantage not enjoyed by similar units in Britain and Canada. In the latter countries, budget units must trust cabinet secretariats to allow them plenty of time to comment on the expenditure implications of departments' intended statements and actions. In the United States, the operation of the early warning system right inside OMB allows budget examiners automatic access to vital intelligence on departments' policy initiatives.

Fall and Spring Reviews
Although to date the Reagan administration has been remiss in observance, the work year of US budget examiners breaks into two major exercises, spring and fall reviews. For the fiscal year beginning in October 1984, OMB would conduct a review in the spring of 1983. This would look closely at the main expenditure issues that the president must face in developing his program to present to Congress in January 1984. From the spring review come the letters to each department outlining the level of expenditure that will likely receive administration approval for the 1984 budget. The fall review involves OMB's assessing departments' proposed programs for fiscal 1984–5. From this stage come various recommendations for modifications whereby departments' plans might better fit the president's specific program priorities and expenditure objectives.

The Budget Review Division serves as the nerve centre for both exercises. It includes branches responsible for financial management, federal program information, budget preparation – including links with appropriations committees in Congress and with resource systems, such as accounting and monitoring and fiscal analysis. The latter branch handles most of OMB's contribution to fiscal policy and actually drafts the president's annual budget message, including sections concerning assessment of the economy and the administration's plans for it. On one level, the division makes a technical contribution to the spring and fall reviews. Someone must put the numbers together. Budget Review assumes a ringmaster's role by providing central guidance for technical procedures to be followed in budget submissions, monitoring actual spending, detecting systematic shortfalls and overruns, translating economic forecasts into guidance on the repercussions for various types of spending, and monitoring day-to-day budget decisions to assure that departments individually and collectively are coming out where the president wants them to be. Under David Stockman, an especially strong emphasis on monitoring has propelled Budget Review into exceptional prominence as essentially the director's staff.

Buried in this world of numbers, one finds a missionary role for Budget Review that transcends simply bringing the figures together. This role entails getting information on the administration's view of the economy out to departments. In this respect, the words of a top official in Budget Review about his role during the Carter administration highlight the importance of the link the division provides between budget review and the objectives set forth by the president: 'You recognize that inflation is such a large problem now that we have got to find a way to reduce it below current policy levels. I will be laying out an outline so my principals can tell all of the examiners that they have got to find a way to reduce rather significantly – just as we did last year ... Within the next two or three weeks we will have discussed that outlook with the president ... We know that he will tell us, just as we are already telling ourselves, that we have got to hold the budget down in a very restraining way. But he may be somewhat more specific than we now are.'

Budget Review's work thus touches on the sensitive relation between macroeconomic policy and expenditure budgeting. One respondent cited a case in which the president had to decide whether certain quasi-governmental agencies excluded from the budget should be added. The president decided against such a move on the grounds that it would set him $12 billion behind in the quest for a balanced budget: 'It's purely a presentational issue. There are things that look like federal agencies, they smell like federal agencies, they taste like federal agencies, but they're not put in the budget. And it's our job to say that's wrong. As technicians, we look at these things and say they belong in the budget. And it is the job of our political leadership to say, "Yeh, but that was true when we inherited this budget and we're not going to be the ones to take it out."'

As we have seen, eight budget examination divisions concentrate their efforts within specific policy fields. Spring and fall reviews usually determine their annual work cycle. However, with each new president, subject-matter divisions will engage in intensive efforts to re-evaluate the programs of their department(s) in light of likely changes in priorities. In national security, such exercises have resulted in sweeping changes. For instance, the Nixon administration decided to pare down American defence capability. The Carter administration brought renewed emphasis to the American commitment to NATO. One respondent described the process at the early stage of a new administration. Along the way, he took strong exception to the view that long-term reviews rarely overcome the incremental nature of budgeting: 'I don't agree with that because of the impregnation problems. The Nixon administration made a fundamental shift which has become "the law of the land" ever since. Before then we were planning on what we called the two-and-a-half-war strategy. This says that we're going to fight the Russians and the Chinese and a small war all at the same time. The Nixon strategy said: "Hell, the Russians and the Chinese don't like each other. It's a little hard to believe that we'll have to take on both of them at one time." So, we shifted to what we call the one-and-a-half-war strategy. Policywise, the broad strategies are something that get adopted and get bought.'

With its clear commitment to increasing US defence expenditure the Reagan administration ushered in another substantial shift that reversed much of the retrenchment of the three previous administrations. To the chagrin of career officials in OMB, the significant alterations came almost entirely from the administration's directives communicated, early on, by David Stockman. The career staff found their new political masters had no time for or interest in more thoroughgoing assessments of spending levels and options: 'We were quite disappointed in the first year. There was no big assessment of defence. It was like they just didn't want to do it. They just wanted to add dollars, which they did. Our advice to the administration when they came in was ... add a few billion bucks – from five to ten, depending on how far you want to go – then do a big study and decide how to allocate ... But they didn't follow that advice. They just added twenty-six or so billion. This was beyond our wildest imagination.

It probably was even beyond the wildest expectations of the defence establishment ... There was no substantial new initiative. It was just a lot more of the same.'

Apart from bringing a new administration through major reviews of defence expenditure and/or programs, all through a term the budget examination divisions will watch for less earth-shaking issues that none the less require firm guidance from the president. Spring reviews provide a mechanism in which OMB can press departments to look at issues with significant budgetary implications. Under the Carter administration, the National Security Division, early each year, isolated four or five such matters and put teams of budget examiners to work on in-depth reviews of each. Similarly, the Health and Income Maintenance Division used spring reviews to force the Department of Health, Education and Welfare to work into its long-term expenditure plans various options for national health insurance. In this instance, OMB imposed 'reality therapy' on HEW that prevented it from developing proposals without due consideration of the objections that might be raised on economic grounds.

Fall reviews involve much greater detail than the spring exercises. In the former, the OMB director develops guidance, which he communicates to each agency, on the dollar level at which they are expected to prepare their budgets. The budget examination divisions will then work closely with departments by developing positions on the implications of the guidance for programs and reviewing actual budget submissions. Formal reviews take place in several hearings, usually held in OMB, in which individual departmental bureau chiefs, accompanied by their assistant secretaries, present their plans before program budget examiners and their branch chiefs. Variations occur here. Officials in the National Security Division have long set up shop for much of the fall review in offices located in the Pentagon. Thus OMB conducts a joint exercise with the Department of Defense that essentially views the various armed services as separate expenditure departments. This arrangement provides one clear benefit for the National Security Division, namely unparalleled access to internal departmental information. Respondents elsewhere in OMB accept the necessity of National Security's cheek-by-jowl relations with Defense on the grounds that the department is really an amalgam of several others. However, they recognize the inherent dangers that such arrangements present. In the words of an official in the International Affairs Division with some experience on joint reviews, under such circumstances spending departments can co-opt OMB into their own agendas: 'I think that the OMB has a greater autonomy in calling the shots in non-joint reviews. So far as the State Department is concerned, I think we are pretty happy that we do that non-joint. When you do a joint review you get dragged into their terms of reference.'

The Review Escalator
Ultimate authority for an administration's expenditure budget rests with the president. (This constitutional principle differs from that prevailing in Britain and Canada whereby the cabinet serves as the ultimate authority on government spending plans.) However, one OMB division experiences this constitutional principle somewhat more profoundly than the others. The National Security Division operates under a convention whereby the president reserves to himself even the first-round decisions about defence expenditure. On the domestic side, the OMB director usually takes these without resorting to the president.

Presidential, as opposed to collective cabinet, responsibility for the budget produces very real dangers of overloading one person. Departments not happy with OMB officials' decisions on a key matter will attempt to 'escalate' the issue. Such efforts will involve a search for a sympathetic ear on the political level. Departmental assistant, under-, and deputy secretaries will take their grievances to political appointees in OMB from the associate directors up to the very top. Cabinet secretaries will press their views on the director or even the president. Faced with departmental efforts to bring matters to the political level, OMB has to resort to tactics designed for keeping issues at as low a level as possible. For instance, senior budget examiners routinely send memoranda back to departments under the signature of officials in Legislative Reference. One respondent, a Carter political appointee, spoke of the constant battle to prevent technical matters from rising to the political level: 'A hell of a lot of issues, which can become terribly political once they get to the president, can be settled on a much more managerial, and, if you will, technocratic level. Sometimes, that's better.'

In theory, keeping technical issues out of the higher levels ensures that the president considers directly only a very limited number of issues. However, two factors place in question the workability of such a distinction. First, technical matters can generate highly sensitive political problems. One respondent, citing the example of funding for a refined coal demonstration plant, takes us through the process whereby technical matters can turn into political minefields:

Politics is a matter of equity. Analysis is a matter of efficiency. We frequently find those running head to head. For example, there ought to be two solvent-refined coal demonstration plants, each costing $800 million. Fundamentally, we're not certain whether one of them is going to produce anything that's very good. But we're willing to run a test of that. But the analysis from our energy people would strongly argue that it's a waste of $800 million to produce two. The congressional delegations from Kentucky and West Virginia don't regard that as a relevant fact. And they're willing to say to you: 'Hell, there are $800 million of waste in the government. Find it. But, we want a coal demonstration plant.' The majority leader of the Senate [Robert C. Byrd] is from West Virginia. So, you start with the given. If there's going to be *one*, it's going to be in West Virginia. And the question is, "How much do you want to offend the Kentucky delegation?" Is [Walter D.] Huddleston's vote critical on SALT? Or, is it just a little bit important? And, if it's really critical, is there something else that's coming down the pike that makes sense to give him?

Second, as Carter demonstrated, the system places few checks on development of a hyperactive appellate process. Outstanding issues between departments and OMB officials rise as a matter of course in spring and fall reviews. Cabinet secretaries meet with the OMB director and top aides in an effort to iron out the most contentious matters before going to the president. However, the thorniest issues might pass readily through this screen. Thus, in the fall of 1978, a year when the OMB director tried especially hard to cut down on appeals, Carter spent some twenty-five hours in review sessions just in national security and international affairs. The constitutional principle whereby the president shoulders sole responsibility for the budget combined with the relative absence of checks on the appellate process to produce a narrow neck in the funnel. Lamenting this fact, one respondent said it would be senseless for OMB to pursue its issues in greater technical depth: 'What type of review is adequate? It's a trade-off between what is possible in terms of human attention and what would be nice if we didn't have to have one man who has to make all the decisions.'

Jimmy Carter
In chapter 2, the reader finds a relatively detailed effort to assess Jimmy Carter's presidential style. The discussion asserts that he deceived himself in thinking that he was following the spokes-in-a-wheel model of executive leadership. The model in fact corresponds to broker politics whereby a president and his advisers choose more to track and guide interdepartmental conflicts than to resolve them personally. Chapter 2 also puts forward the view that Carter's interest in the budget contributed to his failure to implement broker politics. The importance he attached to

his campaign commitment of a balanced budget and his desire to run an open administration produced an almost compulsive immersion in budget reviews. Although in a sense just symptomatic of a profound inability to keep out of technical details, Carter's deep involvement in budget-review sessions seemed to have taken a greater toll than other misuses of his time.

One respondent, who has already seen this argument in a preliminary paper, took this analysis to task.[1] His view bears quotation at length: 'I do not find your criticism about his attention to detail particularly convincing ... Had President Carter simply dealt with the general policies and left the details to the agencies, the DPS and OMB, it is not clear that the results would have been better. They might have been worse. He would have ended up being criticized for not doing the things you criticize him for.'[2]

An answer to this assertion requires two lines of approach. On the negative side, several respondents left an unquestionable impression that Carter's involvement in the budget greatly exceeded that of other presidents. Career officials glowed as they recounted review sessions, usually off-limits for their grades, in which the president delved with them in the details of programs. As well, many respondents saw a clear heightening of OMB's role resulting directly from the level of personal interest in the budget maintained by the president. The following serves as an example of these views: 'The whole milieu that we operate under is a function of the president. In the national security world it's the president, the national security adviser, the secretary of defence and the budget director. And, I'll add, off to the side, the State Department – sometimes. Go back over time and the following relationships take place. President Kennedy and then President Johnson had a very strong relationship with the secretary of defence, Robert McNamara. They had a very small, kind of selectively issue-oriented national security adviser staff. And they did not use the OMB staff at all. The president, in effect, delegated all major decisions on defence, normal decisions on defence, to the secretary.' One OMB associate director working on domestic policy even asserted that the president, at the outset, made himself more available than did Bert Lance, his initial OMB director. This arrangement, he noted, greatly affected OMB's view of personal accountability to the president.

On the positive side, one must recognize a legitimate point made by our OMB critic. Any president would leave himself open to an accusation of benign neglect if he did not involve himself in budgetary review to some significant degree. Given his goal of a balanced budget, we must assume that Carter would have become especially involved in reviews. None the less, Carter failed to define limits to the depth to which he would delve into the budget. Further, until the summer of 1979 he maintained a loosely structured and poorly disciplined White House that could not check the influx of options and produce coherent policies. One OMB respondent gives a particularly good perspective on the administration's internal drift: 'You have political appointees in this administration who are in government clearly to work a personal agenda ... It's fairly easy, in order to keep a battle raging – even though you know where the president is on an issue – to send it to him so that the material presented and the decision he makes leave a number of things open. Whenever we put together one of these memoranda, our job, as career staff, is to try and make sure that that doesn't happen – that, in fact, you get a definitive opinion out of him. The people that are working on their own agenda of course want to waffle things. So, they want to go on and do whatever the hell they want to anyway. The president is not aware that he is being "wide-sided."'

Any president must grapple with the issues embedded in the budget if he hopes to alter the course of government. Carter should have watched closely only issues that struck at the heart of the positions with which his administration was identified. Instead, he let himself get drawn into the details of disputes over the budget. OMB gained in the process because it maintained the attention of the president, even far down into the career ranks. However, the entire relationship represented the drift inherent in the administration. It let through the 'iron fence' and into the Oval Office issues that belonged outside.

THE UNITED KINGDOM

We have seen in chapter 6 that HM Treasury houses the leading units for economic analysis, domestic and international finance, fiscal policy, and public expenditure. In this respect, it controls functions comparable to the combined roles of the US Treasury, the Council of Economic Advisers, and the Office of Management and Budget. Treasury public-expenditure functions come under two second permanent secretaries, the heads of the Public Services and the Domestic Economy sectors, respectively. The former sector contains groups responsible for aggregate budget and accounting functions, review of expenditure programs (excepting those related to industry and agriculture), and control of civil-service manpower and general administrative expenses.[3] The latter sector, as we saw in chapter 6, assumes general responsibility for domestic economic policy. However, three groups within the sector review expenditure budgets for government support of nationalized and private industries and of agriculture.

Unlike the situation in the United States whereby executive authority over the budget ultimately resides in the president, the British cabinet maintains collective responsibility for expenditure plans. However, convention largely devolves this authority. Here various practices prevail at different times. Chancellors of the exchequer certainly maintain a very large say in the economic policies and fiscal frameworks that determine the broad outlines of a government's expenditure budget. In addition, they do, from time to time, take a strong personal interest in specific issues arising from departmental proposals. More usually, the second most senior Treasury minister, the chief secretary, will fulfil the chancellor's responsibilities toward general expenditure review exercises and the specific matters that call for ministerial attention.[4] The current practice that allows the chief secretary a seat in the cabinet adds considerably to his ability to act convincingly on the chancellor's behalf.

The British arrangement provides better barriers than found in the United States against spending ministers who wish to appeal their decisions to the highest court. First, collective cabinet responsibility provides a wall that obscures the prime minister's potential discretion in discerning the cabinet's will in expenditure matters. With relative ease, she can deflect direct appeals by reminding ministers that the cabinet ultimately decides outstanding expenditure issues. Second, the delegation of the chancellor's responsibilities for developing expenditure plans to the chief secretary serves as a moat that protects the chancellor's overall fiscal policies from piecemeal assaults by spending ministers. As we will see, the system does not work perfectly. However, in times of fiscal restraint it operates much better than the American arrangement.

In the United States, the president essentially serves both as his own chancellor and chief secretary. He alone can resolve many disputes arising from the fragmentation of fiscal and economic policy. Three agencies – the Treasury, OMB, and the Council of Economic Advisers – each with its own cabinet-level head, generate hosts of conflicts for his resolution. Under the British system, many of these would remain on the departmental level in HM Treasury. More important, the buck stops with the president. US convention simply has not seen presidents employ the concept of collective cabinet responsibility. Thus heads of spending departments usually escape situations where their special claims receive scrutiny from the standpoint of the 'common good.' As a result, US practice all too often leaves presidents inundated by pleas based on 'special-case' argumentation.

The various units involved with public expenditure in the United Kingdom maintain staffing levels below those of comparable units in OMB. For instance, the eight budget examination divisions in OMB break into two to five branches, each of which usually contains about seven professional staff. In HM Treasury, four expenditure review groups in the Public Services sector and two more in Domestic Economy break into two or three divisions each housing about five professionals. However, some divisions within Domestic Economy handle both investment and financing policy relating to nationalized industries.

One could argue that the smaller staffing in Britain corresponds to the fact that its population is about one-quarter and its total expenditure budget about one-third of the American. Of course, responsibility for much more extensive grants to local government bodies greatly inflates the British expenditure budget. Thus we can conclude from the available figures that HM Treasury does not fall seriously short of OMB in terms of personnel available per 'dollar' of expenditure. In fact, one receives almost the opposite view when looking at specific policy fields. If we recall that in 1979 only six OMB officials reviewed expenditure proposals for the Air Force budget of some $40 billion, the seven senior officials working in HM Treasury on review of Britain's $28 billion defence budget strike one as relatively generous staffing. Also we should remember that senior staff in HM Treasury usually have at least one junior professional colleague working for them.

Starting in the spring of each year, the Public Expenditure Survey Committee (PESC) develops an overview of public expenditure based on the plans for the current fiscal year and projected forward to future years. A Treasury deputy secretary chairs PESC, which consists of the senior financial officers of all departments. PESC reports used to extend into four years beyond the base year. The Thatcher government has reduced this span to three years. PESC focuses on the fiscal year immediately ahead. Thus, in the spring of 1982, it would look especially at plans for the spending period beginning 1 April 1983 and ending 31 March 1984. In working out the overview for future years, PESC, of course, keeps in mind across-the-board increases or decreases that the cabinet wishes to achieve as well as its program priorities. The Treasury deputy secretary who chairs PESC takes the lead in the process whereby financial officers develop and communicate back to their departments the rules they must follow in making bids for additional spending or identifying savings. PESC's operation thus lays the groundwork for collective cabinet responsibility toward the budget. It contributes greatly to Britain's relative success at keeping bilateral squabbles between departments and Treasury away from the cabinet and the prime minister. Under the deputy secretary's guidance, potential disputes receive early identification in a collective exercise. Here exceptions must be argued before the entire Whitehall village.

Three groups under the deputy secretary who chairs PESC operate as nerve centres for various aggregate functions connected with public expenditure. Concerning the administrative politics surrounding PESC, the under-secretary in charge of the General Expenditure Policy Group occupies the most strategic ground. He supervises two divisions responsible for co-ordinating PESC, developing annual estimates, and setting and enforcing rules regarding base-year prices and allowances for inflation. Thus his units serve essentially as a PESC secretariat.

One must not overstate, however, the formality of the process. PESC operates as a point of contact for departments during expenditure review. However, the General Expenditure Policy Group ensures that Treasury maintains in-house discussions providing considerable guidance over bilateral negotiations between review divisions and departments. An official gives us an idea of its pivotal role in keeping, with as few exceptions as possible, a central Treasury line on expenditure:

The group prepares what are called the guidelines for the survey. And it produces a draft first of all. Then we discuss it with the specific expenditure divisions. They will say: 'Hey, that won't do for schools. There is a particular factor about schools which you haven't taken into account. You will have to make an exception there.' The group dialogues with them and reaches an agreement. Then the Treasury tries the rules on departments at the official level. There is a discussion among the departments. On the whole though you have pretty well gone over the ground, you hope, in Treasury. It's unusual that they would surprise us ... Then the whole thing goes to cabinet and is approved. The actual survey figures are then drawn up by departments and negotiated with the expenditure divisions. They both come back on questions of interpretation of the rules ... The group co-ordinates the final report and makes sure that it is fair between departments.

The maintenance of a central line gives officials in General Expenditure Policy a clear sense that they operate as ministers' surrogates in all but the most intractable issues: 'The group tries to assist ministers to come to the decisions which they will want to take. It interprets their guidance. It also assesses who has the best case and how it is going to come out. In the end, it narrows things down to quite fine issues that cabinet has to decide.'

Does the Buck Always Stop Here?

Obviously, the Treasury has organized public expenditure review in such a way that the cabinet is protected as much as possible from having disputes percolate through to it. The Cabinet Office automatically refers to the Treasury documents with expenditure implications unless these state explicitly that the Treasury has already been consulted. If officials fail to reach agreement on contentious matters, the chief secretary, much more often than not, puts an end to the issue once he has decided for or against a recalcitrant department. Special pleading meets a further obstacle in the fact that the chief secretary may attend any cabinet committee reviewing proposals for additional spending. In such sessions, he maintains a suspensory veto which departments can bypass only by recourse to the cabinet: 'The chief secretary is where the buck stops unless the minister wishes to take the issue to cabinet ... He cannot be overruled by the committee. The majority may want to go ahead. If he says no on expenditure grounds ... even if he is the lone voice, it must go to cabinet. A committee cannot overrule the chief secretary ... Only Cabinet can do that.'

Fairly detailed information deriving from discussions both within one department and the Treasury review division responsible for its expenditure gives us an excellent idea of how the process operates. The department, which must remain anonymous, started in early January 1978 its involvement with PESC. The department's finance branch asked other branch heads to project additional costs or savings based on three scenarios, namely, resources would remain the same in each year, rise 2 1/2 per cent, or decrease 2 1/2 per cent. The actual PESC guidelines fitted well the dry run. Departmental projections were to follow established figures for 1977, allowing increases totalling 2 per cent, and then identify savings amounting to 2 1/2 per cent against the new figures. PESC approved the department's submissions for the final draft of PESC in early June.

On 28 June, the chief secretary circulated the final PESC report, which clearly stated that no allowances would be made for net increases beyond the agreed figure of 2 per cent. The cabinet reviewed the report on 6 July. Although several ministers had argued for a faster rate of increase, a majority held sway in endorsing the chief secretary's position. At the same meeting, our department's secretary of state circulated a paper seeking approval of resources for a new program that the cabinet had already endorsed in principle. The cabinet agreed only to charge the secretary of state, with the lord president's concurrence, with drafting the enabling legislation for the program.

Pressing in on the department as well was the budget speech's reversal of a 1977 PESC agreement that substantial increases would be imposed in charges to the public for a popular program largely funded by the department. As the Labour government then viewed 1978 as a likely election year, thought had turned to the fact that such increases could lead to lost votes that would hurt candidates in some swing constituencies.

Although it looked sympathetically on the department's efforts to fund the new program with savings from others, the Treasury stipulated that the program, rather than new ventures, would have first claim on any resources freed by savings elsewhere in the department. The results of a meeting between the secretary of state and the chief secretary in late September further disappointed the department. The chief secretary adamantly maintained the view that the popular program would take first claim on all savings accruing from spending shortfalls and cuts. He reiterated as well his opposition, first expressed in May, to the department's proposed program.

Early in October the department's policy steering group took stock. It believed it still should attempt a limited rendition of the desired program. In a cabinet meeting on 10 October the secretary of state took a hard line in a new paper displaying sixteen additional bids. These totalled £100 million to be paid for by savings estimated between £90 million and £160 million. If the cabinet wanted the department to contribute more to the popular program, it would have to dip into the general contingency reserve. However, the secretary of state did not get the desired result from the tough paper. On 17 October, the cabinet deducted £100 million from the contingency reserve and distributed £43 million without even discussing our department and one other. In a subsequent meeting with the Treasury's chief secretary, the secretaries of state of the excluded departments protested this apparent violation of the principle of collective decision-making and received an apology. However, the chief secretary responded less favourably to the departments' agreement to split evenly the remaining resources drawn from the contingency reserve. He would recommend to the cabinet that the entire £57 million go to the other department on the grounds that demographic factors had hit it badly. On 26 October, the cabinet arrived at a slightly softer position. Our department would receive £19 million, that is, £7 million from the resources already released and another £12 million directly from the contingency reserve. None of these new resources would go for the proposed project. Still not prepared to give up, the department found an additional £12 million in savings and some funds that a third department, with similar interests, promised for a pilot project of the desired program. The cabinet, against the continued opposition of the chief secretary, finally approved £15 million for the experimental venture. Of course, this program was the first to go in May 1979 when the new Conservative government introduced radical cuts from the agreed amounts in the 1978 PESC.

This account of one department's experience with PESC reveals a paradox. The cabinet both assumes collective responsibility for the expenditure budget and carefully limits the actual time it devotes to settlement of disputes. The latter accomplishment stems from two factors. First, it farms out much of its authority for framing the expenditure budget to the Public Expenditure Survey Committee. Second, it allows the chief secretary of the Treasury very great latitude both in directing PESC and in settling disputes with and between departments. Thus, in our example the cabinet had to step in only at the very end of the process. By that time, it worked more to sooth offended pride by helping out at the margins than to reshape its stance towards the department. After agreeing in the spring to the survey's guidelines and endorsing the PESC report in July, it generally stood by its decisions. PESC, we will see, does not always work so smoothly. However, in relative terms, it accomplishes a co-ordinated review of public expenditure much more effectively and with much less fuss than the systems used in the United States and Canada.

James Callaghan

As we have noted in previous chapters, James Callaghan inherited a government with little latitude for manoeuvre. The need for day-to-day crisis management forced him immediately into survival politics. Callaghan's personality lent itself to this style. By nature, he took issues, large and small, to heart and pondered over them before coming up with decisions. As the preceding narrative suggests, however, Callaghan revealed uncharacteristic restraint by keeping pretty much out of detailed expenditure reviews. To be sure, he involved himself heavily in a related field: his personal interest in pay policy touched in large part upon public-service wages.

An even more remarkable dimension of Callaghan's government rests in the fact that it relied very heavily on a relatively automatic device for control over government spending increases due to inflation. This instrument involved cash limits covering some two-thirds of government spending. The first of these, employed in the fiscal year 1974, responded to the rapid escalation of land and property costs and applied to government construction programs.[5] As we saw in chapter 6, Callaghan took the helm just as the International Monetary Fund had prescribed very strict expenditure control as one of its conditions for assistance to the collapsing British economy.[6] By this time an extended cash-limits program fit nicely the government's central economic strategy. This involved pay limits beyond which wages could not increase. With inflation in 1975–6 approaching 25 per cent, the Treasury could no longer sustain the traditional process whereby departments with cost overruns submitted supplementary estimates for parliamentary approval. In the view of one respondent: 'The advantage of cash limits is that people understand cash. If they are given a certain amount of cash and told that's what they have got for the year, that's the thing everyone understands.'

The Treasury attained much greater success in employing cash limits as a restraint device than it did with pay. First, cash limits apply to annual votes based on estimates to be submitted to Parliament rather than to PESC. The Treasury thus arrives at cash limits in a process operating independently of collective cabinet consideration of long-range expenditure plans. Second, the chief secretary holds very closely to himself authority over cash limits. Virtually no discretion over cash limits resides in the review divisions proper. Third, cash limits leave departments little room for appeals. In the case of base-line figures for current costs, departments can beg off on the grounds of exceptional inflation already realized within specialized areas of the marketplace. Under such circumstances, the Treasury finds itself in an awkward position. Often it will lack detailed information on costs within various sectors. Cash limits turn the tables on departments. Relying on forecasts of inflation, they cross into a base of knowledge presided over by Treasury economists: 'The Treasury will say to the divisions and department: "These are the factors that you ought to apply for the movement of prices for the year ahead ..." Whereas they know better than we do what is happening to their prices, they don't know better than we do what is going to happen. The cards are in our hands on that.' Fourth, the Treasury adopted a conscious 'bloody-mindedness' about cash limits and severely restricted exceptions on the grounds that they would negate the entire purpose of the instrument: 'If you say "yes," particularly in the early years, the departments are watching this like hawks. They collect all the precedents. You make sure that nobody at a junior level agrees to something allowing other departments to say, "Well, if you let them, why not us?"'

Margaret Thatcher
In two previous chapters, we have noted that Margaret Thatcher has taken a much keener interest in macro- than in microeconomics. Following an administrative style of leadership, she has operated largely under the assumption that matters of detail would fall into line once her government won widespread acceptance for its economic strategy. On expenditure budgets, initial cuts won ready acceptance because they were anticipated and not so severe as feared. Ultimately, the new government hoped, the salutary effects of its economic strategy would change even

willy-nilly assent into co-operation. When disputes over expenditure budgets arose, they would rarely rise to the cabinet and certainly not involve the prime minister. The whole thrust of Thatcher's view of ministers' responsibility toward their departments would dictate that they assume personal responsibility for checking the expansion of bureaucracy and its programs.

Five significant developments under Thatcher have reflected her government's view of the expenditure review field: 1) the altered relation between development of macroeconomic policy and the establishment of the fiscal framework and expenditure budgeting, 2) the cutting of PESC from four to three years beyond the base, 3) the linking of pay increases in the public sector to cash limits, 4) the setting of limits to assistance to nationalized and private industries and agriculture, and 5) the use of 'star chamber' groups of ministers to deflect departmental appeals from the entire cabinet.

The changes in the relation of macroeconomic policy with the fiscal framework and expenditure budget and the reduction of PESC projections from four to three years reflect the Conservatives' view of economic planning. The PESC process emerged from the concern during the 1960s that the Treasury had not adequately integrated macroeconomic management and expenditure budgeting. It imposed greater discipline on the latter by linking growth to the anticipated performance of the economy and to whatever exceptions, within the fixed aggregate, ministers were willing to trade for.[7] Of course, these developments occurred in happier days when governments actually projected sizeable economic growth. For instance, the 1964 PESC assumed a 4 1/4 per cent annual rate. PESC, however, did not anticipate the economy declining in real terms while double-digit inflation made it prohibitively costly to maintain existing levels for government services.[8] Yet the 1970s saw several quarters in which this most adverse of economic conditions for advocates of increased public expenditure occurred.

The Conservative government complemented the cash-limit program by placing PESC in an entirely new perspective. Over the years, expenditure budgeting under PESC took on an entrenched character. Departments viewed four-year projections as pledges of continued support complete with written-in provisions for expansion. Thus expenditure budgeting commitments greatly affected the outlines of fiscal policy and overall economic strategy. The Conservative government's approach tried to stem this process. As one respondent noted, the flow in the relation between economic, fiscal, and expenditure policy now moves much more in one direction. The government's monetary policies clearly take precedence over expenditure commitments: 'The principle which sums it all up is that finance determines expenditure rather than the other way around ... They start from an objective for the growth of the money supply and regulate everything to put into that.'

Although the Treasury, before Thatcher, had successfully applied cash limits to non-human resources, wage settlements for various public service groups had largely escaped the regimen. The 1980 negotiations with public service unions, however, produced settlements much more consistent with cash limits than thought possible. The government had linked public service settlements to cash limits by making it clear that agreements beyond an accepted percentage increase would result in departments having to find economies through reduced services. It chose 6 per cent as its 1981 wage ceiling. Early indications suggested that unions would not accept this constraint on their bargaining, especially since the private sector enjoyed newfound freedom from limits. Although a number of settlements came in at 7 per cent or more, economies kept the total wage-bill increase to within 6 per cent.

Accompanying the Thatcher government's view that it should stress macro- over microeconomics was a strong position against further assistance to industries. In fact, one of our respondents, citing sharp 1979 staff reductions in Treasury units dealing with assistance, observed that the government appeared, at that time, to lack an industrial strategy. Events have overcome the government in this regard. The economy, quite apart from not showing improvement under Thatcher, has actually seen a severe downswing which has taken a very great toll in bankruptcies. Starting in early 1981, the government had to reverse one of its most solemn promises. It came to the aid of nationalized industries by providing rescue funds. Predictably, the Treasury units working within this field soon experienced some return to prominence.

Thatcher's institution of a star chamber for handling recalcitrant ministers emerged during the successive cutting exercises following the formation of the government in May 1979. The government immediately sought £3 1/2 billion in savings from the 1978 PESC projections for the fiscal year 1979. The chief secretary at the time, John Biffen, found that he could not get desired cuts from some departments. A committee consisting of the chief secretary, the chancellor, and the financial secretary from the Treasury along with the lord president of the council and the secretary of state for trade tried its hand at an additional round of cuts. Subsequently, the 1979 PESC failed to produce desired cuts as late as November 1979. Thus another star chamber came into action. In addition to the same Treasury ministers, this body consisted of considerably more prestigious representatives from non-Treasury ministers. Sir Keith Joseph, the hard-line secretary of state for industry, and William Whitelaw, the home secretary, replaced the original members from outside the Treasury. The group had sessions with the secretaries for defence, environment, social services, and education and science.

Although the practice has occurred in previous governments, it does depart from the concept that the 'buck stops with the chief secretary.' In star chambers, broader political considerations can enter discussions at a point where normally the Treasury would continue to insist that savings must be found. For example, one official in a spending ministry told how the home secretary saved his department from serious cuts to one key program. He convinced the star chamber that reduced support would result in political fallout that the government had best avoid. Mrs Thatcher has continued to use star chambers. They allow departments' special pleading to be heard by ministers swinging sufficent weight to settle disputes without confrontation in the cabinet proper. Departments tend to settle 'out of court' because they realize they have little chance of overturning in the cabinet a star chamber decision.

CANADA

Political scientists live constantly with the threat of their books becoming history before the ink is dry on the pages. This applies more to coverage of the expenditure review agencies in Canada than to anything else discussed in this volume. An extremely experimental attitude to expenditure review has brought to this field a dizzying succession of major institutional changes.

Ironically, our story starts in 1867, the year of Confederation. An order-in-council set up what we have seen Margaret Thatcher resort to – a star chamber of ministers that would review on behalf of the cabinet disputes over public expenditure. The Canadian body, dubbed the Treasury Board, took on a statutory life in 1869. Subsequent legislation affected its mandate in 1878 and 1951. The board operated with varying degrees of regularity through the years. At the time of our interviews (1976), it met almost 100 times a year. Traditionally, it has consisted of 'non-spending' ministers. This nomenclature misleads slightly. No minister totally lacks a budget. However, the Treasury Board has in recent years consisted of its own president, the minister of finance, and four junior ministers. The minister of finance, in deference to the president, does not attend meetings. The continued existence of this body since 1867 thus evokes the picture of stability.

Experimentation creeps into our account in 1962. In that year the Glassco Commission on government organization took the view that the secretariat for the Treasury Board, then housed in the Department of Finance, would operate much more effectively if it moved to the Privy Council Office.[9] The proposal corresponded with the commission's catch-phrase 'Let the managers manage.' It pressed the view that the details of control and guidance of bureaucracy should be left to operational departments. PCO would provide a much better base for the Treasury Board's secretariat because it alone focuses on the bigger picture: 'It must be recognized that the essential task of the staff is to assist ministers in discharging their collective responsibility for program priorities and administrative standards. Their present location in the Department of Finance tends to encourage among the staff a preoccupation with the detailed scrutiny of expenditures.'[10] The new managerial ethos held that, left to their own devices, spending-department officials could find economies just as easily as the secretariat for the Treasury Board. The secretariat should confine its activities to the guidelines for expenditure and development of management policy.

Needless to say, officials in Finance greeted the commission proposals with a jaundiced eye. Much like today's British Treasury, Finance believed management of the nation's economy required 'hands-on' control of all key economic instruments. Ultimately a compromise emerged. The minister of finance would no longer chair the Treasury Board. Instead, another cabinet minister would assume the presidency. As well, an official at the level of deputy minister would serve as secretary of the Treasury Board. However, the secretariat would not move to PCO. Instead, it would become an autonomous central agency. The Financial Administration Act of 1966 finalized these arrangements. In time, the Treasury Board Secretariat (TBS) would rival Finance in size and status. Today, two officials at the level of deputy minister report to the Treasury Board. The first of these, the secretary, heads units responsible for administrative, personnel, and official languages policy as well as the staff on expenditure control housed in the Program Branch. The second, the comptroller general, directs four large branches responsible for financial administration including the evaluation of effectiveness and efficiency and the improvement of accounting practices.

With respect to TBS's responsibility for public expenditure, our story does not end happily. The Financial Administration Act gave the Treasury Board clear responsibility for expenditure budgets: 'The review of annual and longer-term expenditure plans and programs of the various departments of government, and the determination of priorities with respect thereto.'[11] None the less two conventions constrain the board's authority. First, the minister of finance continues to advise the prime minister on the fiscal framework and, therefore, holds considerable sway over both the total amount of the expenditure budget and recommendations about areas of public expenditure that deserve priority on the grounds of economic management. Second, the priorities and planning committee of the cabinet sets the guidelines for annual expenditure budgets.[12]

These two conventions put three bureaucratic contenders into the control of expenditure. The Department of Finance maintains its traditional access to public expenditure as an economic instrument; PCO uses its proximity to the cabinet and the priorities and planning committee to assure that expenditure guidelines fit the overall goals of the government; and TBS flexes its muscles in matters relating to the government's commitment to improved management of physical and human resources.

The Way It Was: 1967–78
Notwithstanding the competing roles of Finance and PCO concerning the aggregate and priorities of public expenditure, TBS maintained, for twelve years after its creation, direct responsibility for budget review. The Program Branch managed this activity. It advised the Treasury Board through both annual reviews of departmental estimates and assessments of the expenditure implications of proposed new programs. Its schedule, in addition to following closely the annual budgetary cycle, fit the relatively routinized procedures of the Treasury Board itself. As George Szablowski and I have noted, the Treasury Board operated essentially as a tribunal during meetings occurring at least weekly:

The president and four members of the board sit at one side of the table facing a group of TBS officials headed by the secretary. They have previously read submissions prepared by a particular department requesting either an approval of a substantial expenditure from the allocated budget or an increase in the proposed budget level. The minister and the officials representing the department are asked to join the meeting and to address the board. When they do, the board members, as well as the secretary, interrupt frequently with questions and observations. When the discussion is over, the departmental delegation – including the minister – leaves the room. The board then deliberates under the direction of its president with active participation of the secretary and his staff. If unanimity is not obtained, the president may ask for a vote. Once the decision is made, it is communicated to the department, immediately and in person, after the minister and his officials have been invited back into the room, and later in writing.[13]

At the time of the interviews for the Canadian phase of this study (1976), the Program Branch maintained an extremely healthy complement of officials responsible for budget review and maintaining aggregate figures. On the career side, it consisted of a deputy secretary, two assistant secretaries (the equivalent to under-secretaries in Britain), and eight directors (assistant secretaries), plus numerous other professionals, bringing the total non-clerical staff to about sixty. Considering the fact that OMB, with responsibility for roughly ten times the expenditure budget, houses fewer than 200 budget examiners, TBS comes off very well by comparison. At the time, each director headed a division. Five of these units divided among themselves responsibility for clusters of government activity: industry and natural resources; defence and external and cultural affairs; social and manpower policy; transportation, communication, and science; and general government services. The remaining three managed separate aggregate functions including compilation of estimates, analysis of expenditure, and management information systems.

One might expect that with the structured and definitive nature of the Treasury Board's work and the relatively bountiful staffing our respondents would have found life in the old TBS sheer bliss. On the contrary, the interviews struck two seams of discontent. First, Canadian examiners, like their American and British counterparts, often remarked upon the difficulty of finding analytic grounds for their positions and making cuts 'stick.' To quote two respondents: 'If we see an ineffective unit, we'll cut it out ... Well, perhaps that's a bit strong. Even if we wanted to, it would make no sense to just cut out a unit. A department can use slippage and attrition to make it appear that they have responded to us when actually they haven't. But, we can flag a problem.' 'You become sort of an investigative journalist here. It's a seat-of-the-pants operation.'

Such qualms realistically acknowledge the incremental dimensions to expenditure budgeting. Officials who believe that a mandate to review the budget, even when accompanied by generous staffing, can accomplish any more than nibbling around the edges of the 'politics of the budgetary process' should reread Aaron Wildavsky.[14] More-than-incremental change in expenditure budgets requires apocalyptic conditions that force the entire cabinet to put its weight behind deep cuts and/or sharp changes in priorities.

The second sign of discontent uncovered by the interviews links directly to the first. In cases of conflict, the will of the cabinet or its executive committee – priorities and planning – will prevail over the Treasury Board. In good times, this fact gives a field-day to spending departments wanting to circumvent the Treasury Board by making direct

193 Review and approval of expenditure budgets

appeals to the more senior brethren either in the cabinet or in priorities and planning. When a government operates under expansionary conditions it finds it difficult to say 'no.' It begins to overlook the economic pitfalls to granting an exception for yet another politically attractive proposal; it tends to hand out stays of sentence to ineffective programs which, none the less, an important segment of the electorate wants continued. To add to these points, one must note that even times of stringency border on times of expansion in such a young and growing country as Canada. For instance, the Liberal budget speech in October 1980 projected 12.3 per cent growth in expenditure for the fiscal year 1981 as against 10 per cent inflation. The forecast deficit of $13.7 billion equalled 26 per cent of anticipated revenues.

If we compare the circumstances of TBS to HM Treasury, we must conclude that the latter demonstrates much greater success in asserting its authority. Part of this success derives from the fact that the chief secretary acts on behalf of the chancellor of the exchequer, clearly the most powerful member of the cabinet short of the prime minister. Further, even when the chief secretary fails to persuade and the prime minister institutes a star chamber, this body usually contains other senior ministers capable of enforcing their collective will. Canada perhaps erred by *both* separating TBS from Finance and appointing mainly junior ministers in charge of relatively minor portfolios to the Treasury Board. Even more fundamental, it provided TBS with adequate access to cabinet documents only very late in the agency's development.

We have already seen how the Legislative Reference unit in OMB provides budget review divisions in Washington with near-instantaneous access to documents with expenditure implications. The Cabinet Office in Whitehall circulates papers affecting expenditure to the Treasury as a matter of course. These conditions did not prevail in relations between PCO and TBS until January 1976. Before that time, proposals involving significant expenditure could win approval in cabinet committees without TBS even having seen the relevant documents. Once such proposals reached the cabinet agenda they would go over to TBS. Such time lags, by often leaving TBS struggling in the eleventh hour to come up with even cursory assessments, provided a distinct edge to PCO in getting its way with ministers.

The change in January 1976 gave access to all cabinet documents requested by the president of the Treasury Board at the time they entered PCO for processing. One of our respondents noted that this change had appreciably improved his position vis-à-vis PCO: 'Recently, a proposal came up that I knew I had to get stopped. We didn't have time to do an analysis of our own. We did have time, however, to raise enough questions that it was referred to an interdepartmental panel. Of course, they didn't do an objective study either. An interdepartmental conspiracy developed to kill the proposal. But if I hadn't seen that thing coming down the pike when I did, it might have gotten through cabinet.' As we will see in the section which follows, our respondent's new-found confidence was premature.

The World of Expenditure Envelopes
In the summer of 1978, Pierre Elliott Trudeau returned from the economic summit in Bonn and imposed, without consulting the cabinet, the minister of finance, or the president of the Treasury Board, $2 billion in cuts for the fiscal year 1978–9. In addition, he put pressure on ministers to come up with $300 million in savings to be earmarked for economic development. Given the shock waves that were still rippling through departments after the major cuts, the basket of 'new' money sparked stiff interdepartmental competition.

The Treasury Board, traditionally operating within a structure of bilateral negotiations with departments on changes in expenditure, simply could not handle the immense competition for the new money. PCO saw an opportunity for institutional alterations aimed at establishing a community of interests among ministers within the economic development sector. Such a community would foster an environment in which departments would in fact trade off resources in return for the opportunity to accomplish more concerted objectives. The concept, dubbed 'expenditure envelopes,' gave an incentive to ministers to find economies in their departments. Newly freed funds would at least stay in the economic development sector.[15]

In addition to the intense competition for the $300 million, several factors accelerated the gestation of the envelope system. First, the government had found it difficult to give central guidance to a lengthy consultation process between business and labour over economic development in various regions and sectors. Although the Department of Industry, Trade and Commerce assumed the lead for the project, the several microeconomic departments created since the 1960s refused to defer to its age and size. Second, the government felt itself under extreme pressure to restore public confidence in its economic programs. The palpable sense of drift showed up in public opinion polls indicating that the Conservatives would win the next election. The Liberals had to come up with some highly visible effort that would convince voters that they could turn the economy around. Third, all signs pointed to a rough road for the bureaucratic establishment in the spring of 1979. By then, the Royal Commission on Financial Management and Accountability would publish its exhaustive critique of the public service. PCO and TBS sensed especially keenly the need to mitigate the adverse effects of the report by pointing to improvements in the machinery of government already being undertaken.

Matters came to a head when the government decided in November 1978 to establish the Board of Economic Development Ministers (BEDM). This new body differed from other policy-sector cabinet committees in that its chairman, the president, would head his own central agency, then styled the Ministry of State for Economic Development. As the government line went, the ministry, headed by a top mandarin, Gordon Osbaldeston (a former secretary of the Treasury Board), would house about 100 staff supporting BEDM as it sifted through various bids for government expenditure on economic development. But even BEDM formed only the tip of an iceberg of elaborate reorganization plans that PCO planned to keep submerged until after the general election in the spring of 1979.

PCO was drafting plans for additional secretariats, each attached to committees of the cabinet, which, in turn, would decide expenditure matters within envelopes. One insider even asserts that the prospect of a Conservative interlude held out hope for an idea that had caught the fancy of PCO's institutional engineers in the early 1970s. Subject-matter cabinet committees, rather than the Treasury Board, should control public expenditure within policy sectors: 'The possibility of the creation of sub-budgets for various policy sectors had been considered in Ottawa on and off since at least the early 1970s. However, it implied a significant institutional realignment and, given the rigidities inherent in all large institutions, could not be implemented until the appropriate conjunction of forces appeared. This conjunction was afforded by the arrival of the new Progressive Conservative government in 1979. Newly appointed ministers, without long-established turf to defend, were much more likely to accept a new expenditure management system with its attendant new distribution of power than was a set of ministers long in place.'[16]

The Conservative victory on 22 May 1979 set the stage for PCO to unveil its bold new plans. The new government had emphasized during the campaign the need for reorganization of the cabinet and cuts in both public expenditure and the size of the bureaucracy. Its commitments along these lines provided fertile ground for the reorganization plans to flourish. Remarkably, PCO pursued its program of reforms while making it appear as if the Conservatives had developed them. A group of outside consultants brought in to advise Joe Clark during the transition had provided a perfect smoke-screen. Overnight, *inner cabinet* and *expenditure envelopes* entered the Canadian political lexicon. The ideas struck even informed observers as so revolutionary that they must certainly have been promoted by the outsiders. Only after the government fell and formerly high-placed Conservatives hit the university lecture circuit did observers find that PCO had developed the 'Clark reforms.'

The envelope system remains the most enduring legacy of the short-lived Conservative government. Currently, it places responsibility for public expenditure plans in ten envelopes residing in five cabinet committees. Here the priorities and planning committee maintains control over financial relations with other governments and public enterprises and over the public debt; economic development, over economic development and energy; social development, over social policy and justice and legal affairs; foreign and defence policy over external affairs and defence; and government operations over Parliament and services to government. Under Clark, the system termed economic development and the other policy-sector groups as *committees* rather than *boards*. In addition to the Ministry of State for Economic Development, a special secretariat for the social development committee emerged in September 1979.

Gordon Smith, then a deputy secretary to the cabinet in PCO, masterminded the new system. He had planned one additional ministry of state. This would have served the foreign and defence policy committee. However, Allan Gotlieb, the under-secretary of state for external affairs, frustrated Smith's attempts. Gotlieb, like any deputy head of a senior operational department, saw that External Affairs could stand to lose a great deal if a secretariat developed around the foreign and defence policy committee. Fifteen ministers belong to the committee. Currently, the secretary of state for external affairs chairs the body. A relatively modest, in-house External Affairs secretariat supports the under-secretary for external affairs in his capacity as chairman of the deputy ministers' group that shadows foreign and defence policy.

Where do these new arrangements leave TBS? First, we should look at the distribution of expenditure review functions now outside TBS.[17] PCO benefits the most through direct linking of expenditure review to cabinet priority exercises. It now takes the clear lead in two areas where it previously shared jurisdiction with TBS: maintaining the integrity and functioning of the overall expenditure review system and managing the process, and advising ministers on settlement of cross-sectoral issues that cannot be resolved within subject-matter cabinet committees. The Department of Finance maintains its leading role in advising priorities and planning on the overall fiscal plan – the economic policies that serve as the basis for aggregate and envelope expenditure targets. It receives express responsibility for advising priorities and planning on tax expenditures. Previously, TBS would have claimed a role here as well. The ministries of state for Economic and Regional Development (as renamed in 1981) and for Social Development conduct major expenditure reviews within their sectors. Their mandates include development of sectoral strategies and priorities, the allocation of resources among departments, and the evaluation of the effectiveness of programs. The Treasury Board and, therefore, TBS lose almost all their mandate from the Financial Administration Act of 1966 concerning expenditure budgets.

The current system limits TBS's role with regard to substantive expenditure review to support of the Government Operations Committee in review of its envelopes. The committee, in fact, lacks a separate secretariat for its sector. In other policy sectors, TBS confines itself to the more technical aspects of the expenditure budget. It:

1. maintains the accounts for the envelope system and an overview of government expenditures;
2. develops management standards and systems (financial, personnel, and administrative) including those used in implementing decisions of policy committees;
3. reviews operational plans to assess the level of resources required to carry out currently approved policies and programs;
4. briefs on the costs and resource implications of program and policy proposals for policy committees, including cross-envelope implications;
5. analyzes and advises on the efficiency aspects of programs.[18]

In sum, if TBS were Washington's OMB, we would say that it had lost most of its 'B.'

One would expect that TBS would have shed staff proportionate to its diminished responsibility for budget review. A look at the current organization of the Program Branch indicates the opposite. In 1981, the branch housed ninety professional-level officials – fully 50 per cent more than it contained in 1976. However, the increase tells only part of the story. The ministries of state for Economic and Regional Development and for Social Development have acquired fifty-five and thirty-five professional-level positions, respectively. Each of these ministries, as well, attained very high 'brass' complements. Former deputy heads of key departments in their sectors, Gordon Osbaldeston (former deputy minister of industry, trade and commerce who previously served as secretary of the Treasury Board) and Bruce Rawson (former deputy minister of health and welfare), became the first occupants of the ministries' top career positions. Further, each ministry had obtained three positions at the level of assistant deputy minister. Taken together, the three ministers and deputy heads, seven assistant deputy heads, three assistant secretaries, twenty-five directors, and 143 other professionals in TBS, MSERD, and MSSD probably exceed both in 'brass' and numbers OMB's commitment to budget review. However, the government of Canada spends approximately one-tenth as much as the United States. Quite apart from the organizational issues emerging from the new system, the logic behind a stringency-conscious government allowing a tripling of resources for expenditure review in the course of four years escapes the credulity of even the most favourably disposed observer. The fact that a country one-tenth the size of the United States perhaps assigns more personnel to budgetary review than the latter does is extraordinary.

In addition to asking why it is that Canada has allocated such incongruous resources for expenditure review, we should examine the practicability of the envelope system in relation to its expressed purpose. It attempts to integrate the cabinet's consideration of policy and of expenditure so that decisions taken on either side correspond to one another. The line of attack follows two prongs. First, the fiscal plan now includes figures for the current year plus four future years including the coming year for which estimates are being prepared. This exercise takes root in the assumption that the various committees can develop and harmonize macro-, sectoral, and micro-fiscal policies that will work.[19] However, the British experience with PESC, as well as the American experience with less ambitious formats, suggests two defects in multi-year plans that spur rather than check expenditure.[20] Experience has shown that multi-year plans too often paint economic oases in the later years that turn out to be mirages. As well, by providing the option of projecting rather than making difficult cuts, they run the danger of further entrenching too many questionable programs.

Second, the new system attempts to get ministers to plan along sectoral lines and not just according to individual departmental cases for a larger share of the pie. Here the rationale moves into game theory. Supposedly, ministers working within policy sectors will obtain a collective sense that will neutralize their instincts towards empire-building. A common purpose will emerge that will result in ministers making sacrifices that hurt some of their own programs. Since newly freed funds stay in their sector, they will more willingly point up possible savings. In other words, they will bank on the improved odds. With only sectoral claims to compete with, the likelihood increases that a department's savings will return by way of increases for its truly deserving programs. Pressing the theory a bit further, they might even grasp the advantages to helping out a colleague pleading for more resources for his program on convincing grounds of mutual interest. Keeping money freed by one minister in the envelope provides, thus, the emollient that will push ministers toward relatively altruistic behaviour: 'Because envelopes are smaller than the entire government budget and because allocation within envelopes is handled by the ministers responsible for the envelope, ministers would be more willing to identify their own programs for termination because they would stand a better chance than under the previous system to receive the money back to pursue other priorities. It could even be hoped that the Cabinet committees could develop a practice of "logrolling in reverse," whereby ministers would agree to give up certain of their own programs if other ministers on their committee would do likewise, so that together they could reallocate funds.'[21]

How does one handle logic that goes so far towards assuming the best of ministers? One tack might stress that even the most altruistic acts rarely reverse logrolling. We might recall here the British incident in 1978 cited above in which two ministers proposed a fifty-fifty split of resources remaining in the contingency fund. This accord ran into a brick wall. The chief secretary did not support one department's bid for additional resources and got the cabinet to back him up most of the way. The minister, department, and program in question simply did not have enough political weight to seal the 'altruistic' exchange. In this respect, a confidential paper provided for the Department of Finance by an outside consultant suggests that expenditure envelopes provide just another environment for the same logrolling cultures that have thrived in the cabinet and its committees before: 'Alliances are made and logrolling becomes an inherent part of the decision making process. "I'll support your program A if you'll support my program B." And ... virtually no program does not have beneficiaries. Unless they are compensated (which greatly reduces the net gain from the reduction or abolition of a program!) the screams rise to a hysterical pitch ... Ministers soon lose their taste for changing the old and come to rely more heavily on bureaucratic advice: an old program is a good program.'[22]

Our outside observer takes us one step further by pointing out an even more fundamental flaw in the theory behind the new system. The priorities and planning committee of the cabinet allocates resources between envelopes. Policy-sector committees submit to priorities and planning the expenditure options within their envelopes. Here rests an opening for a ruse just as readily employed by policy sectors as by departments: 'It is difficult to envision that the committees would not play games in selecting the programs for the lower margin – putting forward for potential cuts items which were *politically* uncuttable.'[23]

Despite dissatisfaction with the role of the Treasury Board in reviewing expenditure plans, the old system allowed for much more communication between policy and budgetary considerations than the framers of the new system will admit. Ministers in policy-sector committees, in the priorities and planning committee, and in the cabinet certainly involved themselves in trade-offs. Presumably the framers would not argue two views at once: TBS was a heartless monolith that chewed up departmental programs and refused to spit them out; departments were 'end-running' TBS with abandon by getting what they wanted from the cabinet and its committees. Yet these contradictory assertions appear in PCO's discussion notes on the new system: '[The] desire to stay within [the] overall expenditure limit led [in 1976] to the procedure of referring Cabinet documents having financial implications to Treasury Board for financial consideration before Cabinet decision. This tended to: (1) undermine committee decision making; (2) *play havoc with departments when they were told to absorb but not give policy direction on what programs to reduce or terminate;* (3) *required that Cabinet become a "court of appeal" reconciling divergent committee and Treasury Board reports*; and (4) generate unnecessary conflict and frustration for ministers [my emphasis].'[24]

Of course, that the practice whereby TBS could demand documents with expenditure implications as soon as they entered the cabinet committee system developed only three years before PCO instituted envelopes. Further, one could argue just as intensely that, given sufficient time, TBS's new access could have improved its bilateral relations with departments and reduced special pleading with cabinet committees. If departments knew at the outset that their proposals would receive scrutiny from TBS, they would begin to consult its officials more regularly at the internal drafting stage. If committees could tap TBS's views on the expenditure implications of a proposal as well as PCO's position on the inherent policy goals, ministers could identify conflicts at an earlier stage and leave fewer outstanding issues for the cabinet. The system seems to operate well in Britain. However, Whitehall does not labour under the burden of a cabinet secretariat as jealous of its prerogatives as PCO is.

CONCLUSION

A thorough study of review and approval of expenditure budgets in our three countries suggests that even here our systems differ considerably.

We saw that the Office of Management and Budget has over the years proven to be an exceptionally strong budget department. Regarding integration of economic and fiscal policies, it has developed and maintained a sharp delineation between its role and Treasury's. Several of its most recent directors have commanded especially high standing in the cabinet and with the president. As well, OMB benefits considerably from the combined effects of a relatively senior complement, which adds a 'brass' factor to its dealings with other departments, and the exceptionally long tenure of its career officials, which makes it difficult for departments to use subterfuge. As well, OMB's control of the legislative clearance process in the Executive Office of the President provides it an early warning system against departmental efforts to win agreement on policy initiatives without an assessment of the implications for the budget.

The actual operation of budget review in the United States seems more to weaken than complement OMB's strong performance as a central agency. As a nagging reality, the fact that Congress often frustrates the best-laid plans even of a united and decisive executive branch makes co-ordination and control of the budget elusive in the best of times. Even after allowing for Congress's exceptionally strong role, the observer still comes away wondering why the United States has not done more to reduce the frequency with which budget issues grow from departmental concerns to major encroachments on the president's precious time. Here some remedies come to mind. Even if presidents insist upon the quest for a balanced budget as a central administration theme, they should restrain themselves from personal immersion in detailed review. Relatedly, the chief executive should make it clear at the outset that his budget director is the appellate judge and that only issues with earth-shaking importance to the administration will receive presidential attention.

In the United Kingdom, the budget review function operates in HM Treasury. This arrangement strengthens considerably the relation between expenditure and other economic policies. As well, it contributes to the clout of budget examiners with departments. They act on behalf of the chancellor of the exchequer who, in turn, normally enjoys prestige second only to the prime minister's. Leaving still less to chance, the British have given the Treasury an additional cabinet-level minister, the chief secretary. His job is to keep as many budget disputes as possible on the level of bilateral discussions between budget examiners and departments. On the technical level, other practices contribute to a relatively smooth process. The Public Expenditure Survey Committee, a body chaired by the Treasury and including the head financial officers for departments, hammers out points of consensus even before departments have developed their annual expenditure plans. As well, a 'cash limits' system has required departments to live within agreed allowances for inflation worked out through the PESC exercise. Expenditure review does not work perfectly in Britain. However, the British have mastered pretty well the importance of protecting both the cabinet and the prime minister from devoting an inordinate amount of time to appeals.

Canada claims a long history of resorting to collective authority to resolve issues surrounding the expenditure budget. In fact, the Treasury Board of the cabinet dates back to 1867. Until 1966, the secretariat supporting the Treasury Board operated within the Department of Finance. Working from the presupposition that improved management in the public sector would greatly advance control of government spending, the Pearson government (1963–8) created an autonomous secretariat for the Treasury Board designed to review administrative policy as well as departmental budgets. Although the new agency clearly took the lead in annual expenditure reviews, the Department of Finance advised the prime minister on the fiscal framework and the Privy Council Office assisted the cabinet's priorities and planning committee in developing spending guidelines. By the mid-1970s, fiscal pressures resulting from the less buoyant economy severely frayed the 1966 division of labour. Here Trudeau's highly experimental attitude toward central agencies came into play. He instituted two new expenditure-review agencies that would support cabinet committees responsible for economic and regional development and for social development. The committees, in turn, would exercise virtual control over the expenditure envelopes within their respective sectors. Trudeau and his machinery-of-government advisers have attempted in these reforms to redistribute collective authority over expenditure into communities of interest in which ministers would offer savings from their departments in order to advance the objectives of a policy sector. One wonders if the game theory behind such expectations has taken flights of fancy. Even granting the framers' optimism, the new system provides precious little assurance that sectoral communities will not adopt the same techniques employed by departments to avoid suffering the full impact of stringent policies regarding the entire expenditure budget.

9

Improving effectiveness and efficiency

This treatment of central-agency roles relating to effectiveness and efficiency in government will focus on four sub-functions: evaluation of effectiveness, machinery of government, evaluation of efficiency, and probity and prudence. Effectiveness evaluation enjoys the strongest connection to expenditure review. It involves analysis of whether existing programs accomplish agreed policy objectives and whether proposed programs will probably achieve their stated goals. Machinery of government involves macromanagement issues. Do the division of labour among departments and agencies and the co-ordination of their work fit the organizational requirements for effectiveness? Efficiency evaluation entails micro-management issues. Assuming that a program or service is effective or, at least, desirable, what can be done to improve delivery? Can changes in the organization and operation of a program increase its benefit in relation to costs? For example, a 'wide-gauge' efficiency evaluation would ascertain whether armed services should acquire food supplies independently or work through a common purchasing agent; a narrower project would assess whether social benefit offices process the optimal number of clients given specific staffing levels. Finally, probity and prudence concern maintenance of managerial responsibility. Here we find several disciplines. More generally, good financial management requires that officials use resources for the purposes for which they were appropriated. Under this principle, governments will set down norms that are used to ensure that officials account for what they spend. They will also establish specific guidelines for acquisition of goods, services, and real estate and for entering into contractual relations with suppliers.

Improvement of effectiveness and efficiency of government relies heavily on links with expenditure review. In the United States, the Office of Management and Budget, even before it took on the 'M' side of its title, housed the principal central agency units concentrating on effectiveness and efficiency. From 1968 to 1981, the United Kingdom operated the management side in an autonomous central agency, the Civil Service Department (CSD). However, CSD exercised authority, delegated by the Treasury, over public expenditure for government employees, manpower substitutes, and administrative expenses. In Canada, a fragmentation of responsibility for management policy has accompanied the dispersion of TBS's former leading role in expenditure review. Here PCO has assumed most responsibility for machinery of government. Although the Office of the Comptroller General has inherited some of TBS's responsibilities for effectiveness evaluation, the ministries of state for Economic and Regional Development and for Social Development have installed rival capabilities in their own operations.

Continuing debates and institutional reforms suggest an important issue for our assessment of the relation between management policy and expenditure review in the three countries. One gradually becomes convinced of the inherent incongruity between the organizational objectives and methods of the two policy fields. This asymmetry places clear limits on the capacity of institutional arrangements for improving co-ordination between the two functions. This observation applies directly to OMB's experience with management policy. Organizationally, OMB provides an optimal situation. Budget review benefits from being conducted in a strong agency that is independent of other key institutions involved in setting economic policies; here various disciplines connected to advancement of government effectiveness and efficiency operate in harness with budget review. However, what looks like a nearly perfect arrangement actually generates a great deal of internal strife. Put simply, the 'MS' and the 'BS' do not get along all that well even when united by a single mandate.

Such conclusions stay with us throughout this section. Issues directly related to effectiveness and efficiency normally account for only a small proportion of any expenditure program. First, even after identifying ineffective programs, one faces the fact that these are difficult to alter, much less terminate. Except in times of fiscal crisis, political considerations will normally outweigh data from even the best-executed effectiveness analyses. Fiscal crises often force political masters into such dramatic cutting exercises that they find little or no time to incorporate effectiveness evaluations into their budget decisions. Second, with respect to efficiency, management per se accounts for perhaps 10 per cent of public expenditure. Any budget examiner would instinctively view promises of savings around the edges of one-tenth of the aggregate as not meriting closest attention.

THE UNITED STATES

OMB has experimented with several configurations to provide its management side greater profile. Administrative Management formed one of the five divisions of the old Bureau of the Budget (BOB). In the early 1950s, it became clear that the old Estimates Division was not taking Administrative Management seriously. Many believed the attitude of Estimates needlessly delayed promotion of modern management techniques in the public service. Therefore, BOB moved a number of Administrative Management staff to newly created budget divisions so that the two functions could operate in tandem. As one old-timer indicated, the management specialists soon imbibed the ethos of budget examiners. The reforms foundered.

Variations on this theme have arisen several times since. For instance, in 1970 the Nixon adminstration tried to heighten the role of management policy by changing BOB's name to the Office of Management and Budget. It followed through on this symbolic move by instituting an ambitious program termed *management by objectives*. Budget examiners were to base their recommendations on the ability of departments to demonstrate that their programs met the standards of cost-benefit analysis.[1]

The revamped budget department created special studies divisions that would provide examiners with the managerial expertise that the new evaluation systems required. Within a short time, Nixon's 'administrative presidency,'[2] which had fostered an exceptional status for managerial criteria, collapsed in the face of the Watergate scandal. The special studies divisions gradually attuned themselves to the interests of budget examiners. They became oriented much more towards effectiveness evaluation than simply management by objectives.

Finally, the Carter administration made a firm commitment to a major reform of machinery of government. It established five divisions in OMB designed to provide staff for several massive reorganization efforts in various sectors of the public service. These divisions found the going rough. The administration had limited their mandate to three years and they staffed themselves largely with contractual appointees from outside government and secondments from operational departments.

The Special Studies Divisions
Currently, four special studies divisions report to OMB associate directors responsible, respectively, for national security and international affairs; economics and government; human resources and veterans and labour; and natural resources and energy and science. A deputy associate director, rated at the highest level in the career ranks, heads each of the special studies divisions. Four to five other professionals round out the relatively small complements. In their choice of personnel the divisions reveal a marked preference for economists, systems analysts, and operational researchers.

The special studies units try to maintain a certain level of isolation from the budget divisions. They attempt to stand aside from routine reviews. Ideally, they come into play only when issues require in-depth study and/or raise questions that cut across the interests of more than one division. In-depth studies usually centre on a major adjustment within a sector of US policy. For instance, around the time of the interviews, the division under national security and international affairs had just completed a major study of the effectiveness of the all-volunteer program of recruitment to the armed services. Meanwhile, the unit operating under economics and government was conducting an independent assessment of conflicting views from the Department of Housing and Urban Development and an OMB review division about future housing needs. Cross-cutting studies provide special divisions a steadier diet of problems. They usually operate in a policy sector that requires co-ordination between budget divisions. In 1979, national security and international affairs took the OMB lead in co-ordination of nuclear non-proliferation and space policies while economics and government played an integrative role in budget issues relating to Carter's urban policy.

All special studies divisions face more claims on their time than they can satisfy. Political masters right up to the president assign special projects studies to them. As well, budget examiners in review divisions regularly submit suggestions for in-depth or cross-cutting studies in their problem areas. A respondent said that one review branch alone had submitted eighteen proposals for studies. Thus the divisions must be extremely selective when taking on projects. Short of a special assignment from higher up, the priorities of the associate director and the specialties of division officials will play a crucial role. As well, the division will take a hard-nosed look at what the study is likely to produce by way of information that will actually help decision-makers: 'Is this issue going to be decided on analytic grounds? There are a number of very important public issues that there isn't too much you can do with in terms of analysis ... Are the data available? Should we get directly involved in a study or should we mandate an agency to build a data base? Is someone else available to do it?'

Individual officials in special studies divisions exercise some discretion in the use of their time. One respondent commented that officials will take up studies on their own initiative in order to elucidate a vital problem that has not penetrated conventional OMB wisdom: 'A remark during a meeting about multi-family housing caught my attention ... I decided to look into it because I thought the secretary for housing and urban development was right and OMB was wrong. That is, that multi-family housing was a future need. It turns out though that the OMB work was very superficial. They didn't know whether there was a need or not. There was just the institutional framework in which we operate which is to always say, "No." I decided I would look into it, on my own time at first.'

Although the special studies divisions concentrate their efforts on effectiveness evaluations, they do take on issues involving efficiency. In 1979, national security and international affairs undertook a large comparative study of the organization of foreign aid agencies. The project looked especially at whether administrative procedures and institutional structures employed in other countries might, if adopted by the US Agency for International Development, result in less labour-intensive delivery of foreign assistance. In the same year, economics and government brought its analytic resources to bear on a dispute between the Veterans Administration and the General Services Administration over storage of veterans' records. Normally, however, special studies divisions eschew such projects.

The outside observer receives mixed signals on how well the special studies divisions integrate their work with the rest of OMB. Most of the praise for the units comes from associate directors – political appointees – each of whom supervises the work of two budget review divisions with no personal staff. They clearly found then that special studies divisions served as powerful surrogates for staff. However, there are pockets of hostility toward special studies in budget divisions. One budget examiner working on the domestic side of the space program registered feelings which, although atypical, reflect the potential depth of conflict:

The space cross-cut now is bigger than the whole NASA review and it says nothing because all that you can report at this point is that studies are ongoing and the results aren't anticipated for a number of months ... In that sense, special studies decisions can be downright counter-productive ... The politicals see all of this stuff in the spring review and they say, 'So what?' And then they come to NASA and they have already got a 'so what?' attitude about this whole business. But we have got some serious problems. One [the space shuttle] could really blow up to be a major embarrassment to the president right now. We are trying to deal with and keep the lid on the damn thing. My examiners, rather than dealing with that, had to take some time off and work on the cross-cut.

It would be foolish for us to take sides in such debates. They originate from the different perspectives and time frames of the budget examination and special studies divisions. So long as it remains relatively civil, the countervaillance of the two views of analysis provides astute associate directors with more creative sets of options.

The President's Reorganization Project (PRP)

As already noted, Jimmy Carter set as one of his top priorities the comprehensive reorganization of the executive branch. A recently published book based on accounts of various officials involved in the project chronicles it in detail.[3] We can focus here on its highlights.

PRP took on three goals. First, it sought to reorganize the management of public service personnel. Second, it undertook sweeping efforts at regulatory reform and the elimination of paperwork. Third, it attempted to improve the organization of various policy sectors by upgrading mechanisms for co-ordination or by creating new departments and agencies. When its three-year mandate expired in 1980, the project appeared to have failed. Yet it achieved success in some respects. For instance, it produced the Office of Personnel Management which, as we will see later in this chapter, pursued a number of innovative policies affecting public servants. Efforts toward deregulation yielded some fruit, most notably in the airline industry. Under Ronald Reagan, a separate office for information and regulatory affairs now enshrines the project's interest in both deregulation and reduction of red tape.

With regard to reorganization affecting the division of programs between departments, the project spawned the departments of Energy and of Education. However, it failed in efforts to create a Department of Natural Resources. It simply could not achieve an amicable settlement of boundary disputes between departments affected by the proposal. The project obtained only modest success in efforts toward improvement of co-ordination between departments. For instance, it encountered mostly frustration in efforts to revamp integration of domestic economic development and of trade policy and programs. The Department of Defense managed to exempt itself from direct scrutiny by the project and thus successfully fought off substantial internal reforms. More generally, it used its special status to frustrate OMB efforts toward improved co-ordination within national security and international affairs.

Two factors contributed to the aura of failure that enshrouded the President's Reorganization Project. First, notwithstanding incessant citizen outrage about bureaucracy, the program took on more than could be sustained by public opinion: 'I think that the emphasis on major cabinet-level reorganization is difficult to sustain in today's political climate; there is just too little grassroots support organized for it and the interest groups are unbelievably difficult to deal with.' A more modest and better-focused program, that tapped clearer public sentiment supporting narrower courses of action, would probably have worked more smoothly. Carter wasted a great deal of time on efforts that were hopeless from the start. One official, for instance, reported that the economic development reorganization took 'at least 50 per cent' of the president's and the senior staffs' time for a period of two weeks. In the end, it produced little. A similar administration effort to seal plans for the Department of Natural Resources resulted in a precipitous decision to cut losses by abandoning the proposal. This move, taken solely by the president and his closest aides, left top OMB officials reeling as they read about it for the first time in the *Washington Post*.

Second, the project's difficulties related to the way in which it was grafted onto OMB. Essentially, the administration created five additional OMB divisions and put them, along with the traditional management units, under an executive associate director. Political appointees headed each of the five divisions. They staffed their units with both consultants from outside government and secondments from departments. This rubbed against the grain of the more staid, career elements of OMB, as one budget examiner noted in no uncertain terms: 'The OMB director was put in a very funny position ... That situation will take care of itself I imagine when PRP goes away as it eventually will. You see, an organization like PRP has to operate very differently. They have to be essentially political salesmen. It has been a strain on the OMB director to be part political salesman and part analyst. He's schizophrenic.' Respondents seconded to the project from other departments found it extremely difficult to operate effectively in OMB. They simply did not gain access to the club: 'OMB is like any institution. It has a bureaucracy and the old-timers want to hold on to their prerogatives and it's very difficult for a new guy ...to suddenly have all the doors opened to him and everyone saying, "Joe, I want you to do this and do that and go talk to the director." No, everybody's too concerned that you are going to bypass them.'

Management Policy

Management policy touches on narrower issues of efficiency in government organization. Under Carter the role came under the associate director for management and regulatory policy. Divisions responsible for management improvement and evaluation, federal personnel policy, regulatory policy and reports management, information systems, and intergovernmental affairs reported to the associate director. Early on, the Reagan administration split this associate directorate into two units, namely the Office of Information and Regulatory Affairs and the Office of Management. The latter retained all the units it had under the old arrangement except regulatory policy and reports management and information systems. It added a unit responsible for organization and special projects.

Officials in the various management divisions work very much to political agendas requiring follow-through on an organization level. From time to time, they will take on evaluations of existing programs that have run into trouble. Further, they will operate as a clearing-house of information on evaluation of programs and operations and on management improvement. The management divisions thus promote efficiency by ensuring that new departments and agencies are properly set up, that particularly derelict programs receive attention, and that departments generally may obtain guidance on criteria and measurements used in new management techniques. The management divisions usually do not conduct evaluations within departments and do not monitor departmental programs designed to improve efficiency.

Considering the relatively modest staffing of the management divisions, one can understand why they work within these constraints. The reason for control of the management divisions' resources becomes clear when one raises the issue with officials in the budget divisions. Examiners there simply believe that they possess the requisite relations with departments and analytic skills to ensure that efficiency evaluations enter into reviews. One examiner made this point particularly strongly: 'I think our division can do the full range of the Ms and the Bs that the president is interested in. There is some role for selected areas of M. There's probably a role for some guy with a great computer talent. None of us are computer experts. There's some guy on their side worrying about computer policy. They suffer, as do all management sides, from a lack of a mailbox. That's the ultimate in this town, "Where will you go with whatever you have and what will you do with it?" And that's the problem with the M side. It always has been.' In contrast, a respondent in a management division presented a ringing indictment of the view that the budget examiners can handle most management issues themselves. He based his remarks on the firm belief that expenditure review simply does not touch on many of the more creative dimensions of management as a science: 'It's one thing to constrain. It's another thing to create ... A lot of the problems that we have in government go beyond the budget as an instrument of control. It is one thing to tell a person that they are not doing well and that their budget will be decreased, or that they are not doing well but their budget will be increased. It's another thing to tell them *how* to do better. That's where I think OMB needs more work, on solutions to systemic problems.'

Thus, yet another debate wages within OMB on the relation between expenditure review and management policy. Notwithstanding several attempts to increase the influence of management specialists vis-à-vis budget examiners, the latter continue to control the 'mailboxes,' thereby relegating the former to the status of ancillary service.

Financial Management and Federal Procurement
These two units operate in the world of probity and prudence. The first, which has recently moved under the associate director for management, takes a very narrow view of financial management. We will see when we look at the Canadian arrangement that there the field includes performance-oriented accounting: Canada's Office of the Comptroller General monitors departments' adoption of the most modern financial-management systems. These, in turn, provide standardized data that feed into evaluations of effectiveness and efficiency. In the United States, the General Accounting Office (GAO), an agency reporting to Congress, formally approves departmental accounting systems. However, it exercises this role unevenly. The financial management unit in OMB thus simply advises departments on accounting, auditing, cash management, and debt-collection systems that might help simplify the work of budget reviewers. It does, however, wield one sharp instrument. Under the Anti-Deficiency Act, it approves departments' and agencies' systems for ensuring that they do not overspend congressional appropriations. Prevailing executive-legislative relations give appropriations considerably greater weight than in the United Kingdom and Canada.

The Office of Federal Procurement also takes a more promotional than a monitoring role. It has worked for several years now toward a common procurement statute for the entire public service. As well, it has gradually integrated acquisition regulations affecting the Department of Defense and the General Services Administration.

The emphasis placed on various techniques related to promotion of effectiveness and efficiency in the British government has fluctuated greatly under different governments. Starting in 1970, Edward Heath introduced program analysis and review (PAR). This method for in-depth study of existing programs centred on effectiveness evaluation. Both Wilson and Callaghan retreated somewhat from the innovative and bold approach to effectiveness promoted under the Heath government. During their governments, PAR eventually fell from grace.

Margaret Thatcher has followed the lead of her Conservative predecessor and brought a new technique, this time styled *scrutinies*, to Whitehall. Introduced by Thatcher's special adviser, Sir Derek Rayner, scrutinies focus on the efficiency with which departments administer their programs. We will see that the emergence of scrutinies occasioned yet another debate over the best institutional arrangements for the relation between administrative policy and expenditure review. Thatcher, at Sir Derek's suggestion, pressed through much of 1980 for transfer of all or most of the Civil Service Department (CSD) back to HM Treasury. Sir Derek had argued that management policy operates better when brigaded with expenditure review. A year's reprieve came when the prime minister softened slightly in the face of arguments that management policy simply dies on the vine if absorbed by an omnibus department preoccupied with performance of the economy.[4] However, the failure of CSD fully to enforce the government's limit on pay increases for the 1981 round of negotiations with the civil service unions steeled Thatcher's resolve. In November 1981, she split CSD. The most vital public expenditure parts, those divisions responsible for pay and complementing policies, went to the Treasury. The units responsible for civil service organization and personnel policy formed a new department, the Management and Personnel Office, that reports ultimately to the secretary of the cabinet in his capacity as joint head of the home civil service.

Edward Heath's PARs

To understand the origins of PAR one must look to the optimism of the 1960s toward government decision-making. At the time, the belief prevailed that modern science, especially vastly improved information systems, had ushered in a new era in which decision-makers could achieve much greater rationality. Harold Wilson had relied heavily on the widely accepted potential of modern science in a speech to the 1963 Scarborough

Conference. He asserted: 'Britain must harness Socialism to science, and science to Socialism.'[5] In practice, the Conservative party took much more to heart the promise of science. This fact largely derived from the working acquaintance many bright young party activists had with the introduction of modern management science to business.

One thing became clear as the Conservatives cooled their heels during the years of Labour government from 1964 to 1970: when they took charge again, they would have to do battle with Whitehall mandarins. These, for the most part, tended to view management science as a passing fad. One Conservative recounts for us some of the antediluvian thinking that prevailed in Whitehall at the time when he and his associates worked in the party to prepare it for the technological revolution: 'I remember at the time [1964] being told by a senior man in the Ministry of Health, when I was chatting with him about the possible applications for computers in British hospitals ... "Well of course before we start spending money on computers in the health service we have got to be sure that they are here to stay."'

The main thrust toward incorporation of plans for new management technology into the Conservatives' preparations for their next government came from a privately financed body, the Public Sector Research Unit. Headed by Ernest Marples, the shadow minister for technology, and staffed by David Howell, now secretary of state for transport, and Mark Schreiber, now with the *Economist,* the unit made an exhaustive effort to explore public-sector applications of modern management techniques.[6] It embarked on a three-month tour of several countries that focused on various governmental institutions and techniques designed to improve policy decisions.

Ultimately, the group took improvement in review of public expenditure as one of its main interests. A strategy emerged whereby the next government would bring along as advisers a cadre of executives from the private sector whose absence from their home companies would 'hurt.' These individuals would spearhead the program analysis and review system. Here each department would undertake fundamental review of two programs, the selection of which would depend on three criteria: 1) the volume of resources allocated to it, 2) the length of time since it had been evaluated from the standpoint of first principles, and 3) the relevance of its objectives to the priorities of the government.

When the Conservatives came to power in 1970, the PAR system was only partially instituted. The government did bring in six managers from the private sector and mandated several studies. However, it failed fully to install the linchpin of the system. Under the original concept, the Central

Policy Review Staff would have selected and co-ordinated PARS and shouldered responsibility for advising the cabinet on responses to the results of the various studies. However, this plan would have encroached on the territory of the Treasury, the Civil Service Department, and the Cabinet Office. As one Conservative involved in the process recounts, Whitehall was well prepared to protect itself from an overly experimental approach on the part of the new government: 'The cabinet secretary, Burke Trend, and the head of the civil service, William Armstrong, had talks with me. They said: "This is all very interesting, your views. We watched them develop while you were in the opposition. We agree with you. We have been thinking along the same lines. In fact, we have all sorts of plans setting up essentially the same things." I became very suspicious.' As it turned out, Whitehall inserted in the Conservatives' plans several key safeguards of entrenched prerogatives. The provision that the Treasury, rather than CPRS, would take the lead on PARS worked especially well to secure the traditional role of the department within the public expenditure field.

By the time of the British interviews, PAR had seen better days. At first, a special cabinet committee selected and co-ordinated PARS; in 1978, the Public Expenditure Survey Committee had absorbed this responsibility. Although the Treasury maintained custody of PAR as a technique, the view clearly had developed that too frequent use in the early days had blunted the instrument. Just about every conceivable program had coped with a PAR. A sense emerged that it had covered the waterfront and produced very little for the effort. Nonetheless, PAR operated behind a veil of secrecy. Whitehall believed that publicity would only flag internal problems best kept under a lid until a consensus jelled around what to do.

At the heart of problems with PAR rests a fundamental limitation. Governments can only achieve so much in economies through in-depth analysis designed to identify ineffective programs. Especially in times of restraint, only very concerted political pressure can force the difficult decisions necessary to reduce the aggregate sizes of expenditure and bureaucracy.

Notwithstanding the demise of PAR, we should look briefly at the types of exercises engaged in at the time of the interviews. One CPRS official reported two PARS, one looking into the adverse effects to industry of alcohol consumption and the other into penal policy. Another CPRS official told of a study on medium-term unemployment as related to economic policy. An official in an operational department had been involved in a PAR on school buildings. On the face of it, these studies do not appear to have warranted a veil of secrecy. Indeed, many PARS eventually saw the light of day in white papers announcing new government initiatives in one or other area.

The Conservative cabinet specifically set aside PARS in 1979 when it introduced scrutinies. However, this has not brought an end to in-depth studies of various issues faced by the government. For instance, during the summer of 1980, one official told of two major in-depth studies in one department. One of these focused on plans for assistance to youths who have remained in school as compared to those who have left but not found jobs; the other projected the diseconomies resulting from smaller school enrolments. However, one Treasury official noted that the constant pressure from the Conservative government to seek economies has left relatively little time for in-depth study: 'Fundamental reviews have been out of the question. The whole effort on our part was directed to getting down to revising the public expenditure programs. We have been doing this day-to-day work instead of sitting back, as one sometimes does, and thinking, "Is a particular part of the service functioning as it should?"'

The 'Mini' in London Traffic
We have already seen the efforts under Jimmy Carter toward improvement of machinery of government. The staffing behind the President's Reorganization Project certainly stands as a bench-mark for institutional resources directed to reforms of machinery. As well, PRP adopted a scope that left virtually every department and agency having to respond in some way to its initiatives. In the Canadian case, we will find a seemingly relentless effort continually to revamp machinery assisting the cabinet in its decision-making. This has stretched now from the mid-1960s to the present.

The American and Canadian emphases on machinery of government prove to be a poor preparation for what one finds in Britain. There the era of experimentation during the 1960s and early 1970s has come to an abrupt halt. The push to integrate some ministries into superdepartments has come and gone. It produced mixed results. At the centre, a clear bias has developed against alterations in existing central agency structures. The return of direct responsibility for civil service pay and complementing from CSD to HM Treasury appears as a partial retreat to the 1968 status quo. Further, nobody talks about creating new institutions to assist cabinet decision-making. All this leaves the Machinery of Government Division within CSD's successor, the Management and Personnel Office (MPO), with very conventional work indeed. It reacts principally to policy initiatives that have implications for relations between portfolios. It usually does not take on major reorganizational efforts. As one official put it, we can liken its role to 'a "mini" in London traffic': 'We nip in for a couple of meetings to express a view or exchange views about the organizational implications, then out again, before we get sucked into a good deal of discussion which is not of direct interest to us.'

The British public service may point to a long-standing tradition of gradualism in matters related to machinery. Richard A. Chapman and J.R. Greenaway attribute this to Whitehall's innate conservatism whereby change occurs but must not appear to be taking place too rapidly.[7] Thus, superdepartment proposals put forward in 1917 did not come to fruition until the 1960s.[8] Meanwhile, sixty-two years after Lloyd George took on six partisan policy advisers and housed them in No. 10's famous Garden Suburb, Margaret Thatcher dithered before adopting a similar arrangement that had been reverted to under Harold Wilson.[9] Thus, dramatic moves, such as Edward Heath's creation of the Central Policy Review Staff in 1970, come off as lapses which prove the rule. Behind the British view of machinery of government rests a firm conviction: change must only occur when the benefits of a new arrangement will clearly outweigh the costs of disruption. One respondent who has witnessed many an organizational change offered these reflections: 'You've got to decide what it is you're going to do and stick with it for a reasonable period of time. The one thing that does reduce efficiency is changing the machinery. Even if you make quite a definite improvement, it's a few years before you collect your payoff. You've got to develop some sort of new *esprit de corps* so that the staff know who they are and what they are. And I think we've not had that sufficiently in the front of our minds in the last twenty years. We've chopped and changed around with pretty gay abandon and not considered sufficiently the losses that you do incur. Human beings aren't that adaptable. They do need time to decide where their loyalties are and the rest of it.'

The Machinery of Government Division in MPO lacks a complete mandate within its field. The Cabinet Office assumes responsibility for advising the prime minister on matters relating to machinery for interdepartmental decision-making. This arrangement leaves MPO with the leading role in advising the prime minister on the division of functions among portfolios. This responsibility extends to organizational issues within departments that might occasion the intervention either of officials in other areas of MPO or the secretary of the cabinet in his capacity as joint head of the home civil service.

The Road to Rayner Scrutinies and beyond
The search for efficiency in government has received renewed impetus under Margaret Thatcher. We have already seen that she upholds the

view that ministers should take more responsibility for the day-to-day administration of their departments. If they took this part of their obligations more seriously, Thatcher believes, they would more readily identify various savings that could cut both the cost and size of their bureaucratic establishments.

To promote the ministers' search for economies, Thatcher installed Sir Derek Rayner in No. 10 as a part-time adviser on efficiency. Sir Derek currently serves as well as vice-chairman of the retail chain Marks and Spencer. He has spent a stint in government before. In 1970, Edward Heath took him on as one of the six executives from the private sector who were to help introduce modern management principles to the civil service. Concentrating his efforts on reorganization of defence procurement, he even served in the Ministry of Defence as chief executive for procurement in 1971–2.

Sir Derek's presence in No. 10 complicated somewhat CSD's special claim on questions of efficiency. However, even without Sir Derek's presence, one might have asked whether officials in the expenditure divisions of the Treasury had more of the intimate knowledge of departmental operations necessary to prod them on efficiency than their opposite members in CSD. At least one senior Treasury official suggested this in clear terms: 'The second function is to try to get value for money, to eliminate waste and to help the department apply the techniques of good financial management. For example, do they use cost-benefit analysis and discounted cash flow and other techniques of this kind for appraising investment projects?'

Just the same, CSD had gained a strong presence in the advancement of government efficiency. Two units in particular were operating in this field before the Thatcher government. One of these conducted a series of management reviews of individual departments that had been running since 1972. The other took its roots in the organization and methods division that had operated in the Treasury for twenty-seven years prior to its moving to CSD when the latter started up in 1968.

The management review program operated with four assistant secretaries. In essence, these officials ran a consultancy service for departments wanting a top-to-bottom assessment of their organization, methods of work, and arrangements for internal planning. As one respondent noted, the concept originated with the Heath government's desire to go beyond Whitehall efficiency studies by introducing private-sector techniques. As happens in these matters, the actual CSD program deviated from the Conservatives' idea by staffing the consultancy with career officials instead of businessmen. Thus the CSD consultants did not bring to their work highly developed knowledge of mangement techniques in use outside government. They traded more on their direct knowledge of the civil service and similarity in background to that of the more senior officials whose departments they criticized: 'I think there are two broad reasons for this approach. First, as you know, there has been this long-term resistance on the part of senior civil servants to the idea that management theorists have a great deal to bring to the management of government operations. Second, I think there has also been a firm conviction so far that in a situation where you may have to advise a very senior official on a personal basis he is more likely to take that from someone who looks something like himself when young than not.'

A division responsible for organization and methods focused on relatively technical matters relating to the efficient operation of such internal services as typing and transport. At the time of the interviews, this unit was focusing especially on services such as stationery that departments draw upon from a central supplier without having to account for the expenditure.

Sir Derek Rayner set out under the current government with a relatively modest scheme. At his suggestion, ministers commissioned some twenty-nine projects in which departments conducted their own studies of areas where administrative costs might be reduced. Clive Priestley, a csp under-secretary on secondment, and David Allen, a Treasury economic adviser, monitored the various scrutinies. During the first batch, Sir Derek kept fairly close tabs on the officials (nearly all of them principals) conducting the scrutinies for departments. Their reports did not filter back through the divisions being studied. Rather, they went directly to a department's permanent secretary, the minister who had assumed responsibility for a specific scrutiny, and Sir Derek. The pilot projects proved very successful. For instance, one in the Ministry of Defence focused on the supply of food to the three armed services as a means to assess the efficiency of the 'non-warlike' purchasing and distribution chain. The study resulted in rationalization of the supply systems. For instance, the ministry placed them under the authority of a single official.

The Civil Service Department assumed responsibility for spotting economies resulting from such moves and asking the Treasury expenditure divisions to press departments with similar operations to produce comparable savings. Indeed, csp, detecting a growth sector, regrouped so as to provide more concerted follow-through on Rayner scrutinies. Here it created the position of under-secretary for functions and programs. This person supervised divisions the activities of which focused largely on the applicability of findings from scrutinies elsewhere in the public service. From the outset CSD tried to avoid bureaucratizing the Rayner method. As one CSD respondent noted, standardization of such exercises would defeat their purpose by evoking only routinized responses from departments: 'That's the dilemma of standardization because it stops being fresh. You tell people you must do annual scrutinies of their activities and really examine closely what your activities are for. Round it comes to that time of the year and the weary chaps who have been bogged down with day-to-day tasks say, "Oh, I've got to do this tomorrow ... the form A23/B/C50 has got to be returned to the establishment officer by the 25th of May." Once one is relying on that kind of thing it's lost.'

For his part, Sir Derek tried to prevent his scrutinies from being swallowed up by CSD. Despite his stated intention to spend only a year at the disposal of the prime minister, he remained heavily involved in No. 10 even after CSD was split. During 1980, he took on thirty-nine scrutinies including a 'trans-Whitehall' study of the Governmental Statistical Service. He conducted thirty-seven in 1981 which involved, in addition to thirty-five departmental projects, cross-cutting investigations of support staff for research establishments and of form-filling in the public service.[10]

In April 1982, Sir Derek reduced his commitment of time as the prime minister's adviser on efficiency. None the less, the scrutinies program continues to operate out of No. 10. As well, Clive Priestley, Rayner's top civil service assistant, has taken over the efficiency divisions of the Management and Personnel Office. Although he now reports most immediately to John Cassels, the second permanent secretary with day-to-day responsibility for MPO, he no doubt will keep in close contact with Sir Derek. Priestley has consistently complemented Sir Derek's commitment to advancing government efficiency with exceptional adroitness at getting results from even the most recalcitrant pockets of Whitehall. Meanwhile, Priestley's MPO predecessor, A.W. 'Sandy' Russell, has taken direction of the Financial Management Initiative (FMI). This program will attempt to bring departments to adopt performance measures designed to increase officials' accountability to civil-service superiors and ministers for efficient management.

Sir Derek, the Comptroller and Auditor General, and Probity and Prudence
Especially in comparison to Canada, the United Kingdom has dedicated sparse resources to central-agency units responsible for improving probity and prudence in government. The Treasury has dedicated three relatively small divisions to this area. One of these maintains relations with Parliament, with the Public Accounts Committee, and with the comptrol-

ler and auditor general (one person) and generally sets policy for public accounts within the civil service. One focuses on financial control and purchasing policy. And one provides advice and information to departments on management accounting and internal audit.

As already noted, part of Sir Derek Rayner's vision of central-agency machinery for advancement of efficiency in the public service had all of the old CSD moving back to the Treasury. His view hinged on the assertion that financial and managerial responsibilities formed part of a seamless garment that should not be divided. As Sir Derek noted before the Treasury and Civil Service Committee of the House of Commons: 'The principle that the permanent secretary is also the accounting officer for the department's votes reflects the principle that finance is inseparable from good policy advice and implementation, good organization and good management ... Any headquarters organization must surely be weakened in its functions of central control if the two parts brought together so clearly by the permanent secretary are separated in the centre of government.'[11]

Even before the split of CSD, Sir Derek made some significant progress in seeing his ideas on the financial management front largely adopted. We should note here that two successive reports by the previous comptroller and auditor general, Sir Douglas Henley, in 1980 and 1981 have taken Whitehall to task for its poor standards of accountancy and internal auditing. Sir Douglas had stressed in particular the paucity of professional financial-management staff in both departments and central agencies and the lack of clear guidance from the centre on matters of policy. The first of Sir Douglas's reports gave Sir Derek much-needed ammunition in arguing several of his most vital concerns: 1) that ministers and permanent secretaries should have to account for services drawn from common resources as well as departmental ones, 2) that candidates for ministerial and permanent secretary positions must have demonstrated their ability to manage money and manpower, and 3) that the government must entrust to a single central agency the responsibility for improvement of financial management.

On 12 February 1981, the government transferred the Financial Accounting and Audit Division of CSD to the Treasury. It established as well a Financial Management Coordination Group, an interdepartmental body chaired by a Treasury deputy secretary.[12] The committee has been developing policy toward the following goals:

1. more effective planning and control of the cash cost of programs of public expenditure;

2. further development of financial responsibility and accountability in line management;
3. better matching of the financial information needed for the Public Expenditure Survey and the Estimates with that required for management;
4. the strengthening of internal audit in departments.[13]

CANADA

Readers probably have already accustomed themselves to the never-ending flux we encounter when looking at Canadian central agencies. Policy on effectiveness and efficiency will not disappoint those who have become connoisseurs of bureaucratic experimentation. Along the way they will find that, in Canada, reform efforts come and go in this field with roughly the frequency of governments in Italy.

The Planning Branch of the Treasury Board Secretariat: RIP
Our discussion starts with an institutional obituary. In 1970, TBS established the Planning Branch around Douglas Hartle, a prominent economist from the University of Toronto who had entered government to upgrade quantitative policy analysis. Hartle took a very broad compass in his view of analysis. Units under him eventually included effectiveness, efficiency, *and* organizational evaluation. The latter division attempted to gain a toehold for TBS in matters concerning machinery of government.

Within the Planning Branch, the Effectiveness Evaluation Division stood out. By 1976, it consisted of five directors who headed teams servicing major interdepartmental studies of policy programs. Each director handled two or three studies at any given time. The directors drew upon an expert staff of some thirty-four professionals, most of them economists, housed within the division. Usually, top officials in central agencies or operational departments would chair the committees undertaking the studies. The Planning Branch essentially provided secretariats to the committees. This arrangement enabled the studies to take particular account of the degree to which the programmatic goals of various departments meshed. The Planning Branch teams provided highly integrative analysis for major interdepartmental studies.

In the United States, OMB special studies divisions struggle constantly with the fact that budget divisions view their integrative approach with scepticism. The belief prevails among budget examiners that special studies divisions operate in a rarefied atmosphere. Identical sentiments emerged during interviews with officials in TBS's Program Branch. Effectiveness evaluations simply required more lead time than normally existed in decisions bound to the cycle of expenditure reviews. However, more than a mere conflict in perspectives stood between officials in the Program and the Planning branches. An affinity grew between the Privy Council Office and the Planning Branch's Effectiveness Evaluation Division that exacerbated the cleavage. As we have already noted, PCO and the Program Branch locked horns incessantly over the expenditure implications of policies being advanced in the cabinet and its committees. In such disputes, PCO found that it lacked the analytic resources necessary to counter the positions taken by the Program Branch. It often turned to the Effectiveness Evaluation Division to provide the analyses it needed. This tack simply added to the Program Branch's insecurity.

The creation of the Office of the Comptroller General (1977) and of the ministries of state for Economic Development (1978) and for Social Development (1979) has left only a remnant of the Effectiveness Evaluation Division. A scaled-down version operates in the Office of the Comptroller General. As well, both of the ministries of state contain evaluation units, the work of which corresponds somewhat to the emphasis taken by the Effectiveness Evaluation Division. Indeed, many former members of the TBS division serve in the ministries' units. Effectiveness evaluation as a technique still maintains a presence in Canadian central agencies. However, too rapid structural change and the resulting institutional jealousies have prevented it from maintaining the same type of sharply delineated profile that it enjoys in OMB special studies divisions.

The Privy Council Office and Machinery of Government

We have touched several times in this book on the emphasis the Privy Council Office gives to machinery of government. Several factors have helped to maintain PCO's presence in this field. The first derives largely from the rationalistic instincts of Pierre Elliott Trudeau, who has always shown a decided weakness for schemes that purport to put the organization of government on a more rational footing. If the prime minister chooses to involve himself directly in issues concerning the machinery of government, it stands to reason that the function will operate out of PCO.

Second, the trust that Trudeau placed in Michael Pitfield helped to account for PCO's emphasis on the machinery of government. Pitfield had an enduring influence on Trudeau, starting even before the latter entered federal politics in 1965. Since Trudeau became prime minister, Pitfield, apart from a two-year stint as deputy minister of consumer and corporate affairs, remained at Trudeau's side in PCO. Indeed, the conditions upon which Trudeau agreed to lead the Liberals into the 1980 election included the assurance that Pitfield would return as his clerk of the Privy Council and secretary to the cabinet. Throughout his lengthy service, Pitfield has produced a string of organizational schemes appealing to Trudeau's quest for a more rationally organized public service.

A third and final factor rounds out our explanation of PCO's stake in machinery of government. The attentive reader will most certainly recall Gordon Smith's relation to Michael Pitfield at this point. As we have noted, Smith rose in eight years from an officer in the Machinery of Government unit to associate deputy secretary to the cabinet with the rank of deputy minister. His background bears a distinct resemblance to that of Pitfield: he was raised in Westmount, the enclave of Montreal's small but prosperous Anglo-Saxon business élite; he attended Lower Canada College and McGill University, both essential stops for Westmount's offspring; and his father was a Montreal investment broker. Smith, thus, evolved quite naturally into Michael Pitfield's closest PCO confidant. In addition, he supplied a well-developed specialized knowledge through which Pitfield could indulge further his interest in organizational structure. Smith has a doctorate from a political science program at Massachusetts Institute of Technology that focuses on the applications of organizational and systems theory in government. Although Smith recently left PCO to become deputy minister of the Ministry of State for Social Development, the observer finds it hard not to conclude that this move occurred as much to give him a direct operational handle on the envelope system he helped create as to cement his status in the deputy-minister community.

The Office of the Comptroller General: Effectiveness, Efficiency, and Probity and Prudence Rolled into One
We noted above that the Trudeau government responded in 1976 to criticism from the auditor general concerning financial management by creating the Office of the Comptroller General. This move involved placing the Planning and Financial Administration branches of the Treasury Board Secretariat under a separate deputy minister, the comptroller general. Subsequently, OCG reduced somewhat the resources allocated to former Planning Branch functions, namely effectiveness and efficiency evaluations. None the less, the office's 1981 complement included, in addition to the comptroller general, who reports directly to the president of the Treasury Board, three assistant deputy ministers, six assistant secretaries, eleven directors, and some eighty-six other professionals.

The development of OCG has benefited greatly from the Canadian instinct to incarnate new emphases in financial and administrative policy through full-blown structural reforms. During the mid-1970s, the auditor general, who reports annually to Parliament on financial management in the public service, riveted his attention onto the need for upgrading programmatic accounting. Partially in response to the auditor general's concerns, TBS enlarged Financial Administration, a relatively small division in the Administrative Policy Branch, to a branch with three divisions.

In the fall of 1976, the auditor general produced a stinging attack on the government's continued neglect of programmatic accounting. It also presented evidence of gross impropriety in the financial operations of Atomic Energy of Canada Ltd, a Crown corporation. The government first attempted to diffuse the issue by creating the Royal Commission on Financial Management and Accountability. However, the auditor general held his ground. Further, the Public Accounts Committee of the House of Commons launched its first-ever in-depth study of the auditor general's annual report. Pressure mounted for the government to adopt the auditor general's principal recommendation. He had urged the creation of an Office of the Comptroller General. This would operate independently of TBS and report directly to the president of the Treasury Board.

OCG has functioned since 1977. Harry Rogers, the first comptroller general, entered the public service with a great deal of fanfare directly from a vice-presidency at Xerox of Canada. He injected a new note of optimism into Ottawa's views of financial management. Making the best of a difficult marriage between TBS's former branches of Financial Administration and of Planning, he stressed the fact that the latter's program evaluations provided the best hope for putting the former on a firmer base. OCG would work to improve the departments' use of program evaluations; decision-makers would find evaluations could serve as useful surrogates for the private sector's indicators of success – profit and loss: 'Human affairs are matters of "more-or-less," matters of opinion. Yet opinion can be informed. There are better and worse gradations of "muddling through." We try to reduce uncertainty by assessing results, weighing and considering alternatives. We have to have a more systematic way of truely [sic] testing the limits. We must, in a way, build *in* our own imprecise, quantitative and qualitative criteria for ensuring survival of the fittest of our imperfect schemes ... The drive to evaluation, then, is an attempt to exert more knowledgeable control over the haphazard propogation [sic] of problems.'[14]

Notwithstanding his enthusiasm, Rogers has encountered serious difficulties even with the operation of OCG. He found that he could not work with either of his deputy comptroller generals, both of whom had headed the former TBS branches that OCG had absorbed. After he had replaced these two, he created a third deputy. By January 1980, two of the three new deputies had resigned their positions. That OCG was now fraying at the edges became transparent in an exceptional disclaimer from one of the departing deputies printed in the column of an Ottawa journalist: 'Notwithstanding your jaundiced view of the Harry Rogers "experience" the past three years have done more to advance the understanding of and commitment to the function of management in the public service than the events following Glasco [sic] in the early 1960's, the introduction of PPBS in the late 1960's and a range of alphabet soup initiatives to the mid-1970's ... Progress will be interpreted publicly as unsatisfactory no doubt, but the harsh realities are that the management of large government institutions is a bloody tough job and useful change will come slowly ... I find your column often informative and occasionally amusing, but as for your demeaning gossip – blow it out your ear.!'[15]

While OCG seems to be foundering, one should not forget TBS's Administrative Policy Branch that housed financial management from 1973 to 1976. Headed by a deputy secretary and brigaded under the Treasury Board Secretariat, the branch encompasses relatively mundane policy matters concerning material and services, real property and accommodation, and information services. With the development of OCG, one might expect that the Administrative Policy Branch would have suffered considerable loss of personnel and responsibilities. OCG might well have absorbed the branch – many of its functions parallel the concerns for management improvement taken on by OCG. On the contrary, the Administrative Policy Branch has experienced an accretion of senior positions. Further, it has assumed responsibility for two additional functions of some importance. These are co-ordination of regulatory reform and development of management standards relating to privacy and freedom of information.

CONCLUSION

With regard to central agency activities connected with improvement of effectiveness and efficiency in government, we have focused on their involvement in effectiveness evaluations, the machinery of government, efficiency evaluations, and the maintenance of probity and prudence. Our examination has stressed the importance of direct links of expenditure review to the actual operation of these various functions. If we take them as all relating to management policy, we have to admit that serious incongruities exist between the organizational objectives and methods of this sector of central-agency activity and those of expenditure review. The latter focuses on aggregate spending and, therefore, will tend to take most seriously exercises that will lead to major savings. Management policy, in contrast, concerns usually less than 10 per cent of expenditure budgets. As well, it upholds less tangible goals than simply reducing expenditure. For instance, inefficient provision of social benefits might cost less than efficient delivery. Thus the department responsible for expenditure review might see this type of management issue as marginal to its concerns.

In the United States, units responsible for review of expenditure and for improvement of effectiveness and efficiency have operated under a single roof. Despite the numerous efforts to clarify their institutional links, the MS and BS within OMB have consistently failed to get along. Budget examiners tend to dismiss the roles of their colleagues in management divisions as needlessly replicating the expertise they themselves have garnered from years of reviewing departments' spending plans. We found that the OMB units responsible for effectiveness evaluations enjoy the best, though far from perfect, relations with budget divisions. Styled *special studies divisions*, these units work under associate directors responsible as well for budget divisions. Functions housed in management divisions find it difficult to establish themselves. With respect to the machinery of government, Jimmy Carter's Reorganization Project, though grafted on OMB, never won credibility on the 'B' side. More conventional units concerned with government efficiency work largely to others' agendas and find too little latitude for creative initiatives. Finally, OMB units involved in advancement of probity and prudence tend to follow relatively narrow terms of reference.

In recognition of the incongruity between expenditure review and improvement of efficiency, the United Kingdom split off units responsible for the function in 1968 and created the Civil Service Department. This arrangement did maintain a leading role for the Treasury in effectiveness evaluations which, until the current government, largely took place as program analysis and review. However, CSD also enjoyed delegated authority over expenditure for personnel and several types of management costs. This responsibility provided it an important point of entry in its efforts to get departments to organize and manage themselves more efficiently. Recently, Mrs Thatcher abolished CSD. She placed the parts responsible for pay and complementing in the Treasury and those concerned with management of civil service organizations and personnel in the Management and Personnel Office. Most insiders believe that this move, by severing the direct link between authorizaton of management-related expenditure and management policy, has greatly weakened the MPO divisions responsible for the latter.

In Canada, efforts to improve effectiveness and efficiency have undergone serious fragmentation. In the mid-1970s effectiveness evaluation operated out of its own branch of the Treasury Board Secretariat and seemed to be thriving. However, the branch of TBS responsible for budget review began to see the Planning Branch as a threat when the latter developed especially strong ties with the Privy Council Office. Ultimately, conflicts between TBS and PCO led to the establishment of the ministries of state for Economic and Regional Development and for Social Development, both of which involve themselves in effectiveness evaluations. The remnant in the Planning Branch moved to another new central agency, the Office of the Comptroller General. Although TBS retains a large stake in matters concerning organizational and management efficiency, its loss of control of review of much of the expenditure budget will require its administrative policy units to adapt to entirely new and largely unfavourable circumstances. PCO, of course, maintains its very firm control of major issues in the machinery of government. We saw that this has stemmed largely from the penchants of the prime minister and Michael Pitfield for experimenting with the organization of the cabinet and the division of responsibilities among departments.

10

Personnel management

The three governmental systems have distributed responsibility for personnel management somewhat unevenly. The general field divides into three subfunctions. First, somewhere within central agencies units allot staffing levels to departments and agencies. Person-years cost money. Thus staffing must link up with annual reviews of expenditure. Second, within the aggregates assigned for staffing governments and administrations try to ensure that departmental and agency complements work with the greatest possible effectiveness and efficiency. As a result, central agencies in our three countries encourage departments to use the principles of advanced personnel management. These should both assist the decisions of those attempting to control staff sizes and improve the use of public service employees on the operational level. Third, senior personnel management receives special attention from central agencies in all three systems. They emphasize this function for three reasons: 1) the personal qualities possessed by senior officials will define in very large part their responsiveness to their political masters and the public, 2) the talents of high-level public servants will greatly affect a bureaucracy's capacity to deliver programs effectively and efficiently, and 3) the establishment of senior executive positions within any bureaucracy produces ripple effects in both the way in which government business is organized and the number of people assigned to it (control of the number and level of senior positions can contribute greatly to the simplicity of organizational charts and the leanness of bureaucratic establishments).

We will find as we look at the way in which central agencies in the countries perform these three functions that boundaries between roles differ sharply along the edges. We see this first with respect to control of staffing levels. The United States lodges this function in the Office of Management and Budget (OMB) rather than in the Office of Personnel Management (OPM). Until recently, the United Kingdom split responsibility over public expenditure so that the Civil Service Department (CSD) exercised authority over staffing levels delegated to it by the Treasury. Canada has recently abandoned a system whereby the Treasury Board Secretariat (TBS) took the undisputed lead both for control of dollar resources and person-years and for the development of management policy, including that related to the personnel.

In the three countries, the various arrangements for the connections between control of staffing and personnel management leave units performing the latter with different types of leverage. With control over staffing lodged in OMB, OPM finds it extremely difficult to affect personnel management within departments and agencies. The personnel management functions operating out of the old CSD found relatively powerful leverage through its Manpower Group's authority over funds for civil service complements. Of course, Manpower's integration with the Treasury has severed this direct link. TBS's continued authority over the operational plans whereby departments expect to implement their programs will maintain only a diminished influence over person-years and civil service management.

Our look at senior personnel management stirs very murky waters indeed. The US system operates under a great deal of ambivalence. First, administrations must appoint and monitor the performance of roughly 2,000 party faithful who occupy 'political' posts in departments and agencies. No administration wants accusations that it has assigned party faithful to jobs for which they lack qualifications or dealt unfairly with appointees who allegedly have 'gone native' by becoming subject to the ethos of their department's career officials. Second, presidents will want to increase the effectiveness and efficiency of senior career personnel. However, their efforts toward this goal must not appear as threats to the merit principle. Britain operates a more straightforward senior personnel system. Ministers' personal staffs provide very few slots for party faithful. Assigning these hardly presents major administrative problems. However, the British civil service maintains a very strong tradition of central control of both recruitment to and progress through the senior ranks. We will find that the activities of MPO reflect this tradition. Canadian practice rests between that of the two other countries. Political appointments in ministers' offices have proliferated to the point where they soon will comprise a growth sector for some enterprising central agency to regulate. Meanwhile, the prime minister involves himself heavily both in setting senior personnel policy and approving appointments. This fact, coupled with the long tenure enjoyed by Pierre Elliot Trudeau, has led to a highly politicized mandarinate.

THE UNITED STATES

The Executive Branch Reorganization Plan of 1978 spawned the Office of Personnel Management. On 1 January 1979, the former Civil Service Commission (csc) divided into three new agencies. opm inherited 'the positive personnel management tasks' including training, productivity, examinations, pay and benefits, and administration.[1] These functions did not derive entirely from the defunct commission. They came as well from omb or represented an enhanced view of the role of central agencies in personnel management. omb retained its control over employment ceilings within departments and agencies. However, it ceded to opm the leading role in executive development and labour relations. The expanded view of personnel management following creation of opm found the new agency revising completely the structure of the executive level of the public service and taking an adversarial role, on the 'employer' side, in management-labour relations. In addition, opm created a group of offices designed to co-ordinate agency relations within governmental sectors. The various offices shadowed the policy fields covered in associate directorates on the budget-review side of omb. Finally, opm had improved upon the former csc capacity for advising departments on the effectiveness and development of the work-force.

Behind these changes, which we will look at in greater detail below, rests the view that the president should take a more active role in personnel management. Even without the transition to the Reagan administration, opm has not operated long enough to allow an assessment of whether heightened presidential attention will result from the reforms. The csc tradition whereby the president remained at arm's length from personnel matters affecting the career civil service still haunts the us system. Further, opm emerged during an ill-fated administration. All this notwithstanding and barring a reversion to a csc-type framework, the opm structure maintains the most significant provision of the Carter reforms. It brigades all key policy functions relating to personnel management under a single head who reports to the president: 'The change from a commission form to a single-headed agency, with direct responsibility of the head of the agency to the president, has given a different kind of mandate that has provided a change from what I would call a neutrality role to a positive kind of aggressive role. It gives to all the traditional personnel functions a much larger management orientation than had been true previously.'

The Agency Relations Group and the Hope for Greater Involvement with OMB
As we have noted, OMB has maintained ultimate responsibility for advising the president on staffing ceilings in the public service. OPM realized at the outset that this comprises a serious restraint on its activities. During 1979, it pursued discussions with OMB about developing joint responsibility for review of budget requests. It also created a large agency relations group organized so as to shadow the sectors covered by OMB budget examination divisions. The agency provided a rationale for its efforts similar to that offered by OMB officials in the management divisions when arguing for greater recognition of their discipline. OPM planned to use better productivity measurement as an analytic base for its efforts towards improvement of departments' personnel management.

OPM recognized that departments would eschew productivity improvements that might only lead OMB to conclude that their personnel should be cut. Of course, OPM respondents acknowledged the intractable tendency of public servants to base their self-esteem on the size of the organizations they head. As well, OMB cuts following upon improvements in departments' productivity could prevent managers from expanding into worthy activities. OPM argued that OMB should not take decisions on staffing ceilings without due consideration to departments' efforts toward improving the productivity of personnel. Since OPM assumed responsibility for productivity, it should have, in the view of many 1979 respondents, achieved a genuine partnership with OMB in review of staffing requests. As one official put OPM's case: 'The interaction between budget and management effectiveness is one that we're going to have to work out. I am convinced that we have got to get in place an effective and useful productivity measuring system and that the performance of agencies in productivity must be taken into account in the budget process.'

Judging from the attitude of OMB budget examiners to the view that their own specialists in management policy should gain greater access to expenditure review, I do not hold out much hope for the OPM understanding of their potential role. Budget examiners believe that they possess just as much expertise in management issues as do the specialists housed either on the 'M' side of OMB or in OPM. In addition, they benefit considerably from their detailed knowledge of the operations of departmental programs that derives from both their relatively long tenure and their day-to-day exposure to line managers. In the end, the Agency Relations Group shrunk to a small staff reporting to the director's office.

Bringing Life back to Personnel Management

Long before its demise, csc had become pretty moribund. Alan K. 'Scotty' Campbell, the first opm director, and the rest of the shapers of the new institution realized that it would have to revitalize a host of atrophied functions. These included senior personnel management, labour-management relations, affirmative employment programs, intergovernmental relations, compensation, and staffing services. Campbell decided to stress labour-management relations and senior personnel management among these existing personnel management groups. He also created an entirely new unit responsible for effectiveness and development of the work-force.

The Office of Labor-Management Relations has experienced a marked change in its orientation owing largely to the emphasis Scotty Campbell wanted it to take. One respondent in this office had briefed himself particuarly well on labour-management relations in the United Kingdom and Canada. Thus he provided especially worthwhile insights into how what he and his colleagues were attempting contrasted with this sector of activity in our two other countries.

Labour-management relations have not developed along nearly so structured lines in the United States as they have in the United Kingdom and Canada. As became clear in the aftermath of the air-traffic controllers strike in the summer of 1981, unions do not enjoy the same level of recognition as management in the eyes of the law: 'We've never fully admitted that we're in collective bargaining. We're trying to be a little pregnant and a little virgin at the same time. That's very difficult to do. We don't bargain wages. We don't permit an agency shop. We don't permit bargaining on government-wide regulations.' On the union side, leaders find it difficult enough to enlist dues-paying members: 'We've got 1.2 million people in exclusive bargaining units. But the employees don't have to belong to the union. And the union doesn't bargain for their wages. End result: the employees don't join the union. So they might have a third of the 1.2 million signed up as dues-paying members.'

Individual departments, rather than opm, serve as the units in management responsible for bargaining with unions. However, the Office of Labor-Management Relations has tried to move toward providing 'hard guidance' to departments on their relations with unions. Its efforts have involved five types of activities. It advises other opm units on labour-management issues that affect other aspects of government-wide personnel management, it has heightened consultation with unions about personnel problems, it serves as the management-side advocate in matters that come before the Merit Systems Protection Board and the

Federal Labor Relations Authority, it tries to co-ordinate departmental views of issues that arise throughout government, and it collects systematically and shares information concerning labour-management relations in various departments and agencies. Notwithstanding these intentions, we should not take too sanguine a view of what the Office of Labor-Management Relations might achieve.

The Workforce Effectiveness and Development Group (WEDG) tried to take OPM farther toward linking productivity with personnel management than CSC ever went. On the level of principals, the director of OPM is co-chairman, with his opposite number in OMB, of the President's Management Improvement Council. WEDG attempts to provide data with which the director and others can press government-wide improvements in employee productivity. Under Campbell, the group took on two new types of activities. First, it pursued with the Bureau of Labor Statistics and OMB efforts to improve measurement and analysis related to the federal work-force. Second, it initiated an extensive research and development program. For instance, its organizational psychologists examined a number of factors related to the effectiveness of bureaucratic organizations. Such projects included studies of the effectiveness of group incentives in operational units such as social service offices. Another type of exercise operated similarly to Rayner scrutinies in the United Kingdom. OPM officials identified improvements in the productivity and speed of work that have taken place in specific departments or agencies. They then developed test designs for field experiments that demonstrated the wider applicability of such improvements throughout government.

Senior Personnel: Taming the Two-Headed Monster
Two sharply contrasting groups comprise the senior ranks of officials serving any administration. On the one hand, over 2,000 appointees take up important departmental and agency positions as well as assignments in the White House and the Executive Office of the President. The best posts – sub-cabinet, at executive level – offered salaries in 1982 ranging between $57,500 and $69,630 (US). Additionally, close to 800 top positions within the new Senior Executive Service, in which posts pay between $54,755 and $58,500, go to non-career candidates. About 6,300 career public servants fill the remainder of SES assignments. The non-career and career ranks combined total, then, about 9,100 senior officials.

All US presidents since John Kennedy have set up personnel offices within the White House.[2] These units have focused their work on the most important political appointments. They have tried to spread the recruitment net as widely as possible – so as to not overlook individuals with the most appropriate talents, to screen candidates systematically, and to ensure that appointees remain loyal to the president. During the term of an administration, the units have undertaken assessments of the competence and loyalty of appointees with a view to replacing those whose performance has proven less than satisfactory.

The activities of White House personnel units have stirred controversy during some administrations. Most notorious here was the group headed by Frederick V. Malek during the Nixon administration. H.R. Haldeman, Nixon's chief of staff, hired Malek in 1970 to identify disloyal appointees and replace them with management-oriented recruits with proven fidelity.[3] Carter tried desperately to avoid even the appearance of such a purge during the first two years of his term. However, his most trusted advisers convinced him in the spring of 1979 that appointees' disloyalty had reached epidemic proportions. Carter initially responded by setting up a secret White House study of the performance of his appointees. In conjunction with this project, a professional recruitment consultant, Arnold Miller, took over the personnel office. Miller began a search for replacements for those whom the administration planned to fire. The process came to a head in mid-July when four cabinet secretaries left the administration. By that time, the systematic search for the incompetent and disloyal had formalized itself in the shape of structured questionnaires.

Under Ronald Reagan, E. Pendleton James, like Miller a professional 'head-hunter,' directed until 1982 the search for appointees. His unit included eleven officials. Some observers faulted James's performance.[4] Such concerns reflect how much is at stake in an administration's selection of senior personnel. A president's ability to get the greatest possible return from his power of appointment suggests how he will fulfil other functions connected with his office. In this regard, the Reagan administration's caution explained in large part its apparent slowness in making appointments. James cleared each appointment with the candidate's prospective cabinet secretary, the counsellor to the president, the White House counsel, the chief of staff and his deputy, either the national security adviser or the assistant for policy development, and, finally, the president.

Although system- and department-wide *esprit* generally falls short of British and Canadian standards, the power of the individual career units in the US departments provides a driving force behind any administration's efforts to find appointees who will fulfil its requirements for competence and partisan loyalty. Often career officials spend most of their public service years in a single unit within a department and rise only slowly in the unit's hierarchy. Units even enjoy some leeway both in creation of senior positions and management of their officials' development. Thus career public servants find themselves much more beholden to specific units than do their opposite numbers in Canada and the United States. The US arrangement ensures continuity in an otherwise volatile executive-bureaucratic system. In fact, it may provide too much stability. Each administration fears that its meticulously selected appointees will 'go native' once they have come under the spell of the career officials who preside over domains of departmental activity.

Hugh Heclo's 1977 book, *A Government of Strangers*, contributed greatly to an understanding of the tense relations between appointees and career officials in the United States.[5] Heclo promoted the view that many top appointive and all senior career positions should collapse into a single senior executive system. Such a move, he argued, would mitigate the adverse effects of the dichotomy between appointees and career staff. It would acknowledge that many career officials involve themselves in policy work, it would provide them access to a wider range of executive positions, and it would install a service-wide personnel management system that would counter the parochial career development prevalent in departments.

The Senior Executive System (SES), similar to that recommended by Heclo, came into effect in 1979 as part of Carter's civil service reforms. The Office of Personnel Management has assumed responsibility for implementing the program. The Executive Personnel and Management Development Group advises the director on all matters connected with SES. The fact that OPM exercises authority over the number of senior posts in each department and agency provides the group some added leverage. Previously, the Civil Service Commission exercised control over only a small proportion of senior positions. The success of departments in appealing to Congress for provision of senior posts had greatly inflated their number while reducing CSC's sway over the uppermost echelons of the career public service.

A number of OPM initiatives tried to exploit its new authority. First, OPM altered the pay system. With the highest career salaries pegged to those of congressmen, the top grades under the old system, GS16-18, were bunched together at a single rate. The SES categories, ES1-6, provide for slight gradations of salaries from $54,755 to $58,500. Second, SES allows for bonuses to senior executives who have attained demonstrably distinguished performance. Originally, up to 50 per cent of officals in any agency could receive bonuses amounting to no more than 20 per cent of their base pay. One and 5 per cent of SES members would receive, respectively, $20,000 and $10,000. In 1980, the first bonus exercise actually yielded less than half the number of awards initially mandated by Congress. Since OPM played a part in this reneging, Sally Greenberg, the associate director of the Executive Personnel and Management Evaluation Group, resigned her position.

THE UNITED KINGDOM

Before being abolished, the Civil Service Department stood pretty much in the same place regarding personnel management that OPM would like to occupy. Its three manpower divisions exerted authority over public expenditure for staff and manpower substitutes for the entire civil service. This function provided relatively strong leverage to the views put forth both by divisions responsible for personnel management policy and for pay and superannuation. Most notably, CSD shouldered with departments joint responsibility for the selection and future career development of members of the 'open structure.' All officials at the level of under-, deputy, and permanent secretary belong to this body of senior officials whose management transcends departmental bounds. CSD also housed the Recruitment Group. This unit services the Civil Service Commission, the body that certifies civil service appointments.

Control of Manpower
Three CSD divisions reviewed complementing and administrative expenses for as many clusters of departments. Headed by assistant secretaries, the units made no clear effort to shadow the organization of expenditure review functions found in the Treasury. However, since the Manpower Group oversaw only about 6 1/2 per cent of public expenditure, it actually enjoyed better staffing per pound of expenditure than the Treasury. It reviewed all estimates for salaries, wages, and overtime allotments for permanent employees and personnel substitutes (including casual staff, temporaries, consultants, and agency staff) and for telecommunications, travel, and several other related costs.

Individual officers in the Manpower Group exerted a large amount of discretion in putting forth their recommendations. In 1981, assistant secretaries could approve up to £15 million. Larger sums would require the signature of the minister of state in the Civil Service Department. Here conflicts arose. However, a concordat between CSD and the Treasury placed a premium on the two working in harness.

The Manpower Group watched very carefully decisions being taken at CSD's behest in the Personnel Management and Pay groups. With respect to the former, Manpower kept an especially close watch on creation of senior positions in departments. These frequently telegraphed to its officials a department's plans to expand a sub-function into a full-blown division or group. CSD had to approve all new posts at the rank of assistant secretary and above. However, excessive pressure for new positions from ministers and permanent secretaries could undermine this authority. In fact, one respondent believed that CSD yielded too frequently to such pressures.

Apart from control over creation of positions from assistant secretary up, CSD looked at the staffing implications of all cabinet proposals and government bills. The department housed, in another group, a division that usually simply monitored staff inspections carried out elsewhere in Whitehall. This unit provided analytic support to CSD's reviews of departments' staffing bids. Thus, CSD's expertise on staffing and the requirement that cabinet papers cover staffing implications combined to assure that departments at least ducked their heads when submitting material that had to pass under Manpower's surveillance.

The Manpower Group, under the 1981 reforms that abolished CSD, operated for some months as an autonomous part of the Treasury. However, its officials were absorbed by the expenditure review divisions of the Public Services Sector in the summer of 1982. Before the group's dissolution, two developments under Thatcher perhaps argued for its survival as a separate Treasury unit. First, the Thatcher government had stiffened the application of cash limits to staff and management costs. Most dramatically, this move involved the effort to link wage settlements in the public service to cash limits. In other words, the government set for the 1981 round of negotiations a specific percentage increase for the entire wage bill. Settlements beyond this ceiling resulted in staff cuts that, in turn, kept departmental bills for civil servants within assigned cash limits. Second, the government had set a specific target for reductions in the size of the bureaucracy that must be reached by 1984. Normally, as one respondent put it, only a 'Treasury saint' would spend much time focusing on the concerns of the Manpower Group. Its authority involved too small a proportion of the entire expenditure budget. The prime minister's target tended to concentrate Treasury minds on the sliver from the expenditure pie that usually escapes its close surveillance. Manpower's officials who had moved to the Treasury from the disbanded CSD argued that the prime minister's target required concentration of their expertise on complementing in a separate Treasury group. However, by the summer of 1982, the Treasury view that such specialization was a luxury won out.

Did the Old Arrangement Provide Personnel Management with Clout?
Personnel management includes here recruitment, training, pay policy
and negotiations, and co-ordination of these sectors with reference to
specific segments of the public service. Viewing this compass of activities,
we find that CSD involved itself somewhat more with service-wide
personnel management than does OPM in the United States. It did so
through three large units, each headed by deputy secretaries. These were
the Personnel Management, Recruitment, and Pay groups.

The Personnel Management Group consisted both of policy and service
units. Among the former, three divisions, headed by an under-secretary,
developed, respectively, overall personnel policy, policy related to the
integrity of the civil service (including security), and common services
(such as catering, health, and accommodation). Three divisions, directed
by another under-secretary, handled management of segments of the
public service. These divided into senior executives, supporting grades
(such as administrators and secretaries), and specialist groups (including
professionals and technicians). A seventh division, run by an assistant
secretary but reporting to an under-secretary, developed training policy
for the public service.

With respect to training, the department centred its involvement on
supervision of the Administration Trainees (ATs) Program and operation
of the Civil Service College. The former, now administered by MPO, still
serves as the gestation period for new recruits to the senior-executive
ranks who undertake a two-year development program designed to
prepare them for promotion to higher executive officer. Apart from the
ATs, departments manage career development for officials pretty much
on their own. However, the Civil Service College mounts courses geared
to service-wide training requirements.

The Recruitment Group, also now part of MPO, works in conjunction
with the Civil Service Commission. The CSC consists of five members.
Three of these, of whom two work full-time in recruitment, come from
the ranks of the career civil service. Officially, the CSC is not part of the
government. In 1977, the House of Commons Expenditure Committee
questioned the CSC's independence in view of the fact that all commissioners serving at the time were career officials.[6] The committee recommended that part-time outside commissioners should form a majority on a
reformed CSC. The Callaghan and Thatcher governments have met the
committee half-way by appointing two part-time members from the
private sector to the CSC.

The bulk of the CSC's work centres on competitions for vacancies on the
initial rungs of the top two levels of general-category positions. The first

of these rungs includes positions for administration trainees, economists, statisticians, inspectors of taxes, clerks for both the House of Commons and the House of Lords, and principals. The principals' competition takes in civil servants and outsiders who apply for admittance to the senior ranks at mid-career. For all competitions, certification occurs only after candidates have passed through a stringent set of examinations and personal interviews at the Civil Service Selection Board in London.

The second level of direct interest to the CSC takes in candidates for executive officer positions. Although university graduates currently take more than half the posts filled each year, the competition still requires only a minimum of two passes in A-level courses from students who have left the British equivalent of high school at the age of eighteen. Selection of candidates for these posts involves an interview as well as a written qualifying test. The CSC runs both the interviews and tests out of several regional offices. Notwithstanding this gesture toward decentralization, the CSC goes to great lengths to ensure that regional interviews follow uniform norms. The CSC runs other recruitment schemes, usually involving only an interview, for various specialist posts at or above the executive level. Departments, on authority of the CSC, undertake, on their own, recruitment to secretarial and clerical grades as well as junior scientific and technical positions.

The CSD Pay Group, now part of the Treasury, consisted of five divisions responsible for salary and superannuation issues relating to the various grades in the civil service. The group took the lead both in setting pay rates and negotiating settlements with unions. For example, its deputy secretary was the top career official involved in the annual face-to-face negotiations during the Civil Service National Whitley Council during the 1981 disputes over the government's pay limit.

Under the previous dispensation, the Personnel Management Group took up with departments and unions ways of co-ordinating policies on recruitment, training, pay, and a host of related issues. This comprised no small task. On the one hand, departments viewed literally the principle that officials below under-secretary belong entirely to them. On the other hand, unions have become much more formidable contenders for power over the civil service in the United Kingdom than they have in the United States. They include virtually every civil servant in the country. They also have organized themselves into a conglomerate, the Council of Civil Service Unions (COCSU), which constitutes the trade union side in the Civil Service National Whitley Council.

With reference to both departments and unions, CSD's authority over staffing and pay rates 'lubricated' negotiations. However, when one asked around among personnel managers in operational departments and union leaders, one developed the view that the two increasingly undertook discussions without CSD involvement. CSD, many believed, failed too often to muster the leverage to deliver the concessions it purported to have gotten from unions for departments or vice versa. In the words of one union official: 'Our great criticism of the CSD is that they can't make things happen. They can't get their way with departments. Departments regard them as a nuisance. They have their own problems. They have their own work to do. They want the CSD there if, of course, there is a problem like a redundancy or something of that kind ... So, the poor CSD is really in an impossible situation. I mean we're beating it away to do things all the time. Every time it goes to the department they just say, "Well you are just acting as a lapdog of the union" ... We have come to the conclusion that under the circumstances we will have to negotiate much more directly with departments ... especially the big ones which will not accept some kind of collective responsibility across the civil service for personnel management.'

The 1981 reforms resulted in the halving of the divisions operating under Personnel Management and the brigading of these under one deputy secretary responsible also for recruitment and training. More critically, Personnel Management operates out of MPO while jurisdiction over manpower and pay has moved to the Treasury. Events since these changes suggest that personnel management, as a central-agency function, has lost much of its former, albeit tenuous, leverage. This point becomes especially clear in the rationales provided by the Treasury for its stance during the 1982 round of pay negotiations. Dismissing the view that pay increases should be linked to specific standards of living, the Treasury asserts that increments should reflect conditions in the labour market.[7] Efficient civil service management requires 'that the levels of pay offered ... should be sufficient (but no more ...) to recruit, retain and motivate the staff needed to conduct public business in an official manner.'[8]

By following this principle, the Treasury sets aside key concepts in personnel management. The surfeit of applicants for civil service jobs justifies young officials and those at the bottom of their grades receiving no increase even if they fall behind the cost of living: 'The Government does not consider that the pay of civil servants, or any other group, should be determined by the needs of the individual. In general terms, pay is a matter for the market place, and social needs are the province of the social security system.'[9] The same market forces destroy the principle that government pay should compare fairly with that in the private sector:

'Comparisons with outside pay are one, but only one, factor in the labor market situation within which an employer must operate, and indeed for practical purposes can be regarded as subsumed in the general signals an employer receives from the market when he seeks to recruit staff or retain those he has.'[10]

The summation by the Treasury deputy secretary responsible for pay, as quoted by the *Guardian*, puts succinctly the current Treasury stance regarding the relation between pay and broader concerns in personnel management: 'Morale cannot be bought.' We should be quick to note that such Treasury views correspond perfectly with the inclinations of the department's current political master. However, one finds it difficult to conceive of a Civil Service Department pay unit this complacent about the near-total submission of elements essential to personnel management, such as adequate and comparable pay, to forces in the labour market.

Senior Personnel Management, or 'How to Run a Good "Religious Order" without Really Trying'

In the mid-sixteenth century, St Ignatius of Loyola looked at the disarray of the Roman Catholic clergy throughout Europe and decided to start a new religious order, the Jesuits. He followed a very simple principle: next to spiritual gifts, intelligence and discipline would serve as the most potent antidote to the corruption of the Roman Catholic church that had spawned the Reformation.

The bills of indictment against the élitism of the Jesuits are legion. Few, however, have taken the Jesuits to task for not knowing how to select, train, and manage their members. Four senior members of the order interview each candidate in private session. A psychologist performs an in-depth assessment of the applicants who pass through the interviews. The order assumes aspirants possess a high potential for sustained academic performance. University education serves as the backbone of its training program. Although the order gives credit for academic work done before admittance, every Jesuit must complete before ordination a multi-phased formation that usually takes between ten and thirteen years. Career advancement of ordained Jesuits follows equally rigorous lines. Regional superiors meet privately each year with each of their men; members of the order familiar with a candidate for a position of leadership submit evaluations of his strengths and weaknesses; the general of the Society of Jesus personally approves appointments to the leadership all the way down to and including the directors of major works and communities on the local level.

The senior civil service of the United Kingdom provides more than a few parallels to the Jesuit order. We even find a 'saint,' namely Sir Charles Trevelyan. In 1840, at age of thirty-two, Sir Charles became the civil service head of the Treasury, and set out on a career-long campaign to rid the British bureaucracy of patronage. Among his many accomplishments toward his goal, Sir Charles prepared with Sir Stafford Northcote the Trevelyan-Northcote report of 1854. This work set out a vision of a civil service which, in the words of Richard A. Chapman and J.R. Greenaway, would 'be free from corruption and patronage, recruited by open competition, divided by grades and centrally directed.'[11] Chapman and Greenaway, in fact, make much of the link between the qualities required of those seeking holy orders and those that had attracted Sir Charles to Oxford graduates as prime candidates for the civil service. In a rapidly secularizing England, educated young men sought careers outside the church that placed a similar premium on learning and dedication:

[Benjamin] Jowett [a tutor at Balliol College] argued strongly that Oxford graduates should have a chance of the Indian [Civil Service] appointments. This new opening for graduates 'would provide us what we have always wanted, a stimulus reaching far beyond the Fellowship, for those not intending to take [holy] Orders ...' Trevelyan was impressed by these arguments ... The Whig ministers ... [modified] their proposals for the Indian reform, so that the universities secured a virtual monopoly in providing applicants. Jowett and his allies in the educational world saw no reason why their proposals for the reform of the Indian Service could not equally well be applied to the British government departments and thus regenerate the universities, which, instead of being ivory towers, would in the future become pioneering centres for reform.[12]

When institutions turn to the brightest and best to perform tasks thought essential to their governance they will certainly encounter a difficult trade-off. St Ignatius's model for training Jesuits has served the institutional church well. However, its products have often been viewed as excessively intellectual and slow to respond to the needs of rank-and-file Catholics, most of whom never see the inside of a college preparatory or a university.

Sir Charles's dream of an efficient and scrupulously honest civil service certainly came true. However, many observers have registered alarm at Whitehall's lack of accountability either to Parliament or the people of the United Kingdom. Certainly, the Fulton Committee, which was appointed in 1966 to examine alternatives for modernization of the civil service, stands as clear indication that even a congenial mix of outsiders, some with experience in government, and four senior civil servants can serve up incisive critiques of the status quo. In its 1968 report the committee proposed reforms along several important lines. First, recruitment to the senior ranks should broaden its net to take in more candidates with degrees from universities other than Oxford or Cambridge. Relatedly, Whitehall should facilitate direct entry of individuals with experience in the private sector. Second, training should place greater emphasis on development of management skills. Third, an 'open structure' system should enable qualified specialists to move more easily into senior executive positions. How much of Fulton has actually come to pass?

One finds it hard to point a finger to the real culprit in perpetuation of biases in recruitment. University graduates who seek eligibility for the administration group pass through a three-phased examination. This includes a written qualifying test, a series of interviews and additional written exams at the Civil Service Selection Board (CSSB) in London, and an interview session before the Final Selection Board. In 1978, 93 per cent of those who reached the last stage passed it. The biases, thus, reveal themselves mostly in the qualifying test and in the exams and interviews at CSSB.

Although the qualifying exams are marked anonymously, the results clearly reflect biases toward graduates of independent and direct-grant college preparatories (in 1978, 37 per cent of those from such institutions who wrote passed, as opposed to 25 per cent of those from 'maintained' schools), Oxford and Cambridge (50 per cent v 22), and arts curricula (33 per cent v 23 and 29 per cent for, respectively, social sciences and science and technology).[13] The CSSB examinations and interviews appear to sustain much the same pattern: 61 and 56 per cent of former direct-grant and independent school pupils who advance to CSSB pass, while only 45 per cent of maintained school students succeed; 63 per cent of 'Oxbridge' graduates proceed to the Final Selection Board (FSB) after CSSB while only 42 per cent of other university candidates do so. However, nearly identical proportions of arts (50 per cent), social science (51), and natural science (50) graduates make it to the FSB.

These figures perhaps understate the impact of an Oxbridge background on candidates' rate of success in the qualifying test and at CSSB. A closer look reveals that the graduates of maintained schools improve their chances of passing the qualifying test from 21 to 46 per cent if they have gone on to Oxbridge. Comparable improvements from 26 to 58 and 26 to 50 per cent accrued to direct-grant and independent school pupils who ultimately graduated from Oxbridge.[14] For those who attended CSSB, the success rates for graduates of maintained, direct-grant, and independent schools who studied at Oxbridge improved as follows: from 40 per cent for those who did not go to Oxbridge to 57 for those who did, from 46 per cent to 76, and from 44 per cent to 63.

Any effort to root out biases in the examination process would require reforms much beyond those affecting the selection process per se. Oxford and Cambridge claim, often through closed scholarships, a disproportionate number of students with the highest grades at A level. Other universities have achieved excellence in many programs and often provide students comparable tutorials and lectures. However, they find it difficult to match other Oxbridge resources, especially libraries and social facilities.

Short of reforms of the university system, one who has observed a CSSB in operation can offer some recommendations for making it run in a way that is fairer to candidates. Doubtlessly Whitehall readers will wince at this. They generally believe that above all else CSSBs maintain the highest standards of fairness. Peter Kellner and Lord Crowther-Hunt describe the process in glowing terms: 'scrupulous honesty,' 'boards operate to a uniform standard,' and 'the care and compassion of the assessors.'[15] A recent report of a Civil Service Commission committee on recruitment of administration trainees lends authoritative weight to the view that CSSBs operate according to uniform standards of fairness. These derive from effective training and monitoring of board members: 'New assessors now normally have eight full days of training. They receive a day's general instruction in the theory and practice of the procedure and a second day being trained in interview techniques under the guidance of CSSB's chief psychologist; they are given two "dry runs" as board members, sitting in on "live" boards. Once the new assessor has begun boarding his performance is closely monitored and his first reports critically scrutinized.'[16]

I sat through a two-day CSSB in 1978. I did not come away with the impression that CSSB achieves an acceptable level of fairness. Although it includes several written exams during the two-day session, it also allows for a considerable amount of subjective appraisal. Candidates join in a group discussion at the outset, write a lengthy 'appreciation' of a policy issue, draft a letter responding to a representation to a minister, sit in on a moot committee studying a policy issue, take their turn at chairing the committee, and submit to private interviews with each board member. The board members include the chairman (usually a retired civil servant), a psychologist, and a principal. Board members assign scores to each candidate on no less than eleven personal qualities: intellectual penetration, intellectual fertility, judgment, written expression, oral expression, interpersonal relationships, influence with others, drive, determination, emotional stability, and maturity.

One candidate I observed began by performing as well as anyone in the group discussion. Some unsettling early returns came from one board member who found the person restless and blustery. The member brought in certain matters from the candidate's file. In the committee exercise, the candidate did reasonably well – placing third in a field of five. Although everyone agreed the candidate was probably the best chairperson, one member in particular wondered about the person's 'judgment' and whether the candidate would always be 'honest and upright.' Things took a turn for the worse in an interview between one member and the candidate that centred mainly on current issues. Neither participant in the exchange demonstrated sterling mastery of facts. The candidate disagreed with a number of points raised by the board member. This evoked a few embarrassed pauses on the part of the latter. The board member reported back to his colleagues using most pejorative terms: 'flippant,' 'idiot grin on his face,' 'total lack of knowledge of the economy,' 'flippant, idiot jokes and asides.' The committee did not effectively counter this rather one-sided assessment. Indeed, it frequently slipped into similar, though not bitter, subjective discourse regarding all five candidates. Although one should avoid generalizations from a sample of one, this committee's performance suggested to me that CSSB operates much less professionally than the literature normally suggests.

The Civil Service College plays a vital role in providing career-development training for individuals who pass through CSSB and FSB and enter the administration group. First, it commands a total of nineteen weeks of the four to six years before administration trainees become principals. For grades beyond administration trainee, the college offers a number of courses and seminars. It tailors these to current developmental needs registered by departments. Even at the level of under-secretary, about half the entire complement will have taken one of the six three-day seminars offered annually at the college. In general, though, the college has not fulfilled the Fulton Committee's expectations for it. Its courses have tended to follow the classic lines of public administration and machinery of government, to impart dutifully some cognate skills – such as statistics and computers – and to avoid more venturesome course offerings in the field of public policy analysis. In the words of one respondent: 'We are very interested in policy studies. For various historical reasons though, we are doing relatively little in that kind of direction. We do handle the formulation and implementation of policy very frequently in our courses. We don't, at the moment, make very much use of a formal policy analysis framework. This is partly because there is an anti-theoretical, anti-academic bias in the British civil service. In the past our experience has been that theoretically based approaches go down rather badly.'

A secretariat within MPO's Personnel Management Group provides, among other functions, support for development and selection of candidates for the 'open structure.' This umbrella category includes under-, deputy, and permanent secretaries. All recommendations for promotion to the latter two levels must receive the personal approval of the prime minister. The joint head of the home civil service (i.e., the secretary of the cabinet) chairs a committee on senior appointments selection that discusses candidates for vacancies. This body consists as well of the permanent secretary of the Treasury, the second permanent secretary of MPO, and a changeable assortment of other permanent secretaries. Once the committee decides upon nominees, the secretary of the cabinet will have the permanent secretary of the department in question clear the recommendation with his minister. Departments promote their own individuals to assistant and under-secretary positions. However, MPO must review the dozen or so assistant secretary appointments recommended in a given year for officials who have not turned thirty-five. Officials below the age of thirty-two cannot be considered for a post as assistant secretary.

Apart from its role in promotions, MPO monitors the career progress of officials as far down as principal. Each year, the second permanent secretary of MPO visits permanent secretaries in other departments to discuss the progress of their complement in the senior ranks. These visits focus on under-secretaries with potential for deputy secretary as well as deputy secretaries with promise of being permanent secretaries. However, MPO derives from these visits and other work with departments an inventory of high-flyers at other levels. The walls on the room next to the assistant secretary responsible for this function display computer cards containing vital data on the principals and assistant secretaries deemed potential deputy secretaries and the under-secretaries considered prospects for permanent secretary.

CANADA

Three departments contend for control of personnel policy in Canada. The Privy Council Office (PCO) takes the clear lead in recommending to the prime minister nominees for deputy minister and assistant deputy minister. It also takes a very keen interest in policy concerning management of senior personnel at lower levels. The Treasury Board Secretariat (TBS) maintains, by virtue of the Financial Administration Act of 1970, statutory authority for personnel management. This includes responsibility for allocating person-years and for public servants' terms and conditions of employment. However, events have eroded the significance of TBS's authority. Finally, the Public Service Commission (PSC) concentrates its role on operational functions such as staffing, training, and handling appeals.

The involvement of three agencies in this policy sector presents myriad problems. In fact, the 1979 reports of both the Royal Commission on Financial Management and Accountability (Lambert) and the Special Committee on the Review of Personnel Management and the Merit Principle (D'Avignon) strongly emphasized the need for personnel management to operate under a single roof. Currently, internecine struggles hamper efforts toward coordination in many areas, such as senior appointments, where the stakes are high. Meanwhile, PCO, TBS, and PSC tend to neglect fields of personnel policy such as training, where returns are long in coming.

Whither Person-Years?
While writing *The Superbureaucrats* in the late 1970s, George Szablowski and I had no difficulty locating authority over staffing levels in the various departments and agencies of the Canadian public service. At that time, the estimates listed, along with the dollar resources allocated to departments, the human resources assigned to accomplish their programmatic objectives. The Program Branch of TBS advised the cabinet committee responsible for expenditure control, the Treasury Board, on the person-years necessary to carry out departments' objectives. In performing this function, it drew upon the considerable expertise of the Personnel Policy Branch of TBS.

Under the arrangement described in *The Superbureaucrats* ministers and TBS officials alike found themselves in a strong position for co-ordinating priorities in the allocation of physical and human resources. This situation does not hold today. Since late 1978, effective authority over the dollar value of expenditure programs has largely slipped from the aegis of the Treasury Board. Most significant here, two cabinet committees with their own ministries of state, namely economic and regional development and social development, control the expenditure envelopes covering the respective policy fields. Further a PCO secretariat takes the lead in advising the foreign and defence policy committee of the cabinet on distribution of resources within the two envelopes devoted to this sector. Thus, the Program Branch of TBS finds its advisory role towards the Treasury Board limited to two residual envelopes, Parliament and services to government. For all other envelopes, the branch and Treasury Board ministers limit themselves to ascertaining what level of resources, physical and human, will deliver most efficiently the programs and policies chosen by cabinet policy committees.[17] As we will see, this new arrangement brings with it some serious consequences for the viability of TBS's role in personnel management.

Many Chefs, One Stew
Looking at the development and implementation of personnel policy in Canada, we come across an extremely segmented sector of activity. The Personnel Policy Branch of TBS has the greatest amount of weight in matters relating to personnel management. Even under the current arrangement, the Treasury Board serves as the employer of Canada's public servants. Thus, the Personnel Policy Branch contains most divisions for setting policy on personnel. However, matters relating to the senior executives and deputy ministers provide a major exception.

In 1981, the Personnel Policy Branch operated under a deputy secretary. Four assistant secretaries managed the branch divisions. The first of these units, General Personnel Management, handled a number of policy issues relating to the contractual arrangements between the Treasury Board and government employees. These include pensions and benefits, policies concerning management, the armed services and the Royal Canadian Mounted Police, general human resources policy, occupational health and safety, and the terms and conditions of employment in the public service. Another division, Developmental Personnel Policies and Activities, contains groups considering policies toward women, indigenous people, and the handicapped as public service employees.

The General Personnel Management and Developmental Personnel Policies and Activities divisions rely heavily on their ability to sell themselves as consultants in personnel policy. In large part, they must convince deputy ministers and their departments of the need to adopt various changes in public service management. As one respondent put it, this task often involves both clarification of policies and forbearance: 'We simply continue to enunciate the policy and require the departments to make reports. They co-operate with what is reasonable. We can't fire deputy ministers, but we can get compliance through reasonableness.'

However, the diminution of the Treasury Board's control of resources will certainly make quiet persuasion more difficult. This conclusion follows from the remarks of one respondent in 1976. He stressed the clear advantages to having personnel policy operate in-house with control of the purse strings: 'There is a lot more authority attributed by others to our function than we have in fact. We have implicit functions which stem from the purse control, that is, what the Program Branch is most involved in, which really are overblown by others. That's why we are called in so much by other departments. We know how one gets authority and resources to do something in the personnel field. It's a culture we have here at TBS, and people in departments have to know about it to get things done. This is where the trade-off comes. They listen to us because they know that they have to work with us.'

One clear prerogative of the Treasury Board – negotiations with various public service unions and the terms of contracts – comes under the Staff Relations and Compensation Division. Several units here staff collective bargaining exercises. As well, a number of groups provide analyses of pay and benefits, including studies of compensation for employees in comparable jobs in the private sector to those of various categories of public servants.

Normally, the statutory position of the Treasury Board as the employer of the public service provides the Staff Relations and Compensation Division more leverage with both departments and unions than other units in the Personnel Policy Branch enjoy. However, the spectre of the Privy Council Office can loom large in this field. Pierre Trudeau has always viewed his responsibilities toward the public service very widely. Indeed, in 1970 he incensed the president of the Treasury Board, C.M. Drury, by forming, without his knowledge, a cabinet committee to settle a postal strike. Subsequently, both the cabinet and PCO have pursued more openly their special interest in negotiations between the Treasury Board and public service unions. This applies especially in situations that raise threats of or actually lead to the interruption of key government services. After operating with ad hoc committees through most of the 1970s, the prime minister has established standing cabinet committees on labour relations and the public service. Likewise, PCO has recently formalized the attention given to emergencies brought on by strikes.

In 1976, Emergency Planning came under the same PCO assistant secretary who handled security and intelligence. At the same time, an assistant secretary for planning projects worked to assist the priorities and planning committee of the cabinet in studying long-range trends in policy issues. As often happens with the relatively slack resources of futuristic shops, Planning Projects increasingly staffed ad hoc cabinet committees working on disputes in the public service. After 1979, its assistant secretary, W.B. Snarr, shed totally his responsibilities for long-range issues. While still an officer of PCO, he also heads a full-fledged offshoot, Emergency Planning Canada, with eight directors. This agency clearly gives the prime minister the organizational machinery necessary to eclipse somewhat the Treasury Board's authority when labour disputes begin to threaten provision of services deemed essential.

The Organization and Classification Division of TBS centres its activities on the assignment of titles and grades to officials within departments. Although PCO takes a strong interest in the resource implications of major reorganizations and reclassifications, it leaves TBS with many of the issues concerning the distribution of positions and titles within departments. At the lower levels, TBS defines broad policies that departments are left to implement. At the senior levels, it takes a more active role. Recently, officials under this division spearheaded a major reform of the executive grades of the public service so that senior managers not belonging to the top categories, EX1-5 and DM1-3, come under a single classification. Previously, the Treasury Board dealt with policies affecting middle-level executives through fifty-five individual occupational groups and categories.

The Official Languages Branch operates under yet another TBS deputy secretary. It ensures that the Official Languages Act and the subsequent parliamentary resolutions are adequately implemented. It also develops revisions in bilingualism programs designed to better fulfil the objectives of the act. The responsibility for policy on official languages in the public service at one time resided in the Department of the Secretary of State. This ministry assumes overall authority for furthering bilingualism and biculturalism in Canada. However, enforcement of these policies within the public service required more clout than the department had with the rest of the bureaucracy. The Treasury Board, as the employer of public servants, possessed the type of authority the policies needed.

The functions that operate out of the Public Service Commission (PSC), unlike those of TBS's Official Languages Branch, lack profile. PSC remains, in theory, an independent body responsible for staff recruitment, development, and assignment, and all appeals concerning hiring and promotion. In practice, the commission simply puts into operation policies set by the Treasury Board.[18] This arrangement, in the view of the 1979 report of the Lambert commission, sets up staffing and training functions for neglect because they frequently fall between two stools.[19]

Regarding matters related to classification of positions and compensation, the lines of authority for personnel matters derive clearly from the

Treasury Board. Further, TBS administers these activities directly. However, policies concerning staffing and training originate partially from PSC. Further, PSC bears almost complete responsibility for implementation. The Lambert commission therefore recommended that an omnibus body, the Personnel Management Secretariat, encompass all policy and implementation functions currently performed by TBS and PSC. A refashioned PSC would continue to handle all appeals and intensify its auditing functions. These latter would result in PSC's reporting directly to Parliament on departments' adherence to the merit principle. To date, the government has failed to act more than cosmetically upon these recommendations.

How Opening the Senior Levels to Creativity Will Lead to Stagnation
When Trudeau became prime minister in 1968 he set as one of his main objectives increasing creativity in the public service and moved on two fronts. First, he took a direct interest in potential deputy ministers. Second, he drew closer to himself policies on recruitment and promotion at other ranks. Through his involvement, Trudeau set the wheels in motion for unprecedented advancement of young, exceptionally bright, and exceedingly well-educated public servants.

The Superbureaucrats reports very clear evidence that a radical transformation of the senior ranks had already occurred by 1976.[20] The study of ninety-two of the top officials in Canada's central agencies found recruitment biases apparent as recently as the late 1960s had not stood up to the influx of new blood. The ranks of senior central agents contained considerably more French-Canadians, members of ethnic groups, Catholics, Jews, westerners, individuals who did not take their first degree at the most prestigious universities (Toronto, Queen's, and McGill), and the offspring of breadwinners who had not completed high school and/or had worked most of their lives in clerical or blue-collar jobs, than had been the case a few years earlier.

Trudeau's initiatives appeared, in the optimism of an expansionary era, as great strides toward energizing the bureaucracy and making it more responsive to the public. In fact, they produced unforeseen side-effects that may well have made matters worse than they were before Trudeau. First, if changes in the recruitment and promotion of senior officials have reduced socio-economic élitism, they have done so by replacing it with an intelligentsia. Campbell and Szablowski found that the clearest vehicle for upward mobility now is graduate and professional education. Expertise acquired through advanced study accounts in very large part for the decreased relevance of socio-economic distinctions.

The emergence of an intelligentsia in the public service poses very serious problems. We find no more eloquent spokesman for this view than Michael Pitfield, who was clerk of the Privy Council, secretary of the cabinet, and principal architect of Trudeau's reforms. As early as 1977, Pitfield indicated in a public lecture the degree to which recruitment with a heavy premium on expertise was not producing officials with satisfactory aptitudes and skills for public service per se:

The law does not provide the analytic competence necessary to evaluate programs and develop more effective alternatives. Economics teaches few political skills and little about the structure of government. Neither one nor the other provides exposure to managerial skills ... The business graduate came with administrative and problem-solving skills, and a smattering of economics, that made him very useful to government. What he did not have and still lacks, of course, is much of a base in the government systems ... As regards value judgements, where the private sector manager makes his decision with a degree of privacy and according to a comparatively well-ordered set of values, the critical choices that face the public sector manager involve difficult questions of accountability, of choices among competing values, and of the ethical principles that should govern unprecedented solutions.[21]

With this as background, the reader should not find it surprising that Campbell and Szablowski report that Canadian central agents, in comparison to senior public servants in other Western democracies, reveal career orientations much more attuned to personal advancement and use of expertise than to public service.[22]

The second major side-effect has only recently been documented. In a monograph titled *No Where to Go*, Nicole S. Morgan has produced alarming evidence of impending stagnation in the senior ranks.[23] Recruits who entered the public service during the 'Trudeau' influx have created a huge career bubble that has only begun working its way through the system. This bubble forms a disproportionately large segment of the senior ranks. Further, the majority of officials in it have risen prematurely to the highest grades. As a result, a generation of public servants used to rapid promotion now faces the prospect of very little career advancement. In addition, as has happened in new Canadian universities with large numbers of tenured faculty, the relatively small supply of vacancies created by mandatory retirements will most certainly close off careers to many highly capable aspirants in the next generation. Barring radical adjustments, stagnation will seize the senior ranks of the public service.

In view of such deficiencies in management of senior personnel through the last decade, one might expect immense efforts toward improvement of the system. In fact, no dramatic moves have materialized. The absence of decisive action derives in large part from the fragmentation of authority over senior personnel, especially in the development of policies concerning the initial five rungs of the senior bureaucracy. These take in EX1-5s, officials making from $43,300 to $72,300 as of 1 April 1981. Here a committee consisting of representatives from the Privy Council Office, the Treasury Board Secretariat, and the Public Service Commission develops policies governing the EX grades. For instance, Audrey Doerr attributes to the committee responsibility for allowing from 1971 to 1975 annual growth rates in EX positions ranging between 11 and 26 per cent.[24]

Joint PCO-TBS-PSC activities have met with mixed results. On the one hand, the three have come to terms over creation of an integrated management category for officials who have not yet risen to the EX ranks. On the other hand, some long-standing ventures have borne little fruit. Here the lack of response to Pitfield's concern that senior executives receive adequate preparation for careers in the public service provides an example of one field where little movement has occurred.

Pitfield was basing his remarks on hard data. At the time of his talk, an interdepartmental committee had just presented similar conclusions to his based on a study of training in preparation for promotion to senior positions.[25] The committee found that many officials are ill prepared for the senior ranks and placed the blame on the inadequacies of departments' in-house training, including insufficient willingness on the part of managers to assume responsibility for training their subordinates, a low level of use of available courses, and the inadequacy of central-agency stimulus toward service-wide co-ordination of training. However, the committee rejected one proposed solution (already placed before the cabinet three times in the early 1970s), that a National School of Public Policy and Administration (NSPPA) be established to strengthen training for prospective senior executives. It believed that such a move would be élitist. Since 1977, PCO, TBS, and PSC have not found a middle ground between the current disarray and the NSPPA proposal. Even the modest central training facilities of PSC have drawn such low enrolments that its Staff Development Branch has recorded successive deficits.

To complete this discussion, we should touch upon two realms of senior personnel management that operate very close to the centre. The first concerns selection and placement of deputy ministers and assistant deputy ministers. These appointments are made by the governor-general-in-council. The prime minister maintains ultimate authority over assignments to these positions. The Committee on Senior Officials (COSO) advises him both on specific choices and general policy matters.

The reader should not conclude too quickly that COSO parallels closely the United Kingdom's Senior Appointments Selection Committee (SASC) discussed above. First, the three most recent chairmen of COSO, Michael Pitfield, Marcel Massé, and Gordon Smith – none of whom have turned forty-five – all embody the high-flying character of the senior ranks of the Canadian public service. Second, the chairman of SASC, as the joint head of the British home civil service, serves as dean of the select few who, at the twilight of careers in public service encompassing all or most of their working life, have risen to the top of the mandarinate. Third, the framers of COSO have taken care to admit to it many more high-flyers than seasoned bureaucrats.[26] All this fits very much into Trudeau's view of COSO's work. The prime minister has throughout his years in office felt no qualms about reaching far down in the senior ranks to get a particularly promising individual with the right perspective on a fast track to becoming a deputy minister. Most of the current deputy ministers owe their advancement to Trudeau's hand in their careers.

CONCLUSION

We have looked in this chapter at the various ways in which central agencies in the United States, the United Kingdom, and Canada involve themselves in personnel management. In all three systems, officials working within the field have encountered difficulties in efforts toward full-fledged membership in the central-agency community. In each case, success hinges to a great degree on control over distribution of all or part of human resources.

In the United States, personnel management found an institutionally distinct place among central agencies as recently as 1979 when Jimmy Carter's reforms in the civil service led to creation of the Office of Personnel Management. OPM has met with only partial success. The Office of Management and Budget still maintains control over staffing in departments and agencies. As a result, OPM lacks leverage in instituting programs that would focus attention on improvements in personnel management. By way of exception, OPM does approve creation of Senior Executive Service positions throughout the public service. As well, it must certify new appointments to SES. In the exercise of these powers, OPM has encountered stiff resistance from departments and agencies. Finally, presidents' control over some 2,000 senior political appointments leads to centralized management of this sector of the public service in the White House. None the less, casual observers tend to make too much of the power accruing to presidents through political appointments. Career officials in the United States usually enjoy much longer tenure, both in their departments and posts within them, than do their opposite numbers in Britain and Canada. They become especially adept at 'socializing' political appointees into 'native' mores.

Although observers tend to view British management as a neglected field, it operated, until abolition of the Civil Service Department, with much greater effect than is the case in the United States. The Civil Service Department's delegated authority over expenditure for staff and personnel substitutes provided it the type of leverage OPM desperately desires. Respondents both within and outside CSD still complained that it did not always succeed at knocking departments' and unions' heads together. In comparative terms, however, CSD officials accomplished much more than their American and Canadian opposite numbers. Somewhat independently, CSD housed the long-centralized control of recruitment and career development of senior executives. Although the system is undoubtedly élitist, it otherwise has accomplished as much standardization in management of senior personnel as attainable under cabinet government. Reforms directed against élitism hold out little promise of effect unless the British both democratize their university system and change their attitudes toward professional and technical academic fields. We have noted that the severing in 1981 of the direct link between personnel management, recruitment, and training and pay and complementing will greatly harm the viability of the former activities as functions of the central agencies. In the new Management and Personnel Office, personnel management will probably suffer the most. The ethos behind it has failed to win the relatively wide and historic Whitehall acceptance of co-ordination by central agencies that recruitment and training have enjoyed.

Canada has recently dismantled an arrangement whereby the Treasury Board Secretariat maintained a leading role in expenditure budgeting and in management and personnel policy. TBS has lost its leading role for all but the technical aspects of expenditure budgeting. This leaves its officials working in the personnel field with greatly diminished leverage. Regarding senior personnel management, the Privy Council Office has crowded TBS out of development of policy and selection of assistant deputy ministers and deputy ministers. Under Trudeau, the latter PCO involvement has resulted in politicization of the uppermost ranks of the public service. The more PCO has stressed personal advice to the prime minister over its function as a cabinet secretariat, the more its officials with a voice in the selection of senior personnel have favoured candidates with proven loyalty to Pierre Trudeau.

PART FOUR

Central agents are people too

Introduction

So far this book has concentrated on the operation of central agencies in the three countries as it relates to authority in the respective systems and the role preferences of individual chief executives. It has relied heavily on central agents' accounts to describe and assess what they and their institutions do. However, it has only inferred the degree to which officials' modes of operating and their personal attitudes and backgrounds set the stage for the operation of central agencies.

Any chief executives who ignored the probable behaviour and qualities of the people upon whom they rely for advice and assistance would most certainly set themselves up for some jarring experiences. By way of example, Jimmy Carter made a major error by bringing in as his top advisers too many Georgians and youthful Democrats whose only real credentials stemmed from key roles in an exceedingly successful but somewhat illusory presidential campaign. In contrast, Margaret Thatcher knew very well that she could not simply wish her brand of monetarist economics on HM Treasury. Thus, she gave her Treasury ministers three highly competent political aides, appointed a committed monetarist – Terry Burns – as the government's chief economic adviser, and brought to No. 10, at great expense, Alan Walters, a prominent monetarist academic. Joe Clark's case contrasts sharply with Mrs Thatcher's. Notwithstanding campaign rhetoric about the need to depoliticize Canada's mandarins, Clark demanded the resignation only of Michael Pitfield and provoked the resignation of only two others – Bill Hood and Tommy Shoyama. He therefore failed to provide even the illusion of a change of guard.

This part looks behind institutional differences and executive leadership to the types of persons who run central agencies. Chapter 11 will examine three issues. First, where do respondents locate themselves and their units in terms of various roles and functions? Second, how do they view and use the networks through which things get done in their capital? What do they report about inner circles, cabinet and interdepartmental committees, and interactions within the policy arena? Third, what do they tell us about relations with those outside the executive-bureaucratic community? Do they interact with legislators, tap outside sources for advice and information, and come in contact with interest groups? Chapter 12 will look at two issues. First, how do their careers compare? How do they view accountability, what has motivated their careers, and what do their career routes look like? Second, what do our central agents recount about their formative years and current involvement in society generally? What do they tell us about the families in which they grew up and the education they received?

Although Appendix I presents details regarding the selection of respondents for this study, the quantitative nature of the analyses in this part calls for some explanation to assist the reader. Strictly speaking, none of the national groups represents a sample of their central agency cohort. The Canadian segment consists of 92 of 102 senior executives in central agencies at the time of the interviews (1976) and, therefore, nearly comprises the whole. Gatekeepers in the British public service limited my interviews there to 41 officials. Confronted by this limit, I selected respondents on the basis of my desire to cover all major functional areas rather than obtain a sample. In the United States, I applied this same principle. The sheer size of the American cohort, more than 1,000 officials, might have made a manageable sample, 132 respondents, unrepresentative in respect to function. As is clear in Appendix I, the three respondent groups provide reasonably good cross-sections both of functional areas *and* placement in organizational hierarchies. Some readers might register qualms about the use of chi-square, a test of statistical significance, when the analysis does not, again strictly speaking, compare samples. With the efforts to make the groups representative, the data derive from the closest material to a sample obtainable under the circumstances. Chi-square, as a test of significance, provides an 'amber light' that warns us away from making a great deal of cross-national differences that might bear only tenuous importance in statistical terms.

The analysis will follow two straightforward foci. It will look first at cross-national differences in all the factors mentioned above. In each case, it will make a special effort to relate differences that appear between central agents in our three countries and what we have already discussed about the operation of their institutions. Second, the analysis will make use of the unique character of the US segment. Here we find three types of central agents. Sixty-nine career officials entered public service by virtue of the merit principle and rose gradually through the ranks to their current positions; twenty-five politicos held partisan appointments awarded on the basis of performance in the Carter campaign; and thirty-eight 'amphibians' received partisan posts on the grounds of expertise in a subject and/or the right political coloration – even if their involvement in the campaign was peripheral or nonexistent.[1]

11

Modes of operating

Generally speaking, one finds in the communities that make up central agencies a keen sense of being 'where the action is.' However, central agents in the three countries differ somewhat in their specific roles and the arenas in which these become manifest. This becomes clear as we examine our respondents' perceptions of roles, including both their views of their own work and their views of the work of their agency; their views of policy arenas, including their ability to identify inner circles, use networks, and gain access to cabinet committees and to interdepartmental committees; and their relations with legislators and groups outside the executive-bureaucratic community who, none the less, have policy concerns.

ROLE PERCEPTIONS

The Views of Their Own Work
The interviews dwelt at length on central agents' descriptions of their roles. With reference to the three umbrella functions that serve as the foci for parts I–III: what claims do they make for roles in setting priorities within a mandate or administration and making decisions in accordance with these, in co-ordinating economic and fiscal policy, and in determining policy for the allocation and management of human and physical resources? As well, within these wider categories, what sub-functions do they emphasize? Second, how do they characterize the nature of their work? Do they make policy, serve as managers or implementors, and/or try to keep lines of communication open? Third, what compass does their work take? Does it involve all, several aspects of, or just a particular segment of their agency's authority?

TABLE 11.1

Percentage of respondents in each country who describe their responsibilities with reference to central-agency functions

Function	United States (career, amphibians, politicos) $N = 132$ (69, 38, 25)	United Kingdom $N = 41$	Canada $N = 92$	Significance
Priorities/substantive	52 (39, 50, 92)[a]	49	55	
Strategic planning	13 (5, 11, 36)[a]	24	36	a
Substantive policy priorities	45 (32, 42, 84)[a]	49	38	
Intergovernmental affairs	8 (7, 8, 8)	2	12	
Economic/fiscal	39 (46, 47, 8)[b]	39	37	
Tax	8 (7, 13, 0)	5	7	
Fiscal	14 (20, 8, 8)	10	17	
Macro	16 (17, 21, 4)	29	20	
Sectoral	6 (3, 16, 0)[c]	7	5	
International	15 (22, 11, 4)	20	9	
Allocation/management	49 (57, 42, 36)	44	64	c
Expenditure budgeting	24 (33, 13, 12)[c]	17	22	
Organizational structure	12 (10, 16, 12)	5	10	
Evaluation of effectiveness and efficiency	27 (29, 34, 12)	17	33	
Personnel policy	9 (15, 5, 0)	17	23	c
Senior executive policy	6 (3, 8, 12)	7	12	
Administrative policy	0.8 (1, 0, 0)	10	12	a

a Chi-square significant at 0.001 level
b Chi-square significant at 0.01 level
c Chi-square significant at 0.05 level

Perceptions of roles as related to the core functions: Keeping in mind that respondents could claim responsibilities toward more than one umbrella function, we find that between 49 and 55 per cent in the three countries described roles that involved priorities and major policy decisions (see Table 11.1). An even narrower range of cross-national differences occurs with reference to economic and fiscal policy. Here between 37 and 39 per cent of respondents in each country report involvement in the function. Only the proportions in each country registering roles in policies on the allocation and management of resources differ significantly. While 49 and 44 per cent of, respectively, American and British respondents recounted involvement in this field, a much larger 64 per cent of Canadian central agents said they worked to some degree in this sector.

The relatively large Canadian proportion reflects the amount of counter-vaillance present in the operation of this function as discussed in part III.

We come across a number of interesting findings when we look at sub-functions of the umbrella categories. Under priorities and substantive policies, the 36 per cent of Canadian respondents working on priorities *exceeds* the comparable figures for Britain and the United States by 12 and 23 per cent respectively. The Canadian-British difference probably results from the very strong emphasis given by Pierre Trudeau to priorities exercises. The large gap between the United States and the others suggests that presidential setting of priorities requires fewer personnel than under the cabinet-style executive system. With reference to the sub-functions of economic and fiscal policy, no significant cross-national differences appear. However, figures for allocation and management of resources reveal that, under the six sub-functions, the Canadian sample yields the highest proportion of respondents associating with four. These results reinforce the observation that the allocation-management umbrella function operates under extreme countervaillance in Canada.

A number of clear differences emerge from comparisons of accounts of their work by US career officials, amphibians, and politicos. Politicos claim roles in both setting priorities and making major decisions exceeding those of both career officials and amphibians. Amphibians, however, do report involvement in these roles somewhat more than career officials do. Such results echo, although not univocally, the traditional distinction in American bureaucracy between policy and administration. A ghetto effect might operate here as well. For instance, the highly political character of the White House probably imparts a keen sense of being 'movers and shakers.'[1]

Such speculation finds some support in the proportions found under sub-categories of the co-ordination of economic and fiscal policy and the allocation and management of resources. With the exception of policy concerning senior executives, the proportions of politicos describing roles fall short of those for career officials and amphibians. By way of contrast, the amphibians lead both career officials and politicos by larger margins in tax policy, macroeconomic policy, and sectoral economics. Under allocation and management, amphibians repeat their relatively strong performance in two fields, namely policy on organizational structures and evaluation of effectiveness and efficiency. Whereas politicos eschew the nuts and bolts of the economics-fiscal and allocation-management fields, amphibians work effectively at various pressure points.

The considerably greater percentage of career officials than *both* amphibians and politicos (33 *v* 13 and 12, respectively) involved in review of expenditure budgets reflects both institutional and leadership factors. With regard to the former, it corresponds with the tradition whereby OMB considers the budget process a career domain. In view of Carter's strong interest in the expenditure budget, it reveals as well how resilient OMB tradition can be. Here Carter's practice of admitting senior career officials to his budget review sessions takes on new significance. Putting aside the issue of whether he spent too much of his time on the budget, he quite naturally gravitated to career people because they, as one respondent noted, knew where all the skeletons are buried.

The nature of their tasks: As one reads respondents' interview transcripts, one sees that officials in our three countries describe the way in which they carry out their tasks in terms of three operating styles. As two variants of policy-making, respondents told of facilitating decisions and advising political authorities. In efforts to ensure that policies came into effect and achieved desired objectives, many central agents often involved themselves in monitoring policy implementation. Many, as well, spent time managing their own bureaucratic units. By virtue of their strategic location in the policy process, our respondents, finally, might have stressed their efforts toward keeping lines of communication open with those inside and/or outside the executive-bureaucratic community.

Cross-nationally, our respondents overwhelmingly describe their work at least partially in terms of functions relating to making policy (see Table 11.2). As well, respondents in all three countries tend somewhat more to say they give advice than to report that they facilitate decisions. However, more than half of British central agents describe their work in terms of facilitation while fully 90 per cent say they advise. It appears that the highly integrated bureaucratic community in the United Kingdom makes less of the distinction between keeping the policy-making process going and advising political authorities. With reference to management and implementation, both the American and Canadian samples produce 36 per cent of respondents who say they fulfil such tasks. Only 24 per cent of British respondents do so. The British case differs sharply when we look at respondents' views of communication. Officials there fall quite significantly behind those in the United States and Canada, especially in that very few discussed communication with outsiders while elaborating their roles.

The proportions within the three US groups fit reasonably well what one might expect. Fifty-six percent of politicos style themselves *policy*

TABLE 11.2
Respondents' styles as indicated by the ways in which they describe their work

Style	United States (career, amphibians, politicos) $N = 132$ (69, 38, 25)	United Kingdom $N = 41$	Canada $N = 92$	Significance
Policy	96 (97, 95, 96)	100	91	
Policy facilitator	41 (38, 34, 56)	56	37	
Policy adviser	75 (75, 82, 64)	90	67	c
Manager, Implementor	36 (36, 40, 28)	24	36	
Manager	28 (32, 26, 16)	22	33	
Implementor	10 (6, 16, 12)	2	8	
Communicator	31 (23, 34, 48)	12	38	c
Inside	18 (17, 28, 8)	2	27	b
Outside (for United States, includes those outside executive branch)	21 (12, 24, 44)[b]	12	16	

For b and c see notes to Table 11.1.

facilitators while only 34 and 38 per cent of amphibians and career officials, respectively, do so. However, both the latter groups provide more respondents who see themselves as policy advisers. Further, we can readily attribute the mere 16 per cent of politicos who say they 'manage' to the fact that few of them operate large bureaucratic units. As well, the strong tendency of politicos to say they communicate with outsiders reflects these officials' important partisan responsibilities.

Roles in relation to agencies' mandates: In examining respondents' descriptions of their work, we may look at the horizons within which they viewed their roles. Most officials dwelt on one very specific aspect of their central agency's mandate. Many touched upon several such functions. Some even portrayed a situation whereby they became involved in matters encompassing the entire mandate of their agency. The results (see Table 11.3) reveal that over half of US and Canadian respondents centred discussion of their roles to some degree within the bounds of a specific agency function. Also in those two countries, 33 and 37 per cent, respectively, venture into several specific matters taken up by their agency. Very small proportions in each sample see their roles as touching upon the entire mandate of their agency. In contrast, 32 and 41 per cent of British respondents say their work touched on all and/or focused on several aspects of their agency's work. Such figures probably derive from the

TABLE 11.3
Portion of agency's mandate that respondent claims responsibility for

Portion	United States (career, amphibians, politicos) N = 132 (69, 38, 25)	United Kingdom N = 41	Canada N = 92	Significance
Entire	6 (1, 5, 20)[b]	32	14	a
Several aspects	33 (22, 47, 44)[c]	41	41	
One aspect	64 (80, 50, 40)[b]	34	66	b

For a, b, and c see notes to Table 11.1.

tightly knit character of British central agencies. For instance, we noted in chapter 6 the much more extensive efforts to co-ordinate policy in HM Treasury than found either in the US Department of the Treasury or the Canadian Department of Finance.

One might speculate that politicos and amphibians would view their roles within a broader compass than do career officials. The former two must safeguard the positions of the administration on a host of issues while the latter trade more on their grasp of more specific matters. Apart from the fact that four times as many politicos as amphibians see their work as taking in the entire mandate of their agency, the data give very strong support to our expectation.

Views of Their Agency
A series of questions shifted respondents' focus from their own roles to those of their agencies. We may view their responses from two standpoints. First, we may look at their descriptions of what their agencies do. Second, we may examine their evaluations of how well their agencies perform their roles.

Descriptions of agencies' roles: Analysis of respondents' descriptions of their agency's roles focused on three issues, itemized in Table 11.4. First, how do they view these roles in relation to our three core functions? Second, what types of activities do they believe their agency stresses as it carries out its responsibilities? Third, to which political and bureaucratic authorities do they refer in discussing their agency's work?

An examination of the core functions stressed by officials produces one significant result. Canadian central agents tend much more than the Americans or the British to view their agency as working to some degree in setting priorities and making major decisions in accordance with these. This result highlights the exceptional profiles all Canadian central agencies give to mapping out goals for a government's mandate and

TABLE 11.4
Characterizations of the role of central agencies in government

Characterizations	United States (career, amphibians, politicos) $N = 132$ (69, 38, 25)	United Kingdom $N = 41$	Canada $N = 92$	Significance
Role described in relation to core functions				
Priorities/substantive	58 (48, 55, 88)[b]	49	70	
Economic/fiscal	38 (48, 37, 12)[b]	39	26	
Allocation/management	49 (57, 42, 40)	51	52	
Role in the Policy Process				
Initiation	71 (70, 79, 60)	66	47	b
Coordination	61 (62, 61, 56)	83	85	a
Implementation	26 (25, 21, 36)	0	15	a
Role described with reference to position/institution				
Chief decision-maker	85 (80, 84, 100)	59	29	a
Collective executive	7 (7, 5, 8)	34	61	a
Department head	42 (45, 50, 20)[c]	37	25	c
Deputy department head	2 (3, 0, 0)	17	8	a
Legislature	24 (22, 24, 28)	0	4	a

For a, b, and c see notes to Table 11.1.

trying to ensure that major decisions further these. Within the US sample, we find that politicos, much more than career officials and amphibians (88 *v* 48 and 55 per cent, respectively), describe their agency's role in terms of setting priorities and making decisions in accordance with these. However, they tend much less to assign to their agency a part in economic and fiscal policy (12 *v* 48 and 37 per cent, respectively). These results probably tap a tendency among politicos to develop a greater awareness of the relation of their organization's work to priorities and major policy choices.

In describing the types of activities upon which their agency centres its efforts, respondents focused on initiation of policies, co-ordination of decisions, and monitoring of implementation. Under each activity, dramatic cross-national differences appear. Canadian officials stress much less than those in the United States and Britain involvement of their agency in policy initiation. The Canadian cabinet system operates from many more departments and with much more formalized committee systems than even in the United Kingdom. Perhaps Canadian central agents view initial development of policy options as the domain of lower-level departmental and interagency deliberation. Well over half of our respondents in each country view their agency as involved in policy co-ordination. However, the proportions in the United Kingdom and Canada exceed that of the United States by more than 20 per cent. Such results underline the importance of cabinet decision-making in the United Kingdom and Canada. The cross-tabulations of the three central agency activities with the three main groups of US respondents produce only modest results.

An examination of the political and bureaucratic authorities that central agents mention with reference to the role of their agency produces some very interesting findings. One might expect that US officials would focus disproportionately on the president and virtually ignore the cabinet; British and Canadian officials would stress roles relating both to the prime minister and the cabinet. We have no reason to believe that department heads would receive more or less mention in any of the three countries. However, deputy heads, as a rule, enjoy higher profile in the United Kingdom and Canada by virtue of the fact that they stand at the apex of the career public service. Whereas many central agents in the United States perform roles that either fulfil specific congressional mandates or require close legislative liaison, few central agents in Britain and Canada have similar accountability. Thus, we might expect US respondents to mention Congress while describing their agency's roles much more than the other respondents would refer to their respective parliaments.

In fact, the cross-tabulations provide exceptionally strong support for all these rather conventional expectations. One noteworthy anomaly appears. Generally, British respondents stand at a mid-point between their American and Canadian counterparts. They refer to the prime minister somewhat more than do the Canadians and cite the cabinet considerably less. In fact, Canadians provide the only group in which the cabinet, rather than the chief decision-maker, receives the greatest proportion of mentions. Thus, we find once again evidence that Canadians view cabinet government in a much more structured way than do even the British. Turning to our politicos, amphibians, and career officials in the United States, we find that they cite pretty much the same authorities. All politicos mentioned the president in the course of his or her account of their agency's work. However, 84 and 80 per cent of amphibians and career officials, respectively, do so as well.

Evaluations of agencies: A series of questions was set up to ascertain respondents' evaluations of their agency and views on how its perform-

TABLE 11.5
Central agents' evaluations of their agency

Evaluations	United States (career, amphibians, politicos) N = 132 (69, 38, 25)	United Kingdom N = 41	Canada N = 92	Significance
Tone of Response				
Positive	61 (58, 62, 66)	58	43	c
Neutral	19 (23, 13, 17)	20	22	
Negative	20 (19, 25, 17)	22	35	c
Diagnosis of problems				
Deficient or conflicting mandates	42 (44, 50, 28)	29	29	
Organizational problems	32 (38, 24, 28)	42	40	
Inadequate resources	22 (23, 21, 20)	24	17	
Inadequate leadership	12 (15, 11, 16)	7	9	
Prognosis				
Agency needs change	69 (71, 74, 56)	63	62	
Agency will change	42 (45, 37, 40)	29	21	b

For b and c see notes to Table 11.1.

ance could be improved. In examining their responses, analysed in Table 11.5, we focus here on whether our officials provided evaluations that took a positive, a neutral, or a negative tone; the problems that they emphasized; and what they saw as the prognosis for change.

In the United States and the United Kingdom, 61 and 58 per cent of respondents, respectively, adopted a positive stance towards their department's performance while only 20 and 22 per cent, offered negative perspectives. In Canada, however, only 43 per cent expressed positive views while fully 35 per cent cast a negative light on their agency. These findings provide a cross-national gloss to the observation made in *The Superbureaucrats* that a great deal of ferment existed in the Canadian sample about the proper role of central agencies.[2] No striking cross-national differences regarding diagnoses of problems with central agencies appear. Between 62 and 69 per cent of respondents in each country called for some substantial changes in the structure or operation of their agencies. However, less than 43 per cent believe that meaningful changes will actually occur. Here, the very modest 21 per cent of Canadians who remained hopeful about change corresponds with the gloomier outlook of these officials' general evaluations. Whether US officials are politicos, amphibians, or career officials appears to have little bearing on their evaluations of their central agency.

Frequently one sees magazine and newspaper articles that purport to identify the inner circle that wields the greatest influence in a particular capital. Although these items titillate, one has to exercise caution in interpreting their significance. Only the naïve observer would become shocked when reading that formal and informal networks of politicians and officials exert disproportionately great influence in one or other policy arena. One would find it difficult in the extreme to cite situations where humans commit themselves to a common enterprise without some of the participants operating according to special understandings. Such arrangements attempt to ensure that certain individuals work in concert so as to achieve common goals and satisfactory trade-offs between personal objectives. The arrangements can take several forms. For instance, participants may keep them secret or make them known to all. As well they may exclude interested parties or permit all with a stake to join.

As we proceed through this section we should keep in mind some important cross-national vagaries. First, Canada's cabinet committee system has so formalized itself that the bodies and their membership have become public knowledge. As well, most committees include virtually every relevant ministry. Ministers usually attend meetings accompanied by at least one official from their department. Officials even substitute for ministers when they must fulfil conflicting commitments. Canada has also followed the practice of creating secretariats, independent of the Privy Council Office, designed to service some cabinet committees. The United Kingdom maintains a strong commitment to a system of cabinet committees. However, it keeps secret the membership of all committees and the existence of most. As well, it tends to limit the size of these bodies much more than does Canada. Further, it usually does not allow officials either to accompany or to substitute for ministers. In no case has it created an autonomous secretariat for a specific committee. Apart from the highly developed committees linked to the National Security Council, cabinet-level bodies in the United States lack differentiation and continuity both within and between administrations. Further, the centrality of the president to an administration's decision-making and the relative insularity of the spheres of cabinet secretaries result in a much stronger emphasis

TABLE 11.6
Central agents who perceive an inner circle in government, and the characteristics they attribute to its members

Views	United States (career, amphibians, politicos) N = 132 (69, 38, 25)	United Kingdom N = 41	Canada N = 92	Significance
Is there an inner circle?				
Yes: qualified and unqualified responses	83 (78, 92, 84)	85	90	
Yes: unqualified responses	33 (32, 37, 32)	44	50	c
Yes: based on issues	21 (17, 24, 24)	34	25	
Qualities of inner circle members				
Formal position	67 (67, 68, 68)	73	78	
Experience, expertise	45 (48, 50, 28)	51	35	
Trust of chief executive	42 (35, 45, 60)	20	13	a
Political ability outside government	4 (3, 3, 8)	5	15	b
Political ability inside government	8 (4, 8, 16)	2	32	a
Personality characteristics	5 (4, 5, 4)	24	36	a
Positions that confer inner circle membership				
Central agency head	34 (28, 45, 36)	12	19	b
Central agency deputy head	5 (4, 8, 0)	17	26	a
Head of other departments	29 (25, 32, 36)	32	8	a
Deputy head of other departments	1 (1, 0, 0)	5	27	a
Cabinet and its committees	11 (9, 21, 0)ᶜ	49	44	a
Senior officials of central agencies	12 (9, 16, 16)	7	16	
Other senior officials	8 (9, 11, 4)	44	10	a

For a, b, and c see notes to Table 11.1.

on bilateral discussions between the chief executive and departments than found either in Canada or the United Kingdom.

Identifying Inner Circles
Virtually every respondent in each of our countries believed that inner circles exist (see Table 11.6). However, British respondents tend more than Americans and Canadians to qualify their statements. Reservations most often simply underline the fact that inner circles change according to what policy issues command the most attention at a given stage of an

administration or government. In all three countries, central agents attach the greatest importance to formal positions as passports to inner circles. With respect to the other qualities, the three samples provide widely divergent proportions. Both British and American officials give somewhat more weight to experience and expertise than do their Canadian counterparts (51 and 45 per cent, respectively, v 35 per cent). US officials place much more stock in the trust of the chief executive as a factor in inner-circle membership (42 per cent v 20 and 13 per cent for Britain and Canada). Canadians lead the others by large proportions in citing political ability inside and outside government and personality characteristics. Thus, three themes appear to emerge from our results. The more stratified American and British career systems generate a more discernible nod to experience and expertise; Americans give due recognition to the fact that each president brings with him a cadre of loyal advisers who enjoy privileged access; Canadian officials realistically account for the contributions of political ability and personality in a developing executive-bureaucratic community characterized by accelerated upward mobility for especially well-connected and gifted individuals.

Notwithstanding the clear cross-national consensus over the importance of formal positions in access to inner circles, respondents in each of our samples revealed quite different perspectives on exactly which positions contribute the most to a person's potential prominence. American officials lead the others in attributing special access to the heads of central agencies and come a very close second to their British counterparts in assigning similar power to heads of operational departments. As well as placing a stronger emphasis on one's headship of specific operational departments, British officials surpass the Americans, by a very large margin, in stating that membership in the cabinet or one of its more important committees assures access. They also mention, much more than either of the other groups, senior officials, short of deputy heads, who benefit from special opportunities for influencing policy. The disproportionate attention of British officials to positions short of the top of the career ranks might relate to the fact that deputy, rather than permanent, secretaries make up many of the key interdepartmental committees. Although they too acknowledge the importance of positioning within the cabinet committee structure, Canadian respondents deviated from their British counterparts in stressing the privileged access of deputy heads of central agencies and operational departments. They attribute much less importance to the status of senior officials below the level of deputy head in operational departments. Since deputy ministers accompany their department heads to cabinet committees, those in operational departments might acquire high profiles more readily than their counterparts in the United States and Britain.

Focusing on politicos, amphibians, and career officials in the United States, politicos attach much more importance to the degree to which individuals have won the trust of the president. However, politicos offer significantly less than the others the view that posts in the cabinet and key committees at that level contribute to one's standing in Washington. Politicos thus provide responses that correspond to earlier evidence that they view power in the executive-bureaucratic community through the perspective of the presidency.

How Respondents Use Their Networks

The 'man on the street' probably harbours pet theories about who belongs in the inner circle in his capital. Of course, dramatic episodes such as Watergate can earn status as a household word for virtually the entire inner circle. In quieter times, controversies surrounding a single individual can generate notoriety. However, we assume that strategically placed insiders have garnered direct knowledge about inner circles from their own privileged access or from having to exercise executive or bureaucratic authority on a day-to-day basis.

With respect to interactions with chief executives, the first item in Table 11.7, US central agents report in a significantly greater proportion than do the British and Canadian respondents that they interact directly with the chief executive (57, 44, and 39 per cent, respectively). However, a look at the frequency of such encounters suggests a much narrower range of responses in the three countries. For instance, between 22 and 34 per cent in each sample interact with the chief executive at least once a month. The variations contract further for interaction at least weekly, as between 18 and 20 per cent of respondents in each sample attain this level of contact. While American central agents tend more to claim at least some direct exposure to the president, British and Canadian officials who obtain access to their prime minister seem to enjoy about as frequent contact as do their US counterparts.

A look at the settings for interactions between our respondents and their chief executives suggests an explanation of our results concerning the frequency of contacts. Officials in all three countries report roughly the same experience of encounters over the telephone and personal visits to their chief executive's office. References to contacts in the former setting do not exceed 12 per cent in any of our samples; mentions of the latter do not surpass 22 per cent. Thus, the range of citings of official

TABLE 11.7
Level, frequency, and nature of central agents' interaction
with senior government officials

Interaction	United States (career, amphibians, politicos) $N = 132$ (69, 38, 25)	United Kingdom $N = 41$	Canada $N = 92$	Significance
Interacts with chief executive	57 (38, 66, 96)[a]	44	39	c
Monthly, at least	25 (4, 32, 72)[a]	22	34	
Weekly, at least	18 (1, 24, 56)[a]	20	20	
Telephone	5 (0, 5, 20)[a]	12	8	
Personal visits	17 (3, 18, 52)[a]	22	22	
Official meetings	53 (35, 63, 88)[a]	32	30	b
Interacts with own agency head	86 (83, 97, 80)	51	59	a
Monthly, at least	71 (62, 79, 80)[b]	39	50	a
Weekly, at least	60 (46, 71, 80)[b]	20	24	a
Telephone	67 (54, 84, 80)[b]	22	15	a
Personal visits	66 (55, 76, 80)[c]	39	41	a
Official meetings	84 (78, 97, 80)[c]	46	40	a
Interacts with heads of other agencies/departments	68 (51, 79, 100)[a]	68	73	
Monthly, at least	48 (30, 55, 84)[a]	26	67	a
Weekly, at least	29 (12, 37, 64)[a]	24	36	
Telephone	47 (25, 53, 100)[a]	29	21	a
Personal visits	34 (16, 40, 76)[a]	27	23	
Official meetings	65 (48, 79, 92)[a]	61	64	
Interacts with deputy of own agency	64 (68, 63, 56)	71	89	a
Monthly, at least	50 (45, 58, 52)	49	76	a
Weekly, at least	41 (32, 50, 52)	37	55	c
Telephone	48 (42, 55, 52)	42	42	
Personal visits	46 (38, 55, 56)	54	70	b
Official meetings	61 (64, 63, 52)	63	72	
Interacts with deputies of other agencies/departments	47 (33, 61, 64)[b]	78	85	a
Monthly, at least	30 (19, 37, 48)[c]	22	79	a
Weekly, at least	21 (13, 26, 36)[c]	15	57	a
Telephone	41 (28, 50, 64)[b]	29	49	
Personal visits	29 (15, 42 48)[a]	32	41	
Official meetings	46 (32, 61, 60)[b]	·63	67	b

For a, b, and c see notes to Table 11.1.

meetings – 30 to 53 per cent – indicates that in each country many respondents interact with the chief executive only in larger gatherings of cabinet members and/or advisers. The fact that 53 per cent of us officials report attending such meetings corresponds with the finding above: namely, a greater proportion of Americans claim interactions with the chief executive, but when we focus on frequency of contacts they fall closer to the levels attained by the British and Canadians.

As we might expect, politicos in the American sample interact with the president much more frequently than do amphibians and career officials. As well, they make much greater use of the various settings. This appears to be especially the case with personal visits to the president's office. Amphibians' reports of attendance at formal meetings involving the president suggest an especially robust point of access for these officials. In almost every setting, career officials provide much smaller proportions even than found in British and Canadian officials' direct contacts with their chief executive.

A look at central agents' interactions with the heads of their departments and with secretaries or ministers of other departments reveals some strong cross-national differences. While British and Canadian respondents recount close to the same frequencies and settings of relations with their own department heads, their American counterparts outstrip them by far in every respect. Most dramatically, 84 per cent of the us respondents told us that they discussed matters directly with their department heads in official meetings while only 46 and 40 per cent of the British and Canadians, respectively, told us of similar exchanges. A comparison of the responses of us politicos, amphibians, and career officials reveals that amphibians provide the highest proportion that claims at least some interaction with their agency head (97 per cent v 66 and 38 per cent). As well, they keep up with or surpass politicos in each of the other variables of interaction. However, career officials perform much better than the British and American respondents in the case of every variable. Clearly, our data provide evidence that central agents in the United States gain access to their political head more frequently than those in the United Kingdom and Canada.

Turning to interactions with the heads of other departments, we begin to discern the effects of the fact that Canadian officials participate much more freely than the Americans and British in cabinet-level bodies. Some large gaps appear between the proportions of Canadians and the others claiming monthly or weekly contact with the heads of other departments. On most indicators, the Americans fall midway between the Canadians and British. Their use of the telephone and personal visits to offices, however, exceeds that of their counterparts in the other countries. In every case, politicos provide larger proportions under variables than do the career officials *and* the amphibians. This makes sense. We might expect that career officials would perform less well here than they did with respect to interaction with their own department head. They, after all, call upon their agency experience and expertise as their main currency. Amphibians often enjoy the benefit of being hand-picked nominees of the agency head. However, they might lack the performance in the electoral trenches that would give them greater profile with appointees elsewhere in Washington.

Interesting results appear regarding respondents' mentions of interactions with the deputy heads of their departments. Because in the United Kingdom and Canada these posts represent the apex of the career civil service, we might have expected officials in these two countries to report more frequently contacts at this level. The Canadian respondents fulfil this expectation, usually in large proportions, in every case but interaction on the phone. However, the presence in HM Treasury and the Civil Service Department of second permanent secretaries who work with relative autonomy in many areas of their responsibilities apparently tempers the British results. The large differences among politicos, amphibians, and career officials that appeared with reference to interactions with central agency heads simply do not develop with regard to their deputies.

Canadians provide much greater proportions of respondents under all variables concerning interactions with deputy heads of other departments. The British respondents tend much more than the Americans to report at least some interaction at this level. Yet their responses under the frequency and setting items fall considerably short of the Canadians' in most instances. The British do come much closer to the Canadians than to the Americans in citing official meetings as the settings for their encounters with deputy heads from other departments.

Cabinet Committees

Various discussions in parts I–III examine in greater detail the roles of cabinet committees in the functional areas in which our central agencies provide assistance and advice. However, before looking at our respondents' exposure to cabinet-level groups, we should highlight briefly some salient cross-national differences in how these bodies operate.

Canada runs the most formalized cabinet committee structure. For instance, as of 14 October 1981, it had created thirteen standing committees. Most of these bodies appeared to include virtually every minister whose interests it could conceivably affect. The largest committee, economic development, took in twenty members; the smallest, public service, included only six. One committee, priorities and planning, served essentially as an inner cabinet.

Cabinet committees in the United Kingdom differ considerably from those in Canada. First, the cabinet itself operates as a somewhat bloated version of Canada's priorities and planning committee. Whereas twelve of Canada's ministers belong to 'P and P,' twenty-two of Britain's fifty-five senior ministers serve in the cabinet. Second, the prime minister delegates the chairmanship to a senior colleague of 'QL' – queen's speech and legislation. Apart from the cabinet, this committee takes the widest compass. However, it pretty well limits itself to vetting of proposals for legislation and meshing these with the priorities for sessions of Parliament. Other British committees cover large policy sectors such as economic policy, foreign affairs and defence, home affairs, and relations with the European Economic Community.[3] Sub-committees flourish in each of these fields. As well, the prime minister uses a free hand in gathering ministers into ad hoc bodies intended to get to the bottom of particularly intractable problems.

As we saw in chapter 2, the Reagan administration appears to be moving the presidency toward adoption of a structured cabinet committee system. At the time of the interviews (1979 – i.e. during the Carter administration), only the National Security Council and its working groups and the Economic Policy Group operated as cabinet committees in the strict sense of the word. They met on a regular basis throughout the administration and served as the key forums for discussion of long-term issues and emergencies as they arose. This does not imply that other cabinet-level bodies were totally absent. The point remains, however, that the Carter administration did not make much use of ongoing cabinet-level bodies.

In looking at our officials' accounts of their involvement with cabinet committees (Table 11.8), we find that Canadians clearly receive greater exposure to these bodies than do the Americans or the British. In fact, 45 per cent of the Canadians claim they join committee sessions on a regular basis and 33 per cent report having been to two or more different bodies. Notwithstanding the more structured cabinet committee system in the United Kingdom, respondents there indicate about the same amount of exposure to these bodies as do those in the United States. The British convention whereby officials usually only attend committees in order to record the proceedings and decisions apparently operates very strictly.

Respondents' characterizations of their participation in cabinet-level

TABLE 11.8
Participation in cabinet committees

Participation	United States (career, amphibians, politicos) $N = 132$ (69, 38, 25)	United Kingdom $N = 41$	Canada $N = 92$	Significance
Cabinet committee attendance				
Attends meetings of some committees	43 (30, 50, 68)[b]	42	78	a
Attends meetings of two or more committees	13 (4, 21, 24)[b]	15	33	a
Regular attendance	16 (10, 16, 32)[c]	15	45	a
Episodic attendance	27 (19, 34, 36)	27	29	
Type of participation (most active role indicated)				
Observer	4 (1, 3, 12)	17	5	b
Adviser	23 (23, 26, 16)	15	34	c
Discussant	13 (3, 18, 32)[a]	7	30	a
Reason for attending				
Get information	12 (6, 18, 20)	5	13	
Study problems	10 (6, 21, 4)[c]	7	25	b
Influence policy	4 (3, 5, 4)	0	10	c
Implement decisions	10 (3, 11, 28)[b]	2	8	
Learn the ropes	5 (3, 8, 8)	2	29	a
Part of respondent's mandate	5 (1, 5, 16)[c]	20	20	b

For a, b, and c see notes to Table 11.1.

bodies sharpen the cross-national differences. Only small percentages of American and Canadian respondents (4 and 5, respectively) say they attend committees simply to observe and record. In contrast, the largest proportion in the British sample (17 per cent) attends for this relatively limited purpose. Only 7 per cent of British officials admit to acting as full discussants in cabinet committees. The us sample, as well, produces a relatively small proportion (13 per cent) willing to take their roles this far. Thus, the 30 per cent of Canadians who view themselves as full-fledged discussants in cabinet committees proves exceptional.

Consistent with their relatively high level of participation in cabinet committees, Canadian respondents offer the most expansive accounts of their reasons for attending these bodies. They provide the largest proportions who say they use them for keeping informed about others' positions on major issues (13 v 12 and 5 per cent in the United States and the United Kingdom, respectively), influencing the way in which ministers study a problem, especially by lending the perspective of expertise and experience (25 v 10 and 7 per cent), getting their point of view across so as to actually influence policy decisions (10 v 4 and 0 per cent), learning the ropes by watching how various ministers perform and how things get done (29 v 5 and 2 per cent), and simply fulfilling a specific part of secretarial functions by taking minutes and recording decisions (20 v 5 and 20 per cent). With special reference to influencing the study of problems, having one's say on policy, and learning the ropes, the large gaps between the Canadian sample and the others flesh out an important theme. Cabinet committees have become vital forums for any central agent in Ottawa who wants to wield power.

In the United States, politicos, amphibians, and career officials view their involvement in cabinet-level bodies quite differently. As we might expect, politicos lead the others in saying they attend such panels at all (68 v 50 and 30 per cent for amphibians and career officials, respectively), join two or more different groups (24 v 21 and 4 per cent), and attend on a regular basis (32 v 16 and 10 per cent). Amphibians provide proportions that fall between the politicos and career officials. With respect to their characterizations of participation, most politicos style themselves discussants. The largest proportions of both amphibians and career officials believe they limit their participation on committees to providing advice when called upon.

Cross-tabulations of the three US groups' reasons for attending committees provide some important insights into the different perspectives of politicos and amphibians. Politicos contribute disproportionately highly to the emphasis on committees as vehicles for assuring that the administration's policy initiatives come to fruition. Obviously, US policymaking differs from that in Canada and the United Kingdom. No US administration can take for granted that departmental commitments to initiatives will hold up under resistance from Congress. Amphibians provide by far the largest proportion of respondents who attend cabinet committees in order to influence how secretaries study an issue. The findings suggest once again that amphibians trade more on expertise than on political skills.

Interdepartmental Committees
Since our central agents often shoulder special responsibility for resolution of government-wide issues, we might expect interdepartmental committee work to make great claims on their time. We might anticipate as well that committees command the most time in areas where our central agents concentrate their roles. Thus, cross-national differences in the

TABLE 11.9
Interdepartmental committee work

Participation and perceptions	United States (career, amphibians, politicos) $N = 132$ (69, 38, 25)	United Kingdom $N = 41$	Canada $N = 92$	Significance
Participation on committees				
Attends one or more	89 (87, 90, 96)	88	74	b
Attends five or more	24 (16, 24, 44)[b]	12	12	
Chairs committee(s)	25 (22, 21, 40)	29	11	c
Discussant	80 (73, 84, 92)	90	49	a
Delegates responsibilities to others	23 (28, 16, 20)	20	27	
Is delegated by others to attend	18 (20, 24, 4)	5	7	b
Perceives committee work as crucial	62 (52, 66, 84)[b]	68	42	b
Reason for attending				
Part of mandate	73 (65, 76, 88)	73	39	
Delegated	21 (22, 24, 12)	5	7	b
Expertise	63 (77, 68, 16)[a]	51	22	a
Perceived role on committees				
Get information	67 (65, 76, 60)	81	23	a
Represent agency	81 (80, 78, 88)	88	8	a
Use expertise	61 (68, 71, 28)[a]	54	21	a
Use influence	4 (20, 40, 40)	2	8	
Perceived purpose of committees				
Oversight of problems	56 (57, 58, 52)	76	21	a
Prepare policy proposals	71 (73, 79, 56)	88	37	a
Coordinate executive policy decisions	44 (36, 47, 60)	17	27	b
Coordinate legislative liaison	14 (3, 13, 44)[a]	10	1	b
Perceives committees as effective	83 (83, 82, 84)	93	50	a

For a, b, and c see notes to Table 11.1.

focus of committee work will probably reflect areas of intense activity by central agencies in one or more of our three countries.

Generally, as reported in Table 11.9, Canadian respondents de-emphasized roles on interdepartmental committees. Just under three-quarters of Canadian officials say they attend interdepartmental committees, while nearly 90 per cent of Americans and British respondents do so. At a higher level of participation, twice as many US officials (24 per cent) claim membership on five or more committees as do the Canadians and British (12 per cent). The 11 per cent of Canadians who claim chairman-ships of committees falls considerably short of the proportions for the Americans (25 per cent) and the British (29 per cent). Finally, just under half the Canadians say they become full discussants in committee meetings as opposed to 80 and 90 per cent of the Americans and British.

Since Canadians reported much greater involvement with cabinet committees than their opposite numbers in the United States and Britain, their poor showing regarding interdepartmental committees, especially in assumption of the chair, comes as a surprise. However, procedural differences might explain our findings. In the United States, operational departments might assume the chair in policy areas that do not pose serious difficulties or when a major issue remains in the phase before legislative study. However, whenever the administration wants to respond quickly to a crisis or break a deadlock in deliberations that have taken too long, the president probably assigns the chair to someone in the White House. As well, once policies reach the legislative stage, the controversial ones increasingly require an interdepartmental task force, chaired by White House staff, to ensure that congressional relations run smoothly. In the United Kingdom, the Cabinet Office sets up and chairs many committees of officials designed either to monitor major policy areas or resolve conflicts between departments on specific issues. In Canada, the Privy Council Office often encourages departments to set up committees and monitors the progress of these bodies. However, it has tended to avoid the chair.

Our respondents told of a dizzying array of interdepartmental commit-tees. A case-by-case look at individual bodies would simply overload the reader with detail. However, a categorization of committees according to roles in the central agencies and sub-functions within these provides a suitable basis for some cross-national comparisons; Table 11.10 catego-rizes my findings.

Regarding interdepartmental committees involved with setting of priorities and ensuring that major decisions adhere to these, 56 per cent of US respondents said that they participate on such bodies while only 32 and 26 per cent of British and Canadian officials, respectively, do so. In none of our countries do panels working on strategic planning per se account for the greater share of the respondents' involvement in priorities and major policy areas. In the United States, central agents served on strategic committees designed more to co-ordinate departmen-tal 'lines' in light of administration policy than to map out priorities. Thus, this category included in the United States such gatherings as weekly

TABLE 11.10
Interdepartmental committees, categorized by function

Function	United States (career, amphibians, politicos) $N = 132$ (69, 38, 25)	United Kingdom $N = 41$	Canada $N = 92$	Significance
Priorities/substantive	56 (44, 61, 84)[b]	32	26	a
Strategic planning	23 (12, 16, 64)[a]	7	10	b
Co-ordination for the administration	12 (1, 11, 44)[a]	0	0	a
Planning government reorganization	14 (10, 11, 32)[c]	0	0	a
Substantive policy	42 (38, 47, 48)	29	19	a
Energy	16 (13, 11, 32)	2	9	c
Health	7 (3, 8, 16)	0	0	b
Other domestic	8 (4, 16, 8)	0	0	b
Foreign affairs and defence	21 (22, 16, 28)	7	4	a
Intergovernmental affairs	0 (0, 0, 0)	7	1	b
Economic/fiscal	52 (52, 53, 48)	34	45	
Fiscal (including tax)	5 (4, 0, 12)	5	9	
Macro	25 (23, 34, 16)	12	21	
Sectoral	21 (15, 21, 40)	17	26	
International economics	14 (16, 13, 12)	12	9	
Allocation/management	28 (28, 26, 32)	54	32	b
Expenditure budgeting	14 (12, 11, 24)	10	1	b
Organizational structure	14 (10, 11, 32)[c]	27	2	a
Evaluation of effectiveness and efficiency	0 (0, 0, 0)	2	4	
Personnel policy	11 (10, 13, 8)	20	12	
Senior executive policy	0 (0, 0, 0)	27	4	a
Administrative policy	11 (12, 11, 8)	24	15	

For a, b, and c see notes to Table 11.1.

meetings of departmental assistant secretaries for policy, chaired by
Hamilton Jordan; heads of congressional liaison offices, with Frank
Moore; and chief public information officers, with Jody Powell. However,
14 per cent of the US respondents belonged to task forces co-ordinating
various aspects of the president's reorganization project. In our sample,
these included bodies working on economic development, natural
resources, trade, civil service reform, education, regulatory reform, and
foreign aid. Although each of these projects focused most substantially on
structural change, they all required some soul-searching as to the
administration's priorities in these various fields.

Still focusing on strategic planning, the British and Canadian cases present quite different pictures. In the United Kingdom, only one committee of officials, the Future Business Committee – consisting of top officials in the Cabinet Office, No. 10, and the Central Policy Review Staff – looks at priorities centrally. As well, it tends to work within fairly short horizons that limit participants essentially to planning cabinet business. In Canada, at the time of the interviews, an élite group of deputy ministers, DM-10, played a much more significant role with regard to sorting out priorities for the duration of the mandate. Currently, a similar body has adopted the title Senior Co-ordination Committee and greatly expanded and regularized its operations.

The American respondents reveal much more involvement on panels attempting to assure that major policy decisions fit the priorities of the administration than do the British and Canadians. The fact that, on the domestic side, respondents singled out energy and health policy for intense committee work suggests that preoccupations of the Carter administration had dominated this landscape. Task forces tackling one or other issue came into their own only when the administration desperately wanted to bring an issue to resolution. In foreign affairs and defence policy in the United States, the same pattern emerges. A much larger proportion of American respondents than British and Canadians said that they participated in interdepartmental deliberations in this field. At the time of our interviews, some forty interdepartmental committees focused on specific issues relating to foreign affairs and defence policy. Most of these functioned as task forces assigned to study problems that came under the aegis of the National Security Council.

Concerning bodies working on various aspects of development and integration of economic and fiscal policies, we find smaller cross-national differences. The British respondents provide the smallest proportions under the umbrella function and two categories within it. The results probably derive from the fact that HM Treasury enjoys a decisive voice in the use of the most crucial economic instruments. Thus it leaves fewer openings for discussions involving other central agents. In contrast, the US Department of the Treasury and the Canadian Department of Finance, especially the former, must increasingly consult other central agencies and, in some cases, operational departments, before advocating to the chief executive use of one or other economic lever.

Turning to bodies that deal with the allocation and management of governmental resources, many more British officials (54 per cent) than those in the United States (28 per cent) and Canada (32 per cent) told us that they participated on panels working within this field. In Canada at the time of our interviews, the Treasury Board, a cabinet committee, met nearly one hundred times a year to consider matters arising in allocation and management. This intense activity certainly would make burdensome all but the most urgent efforts on the part of officials to co-ordinate their positions before meeting with ministers. Meanwhile, British officials seem to have shouldered much of the British load in this field left by the absence of a cabinet committee comparable in scope to Canada's Treasury Board.

The proportions of politicos, amphibians, and career officials coming under our various umbrella categories and sub-functions simply reinforce some of the observations already made about interdepartmental committees in the United States. Politicos clearly dominate committees involved with priorities. However, task forces working on specific substantive policies provide the three groups reasonably equal access. With one exception, the results under development and integration of economic and fiscal policy suggest access evenly distributed among the groups. The bodies trying to relate economic policies to the claims of particular industrial or work-force sectors provide disproportionately high representation to our politicos. Finally, allocation and management also appear to provide reasonably equal access to our three groups. Only bodies involved with organizational structure favour politicos.

RELATIONS WITH OUTSIDERS

The relations of central agents with individuals and groups outside the executive-bureaucratic community depend in no small part on how our three democratic systems work. In this regard, three factors play vital roles. First, commonality of backgrounds can foster relations between central agents and some outsiders.[4] We might expect two former dons at Oxford, one working as an economist in the Treasury and the other doing similar work for the Confederation of British Industry, to keep in touch. They would meet especially often if they both took lunch at the same club. A former partner at a top law firm in New York, now working on tax policy in the US Department of the Treasury, will no doubt meet with former colleagues representing corporate clients' positions on important issues.

Second, institutional factors can inhibit interaction between members of old-boy networks. However, they might foster ties that would not have developed on the basis of shared experiences. Anyone working in the White House Office will by necessity manifest only the most solicitous concern for the representatives of any group that can make or break the president either on a major policy initiative or in re-election. Thus, one often sees, during visits to the West Wing, top presidential aides serving as glorified tour guides by shepherding group delegations through the White House. However, many economists in Treasury work contentedly with no contact with outsiders except fellow professionals studying similar issues.

Third, the overarching environment of the political system greatly affects consultation with outsiders. In the United Kingdom and Canada, individual and collective ministerial responsibility, accompanied by the emphasis on secrecy, works to discourage contact with outsiders. Until the last few decades, US career officials did exercise restraint in their external relations. Indeed, many of our career respondents in the Office of Management and Budget spoke nostalgically of the golden era when the old Bureau of the Budget maintained strict detachment from the outside world. However, freedom-of-information legislation and the prevalence of sub-governments based on communities of interest between outside groups, bureaucrats, and Congress have forced even these officials to interact more often with outsiders.

In addition to keeping the above considerations in mind, we may tap the findings from a growing body of empirical research focusing on this topic. Robert Putnam suggests that a distinction between politically oriented and classic career bureaucrats proves helpful here.[5] His study of top officials in Italy, Germany, and Britain indicates that in each country politically oriented officials tend more than the others to interact with outsiders. American scholars have tended to view US bureaucrats as fulfilling representational functions similar to those of legislators. In fact, Norton C. Long argued in the early 1950s that legislators have become less representative, responsive, and responsible than bureaucrats.[6] His controversial position hinged largely on the belief that bureaucrats' more pluralistic backgrounds would generate relatively egalitarian attitudes and values.

Empirical tests of Long's assertion have produced results that should make us less than sanguine. Kenneth J. Meier and Lloyd G. Nigro report that eight standard background variables accounted for only 5 per cent of the differences in US bureaucrats' public-policy priorities.[7] Two explanations for such findings present themselves. First, the backgrounds of officials and legislators, though different, do not range along a band wide enough to work an appreciable effect on attitudes and values. Second, the socialization of officials into bureaucracy and their departments might largely cancel out the effects of background differences. Such conclusions find support in a study by Joel D. Aberbach and Bert A. Rockman, which found that congressmen and top officials differ in social background but not in normative orientations and styles of thinking about politics.[8] The finding suggested to Aberbach and Rockman that US officials and legislators pass through a similar socialization. It came as no surprise to Aberbach and Rockman that fully 43 per cent of their senior officials report interactions with members of Congress at least once a week. Further, the authors counsel against our concluding that the encounters take a predominantly adversarial character. Citing Roger Davidson's work, they remind us that most relations occur within the 'cozy triangles' that maintain communication among bureaucrats, congressmen and leaders of interest groups working in the same area of policy.[9]

Officials in Whitehall remain notoriously aloof from British society – and Westminster. In the late 1950s, C.H. Sisson put his finger on two factors contributing to the apparent chasm between British officials and MPs.[10] The former maintain a strong sense of the distinctness of their élite group and manifest almost vocational commitments to their careers. Subsequently, James B. Christoph has found that in comparative terms the top officials, by virtue of their much stronger ties to Oxford and Cambridge, represent an educational élite.[11] As well, they decide upon their careers at relatively early ages and submit to a thoroughgoing process of socialization that fosters isolation from people in other walks of life. Robert Putnam reports that British officials often 'inherit' their careers from relatives who preceded them in the public service.[12] He concludes that many senior officials have brought with them distinct values and mores largely unalterable even by the changing role of bureaucracy in government. Christoph adds his voice to Putnam's observation. He notes that courses to teach senior Whitehall officials economic analysis and management techniques have forced a change only in substantive expertise, not in administrative ethos.[13]

In view of the differences between British and American culture, we might expect that our British central agents will lag behind their US counterparts in interactions with legislators. However, we should not take too jaundiced a view of British bureaucrats' relations with legislators. Significant changes in the British party system in the last two decades have introduced looser party discipline and more powerful parliamentary committees.[14] Even if these have yet to produce dramatic results in studies such as this, officials have taken Westminster more seriously in the last ten years. With respect to outsiders generally, Christoph urges us not to conclude too quickly that the relations of British officials will fall far short of those of Americans. He notes that British officials view consultation with outsiders in a fairly favourable light.[15] They attempt to obtain technical information and to satisfy an unwritten rule that consultation must precede government action.

In his comprehensive study of Canada's élite, John Porter found that those working at the top of the key sectors share essentially the same social and demographic backgrounds.[16] With special reference to senior bureaucrats, he argued that their socialization within the federal public service would ensure that they developed views of the role of government in national development that corresponded to those of legislators. Campbell and Szablowski, however, suggest that commonality of backgrounds and perspectives might only influence relations between top officials and members of the cabinet.[17] The practice whereby senior executives in the bureaucracy regularly attend cabinet committees and freely join in proceedings propels them into the executive-bureaucratic 'big leagues.' Relatedly, Robert Presthus and William Monopoli have noted that most senior officials believe they stoop a bit when engaging in relations with non-cabinet legislators.[18] Nearly half of their respondents opined that MPs do not perform competently in the policy process.

Canadian central agents extend their ambivalence toward interactions with outsiders to representatives of interest groups. In fact, Campbell and Szablowski cite a 'turtle syndrome' whereby the Canadians will interact with outsiders in the pre-legislative stage but close ranks once in the process of deciding upon specific options.[19] In the tax-policy process, for instance, members of the Department of Finance will receive representations from corporations and other organizations concerned about tax policy.[20] However, they make no provision for public forums and do not disclose the nature of representations from various quarters to other interested parties. As they work on the details of the annual budget – a process that may take as long as six months – they operate totally behind the veil of secrecy and eschew contacts with outsiders. After budget day, when in the United States and the United Kingdom outsiders could use the good offices of legislators to force public discussion of tax measures, Finance officials simply move from one controlled environment to another. Although they cease to cite the need for utter secrecy regarding the budget, they resort to the cover provided by Canadian parliamentary practice. This dictates that the committee of the whole in the House of Commons considers motions on ways and means. In this body, MPs may neither question officials nor call upon the testimony of outside experts.

Interactions with Legislators
A question in the interview attempted to ascertain how much and in what settings our respondents interact with legislators (see Table 11.11).

TABLE 11.11
Interaction with legislators

Interaction	United States (career, amphibians, politicos) N = 132 (69, 38, 25)	United Kingdom N = 41	Canada N = 92	Significance
Interacts with legislators of upper house	74 (62, 82, 92)[b]	24	29	a
Monthly, at least	39 (22, 50, 68)[a]	5	24	a
Weekly, at least	27 (13, 29, 64)[a]	0	14	a
Telephone	50 (32, 55, 92)[a]	10	17	a
Personal visits	38 (19, 45, 80)[a]	7	11	a
Official meetings	56 (45, 66, 72)[c]	17	13	a
Interacts with legislators of lower house	77 (70, 82, 88)	59	60	c
Monthly, at least	39 (22, 53, 64)[a]	17	44	c
Weekly, at least	27 (13, 29, 60)[a]	10	27	
Telephone	51 (35, 55, 88)[a]	22	32	a
Personal visits	39 (23, 45, 76)[a]	22	15	a
Official meetings	58 (49, 66, 68)	34	24	a

For a, b, and c see notes to Table 11.1.

Looking first at relations with members of the upper houses in the respective systems, we find what we might expect: British and Canadian officials tended much less than Americans to tell us that they keep in touch with members of these chambers. Both the House of Lords in the United Kingdom and the Senate in Canada play subsidiary roles to the lower houses in each country. However, Canadian officials register somewhat more cognizance of senators than their British opposite numbers do of peers. Previous research suggested that senators, despite their limited roles in the legislative process, perform very important functions relating to organization and fund-raising for their parties.[21] They also have developed a ken for policies that might adversely affect the business community. Thus, officials in the Prime Minister's Office co-ordinating various aspects of party organization will maintain close ties with senators as will those in the Department of Finance who must, from time to time, justify their policies before the Banking, Trade and Commerce Committee of the Senate.[22] The us respondents interact to an almost identical degree and in virtually the same forums with senators as they do with members of the House of Representatives.

Our respondents' reports of their interactions with members of their lower houses present some surprises. About 60 per cent of both British and Canadian officials say that they maintain some contacts with members of their lower houses; this compares with the 77 per cent of American central agents who report some relations. Respondents in all three countries tend to relate frequently with members of the lower house, Americans more so than Britons and Canadians: Americans and Canadians make monthly contact about equally (44 v 39 per cent) and exactly the same on a weekly basis (27 per cent). Their British counterparts register less than half these levels of interactions. A cautionary note comes to mind at this point. First, the American respondents offer much more expansive accounts of the settings in which they interact with congressmen than do Canadians in describing their relations with MPs. Fifty-one as opposed to 32 per cent use the telephone for such encounters, 39 as contrasted with 15 per cent meet in their or legislators' offices, and 58 versus 24 per cent interact in committee meetings and other formal gatherings.

A look at politicos, amphibians, and career officials in the United States reflects the tendency for the first group to involve themselves with political liaison, the third to stand a bit aloof, and the second to fall between the two others. However, we should not draw from this observation the conclusion that career officials become shrinking violets at the thought of contacts with Capitol Hill. In the case of every variable, they provide a larger proportion than do British officials. Only in monthly and weekly contacts with members of the lower house do they fall behind their counterparts in Canada. Of course, we should remember that the British and Canadian figures represent political appointees (in, respectively, No. 10 and the Prime Minister's Office) as well as career officials.

Some interesting differences between amphibians and career officials suggest themselves. The latter come considerably short of the former in monthly interactions with legislators. However, the amphibians appear to meet a threshold on a weekly contact. They produce proportions much closer to career officials than to the politicos. The amphibians thus arrive at mid-points between politicos and career officials in use of the telephone and personal visits in offices. However, they produce proportions very close to those for politicos in contacts in committee and other official meetings. These findings suggest that amphibians rely more on formal interactions with legislators than do politicos.

Relations with Groups and Other Outsiders
Respondents answered a lengthy series of questions on their consultation of outside sources of advice and information (see Table 11.12). In this respect, officials in the three countries hold different views as to the meaning of 'consultation.' Some viewed it as involving direct encounters

with various outside sources; others saw it as indirect efforts to remain aware of the concerns and stances of various elements of society.

Keeping the different understandings of 'consultation' in mind, we find Americans more likely than the British and Canadians to believe that obtaining the views of outsiders forms an important part of their responsibilities as officials (58 v 46 and 40 per cent, respectively). Further, the us respondents have significantly greater direct contact with outside sources monthly (80 v 40 and 34 per cent) and weekly (40 v 17 and 2 per cent). In this regard, the mere 2 per cent of Canadian respondents who encounter outsiders directly at least once a week appears to reflect an especially pronounced aloofness in that sample. The fact that close to half of British officials (46 per cent) state that they consult views only indirectly suggests a strong element of remoteness in that group as well. Obviously, when British central agents say they 'consult' various sources they often as not mean that they make themselves aware of their positions through indirect means.

When confronted with a list of sources of advice and information, respondents first said whether they consult these at all. The first twelve sources included items 'media' to 'polls' in Table 11.12. A thirteenth provided an 'other' category. Here two groups not included in the original list emerged in significant numbers, namely, 'academics' and 'other' professionals.

Moving through the sources in order, we note first that vastly more British respondents than those in the United States and Canada (85 per cent v 54 and 57 per cent, respectively) cite the media as a source of information. Apart from suggesting one reason why so many British respondents stress indirect consultation, the figure appears to reflect the relatively high quality of Britain's best newspapers.

The British lead in consultation of all other sources except religious leaders, leaders of ethnic groups, academics, and other professionals. In the latter cases, the Americans, not the Canadians, equal or surpass the British proportions. The Americans register proportions close to those for the British under all sources except political leaders and party workers, union leaders, friends and acquaintances, and polls. Canadians exceed slightly the Americans' consultation of media (57 v 54 per cent), provincial or state officials (47 v 46 per cent), and polls (22 v 17 per cent). They fall behind the Americans in consultation of all other sources. The gaps prove particularly large for tapping information from business leaders, union leaders, local government officials, religious leaders, leaders of ethnic groups, citizens' groups that cut across socioeconomic, ethnic, and religious lines, academics, and 'other' professionals. Clearly,

TABLE 11.12
Consultation with groups and officials outside the federal/central government

Perceptions	United States (career, amphibians, politicos) N = 132 (69, 38, 25)	United Kingdom N = 41	Canada N = 92	Significance
Consults				
Media	54 (49, 55, 64)	85	57	b
Political leaders, party workers	20 (4, 18, 64)[a]	56	25	a
Business leaders	76 (77, 79, 68)	81	50	a
Union leaders	39 (29, 57, 48)[b]	81	23	a
Farm group leaders	17 (10, 18, 36)[b]	20	16	
Local officials	44 (33, 55, 56)[b]	56	16	a
Provincial or state officials	46 (36, 55, 60)[b]	—	47	
Religious leaders	24 (13, 37, 36)[b]	24	9	b
Ethnic groups (including civil rights groups in the United States)	39 (22, 55, 60)[a]	39	11	a
Friends and acquaintances	49 (42, 53, 60)	71	42	b
Citizens' groups	41 (35, 47, 48)	46	20	a
Polls	17 (6, 24, 36)[a]	51	22	a
Academics	46 (52, 50, 24)[c]	37	17	a
Other professionals	39 (46, 40, 20)	20	19	b
Most reliable sources of the 'public's' view				
Media	15 (15, 13, 20)	22	12	
Political leaders, party workers	8 (0, 3, 36)[a]	10	8	
Business leaders	25 (28, 24, 20)	20	16	
Union leaders	5 (3, 5, 8)	17	2	b
Farm group leaders	1 (0, 3, 0)	0	0	
Local officials	14 (12, 21, 12)	7	1	b
Provincial or state officials	14 (12, 21, 12)	—	17	c
Religious leaders	1 (0, 0, 4)	0	0	
Ethnic groups (including civil rights groups in the United States)	5 (1, 8, 12)	0	0	c
Friends and acquaintances	24 (17, 24, 40)	7	10	b
Citizens' groups	8 (4, 11, 16)	7	3	
Polls	2 (0, 3, 4)	10	5	
Academics	24 (25, 32, 12)	20	7	b
Other professionals	23 (29, 18, 12)	12	7	b

TABLE 11.12 (continued)

Perceptions	United States (career, amphibians, politicos) $N = 132$ (69, 38, 25)	United Kingdom $N = 41$	Canada $N = 92$	Significance
Nature and perception of consultation with outsiders				
Consultation is proper	58 (48, 71, 64)[c]	46	40	b
Frequency of consultation				
Monthly or more	80 (70, 92, 88)[b]	40	34	a
Weekly or more	40 (26, 45, 72)[a]	17	2	a
Most consultation is indirect	14 (17, 11, 12)	46	11	a

For a, b, and c see notes to Table 11.1.

the Canadian figures conjure images of the turtle syndrome. Canadian officials appear very reluctant about taking into consideration the views of outsiders.

A look at respondents' views of which sources prove to be among the most reliable enables us to focus our consideration more precisely. In the United States, roughly a quarter of respondents chose each of business leaders, friends and acquaintances, academics, and other professionals as among the most reliable. The prominence of the latter two groups probably reflects the presence in Washington of a number of highly effective research institutes and headquarters for associated professionals. British central agents dwell on the reliability of the media to the largest degree (22 per cent). This suggests once more that many use the media as the prime source of information on the views of other groups. Business leaders and academics each drew mention from 20 per cent of British officials, while union leaders attracted praise from 17 per cent. British respondents' emphasis of consultation of union views probably reflects the fact that they operated under a Labour government at the time of the interviews. The greatest proportion of Canadian respondents (17 per cent) cited provincial officials as their best sources. The next greatest proportion (16 per cent) gave a nod to business leaders.

Our three American groups again provide very interesting results. Generally, both amphibians and politicos tend somewhat more than career officials to believe that consultation of outside views comprises a major part of their responsibilities. However, 70 per cent of career officials (*v* 92 and 88 for amphibians and politicos) consult outsiders directly at least once a month. Only at the level of weekly contact do career officials *and* amphibians fall greatly behind politicos (26 and 45 *v* 72 per cent).

Looking at specific sources, we find that career officials consult the media, business leaders, friends and acquaintances, and citizen groups about as much as do amphibians and politicos. However, they appear to fall appreciably behind the others in consultation with union leaders, local and state officials, religious and ethnic leaders, and polls. They join amphibians in resorting somewhat less than do politicos to political leaders and party workers, and leaders of farm groups. Similarly they tap somewhat more the views of academics and of 'other' professionals. Thus career officials prove to be relatively chary of consulting with advocacy groups. However, they and amphibians maintain considerably stronger links with experts than do politicos.

With respect to the views of our three groups on the most reliable source of advice and information, career officials place the greatest trust in 'other' professionals (29 per cent), business leaders (28 per cent), academics (25 per cent), and friends and acquaintances (17 per cent). Although local and state officials each attract 21 per cent of amphibians, the group more strongly prefers academics (32 per cent), business leaders (24 per cent), and friends and acquaintances (24 per cent). Politicos most often cite friends and acquaintances (40 per cent) and then political leaders and party workers (36 per cent). Here the media and business leaders tie for a distant third (20 per cent). Thus all three groups give fairly strong recognition to business leaders as preferred sources for advice and information. However, career officials and amphibians appear to place the greatest stock in expert sources. Politicos trust most often individuals of the same political stripe and/or friends and acquaintances.

CONCLUSION

Taken as a group, the US respondents did not differ sharply from the British and the Canadians in their views of their work and their agency. The Americans, along with the Canadians, tended to describe their roles in relation to more specialized aspects of their agency's mandate than did the British. Relatedly, US respondents tended to fault their system for providing central agencies with deficient and conflicting responsibilities. The Americans differ sharply from the British and Canadians in the much greater stress they give to the role of their agency in supporting the chief executive. This emphasis on the president permeated the Americans' views of networks. US respondents attribute the greatest importance to gaining the chief executive's trust as a means to obtaining membership in inner circles. As well, the Americans tend much more than the others to have interacted directly with their chief executive. Of course, concentration of executive authority in one individual diminishes the importance of cabinet-level bodies designed to ease presidents' burdens. Americans do report more than the others involvement with committees responsible for strategic issues. However, these groups attempt more to manage political problems with specific pieces of legislation than to plan annual or term programs. Similarly, the absence under Carter of cabinet-level bodies in major areas of policy seemed to contribute to the balkanization of issue sectors into ad hoc steering groups.

As we might expect from the exigences of relations between the president and Congress and the more pluralistic democracy in the United States, the American respondents reported stronger links to legislators than did the British and Canadians. Closing in the third corner of sub-governments, the Americans tend much more than the others to view consultation with outside groups and interests as part of their responsibilities and to engage in direct contact with these. Their tastes in sources of advice and information prove relatively eclectic: business leaders, academics, representatives of professional groups, and friends and acquaintances lead the list of sources that they trust the most.

The role perceptions of our British respondents differ from those of the others in two important ways. They tend much less than both the Americans and the Canadians to say that their tasks include implementation of policies and communication with outsiders; they also hold wider views of the parts of their agency's mandate for which they share responsibility. We noted that these findings probably derive from their tightly knit village life. With respect to the Britons' views of the roles of their agencies, the effects of cabinet government reveal themselves by no means as clearly as in Canada. Although a greater proportion of British than American respondents refers to the cabinet while describing the remits of their agency, the greatest number cites the prime minister.

Of course, the operation of the British cabinet system provides fewer points of access for British civil servants than their Canadian counterparts enjoy. Committees neither allow for officials to represent ministers nor permit them to become regular discussants in deliberations. Thus, in contrast to the Canadians, British officials stress experience and expertise, rather than political ability, as governing access to inner circles. They also tend more than both the Canadians and Americans to mention fellow civil servants below the level of deputy head as members of the inner circle. Generally, their exposure to the cabinet and to interdepartmental meetings resembles that of the Americans much more than that of the Canadians. They report relatively modest experience with cabinet committees. However, perhaps because lower-level bodies will become more numerous when cabinet-level bodies are less well differentiated, the British respondents engage somewhat more than the Canadians in interdepartmental gatherings. These we find often ran without the participation of deputy heads.

Even with respect to interactions with outsiders, the British continue to provide responses closer to those of the Americans than to those of the Canadians. Although they are the least likely to have direct relations with outsiders and prove to be by far the most reliant on the media, the British easily outstrip the Canadians in their willingness to find out and take into consideration the views of several different kinds of groups.

The Canadian group appears to be the deviant case in this study. Certainly the variables employed in this chapter point to that conclusion. To begin with, Canadians stress much more than the others their role in setting priorities and in allocation and management of resources. The former result corresponds to the heavy stress given under Trudeau to 'rational' decision-making; the latter reflects the fragmentation of authority that occurs when several central agencies involve themselves in crucial issues surrounding the expenditure budget. Struggles over control of the delicate process whereby detailed plans and priorities are converted into substantive decisions that abide by the fiscal framework had reached dysfunctional proportions during the 1976 interviews. The relatively gloomy view of the effectiveness of central agencies given by respondents underlines the seriousness of the conflicts.

We have found so far in this book ample indications of the degree to which the distinctions between ministers and key bureaucratic players have been blurred in Canada. Officials' access to cabinet committees emerged as the principal source of erosion here. In relative terms, we find very strong evidence that the Canadians value highly the ability to operate effectively as political actors in the ministerial-bureaucratic milieu. The degree to which our officials played down the relevance of interdepartmental committees suggests that the more astute central agents concentrate their efforts on gaining a profile in cabinet committees.

Another side to Canadians' immersion in executive-bureaucratic politics suggests itself when we look at their interactions with outsiders. The relative insularity of the cabinet from Parliament and the apparent aloofness of central agents conjure up the image of an impenetrable fortress. Earlier, we resorted to a milder image, the turtle syndrome. Nomenclature aside, insularity permits the Canadians to place considerably less value than the others on consultation of sources of advice and information outside government.

Our look, within the United States, at politicos, amphibians, and career officials yielded some exceptionally clear differences. Focusing first on politicos, their renderings of their roles emphasized involvement in setting strategic plans and making major decisions adhere to these. Since the Carter administration operated with relatively weak structures for carrying out these central agency functions, the politicos' perceptions might stem largely from a 'being there' effect, whereby they associate with tasks that would run from 'the top of the tree' even if these work in a relatively haphazard way. At least, the politicos' stress on facilitating the decision process and maintaining lines of communication suggests more attempts to keep the administration together than efforts toward mapping out priorities and trying to make them stick. Politicos, largely because of their clearer association with the president, both attain higher profiles in various networks and make greater use of them. Regarding outsiders, they maintain the strongest relations both with Congress and with various interest groups and attentive citizens. In contrast with amphibians, their political manoeuvrability comes to the fore both in the regularity and the diverse settings of their contacts with Congress and in their reliance on advice derived from contacts with friends and various partisan figures.

Amphibians do not provide responses that differ dramatically from those of the others to questions concerning their perceptions of their own roles and those of their agency. They tended somewhat more than the others to style themselves as policy advisers and to describe their agency's roles with reference to its head. Both these findings might stem from the fact that amphibians joined the administration because of prominence in a field of policy and, often, close associations with department heads. The latter assertion draws further support from the fact that amphibians remain in more regular touch with their own department head than do the others. With respect to committees, the amphibians receive exposure to cabinet-level bodies less than politicos but more than career officials. The fact that they see their involvement in these panels as attempting to change secretaries' views of problems suggests once again that they approach their work from the perspective of expert adviser. Similar themes recur when we look at the interactions of amphibians with outsiders. They report almost as much exposure as politicos to official meetings with congressmen and senators. These more formal settings – usually committees – normally require expert briefing or testimony. Along with politicos, amphibians tend more than career officials to see consultation with outsiders as forming part of their responsibilities. However, they resort more than politicos to outside views from academics and from representatives of state and local governments.

Career officials in the United States revealed the strongest interest in functions related to expenditure review. However, this finding probably derives from OMB's continued deference to its career complement. Career officials tend much more than the others to focus their activities on narrower segments of their agency's mandate. This notwithstanding, US career officials report more robust relations with their department heads than either the British or Canadian respondents. Generally, they involve themselves less than do amphibians and politicos with both cabinet-level and interdepartmental committees. Career officials tend more than the others to avoid groups and members of the public whom they view as too partisan or narrow in appeal. However, unlike politicos, the Canadians, and, to a lesser degree, the British, they give very high marks to academics and leading professionals as sources of advice and information.

12

Accountability, careers, and backgrounds

The preceding discussion of our officials' views of the role of their agencies, how they relate to key players in the executive-bureaucratic community, and their interactions with legislators and other 'outsiders' all raise questions of their accountability. These, in turn, suggest issues related to how they view public service as a profession and what types of career routes they have followed as well as what their sociodemographic backgrounds are.

When applied to public servants, the term *accountability* refers to officials' belief that they must act in accordance with the norms that they as individuals, society generally, and/or certain institutions uphold as standards of behaviour.[1] Traditionally, students of administrative behaviour have tended to view accountability in the public service as falling along a continuum. While certainly aware of wider societal and institutional environments, *highly subjective* officials would uphold as standards for their behaviour moral convictions, professional standards, and views of democracy that are derived predominantly from personal convictions. At the other extreme, *highly objective* officials would focus on institutional obligations. A sense of public service as a vocation would cause these officials to keep at arm's length the world beyond the executive-bureaucratic community. Upon entering government, they would have set aside former ideological commitments and stakes in the marketplace.

As difficult to obtain as the ideal of objective accountability appears, it has inspired many bureaucrats who believe that they only do what they have received mandates to do. These derive either from political authorities (executive and legislative), or from bureaucratic superiors. If subjective accountability takes root in conscious and unabashed upholding of personalized views, objective accountability stems from the deliberate adoption of loyal obedience as a state of mind. A bureaucratic system that attempts to foster objective accountability sets out a task not unlike that of a religious order. As with religious obedience, it calls upon officials to go beyond simply willingly doing what they are told to do. In addition, it urges them to place their thoughts in harmony with those of their superiors. Such 'piety' enables the official to experience greater peace while obeying. As well, it permits him to use discretion so long as he attempts to operate according to his superior's 'mind.'

In between the two extreme expressions of the meaning of accountability, we find the world of public service in which most officials operate. Here public servants must seek a mix of standards that fits the requirements of their position *and* the system in which they operate. With respect to positions, both the competitive nature of the executive-bureaucratic politics surrounding a post and the amount of discretion left the official can tip the mix in favour of subjective accountability. Most, if not all, central agents face these circumstances.[2] As a group, officials who work in central agencies bring exceptional talent and creativity to their tasks. Thus, individually they must learn to work with colleagues who virtually all manifest entrepreneurial qualities. The strategic location of central agents in government harnesses the energy of their collegial situation. It does so mainly by providing psychic rewards that surpass those available to only the very top officials in operational departments. First, central agents focus on service-wide rather than departmental concerns. Second, they enjoy access to a wider range of information and greater exposure to meta-issues. Third, they benefit from closer identification with the sources, both individual and collective, of executive authority.

Regarding the systems in which officials work, we should acknowledge the influence of conventional thinking on views of accountability. Most important, the concept *ministerial responsibility* holds particular sway in the United Kingdom and Canada. According to this view, ministers report individually and collectively to Parliament for all acts or omissions of the public servants operating within individual departments.[3] Unless their actions have been approved by their minister, officials do not release information to the public or openly express personal views. This convention assures that ministers and cabinets may always project the image of decisive and competent execution of the public interest so essential to winning re-election. In return for their silence, officials receive from ministers a virtually ironclad commitment of protection from unfavourable publicity and continued job security should something go wrong. Normally, only the grossest incompetence on the part of an official results in the loss of these protections.

The potency of such conventions notwithstanding, public servants cannot think themselves into a state of disembodied spirithood whereby they behave only according to the dictates and minds of duly elected and appointed superiors. Allowing for the distinction between personal goals, societal values, and institutional norms as influences on bureaucratic behaviour, all officials will imbibe views of the public interest that have not emerged from executive and bureaucratic authorities. These views and the emphases officials place on them will derive in no small portion from their personal perspectives which includes their familial and societal history as well as their public service career.

This chapter starts then with a plea for realism about bureaucratic power. In doing so, it invokes a major caveat. We should keep in mind the 'myth spheres' of our three systems. Myth spheres protect individuals' traditional views of life by providing automatic translation of experience according to hallowed beliefs. The popular British TV series 'Yes, Minister' takes off from this point. It satirizes the incongruity of Whitehall's continued obeisance to ministers coupled with its officials' exceptional cunning at the art of getting what they want from their political masters. On the other side, Americans overwork their image of government by the people. To be sure, Congress often asserts itself to such an extent that the term *chief executive* appears to be a misnomer.[4] However, strong presidents such as Lyndon Johnson have, at times, proved exceptionally adept at marshalling the bureaucracy and getting what they want from Congress. Thus we must keep a weather eye for traces of myth spheres in our officials' responses.

ACCOUNTABILITY

Several studies have already examined the views of public servants on accountability. For instance, Ezra Suleiman discusses in detail a significant transformation in the thinking of some French bureaucrats about their work. Whereas in previous generations French officials would focus on the technical details connected with implementation of policies, many in the current generation admit to strong interest in policy making per se.[5] The dividing line between those who uphold the traditional and those who uphold the recent views appears to fall between those occupying positions in 'line' departments and those working on the advisory offices ('cabinets') of ministers. The former still tend to see policy-making and administration as dichotomous.[6] Officials in *cabinets* more frequently have abandoned the sharp distinction between those realms. Such officials realize that they must keep in constant view the political implications of the various options that come to light while they attempt to advise their minister.

Robert Putnam addresses the issue by asking whether the dichotomy politics-administration has not already revealed itself to be an illusion. Finding support in works by Richard Rose and Michael R. Gordon, Putnam puts forth the view that bureaucrats can effectively operate as masters of the policy process.[7] Their efforts seemingly centre on elements of administration such as information, technical expertise, and the setting of agendas. However, these provide the building-blocks for policy decisions. When successful at manipulating such resources, officials' presentations of various options and discussions of the implications of these can preordain the decisions of politicians. Putnam reports that officials in Germany and Britain tend now to minimize the distinction between administration and politics. In addition, three of five report that they involve themselves in executive-bureaucratic politics and derive satisfaction from this level of involvement.[8]

Joel Aberbach and Bert Rockman press this line of inquiry a step further. In the test of the dichotomy administration-politics, they compare the role-orientations of top us federal executives and congressmen. They find that the executives view their work from essentially the same perspective as the politicians: 'We want to emphasize the notion that American legislative politicians *and* top federal executives must be well schooled in the arts of politics in a system that provides ample opportunities for both politicians and bureaucrats of an entrepreneurial spirit.'[9]

Our respondents were asked to discuss at length their views of accountability, which are analysed in Table 12.1. Specifically, they were encouraged to consider whether they were accountable to the chief executive, the cabinet, their own department head, their bureaucratic superior, the legislature, the public, and/or their own consciences. We look at our officials' responses to these questions from three perspectives. First, for each of the above, we ascertain the proportions of central agents in each country who consider a possible object of accountability important in their case. Second, we examine the proportions of respondents who consider the various objects of primary importance. Third, in order to develop a profile of their views of bureaucratic accountability, we assess the rationales provided by our officials for each choice.

In looking at respondents' choices of objects of accountability, we may think of four clusters. Officials might have chosen objects on the basis of *hierarchical and personal* commitments to executive-bureaucratic authorities including their superior, the chief executive, and the head of their department. As well, they might have mentioned *collective and political* authorities such as the cabinet and the legislature. In addition, they might have given a nod to *generalized and external* elements, taking in 'the people,' specific segments of the public, and 'the state.' Finally, they might have invoked *individual* considerations involving matters of conscience and professional standards.

With respect to hierarchical and personal accountability, over 80 per cent of respondents in each country cite one or more objects. Between 60 and 70 per cent of officials in the three samples mention their superior. However, such even distributions do not emerge with reference to views of accountability to the chief executive and the head of their department. Sixty-eight per cent of us respondents say they attempt to maintain accountability to the chief executive; 75 per cent refer to the department head. The British and Canadian figures fall between 30 and 44 per cent.

The figures for collective and political accountability provide a range of 16 per cent. British respondents acknowledge objects under this category the most (42 per cent); us officials stress them the least (26 per cent). However, the figures for the entire cluster disguise some important differences. Most dramatic here, 32 and 26 per cent of British and Canadian central agents claim efforts toward accountability to the cabinet while a paltry 2 per cent of us respondents do so. However, the 24 per cent of Americans who say they keep Congress in mind at least doubles the percentage who feel accountable to Parliament in Britain (12) and Canada (10).

Much as with collective and political accountability, the proportions of respondents in each country recognizing the importance of generalized and external objects come reasonably close. A look at specific objects, however, suggests additional cross-national differences. British respondents stress accountability to 'the people' somewhat less frequently than do Americans and Canadians (24 per cent *v* 42 and 35 per cent). Although the small numbers strain statistical analysis, American and British respondents value accountability to specific segments of the public more than do Canadians. Meanwhile, officials in Canada and Britain give stronger emphasis to accountability to the state than do those in the United States.

Sharp drops from the United States to Britain to Canada appear in the proportions for individual considerations. Seventy-four, 56, and 37 per cent of us, British, and Canadian central agents, respectively, hold one or

TABLE 12.1
Accountability

Perceptions	United States (career, amphibians, politicos) N = 132 (69, 38, 25)	United Kingdom N = 41	Canada N = 92	Significance
Accountability is				
Hierarchical/personal	95 (90, 100, 100)[c]	95	83	b
to superior	70 (84, 68, 32)[a]	66	60	
to chief executive	68 (58, 71, 92)[b]	34	32	a
to head of department	75 (67, 90, 76)[c]	44	30	a
Collective/political	26 (23, 34, 20)	42	32	
to cabinet	2 (0, 8, 0)[c]	32	26	a
to legislature	24 (23, 26, 20)	12	10	c
Generalized/external	43 (45, 40, 44)	32	38	
to the people	42 (45, 40, 40)	24	35	
to a segment of the public	6 (4, 5, 12)	5	1	
to the state	1 (0, 0, 4)	5	9	b
Individual	74 (83, 63, 68)	56	37	a
to own conscience	42 (36, 45, 56)	27	11	a
to professional standards	61 (75, 52, 36)[a]	42	30	a
Primary accountability is				
Hierarchical/personal	68 (64, 74, 72)	68	57	
to superior	19 (26, 18, 0)[c]	32	32	
to chief executive	32 (29, 26, 48)	20	20	
to department head	17 (9, 29, 24)[c]	17	7	c
Collective/political	2 (1, 0, 4)	12	10	b
to cabinet	0 (0, 0, 0)	12	10	a
to legislature	2 (1, 0, 4)	0	0	
Generalized/external	9 (12, 8, 4)	2	15	
to the people	8 (12, 8, 0)	0	11	
to a segment of the public	0 (0, 0, 0)	0	0	
to the state	1 (0, 0, 4)	2	4	
Individual	21 (23, 18, 20)	15	14	
to own conscience	7 (4, 11, 8)	0	0	b
to professional standards	14 (19, 8, 12)	15	14	
View of bureaucratic accountability				
Subjective	86 (88, 79, 92)	56	54	a
Moral convictions	37 (25, 45, 60)[b]	22	8	a
Professional standards	60 (71, 53, 36)[b]	30	22	a
Democratic values	46 (36, 50, 68)[c]	22	32	b
Objective	78 (83, 74, 72)	95	97	a
Public service seen as a vocation	29 (49, 8, 4)[a]	22	33	

TABLE 12.1 (continued)

Perceptions	United States (career, amphibians, politicos) $N = 132$ (69, 38, 25)	United Kingdom $N = 41$	Canada $N = 92$	Significance
Concern with mandate/ rules	27 (36, 16, 16)^c	32	44	c
Accountability to career superior	14 (20, 11, 4)	32	49	a
Accountability to political superior	53 (45, 63, 60)	59	58	
Communal	45 (52, 42, 28)	44	16	a
Values problem-solving skills	34 (38, 34, 24)	34	2	a
Believes skills are transferable	20 (20, 18, 20)	2	0	a
Values peer feedback	8 (6, 11, 12)	12	3	
Non-deferential	14 (17, 11, 8)	2	13	

a Chi-square significant at 0.001 level
b Chi-square significant at 0.01 level
c Chi-square significant at 0.01 level

both of the dimensions in this cluster to be important. The same declining order appears under individual conscience (42, 27, and 11 per cent) and professional standards (61, 42, and 30 per cent).

Respondents in each country tended overwhelmingly to resort to hierarchical and personal authority when asked to narrow their allegiances to the most central. Americans reveal a considerable, though not statistically significant, preference for the chief executive. British and Canadian officials select their superior the most often. The Americans just about fade from the picture under the collective and political cluster. The two respondents who gave the nod to Congress comprise the entire US contribution to this category. Twelve and 10 per cent of British and Canadian respondents, respectively, give the highest priority to the cabinet. However, only one British respondent opts for the generalized and external category against the 9 and 15 per cent of Americans and Canadians who register this emphasis. Finally, under individual considerations, between 14 and 15 per cent of respondents in each country choose professional standards above all and 7 per cent of Americans select personal conscience.

In sum, the findings from our look at central agents' objects of accountability appear to echo previous observations both in this book and elsewhere. Americans do report more diverse pressures. However, they tend to resolve these by gravitating to the same cluster that their British and Canadian opposite numbers cite. Most defer to hierarchical and personal authority. In this respect, the Americans' emphasis on the president contrasts somewhat with the others' preference for their bureaucratic superior. However, the British and Canadians differ from the Americans most in the proportions reporting ultimate accountability to the cabinet. The concentrated authority of the us presidency as opposed to the collective responsibility of the British and Canadian cabinet systems probably explains in very large part our cross-national differences.

The data on our politicos, amphibians, and career officials in the United States also resonate with what we have already discussed. With respect to simple mention of hierarchical and personal authority, career officials provide easily the largest proportion opting for bureaucratic superiors, politicos reveal the greatest respect for the chief executive, and amphibians place the most stress on departmental heads. Dramatic differences fail to appear with respect to most other objects. However, a very large proportion of career officials (75 per cent) keep professional standards in mind to some degree (v 52 and 36 per cent, respectively, for amphibians and politicos). The winnowing process amplifies these results with the vast majority of each group saying they would yield to hierarchical and personal authority. Here career officials provide the largest proportion choosing superiors (26 per cent v 18 and 0 for amphibians and politicos). The 48 per cent of politicos opting for the president greatly exceeds the figures for the other two groups. This makes sense. Politicos distinguished themselves as political operatives before assuming their positions.

Embedded in our respondents' lengthy rationales for their views on objects of accountability, we find a wealth of thoughts on the pressures they experience. Such elaborations touched on three major areas of accountability. One element, Don Quixote factors, entered into our discussions when respondents based their choices of objects or qualified these with reference to overriding moral convictions, professional standards, and democratic instincts. Often this dimension emerged essentially as anxiety over maintaining personal integrity in the executive-bureaucratic milieu. Hence, many Americans referred to what they considered the illegal and/or undemocratic activities of the White House under Richard Nixon. They hoped out loud that they would have the courage to 'blow the whistle' or resign if those circumstances developed under their current administration. Others believed in a more positive sense that their remaining in government contributes, albeit in a small way, to the pursuit of moral principles, professional standards and democratic values.

A second element, green-eye-shade considerations, conjures in my mind the image of a senior official whom I interviewed in the British Treasury. When I entered the respondent's office the lights were out. The official was working at his desk by a window through which winter's dim sunlight barely shone. The respondent, who wore braces that suspended both his shirt sleeves, explained apologetically that right-handed officials could save electricity by working close to a window on their left side. All he lacked was a green eye-shade. However, the image received regular use in Washington where respondents frequently referred to career officials as 'green-eye-shade types.' Many career officials prefaced their own views of accountability by invoking the term and then stressing their adherence to the stereotype or maintaining that their perceptions of accountability transcend the concept. At any rate, green-eye-shade considerations include concern with the integrity of public service as a vocation, emphases on mandates and formalized rules, and references to obedience to career and political superiors.

Our third element taps officials' views that neither the Don Quixote nor green-eye-shade formulations satisfies completely the requirements of bureaucratic accountability. Officials here registered at least some tendency toward communal accountability. They told of the special demands placed upon officials working in a high-level bureaucratic community. These centre on such issues as the development of finely honed problem-solving skills, the transferability of these skills from unit to unit, sensitivity to feedback from peers, and non-deferential orientations whereby collegial obligations as well as traditional hierarchical ones come into focus.

Although more than half the respondents in each country stress some aspects of the Don Quixote view, us officials outstrip the others by far (86 per cent v 56 and 54 per cent for British and Canadian, respectively). American Don Quixotes provide the largest proportions for each category comprising the view. Canadians provide the smallest percentages citing moral convictions (8) and professional standards (22) while the British, in relative terms, offer the smallest contingent to those upholding democratic values (22 per cent). Virtually every· British and Canadian official makes some mention of elements of the green-eye-shade view (95 and 97 per cent, respectively), while somewhat fewer us central agents do so (78 per cent). Even in comparison to their British counterparts, Canadians place disproportionate emphasis on mandates and rules (44 v

32 per cent) and obedience to superiors (49 v 32 per cent). With respect to perceptions of communal accountability, US and British central agents provide percentages short of those in the other categories, but still in the mid-forties (45 and 44, respectively). Canadians, however, trail far behind with only 16 per cent referring to one or more aspects of communal accountability.

The Canadian case appears to be anomalous. Through access to cabinet committees these officials have risen to stellar heights in the executive-bureaucratic community. Yet they provide only the most conventional views of accountability. Do myth-spheres play an especially strong role here? Do the relatively unschooled members of a public service that has grown like Topsy pay lip service to conventional thinking while in fact engaging fully in the politics of their executive-bureaucratic milieu? We will return to this issue when we examine the career orientations and paths of central agents.

As has been their wont in preceding sections, the American groups produce responses that differ considerably. Similar percentages in each group manifest one or other Don Quixote trait (88, 79 , and 92 for career officials, amphibians, and politicos, respectively). However, the three types of officials favoured different elements of the orientation. Perhaps symptomatic of an American hangover from the Nixon administration – especially Watergate – politicos, first, and amphibians, second, felt the most compelled to uphold the role of moral convictions and democratic values. As expected, amphibians acknowledged the relevance of professional standards somewhat more than did politicos. However, career officials overwhelmingly favoured this perspective. With the exception of obedience to political superiors, career officials discuss the various aspects of green-eye-shade accountability much more than those from the other groups. The reliance of the three groups on communal accountability suggests that career officials and amphibians place greater stock in this dimension than do politicos.

CAREER ORIENTATIONS AND PATHS

If we go as far back in the literature as the first scholarly attempt to fathom the bureaucratic career, we find Max Weber. Weber considered a career in the civil service to be a vocation.[10] In using this term he made a direct association between the way in which civil servants begin and pursue their careers and the way in which clerics and religious assume their state of life. The latter accept their vocations in response to what they perceive as a special call from God to dedicate themselves in singular service. Weber maintained that, in a similar sense, individuals enter the bureaucracy in order to commit their entire working lives to public service. They usually developed such aspirations while still motivated by the ideals of youth, took studies that prepared them especially well for work in government (in Weber's Germany, law), and, once having landed in a position, viewed it as a lifelong commitment. Under Weber's view of the bureaucratic vocation, few would terminate their careers by moving to the private sector or into politics. As well, virtually no one still seeking advancement would leave a career in business or politics at mid-life to enter the civil service. Notwithstanding Weber's view of bureaucracy as a vocation, he did not delude himself about civil service power: 'Under normal conditions, the power position of fully developed bureaucracy is always overtowering. The "political master" finds himself in the position of the "dilettante" who stands within the management of administration.'[11]

Weber's stress on public service as a vocation dovetailed all too well with the view that public servants were objectively accountable. For instance, the clear demarcation of bureaucratic and political careers in the United Kingdom would, according to conventional wisdom, assure that officials concerned themselves only with administration.[12] In fact, the cleavages between the two communities evolving from the demarcation tended to strengthen the ability of bureaucrats to control policy-making through discreet use of 'administrative' resources.[13]

Recent research suggests that Italian and French officials follow the most Weberian career ladders. Putnam reports in a 1971 study that fully 95 per cent of the senior Italian officials he had interviewed began their careers before 1943.[14] Further, 80 per cent of his respondents had worked in a single department throughout their years of public service. The Italian system, it appears, provides an exceptionally hierarchical setting. It bases advancement in large part on long-term service within one's original bureaucratic organization.

Ezra Suleiman has identified similar preoccupations in France. In reporting his findings, he stresses the vocational character of public service in that country. Twenty-five per cent of his respondents claimed that they aspired to public-service careers before adolescence; 40 per cent recalled having made up their minds before beginning university.[15] Suleiman underlines the significance of these figures by recounting that many of his officials described decisions in favour of career in bureaucracy as a response to a 'call.' Although they did not tend to stay in one department, practically all of Suleiman's officials belonged to three corps of the bureaucracy that provide most of the senior executives.

We have already dwelt at length in chapter 10 on differences in the policies for recruitment and career development of senior officials in the three countries. It is sufficient at this stage simply to reiterate some of the highlights. The United Kingdom prefers to put aspirants to the senior public service on track to such posts immediately after leaving university. Once they start their traineeships, young officials become permanent members of a department. After leaving the fledgling stage, they undergo a number of developmental assignments as they progress through the ranks. Such career planning allows for posts elsewhere in Whitehall – often in central agencies – and, occasionally, stints in the private sector. Generally, officials face a number of restrictions on rapid promotion. For instance, a post as assistant secretary requires an exemption for individuals under thirty-four years old and in no case goes to those under thirty-two.

The United States has attained nowhere near this level of control on career development. However, career officials do tend to remain in the same department for most of their career and individuals in top posts hold on to these for relatively long periods of time. Such practices result in career progress and socialization about as stratified as in the United Kingdom. American presidents, of course, assign many of the top executive posts to political appointees. This convention maintains the double, career-political, tracks in the US bureaucracy which Hugh Heclo dubbed 'a government of strangers.'[16] Many political appointees have served before under previous administrations. Effective presidents know how to use appointees to shake up departments and assure that career officials serve up policy options that fulfil the objectives of the administration.

Although Canadians believe that their senior public service operates more like the British than the American system, empirical research suggests that it follows neither. The 1953 career data used by John Porter indicated that even then senior officials in Canada did not rise through stratified career routes.[17] Only one-quarter had spent their entire working lives in the public service; nearly two-thirds took on senior posts after entering directly from the private sector. Along the same lines, P.J. Chartrand and K.L. Pond report 1967 data that indicate that only 15 per cent of senior officials had worked in government throughout their adult years.[18] The authors found as well that the officials who changed their departments most frequently experienced the quickest advancement to the highest posts.[19]

We have already noted that Michael Pitfield, when he was clerk of the Privy Council and secretary to the cabinet, registered alarm over current recruitment and development of senior officials in Canada.[20] He maintained that it does not adequately prepare individuals for public service. These concerns receive alarming amplification in Nicole S. Morgan's monograph plotting the course of a huge 'career bubble' of officials, still in their thirties and forties, who have reached the top of the public service too early.[21] By occupying almost all the senior positions available, they face stagnation of their own careers. Further, they have cut off the next generation from even gradual entrance to senior posts relinquished through attrition. Canada, of course, permitted this aberration in order to keep up with the steady growth of government since the Second World War. Along the way, government has competed with other sectors, particularly business and universities, for top talent. In order to remain appealing, it has given top officials higher rates of remuneration than available to their opposite numbers in our other countries. As well, its provision of very great responsibilities at relatively early ages has contributed compelling psychic rewards to senior officials who might otherwise find careers elsewhere more alluring.

For the purposes of this analysis (see Table 12.2), career orientations include individuals' views of why they entered government, of expertise, of what they wish to accomplish during their careers, and of what they would miss if they left public service. With respect to their motives for entering government, the factors mentioned by respondents included idealism and a desire to serve the public, academic training, the hope of 'being where the action is,' compatible experiences in a previous career, interests in a specific policy sector, an opportunity for personal advancement, and partisan or political commitments. With the exception of the hope of being where the action is, British officials provide proportions closer to the Americans than to the Canadians. Under the 'action' motive, the British fall 7 per cent above the Americans and behind the Canadians (ie 20 v 13 and 27 per cent, respectively).

In addition to their relatively strong emphasis on being where the action is, Canadians tend much more than the others to say they saw a career in the public-service as an opportunity for advancement and to cite an interest in a specific policy sector. However, Canadians ascribed somewhat less significance to academic training and to partisan or political commitments. In brief, Canadians appear to highlight motives that relate to the fulfilment of *secular* career satisfaction. Motives relating directly to the peculiar nature of public service or of politics played less of a role in Canadians' choice of their careers than they did in the choice of Americans and Britons.

Over 80 per cent of respondents in each sample claimed one or other type of expertise. However, American and British respondents provided

TABLE 12.2
Career orientations

Orientation	United States (career, amphibians, politicos) N = 132 (69, 38, 25)	United Kingdom N = 41	Canada N = 92	Significance
Motive for entering government				
Idealism, public service	29 (32, 18, 36)	37	26	
Scholastic training	28 (33, 26, 16)	27	12	b
It's 'where the action is'	13 (16, 8, 12)	20	27	b
Previous career experience	24 (12, 55, 12)[a]	20	15	
Interest in specific policy sector	8 (6, 11, 12)	2	15	c
Career opportunity	48 (61, 47, 12)[a]	37	63	b
Partisan or political commitment	24 (4, 21, 84)[a]	17	8	b
Respondent considers self an expert	96 (99, 97, 88)	93	80	a
Area of expertise				
Administrative-management skills	22 (25, 11, 32)	22	33	
Administrative policy	14 (16, 13, 8)	10	3	c
Political skills, knowledge	27 (28, 16, 44)[c]	32	9	a
Legal skills, knowledge	10 (4, 13, 20)	0	4	c
Analytical skills	27 (35, 28, 12)	7	3	a
Specific policy sector	12 (7, 26, 4)[b]	7	13	
Economics, generally	17 (23, 18, 0)[c]	27	13	
A sector of economics	13 (15, 16, 4)	10	17	
Interpersonal skills, knowledge	4 (4, 3, 4)	2	4	
Source of expertise				
Academic	68 (71, 74, 52)	37	29	a
Business experience	14 (7, 16, 32)[b]	5	15	
Government experience	85 (94, 82, 64)[a]	78	46	a
Other experience	15 (6, 24, 28)[b]	12	22	
Personal qualities	14 (13, 11, 24)	0	12	c
Respondent has tried to accomplish something while in government	83 (81, 84, 88)	71	64	b
Goals or accomplishments				
Tries to make government responsive	29 (26, 34, 28)	17	16	
Planning-oriented	31 (29, 26, 44)	34	32	

TABLE 12.2 (continued)

Orientation	United States (career, amphibians, politicos) $N = 132$ (69, 38, 25)	United Kingdom $N = 41$	Canada $N = 92$	Significance
Policy-oriented	36 (39, 45, 12)[c]	42	34	
Personnel-oriented	14 (15, 18, 8)	12	14	
Tries to give best advice	27 (33, 11, 32)[c]	32	12	b
Committed to general, over-arching goal	7 (4, 8, 16)	5	13	
Wants to have an impact	11 (9, 16, 8)	5	12	
Desires personal satisfaction	14 (13, 24, 0)[c]	5	23	b
Tries to be a facilitator	9 (3, 11, 24)[b]	10	11	
If respondent left government, he/she would miss				
Impact in specific policy field	18 (10, 37, 12)[b]	0	7	a
Impact, generally	40 (46, 26, 44)	29	38	
Atmosphere	61 (54, 63, 76)	56	60	
Variety	11 (10, 13, 8)	12	16	
Colleagues	9 (9, 5, 16)	22	21	c
Sense of public service	22 (22, 26, 16)	32	17	
Intellectual challenge	8 (4, 13, 8)	20	7	c
Instrumental opportunities offered by the job	13 (17, 11, 4)	10	17	

For a, b, and c see notes to Table 12.1.

somewhat larger proportions than the Canadians (96 and 93 per cent, respectively, *v* 80 per cent). Reasonably large numbers of officials cited the following areas of expertise: administrative and managerial skills, knowledge of administrative policy, political skills, legal skills, analytic skills, knowledge about a specific policy sector, knowledge of economics, knowledge of a sector of economics, and interpersonal skills. Here Canadians stand out once again. They tend to de-emphasize administrative policy and political skills. However, the British join the Canadians in claiming, less than the Americans, legal and analytical skills.

In addition to noting various areas of expertise, our officials traced the origins of these: 1) academic training; 2) experience in the business world, government, and 'other sectors,' including the professions and the military; and 3) personal qualities not connected with education and career backgrounds, including a knack for getting along with people or an especially analytical mind. In each country, the greatest proportions cite experience in government and, after that, academic training. However, a huge gap opens between the 46 per cent of Canadians who attribute importance to experience in government and the 85 and 78 per cent of Americans and British, respectively, who do so. This result reflects starkly Canadians' relatively modest exposure to government work. Even the 64 per cent of US politicos who ascribe some value to their experience in government exceeds the Canadian proportion. However, both the British and Canadians cite academic training less than the Americans do (37 and 29 per cent, respectively, v 68 per cent). We noted earlier the relatively high trust US respondents place in academics as sources of advice and information.

When asked whether they had any particular goals they wished to accomplish during their careers in the public service, our officials cited the following: making government responsive, bringing about better planning, improving policies within a specific sector, attracting and keeping the best personnel, attempting to give the best possible advice to superiors, seeking some overarching goal such as improving the quality of human life, wanting to have an impact on things of great relevance to society, gratifying personal needs such as acquiring greater knowledge of how the system works or being presented with challenging problems, and, finally, facilitating the smooth operation of government. In each sample, roughly the same proportions of respondents appear under most of the goals.

Once more, the Canadians provide most of the apparent heterogeneity in responses. They tend less to make a point of affirming that they try to give the best possible advice to superiors (12 per cent v 27 and 32 per cent for Americans and British, respectively); they single out much more often than the others goals relating to personal satisfaction (23 v 14 and 5 per cent). We find as well some evidence that both British and Canadian respondents value less than Americans the task of keeping government responsive (17 and 16 v 29 per cent). Of the findings derived from respondents' accounts of what they try to accomplish, the Canadians' relative stress on personal gratification best fits our observations above. Canadians lean much more than others toward viewing public service as an opportunity for personal advancement taken in a secular, rather than vocational, light.

Finally, in response to our question about what they would miss if they left government, our officials raised the following aspects of their jobs which they find enjoyable: having an impact on a specific field of policy, influencing public affairs generally, working within such an exciting and challenging atmosphere, dealing with a great variety of problems, being stimulated by exceptionally bright colleagues, finding within one's work a sense of public service, facing so many intellectual challenges, and personal considerations such as life-style and standard of living. One clear result emerges from our respondents' views of what they would miss. Large majorities (61, 56, and 60 per cent for the United States, Britain, and Canada, respectively) would regret having lost a place in such a charged atmosphere as provided by public service at their level. Canadians and the British indicate somewhat less than Americans that they would miss having an impact on a specific field of policy (7 and 0 per cent, respectively, v 18 per cent); and Americans and Canadians acknowledge less than the British the loss of the intellectual challenge to their work (7 and 8 per cent, respectively, v 20 per cent). As well, the Canadians and the British ascribe much greater significance than do the Americans to the loss of exceptional colleagues (21 and 22 per cent, respectively, v 9 per cent).

An examination of differences among our American groups mostly presents straightforward results. With respect to motives for entering government, amphibians gave vastly disproportionate weight to experiences in a previous career (55 per cent v 12 per cent for career officials and politicos). Of course, many of our amphibians had written major books in their area or had held prestigious jobs in the private sector, universities, or one of the think tanks. Interestingly, the amphibians indicate almost as much as career officials (47 per cent v 61 per cent) and a good deal more than politicos (12 per cent) that the opportunities attached to entering government had attracted them. In this respect, their views corresponded with the strong American tradition whereby outsiders serve stints in government in order to improve their knowledge of how the system works. Finally, it comes as no surprise that politicos overwhelmingly cite partisan and political commitments as motivating their joining government (84 per cent v 4 and 21 per cent for career officials and amphibians, respectively).

Amphibians stand out from the others in their views of expertise. They value political skills a great deal less than do politicos *and* career officials (16 per cent v 44 and 28 per cent, respectively) and credit administrative and managerial talents somewhat less (11 per cent v 32 and 25 per cent). However, they ascribe much greater weight to expertise within a policy sector than do the others (26 per cent v 4 and 7 per cent). With respect to the sources of expertise, amphibians come out closer to career officials than politicos. They mention more often debts to academic training and experience in government.

The Americans' views of what they wish to accomplish and what they would miss do not provide so clear a picture as the other career-orientation responses. Both career officials and amphibians singled out goals relating to specific policy fields much more than politicos (39 and 45 per cent, respectively, *v* 12 per cent). However, the almost identical importance attributed by career officials and politicos to making sure they proffer the best possible advice exceeds considerably that given by amphibians. Perhaps amphibians believe themselves sufficiently expert that they do not have to worry greatly about the quality of their advice.

Consistent with our previous finding that amphibians prize especially strongly the opportunity to work in government, these same officials refer much more than the others to hoped-for accomplishments related to personal satisfaction. However, politicos stand out from the rest by citing more often their efforts toward facilitating the smooth operation of government. Except for the fact that amphibians highlight their current impact on a specific field of policy much more than do the others, the three American groups fail to offer dramatically different views of what they would miss if they left government.

Turning to the career paths of central agents (see Table 12.3), only small proportions of officials in each country recall deciding on careers in the public service before going to university (12 per cent in the United States and Britain and 5 per cent in Canada). However, both the American and British respondents still come across as early bloomers in comparison to Canadians. More than twice the proportion of officials in the former samples made up their minds immediately after completing university and/or mandatory military service (50 and 49 per cent, respectively, *v* 24 per cent). By default, the Canadians overwhelmingly contribute to the 'late vocations,' namely, those who opted for work in the federal government after several years in another sector (69 per cent *v* 38 and 34 per cent, respectively).

With respect to years actually served, British respondents yield by far the largest proportions working 11 to 20 (46 per cent) and 21 or more years (37 per cent). The Carter appointees clearly tip the scales in favour of the US contingent among respondents who have served five years or less (38 *v* 15 and 21 per cent for Britain and Canada). However, for a predominantly career complement, the Canadians comprise a remarkably short-tenured group. They have the same proportion as do the Americans with 11 to 20 years service (28 per cent) and actually produce a smaller percentage of officials who have worked in government 21 or more years (15–20 per cent).

Regarding service in their present department, the British do not report very much longer service than do the Canadians. Of course, No. 10, the Cabinet Office, and the Central Policy Review Staff provide only temporary assignments, whether for appointees or career officials. As well, the Civil Service Department split off from HM Treasury fairly recently (1968). These facts no doubt explain in part the similarities between our British and Canadian results. Notwithstanding the very high proportions of US respondents, largely amphibians and politicos, who have spent three years or less in their departments, the Americans produce, by a hair, the largest percentage of officials who have worked in their department ten years or more (25 v 24 and 11 per cent for Britain and Canada). The US practice whereby career officials tend not to stray from their original department probably contributes greatly to this finding.

We may examine as well the experiences of our central agents elsewhere in the national/federal government. The United Kingdom produces by far the largest proportion of officials who worked before in other central agencies (51 v 17 and 19 per cent for the United States and Canada). HM Treasury provides a disproportionate number of Cabinet Office civil servants. As well, many Treasury officials have worked on secondment either in No. 10 or the Cabinet Office. Of course, many respondents working in the Civil Service Department at the time of the interviews started their careers in the Treasury, before CSD split off.

As we might fully expect, the US respondents produce the only significant proportion with experience on legislative staffs (15 v 0 and 3 per cent for the United Kingdom and Canada, respectively). Quasi-official agencies do not contribute large percentages in any of our countries. However, the United States and Canada – especially the latter – make considerable room in central agencies for those with experience in independent agencies (14 and 21 v 0 per cent for Britain). The Americans as a group claim less experience in operational departments (34 v 68 and 50 per cent for the British and Canadians). In keeping with their longer tenure in government, the British respondents report having had many more positions in government than do their opposite numbers in the United States and Canada. In this regard, the latter two groups generate virtually identical figures.

With respect to American career officials, amphibians, and politicos, the latter two groups have spent much less time in government and in their departments and have held fewer posts than has the former. Since such findings fit completely what we might expect, we will not dwell on them. As well, the locations of US respondents' previous posts in government reveal that career officials have passed through the most diversified experiences in departments and agencies. Politicos come with disproportionately more experience on congressional staffs. However, responses to our question on when officials decided on government careers yield one interesting result. Although the figure falls short of significance, a

TABLE 12.3
Career paths

Variable	United States (career, amphibians, politicos) $N = 132$ (69, 38, 25)	United Kingdom $N = 41$	Canada $N = 92$	Significance
Decision to enter federal/central government was taken				
Early – before university	12 (13, 5, 20)	12	5	
After university, military service	50 (64, 29, 44)[b]	49	24	a
In mid-career	38 (23, 66, 36)[a]	34	69	a
Number of years in federal government				
One–five	38 (9, 68, 72)[a]	15	21	b
Six–ten	14 (13, 13, 16)	2	36	a
Eleven–twenty	28 (45, 11, 12)[a]	46	28	
Twenty-one or more	20 (33, 8, 0)[a]	37	15	c
Number of years in present department				
Three or fewer	60 (30, 86, 100)[a]	42	44	b
Four–nine	15 (23, 11, 0)[b]	34	45	a
Ten or more	25 (47, 3, 0)[a]	24	11	b
Previous positions in federal government				
Another central agency	17 (26, 11, 0)[b]	51	19	a
Legislative staff	15 (7, 13, 40)[a]	0	3	a
Quasi-official agency	5 (1, 11, 4)	10	4	
Line department/agency	42 (57, 32, 20)[b]	68	61	b
Reported to minister/ secretary	34 (45, 26, 16)[c]	68	50	a
Independent agency, Crown corporation, etc.	14 (19, 8, 12)	0	21	b
Number of previous positions in federal government				
One or more	69 (73, 66, 64)	81	67	
Two or more	37 (42, 40, 20)	68	38	b
Three or more	15 (19, 13, 8)	59	16	a
Four or more	8 (8, 5, 8)	22	7	b
No previous position	31 (28, 34, 36)	20	32	
Positions outside the federal government				
The professions	24 (16, 29, 36)	10	27	

TABLE 12.3 (continued)

Variable	United States (career, amphibians, politicos) $N = 132$ (69, 38, 25)	United Kingdom $N = 41$	Canada $N = 92$	Significance
Private corporations, business	15 (13, 16, 20)	10	16	
Education	29 (23, 56, 8)[a]	29	25	
Elsewhere in the public sector	25 (26, 26, 20)	17	34	
Other non-profit	21 (12, 37, 24)[b]	5	4	a
Politics	17 (0, 8, 76)[a]	2	1	a
Position(s) outside interrupted federal/central government career	37 (26, 50, 48)[c]	17	7	a

For a, b, and c see notes to Table 12.1.

considerably greater proportion of politicos than the others decided on government careers before entering university (20 *v* 13 and 5 per cent for career officials and amphibians). Perhaps American youths become aware of the possibility of a career in politics earlier than they consider the prospect of becoming a public servant.

The amphibians provide an exceptional profile in that they generated the smallest proportions of US respondents who decided upon their careers before university or after completing college and military obligations. In addition, they contribute by far the largest percentage of officials who saw the potential of government service in mid-career (66 *v* 23 and 36 per cent for career officials and politicos). The profile of their adoption of careers comes very close to that of the Canadians. In this light, we should keep in mind that they, like their neighbours to the north, tend to enter government fairly late in life and with vaguer orientations toward public service as such and/or political life. Further, they stress the contribution that work in government will make toward their personal development and satisfaction.

SOCIODEMOGRAPHIC BACKGROUNDS

Two issues emerge from a consideration of the sociodemographic backgrounds of public servants. First, are their family backgrounds reasonably in line with those of the population generally? Second, what do respondents' accounts of what they did before entering the public service tell us about their preparation for this type of career?

Recent studies have taught us a great deal about the backgrounds of public servants in advanced liberal democracies. For instance, Ezra Suleiman has found that the senior ranks of the French bureaucracy accommodate disproportionately large numbers of individuals with élite sociodemographic backgrounds. An overwhelming majority received part of its education in the Paris area; one-third graduated from élite Parisian lycees.[22] Once completing their high school and university education, nearly all of Suleiman's respondents passed through the exclusive, government-run, École nationale d'administration. Indeed, the ENA reveals a marked preference for graduates of élite schools and, therefore, counts few of humble socioeconomic origins among its students.[23]

Robert D. Putnam's study of top officials in Italy, Germany, and Britain presents a picture similar to that emerging from France. Senior officials in his three countries come predominantly from the middle and upper classes.[24] This applies even in the case of young respondents included in his sample because they demonstrated exceptional promise for reaching the highest levels of the public service. However, the countries differ with respect to the preferred career preparations for entrance to the uppermost ranks. Along classic Continental lines, Germany and Italy still apparently hold that law graduates enter public service with the best background for making administrative decisions. Britain, in contrast, recruits disproportionately large numbers of arts graduates who attended either Oxford or Cambridge.

In the United States, early work by Stanley, Mann, and Doig examined the sociodemographic backgrounds of senior officials in the federal government. These bureaucrats very often hailed from large cities in the east and were mostly well educated, white, Anglo-Saxon and Protestant.[25] In a more recent study, Joel D. Aberbach and Bert A. Rockman looked separately at US appointees and career officials. They came up with the finding that the former come to Washington with higher-status family backgrounds and greater exposure to prestigious universities.[26] However, a disproportionately high number of both appointees and career officials claim hometowns in the Washington-New York corridor.[27] With respect to career preparation, appointees clearly favoured law while career officials stressed studies in social or management sciences.[28]

Canadian studies provide us several snapshots reflecting changes in recruitment to the public service since the early 1950s. John Porter's analysis of 1953 data indicated that senior officials in Ottawa claim family ties to the country's dominant social groups, including leaders in the business community.[29] As well, they counted among their ranks relatively small proportions of French-Canadians, non-Anglican Protestants, and Catholics. P.J. Chartrand and K.L. Pond surveyed virtually every senior Ottawa official in 1967.[30] Their results demolished one myth that, none the less, still maintains an honoured place in folklore about Canada's mandarins. They found that Queen's University in Kingston, Ontario, does not serve as a conduit for the nation's best and brightest gaining access to top positions. In fact, the universities of Toronto, Manitoba, British Columbia, and Alberta, in that order, sent the four largest contingents of the authors' officials. Queen's took fifth place. Finally, Robert Presthus and William Monopoli, while reporting 1968 data, note that fully 40 per cent of senior public servants in Ottawa grew up in upper-middle-class homes.[31] By way of contrast with US counterparts, however, they tend somewhat more to have done their advanced studies in humanities and the natural sciences.

The various studies cited above, albeit not based on central agents alone, suggest three possible avenues for comparative inquiry in this present study. First, individuals with modest socioeconomic backgrounds might experience less difficulty rising to the senior ranks of central agencies in the United States and Canada than in the United Kingdom. Second, central agents in Canada might hail much more than those in the other two countries from 'hinterland' regions. Third, the two North American groups might provide many more spaces for officials who studied the social, management, and natural sciences than does the United Kingdom.

Social Background

Here we should examine our central agents' ages, sex, fathers' occupations and education, religious background, and ethnicity. See Tables 12.4 and 12.5. With reference first to age, two especially notable, though not statistically significant, findings come to light. If we divide our respondents into four age groups including the under-35s, the 35–44s, the 45–54s and those 55 and older, we find the Americans contribute proportionately more to the first age group while the British provide the largest percentage in the oldest. These findings hark back to our previous observations about the relative youthfulness of US appointees and the comparatively long tenure of career officials in the United Kingdom.

Unfortunately, differences in respondents' sex do not offer much basis for discussion. All three samples carry very small female complements (10 per cent for the United States and Britain and 7 per cent for Canada). Clearly, the canons for recruitment of central agents in our countries have made very poor provision for female aspirants.

TABLE 12.4
Social background

Characteristic	United States (career, amphibians, politicos) $N = 132$ (69, 38, 25)	United Kingdom $N = 41$	Canada $N = 92$	Significance
Respondent's age				
Under 35	17 (4, 24, 40)[a]	10	11	
35–44	47 (41, 53, 56)	41	42	
45–54	24 (38, 13, 4)[a]	29	39	
55 or older	12 (17, 10, 0)	20	8	
Female respondents	10 (6, 21, 4)[c]	10	7	
Origin				
Rural	18 (19, 13, 24)	5	7	b
Hometown is a national metropolis	21 (10, 37, 28)[b]	29	30	
Hometown is a national metropolis and/or the political capital	25 (16, 37, 32)[c]	29	36	
Region (see Table 12.5)				
Father's occupation				
Professional-technical	30 (26, 34, 32)	17	28	
Manager/administrator	28 (22, 29, 44)	59	36	b
White-collar (neither of above)	11 (10, 13, 8)	10	15	
Blue-collar (including farm workers)	23 (29, 18, 12)	12	14	
Farmer	5 (7, 5, 0)	0	5	
Father's education				
Some graduate education	28 (25, 32, 32)	5	22	b
Graduate degree	26 (20, 32, 32)	5	22	c
Some post-secondary	25 (23, 29, 24)	22	17	
Undergraduate degree	12 (10, 13, 16)	10	8	
Some secondary school	35 (36, 34, 32)	61	47	b
Finished secondary school	24 (22, 24, 28)	39	14	b
Some primary school	9 (15, 2, 4)	7	12	
Religious preference				
Catholic	24 (30, 16, 16)	10	36	b
Protestant	43 (45, 37, 48)	63	40	b
Jewish	22 (16, 34, 20)	0	7	a
None	11 (9, 13, 12)	24	17	
Atheist, agnostic	1 (1, 0, 0)	7	2	b

TABLE 12.4 (continued)

Characteristic	United States (career, amphibians, politicos) $N = 132$ (69, 38, 25)	United Kingdom $N = 41$	Canada $N = 92$	Significance
Respondent practises his/her religion	28 (36, 21, 16)	24	72	a
Ethnic origins				
Non-caucasian	6 (4, 8, 8)	0	1	
Jewish	19 (15, 24, 24)	5	9	c
English (including 'Wasp')	34 (33, 32, 40)	78	41	a
Irish	30 (38, 18, 28)	17	25	
Scottish	17 (25, 8, 8)^c	20	33	c
Welsh	1 (1, 0, 0)	12	0	a
European continent	53 (51, 61, 48)	12	36	a
French	4 (3, 5, 4)	0	24	a

For a, b, and c see notes to Table 12.1.

In examining data about respondents' town of origin we may focus on two issues. Did officials grow up in a rural area or in a national metropolis and/or the capital city? What region of the country did they hail from? Here Americans told us of rural origins somewhat more than did the British and Canadians (18 per cent v 5 and 7 per cent). Cities qualify as a national metropolis if they operate as the major financial and commercial centres within their country. Thus, New York City, Chicago, Los Angeles, and Houston rate national-metropolis standing in the United States, London in the United Kingdom, and Toronto, Montreal, and Vancouver in Canada. We find that 29 and 30 per cent of our British and Canadian respondents, respectively, claim roots in these centres, while only 21 per cent of Americans do so. The addition of officials from Washington, DC, and Ottawa neither substantially decreases nor increases the gap between the two samples. The Americans thus appear more rural and less metropolitan in origin than both the British and Canadians.

The proportions from various regions of our countries suggest considerable unevenness in this aspect of central agents' backgrounds. Nearly a quarter of US respondents (24 per cent) told us that the mid-Atlantic region was their home. Those from east-north-central states and New England follow a fair distance behind with, respectively, 17 and 14 per cent. Complements from other regions fall far short of these proportions. The mountain states make the poorest showing, with only two respondents. The 11 per cent of officials hailing from the south appears somewhat short of what we might have expected from the Carter

TABLE 12.5
Respondent's origin by region (percentages)

United States (N = 132)		(*career, amphibians, politicos*)
New England	14	(17, 5, 20)
Mid-Atlantic	24	(23, 37, 8)[c]
East north central	17	(19, 21, 4)
West north central	7	(7, 5, 8)
South	11	(7, 5, 28)[b]
Border	8	(12, 0, 12)
Mountain	2	(3, 0, 0)
Pacific and external	9	(3, 13, 20)[c]
United Kingdom (N = 41)		
South-west	5	
South-east	51	
London	29	
excluding London	22	
Wales and Monmouth	2	
West Midlands		
East Midlands	5	
East Anglia		
North-west	12	
Yorkshire and		
Humberside	5	
Northern		
Scotland	10	
Northern Ireland	2	
Canada (N = 92)		
Atlantic provinces	4	
Central Canada	53	
Quebec	14	
Ontario	39	
Western provinces	22	
British Columbia	8	
Prairies	14	

For b and c see notes to Table 12.1.

administration. In the United Kingdom, London and its suburbs clearly dominate the sample with 29 per cent. South-east England, excluding London, adds 22 per cent to bring the entire south-eastern complement to 51 per cent. Other British regions trail a considerable distance behind. Here the north-west and Scotland try the hardest by contributing, respectively, 5 and 4 of our 41 respondents. Meanwhile, Canadian recruitment to central agencies suggests a clear bias within central Canada toward Ontario. The 39 per cent of respondents from Ontario exceeds by far the 14 per cent from Quebec. With respect to the western and maritime hinterlands, the former holds its own by providing 22 per cent of all officials; the Maritimes contribute a pathetic 4 per cent. In sum, all of our countries appear to recruit central agents disproportionately from heavily populated areas close to the capital.

With respect to father's occupation, larger proportions of Americans and Canadians than British officials said that their fathers worked at professional or technical occupations (30 and 28 per cent v 17 per cent, respectively). A wider gap appears when we look at the percentages reporting that their fathers were managers and administrators. Here the United Kingdom provides a vastly disproportionate 59 per cent, while the United States and Canada contribute only 28 and 36 per cent. Fairly low figures, between 10 and 15 per cent, appear under white-collar occupations short of the professional-technical and manager-administrator groups. However, differences widen once again for blue-collar occupations. Twenty-three per cent of us officials say their fathers worked in this sector while only 12 and 14 per cent of British and Canadian respondents claim similar pasts.

The varied nature of these data strikes some familiar themes. The relative rarity of graduate and professional education in the United Kingdom probably preordained that relatively few of our respondents would report that their fathers were professionals or senior technicians. However, successful businessmen, whether they went to university or not, would find themselves in a better position than others to send their children to the quality secondary schools that serve as preparations for Oxford and Cambridge. Although the greater accessibility of us central agencies to the offspring of blue-collar workers falls short of statistical significance, it does clearly echo one of the dominant motifs of the 'American dream.'

Turning to the education of the fathers of our respondents, we see immediately why the British sample provided such a low proportion of respondents whose fathers worked in professional and technical fields. Roughly the same proportions of respondents in each country say their fathers terminated their education with an undergraduate degree (12, 10, and 8 per cent for the United States, Canada, and the United Kingdom, respectively). However, both the Americans and Canadians provide much larger percentages whose fathers completed graduate and professional degrees (26 and 22 v 5). Relatedly, British officials swell the ranks of those whose fathers only advanced as far as secondary school (61 v 35 and 47 per cent for the United States and Canada). None of our samples provides a substantial proportion of respondents whose fathers left school during or after completing the primary level.

The religious backgrounds of central agents suggest that the American and Canadian systems allow for greater diversity. In the United States, Catholics receive representation in central agencies (24 per cent) roughly proportional to their numbers in the population generally. In Canada, where they account for nearly 50 per cent of the population, Catholics comprise a delegation (36 per cent) somewhat short of this figure. None the less, this marks a considerable improvement over Porter's 1953 figures. The United Kingdom provided only four Catholic central agents. Canada produced a proportion of officials from the Jewish faith (7 per cent) approximately that in the population, and the Americans provided an exceptionally large percentage (22 per cent). Remarkably, the United Kingdom provided no respondents claiming ties with the Jewish religion.

The healthy proportions of Catholic and Jewish respondents in the US sample are significant. To be sure, US regions sending the largest proportions of respondents also claim large Catholic and Jewish populations. However, the fact remains that top law firms, financial houses, and corporations have not always welcomed Catholics and Jews with open arms. Some of the older Catholic and Jewish respondents did not mince words when broaching the topic. They said that they joined the public service because it offered a career in which their religion would not be held against them. Although we now live in a more enlightened era, government held out the possibility of careers relatively unencumbered by religious prejudice for young professionals beginning work in the 1950s.

We had best proceed country by country when viewing respondents' ethnicity. The largest proportion of US respondents claim at least some ancestors from continental Europe (53 per cent). This figure places in serious question the conventional view of WASP dominance in the United States . The senior ranks of the public service, at any rate, have provided considerable access to the most recent Caucasian immigrant groups. This observation applies as well for individuals of Irish descent. The complement tracing links to Ireland falls only four percentage points short of that claiming some English heritage (30 v 34 per cent). As we might fully expect, the vast majority of respondents in the United Kingdom told us they had English roots (78 per cent). The proportions of United Kingdom respondents claiming Irish, Scottish, and Welsh backgrounds all exceed by far those of British officials who grew up in the three regions in which these groups concentrate. Canada differs from the United States in a number of respects. Most important, French-Canadians appear to account for most of the officials with continental European ethnic origins. This perhaps reflects the fact that non-French immigration from continental Europe started later in Canada than in the United States. As well, we found a healthy contingent of Scots in Canadian central agencies (33 *v* 17 and 20 per cent in the United States and the United Kingdom, respectively). This probably stems from the fact that waves of Scottish immigrants entering after clearances of the Highlands supplied a major population source for British North America.

In our American groups, the amphibians and politicos find disproportionately high representation in the under-35 age group and relatively fewer respondents in the two oldest age brackets. Strangely, politicos report strong links to rural communities (24 per cent) *and* a national metropolis (28 per cent). This suggests that, in addition to the Georgians who worked with the president while he was governor, big-city natives played significant roles in the campaign. As well, amphibians appear to have benefited disproportionately from growing up in a metropolis or in the nation's capital. A look at the regions from which our groups came suggests similar themes. By far, the largest proportion of politicos fell into the southern category (28 *v* 7 and 5 per cent for career officials and amphibians). In fact, the small proportions of southerners in the other two groups lends some credence to the 'us' *v* 'them' state of mind so pervasive among the Georgians in the interviews.

The occupations of the fathers of our American respondents reveal one statistically significant finding. Politicos claim a large share of fathers who worked as managers and administrators. The fathers of career officials, more than those of the others, worked in blue-collar occupations. The results suggest two possibilities. First, the offspring of managers and administrators might learn by osmosis certain social, organizational, and entrepreneurial skills that prepare them especially well for careers as politicos. Second, the children of blue-collar workers might view careers in public service as assuring, more than others, upward mobility. When we examine our data on father's education, we find that career officials provide a considerably larger proportion of respondents whose fathers ended school at the primary level.

Finally, our American groups do not generate hugely different proportions under various religious preferences and ethnic origins. Catholics seem somewhat underrepresented among both amphibians and politicos. These figures underline the peculiar fact that Carter eschewed Catholic appointees despite their denomination's strong presence in the Democratic party. The fact that Jewish respondents appeared somewhat more in the amphibian group than in the other two perhaps derives from the relatively strong links to the south in the politico group. Among the findings regarding ethnicity, one stands out. Scots reveal a marked preference for career positions. This might reflect inherited biases toward secure careers. More probably, though, the finding takes root in the fact that respondents with working-class origins who hailed from states close to Washington very often gave their ethnic designation as 'Scots-Irish.'

Education

Any examination of the educational backgrounds of our central agents (see Table 12.6) must raise three issues at the outset. First, the United Kingdom relies very heavily on private secondary schools, ironically called 'public,' to perpetuate and replenish its ruling élite. Second, the country as well calls disproportionately often upon graduates of Oxford and Cambridge for the top positions in both public and private sectors. Third , Britain has consistently viewed with scepticism the suitability of specialists for major administrative posts. The United Kingdom's concomitant weakness for generalists has continued to give liberal arts graduates access to jobs in management which, in the United States and Canada, go increasingly to individuals with specialized degrees in the management and social sciences.

With respect to secondary education, 42 per cent of our British central agents attended private institutions. This figure outstrips the 22 and 25 per cent of US and Canadian respondents claiming similar pasts. With respect to the US and Canadian data, we should keep in mind that the large numbers of Catholic respondents who attended parochial schools in the United States and separate schools in Canada inflate our figures. Catholic schools in the United States, though mostly privately funded, are usually not socially exclusive. Canadian schools operate largely on grants from provinces and municipalities.

With respect to highest degree achieved, the British fall far behind the Americans and Canadians in that the majority ended their education with a bachelor's degree (54 *v* 23 and 28 per cent, respectively). Meanwhile, the Americans and the Canadians placed similar value on master's degrees (49 *v* 41 per cent) and doctorates (26 *v* 23 per cent) as preparations for their careers. Oxford and Cambridge enjoy the clearest dominance of their country's educational community. However, the 'Ivy League' universities in the United States and Toronto, Queen's, and McGill in Canada have long maintained reputations for providing relatively large proportions of various elements of the national élite. With respect to undergraduate education, Oxbridge leaves the US and Canadian élite schools far behind by providing fully 63 per cent of UK respondents (*v* 24 and 33 per cent). However, the figures for graduate education indicate that the role of US élite schools in their country exceeds that of their

TABLE 12.6
Respondents' education

Variable	United States (career, amphibians, politicos) N = 132 (69, 38, 25)	United Kingdom N = 41	Canada N = 92	Significance
Level of education				
Bachelor's degree	23 (23, 21, 24)	54	28	a
Master's degree	49 (48, 34, 72)[b]	17	41	b
Doctorate	26 (25, 42, 4)[b]	17	23	
Schools attended				
Private secondary	22 (20, 21, 28)	42	25	c
Elite university: graduate or undergraduate degree	47 (48, 53, 36)	71	54	c
Elite university: undergraduate	25 (23, 34, 16)	66	35	a
US university	24 (23, 32, 16)	0	1	a
British university	0 (0, 0, 0)	63	2	a
Canadian university	1 (0, 3, 0)	2	33	a
Elite university: graduate	40 (42, 45, 28)	37	28	
US university	39 (41, 45, 28)	12	11	a
British university	3 (1, 5, 4)	29	4	a
Canadian university	0 (0, 0, 0)	0	16	a
French university	1 (1, 0, 0)	0	1	
Undergraduate field of study				
Arts	84 (80, 87, 92)	83	70	c
Classics, humanities	8 (4, 13, 12)	22	15	c
Social science	64 (62, 66, 68)	68	51	
Political science	26 (17, 26, 48)[b]	5	13	b
Economics	29 (38, 29, 4)[b]	29	34	
Science, engineering	6 (9, 5, 0)	7	11	
Business	10 (12, 8, 8)	0	15	c
Graduate/professional field of study				
Professional	43 (36, 45, 60)	7	30	a
Scientific professional	3 (4, 3, 0)	0	3	
Liberal professional	41 (33, 42, 60)	7	27	a
Public administration	8 (10, 11, 0)	2	1	c
Law	20 (9, 24, 44)[a]	0	13	b
Academic	57 (62, 63, 32)[c]	42	41	c
Science	2 (4, 0, 0)	2	1	
Humanities	6 (6, 11, 0)	15	4	
Social science	51 (55, 55, 32)	27	37	b
Political science	22 (16, 29, 28)	7	8	b
Economics	29 (41, 24, 4)[b]	17	26	

For a, b, and c see notes to Table 12.1.

opposite numbers in the United Kingdom and Canada (39 v 29 and 16 per cent). Americans appear to compensate for not having done their bachelor's at an élite school by attending such an institution for their graduate work. Still, when we examine whether our respondents ever attended an élite school, regardless of whether they did so in one of the two other countries or their own, we find the British enjoyed far more exposure to this type of institution than did the Americans and the Canadians (71 v 47 and 54 per cent).

Looking at the fields in which degrees were taken, we find the Americans and British placed virtually the same emphasis on arts degrees (84 and 83 per cent), while the Canadians trail behind (70 per cent). However, the Canadians generated the largest percentages with undergraduate degrees in science and engineering and in business. Among the arts graduates, relatively large proportions of British and Canadian officials studied the classics and humanities (22 and 15 per cent v 8 per cent for the Americans). In the United Kingdom, classics still command respect as the pre-eminent field. In Quebec, before the decline of church-run colleges in the 1960s, francophones largely took their bachelor's in classics and humanities. With respect to social sciences, large proportions in each country took first degrees in economics (29 per cent for the United States and Britain, and 34 per cent for Canada). Political science nearly equals economics in the United States (26 per cent); however, it falls way behind in the United Kingdom (5 per cent) and performs relatively poorly in Canada (13 per cent). The United Kingdom figures largely stem from the dominance of the exceedingly wide-gauged degree in philosophy, politics, and economics at Oxford.

The British respondents again reveal their aversion to professional programs when we look at the advanced training of central agents. The 7 per cent of British officials who completed professional degrees proves to be a fraction of the proportions found in the United States (43 per cent) and Canada (30 per cent). Among the professions, Americans and Canadians showed a marked tendency toward law (20 and 13 per cent, respectively, v 0 for the British). As well, the operation, for several decades now, of very strong public administration programs at some American universities, such as Syracuse, has resulted in a relatively large contingent of graduates among our professionals in the US sample. Regarding advanced degrees in academic fields, the Americans tend somewhat more than the others to have completed these (57 v 42 and 41 per cent for the United Kingdom and Canada). The gap appears the greatest in social science fields, especially political science. The Americans place a fairly high value on political science which does not show up in the other countries.

Turning to our American groups, we find that a large 42 per cent of amphibians completed PHDs. This result corresponds well with the view we have developed so far of amphibians as specialists. Remarkably, a very small 4 per cent of politicos claimed PHDs. Concerning the institutions they attended, the groups do not vary greatly from one another. Politicos tended somewhat more to go to private schools. However, they received less exposure to élite universities either at the undergraduate or advanced levels. Their disproportionately frequent southern origins probably help explain the politicos' figures. Although career officials tended less than amphibians to have gone to Ivy League schools for their first degree (23 v 32 per cent), many made up for this by doing advanced work at one of these institutions (41 v 45 per cent).

Their fields of study suggest that politicos tended to prepare themselves as generalists, career officials, as experts, and amphibians, as a mix of the two. For instance, politicos strongly favoured political science for their bachelor's; career officials opted for economics; amphibians chose the two fields to virtually the same extent (26 and 29 per cent, respectively). On the graduate level, politicos preferred, in ascending order, economics (4 per cent), political science (28 per cent), and law (44 per cent). Career officials indicated the reverse: law (9 per cent), political science (16 per cent), and economics (41 per cent). With between 24 and 29 per cent having done work in each field, amphibians evenly distributed their career preparation.

CONCLUSION

The concentration of authority in the president, along with their greater exposure to outsiders, probably contributes to the fact that the Americans cite more than the others multiple objects of accountability. In resolving conflicts, the Americans differ most sharply from the others in not resorting to cabinet authority and in stressing their obligations to the chief executive. Their rationales for focusing on one or other object include by far the highest proportion of references both to professional standards and democratic values. These various findings present clear evidence that the Americans have adopted much more subjective orientations than the others. The cross-currents of the US system no doubt contribute greatly to their viewing accountability as fraught with ambiguity.

One might conclude from the above that the Americans would register less traditional career orientations than the others. In fact, they gave responses almost as Weberian as those of the Britons. They tended, certainly more than did Canadians, to see their careers in a vocational light, to stress motives of public service, and to dwell on the role of previous experience in government as equipping them for their current roles. Such results indicate that the nature of the us system, as well as the types of people staffing central agencies, fosters the Americans' relative subjectivity. This conclusion finds additional support in the fact that the Americans tended about as much as the British to have decided upon their careers at least by the time they finished university and, notwithstanding the presence of the contingents of politicos and amphibians, to boast relatively long tenure in government, their department, and their current posts.

With respect to sociodemographic backgrounds, Americans deviate from the British in a number of important ways. Indeed, the fact that the Americans' social backgrounds parallel more closely those of Canadians suggests a North American factor here. Greater social mobility on the western side of the Atlantic produces central agents more representative of the general population. The stress on graduate and professional education in the two countries serves as a partial explanation of the representativeness. Specialized training serves as a principal vehicle for social mobility in North America.

The British take a mid-point between the other groups by giving more weight, though less than the Americans, to individual conscience and professional standards than do the Canadians. Since most sociodemographic variables suggest that the British respondents are the least representative group, we can hardly attribute their a pparent openness to relatively diverse pasts. However, the British in many respects provided accounts of their career paths and orientations steeped with vocational characteristics. Thus, their openness might derive largely from a bureaucratic variant of functional obligation.

Of respondents from the three countries, Canadians have come to grips the least well with the cross-pressures of modern bureaucracy. In fact, they maintain a near-schizophrenic state. They rattle off the most traditional views about the relationship between politics and administration even though they recounted earlier the most expansive sketches of how vitally they involve themselves in cabinet decision-making. This internal contradiction finds at least a partial explanation in the relative youth, inexperience, and upward mobility of our Canadian respondents. Too many chose careers in the public service in order to advance themselves and gain proximity to power. Even if they manifested more vocational reasons for entering government, too few have served long enough to have imbibed clear norms for how to ply careers in government.

It hardly comes as a surprise that us politicos, while discussing accountability, stress more than amphibians and career officials their commitment to the president. However, their frequent mention of moral convictions and democratic values suggests a post-Watergate awareness of the dangers of blind obedience to the president. By the same token, we find little evidence that politicos suffer disproportionately highly from 'blind ambition.' Although they expressed their motives for entering government with more references to partisan and political commitments, they decided on their careers relatively early in life and tended less than the amphibians to say that the desire for secular career advancement played a large part in their choice. Politicos' backgrounds, while suggesting some characteristics that might apply independently of administrations, appear to reflect mainly peculiarities associated with Carter appointees. Disproportionately more of them came from the south, were relatively young, went to private schools but not Ivy League universities, and were Protestant or Jewish. Possible enduring qualities include father's occupation and respondent's education. The high percentage of offspring of managers and administrators among politicos might provide evidence that they inherit their entrepreneurial skills. That few of them have PhDs and that political science and law were their favourite degrees indicate that politicos rely more heavily on generalist than on specialist talents.

Consistent with what we have seen to this point, amphibians tend more than the others to focus their accountability on department heads. As well, they cite, more than politicos, professional standards as playing a role in accountability. Regarding their careers, amphibians ascribe very great importance both to sharing expertise and advancing themselves. The latter finding, along with the fact that, as a group, they bloomed later than the other two, underscores the similarities between the career orientations and paths of amphibians and Canadian respondents. The amphibians' sociodemographic backgrounds differ from those of the politicos and career officials most dramatically in the very large proportion that have PhDs. However, a PhD does not appear to be a surrogate for social standing. The amphibians do not come from humbler backgrounds than the others.

In discussing accountability, career officials place very great importance on professional standards. In their responses to questions on career orientations, they stressed more the opportunities involved in public service, debts that they owed to academic training and experience in government, and goals related to specialized fields of policy. They, of course, reported the widest and longest backgrounds in government. With respect to their sociodemographic backgrounds, apart from tending less to come from a national metropolis and/or Washington, the career officials show some signs of humbler roots. More of their fathers were blue-collar workers and/or did not go beyond primary school. However, as a group they claimed stronger connections to the Ivy League than do politicos. They favoured training in economics more than did others. They appear to be 'amphibians' who focused their studies more on the applied than the liberal social sciences and professions and decided early on that government provided the best environment in which to pursue their specialties and find stable careers.

Turning government under stress into the art of the possible

The first chapter of this book specifically appealed to the morning-after-the-election president or prime minister in many of us. It set the agenda for a detailed look at the staffing and organization of central agencies which would ask along the way, 'If I were in charge, would I have done it differently?' As one gains experience in watching chief executives and central agents, one senses more keenly what the pressures must be like in the 'cockpits' of advanced liberal democracies. Obviously, chief executives have tackled the toughest political jobs in their respective countries. For their part, central agents run departments and agencies that take on the most difficult co-ordination and control functions in government. Indeed, the evidence suggests that their jobs have become more onerous over the last decade. All three of our countries have had to make major adjustments connected with changes in global politics, have experienced grueling stagflation since the late 1960s, and have faced severe centrifugal and atomizing forces at home. Even in good times, growth in the size and complexity of government, which inevitably accompanies an expansionary period, forces upon both chief executives and central agents the task of taming seemingly unbridled energies.

Assuming that all seasons, good and bad, place those at the apex of executive-bureaucratic power under stress, this chapter sets forth the contours of an 'art of the possible' for central agencies. The treatment attempts to avoid two pitfalls to such efforts. First, realizing that stresses, chief executives, and even central agents come and go, it emphasizes general principles more than specific institutional reforms. Second, it tries to avoid enshrinement of the status quo by not dwelling excessively on the inherent intractability of some problems that central agencies face.

Thus, the various points made below reflect an effort not to come across, on the one hand, as a naïve optimist about specifics and to eschew, on the other, the fatalistic view that 'they've got it all "wrong," so we'll just have to ride this one out.' In other words, somewhere in between these extremes, we might just find an art of the possible.

In search of this, the sections that follow tackle three issues. First, given certain forces bearing on a chief executive's style of operation, what have we found in this book regarding the use he or she should make of central agencies? Second, looking more at the long-run requirements for improving control and co-ordination of bureaucracy in all advanced liberal democracies, what types of general principles should guide chief executives as they attempt to improve central agencies? Third, acknowledging the peculiar requirements of each of our countries, what types of specific reforms should chief executives in the United States, the United Kingdom, and Canada seek?

THE STATE OF AN ADMINISTRATION/GOVERNMENT

Throughout, this book has attempted to relate what we have found about the organization and operation of central agencies to the styles of chief executives. First, presidents and prime ministers might adopt a priorities-and-planning style. Here they attempt to maximize the accomplishments of their administration or government by challenging departments to come up with innovative and cross-cutting policy alternatives and by employing central agencies to help bring these together in a detailed strategy. Alternatively, they can adopt broker politics. Here they attempt to keep many important policy decisions at a lower level, ie either in departments or interdepartmental committees, and use central agencies as managing and tracking mechanisms that commit their problem-solving capacities only during crises and deadlocks. As well, chief executives might prefer administrative politics. Here they rely so much on individual cabinet members' management of their respective departments that cabinet members gain near-hegemony in their own domains. Such circumstances sharply curtail collective decision-making, thereby reducing proportionately the workload of central agencies. Finally, political leaders may choose the politics of survival. In an attempt to impose strict discipline on government, they simultaneously alter the routing of issues so that virtually every matter of importance receives vetting in central agencies and limit authority over subject areas to single units within the central-agency complex.

Earlier, we examined the various influences on the styles selected by chief executives. Three of these, secular trends, metacycles, and term-cycles, concerned the circumstances and public attitudes found in the political environment. Taken together, these factors coalesce into 'good' or 'bad' times. A fourth influence is the partisan situation of an administration or government. Both the ability of the chief executive to get what he wants from legislatures and his party's performance in recent elections and likely strength in future outings contribute the most to an assessment of his partisan situation. A fifth factor is the ex officio situation of the president or prime minister. In this regard, some variations between the United Kingdom and Canada exceeded those between the two parliamentary systems and the American system. Thus, we have watched throughout this treatment for oversimplifications that view the three countries' central agencies through Westminster and Washington lenses. A final factor is the chief executive's personality. It can play a decisive role. In fact, it can reverse the best-laid plans of an administration. For instance, chapter 2 argued that Carter spoke as if he had set out on broker politics, organized his central agency support as if he was running an administrative presidency, and used his own time as if he were immersed in priorities and planning. This book has chronicled several other instances in which chief executives have failed, largely through quirks of personality, adequately to mesh their styles with the organizational and behavioural tacks suggested by the other influences on their administration or government.

This section attempts to give some rules of thumb for how chief executives in each country should organize and employ central agencies under various circumstances. This effort once again appeals to the latent chief executive in all of us. I hope it will clarify the options available to incumbents enough to enable attentive observers to evaluate better and earlier a chief executive's performance.

When taking office, chief executives must set their minds on an appraisal of overall conditions in the political environment and their partisan situation. For our purposes, good times prevail when the government sees multiple options for creative and positive-policy making and the public generally supports expansionary efforts. Pessimism over the performance of the economy, the high costs of the desired level of national security, a stated or implied assumption that economic programs call for more attention than social services, and the unmet infrastructure requirements connected with public-service and/or national expansion might constrain the options of chief executives. Intense pressure on all or several of these fronts presents an administration or government with 'bad' times.

In the partisan realm, a majority government with a strong electoral mandate provides the best circumstance in the United Kingdom and Canada for a chief executive who plans creative ventures. Landslide victories, especially those which help his party secure both houses of Congress, can provide us presidents with a comparable power base to that of a majority government. Notwithstanding the original situation of a government or administration, losses of support among legislators and clear signs of public disaffection can, in the United Kingdom and Canada, turn a majority government into one that looks as if it will lose the next election and, in the United States, make a formerly strong president look weak. In this regard, chief executives must always scrutinize the action and measures proposed to them in terms of 'risk factors': are these likely to detract from voter support of the administration or government? If so, is there enough time left in the term to ensure that voters will have forgotten an unpopular initiative before the next election? As the time left gets shorter, the permissible risk factor for potentially unpopular positions contracts.

Allowing for differences in party platforms, a chief executive who enters office in a strong partisan situation during good times should give consideration to a priorities-and-planning style. Expectations that a strong administration or government will operate creatively normally accompany expansionary times. Here chief executives will experience considerable pressure to develop, from many shopping lists, a comprehensive program that appears to capitalize on the times.

A us president finds himself at a considerable disadvantage should he decide upon a priorities-and-planning style. Even if his party commands a majority in both houses of Congress at the outset of the administration, the ground under this position often erodes during mid-term elections. Of course, the relative absence of party discipline in the United States makes detailed legislative programs risky at best. As well, the weakness of mechanisms for collective cabinet decision-making suggests that presidents who embark on priorities and planning will find much of their time pre-empted by battles surrounding the installation of requisite organizational baggage. However, one aspect of the us institutional landscape would strengthen the position of a priorities-and-planning president. The relatively large number of partisan positions in central agencies and operational departments gives an incumbent an opportunity to assign positions according to individuals' adherence to the strategic objectives of the administration.

A president who chooses priorities and planning must recognize that, while institutionally the decision process in the United States has at best geared up for walking, he has opted for running. Thus he should content himself with a scaled-down variant of the style and devote some of the remaining effort to improving machinery. He should remember that, in a developing system of collective decision-making, he need not introduce new machinery for every central-agency function. Although he will want to further institutionalize cabinet committees and improve through appointments and organization, but not necessarily expand, secretariats operating out of the Executive Office of the President, expenditure review should function under the headship of a strong director of OMB. Otherwise, the administration will see its overall strategy dissipate in 'end-run' appeals to the president.

Regarding assignment of partisan posts, a priorities-and-planning president will find himself on a tightrope. On one hand, his chosen style demands that his appointees will follow the administration line when conflicts with departmental and agency goals arise. On the other hand, selection based too much on policy views could undermine the coalitions that helped win the election by failing to ensure that the groups that contributed significantly to the victory receive satisfactory representation. If an incumbent tends by nature to lose himself in detail, he had better double, even triple, his safeguards against taking on too many issues; such a person might reject at the outset priorities and planning as a possible style.

Under the appropriate circumstances, neither British nor Canadian prime ministers face the same obstacles to priorities and planning that US presidents experience. As a sine qua non, they would have to emerge from the election with a strong majority mandate. Granting this condition in the United Kingdom appears increasingly questionable. The emergence of the SDP-Liberal coalition appears only to add to the obstacles to a majority government emerging from the next election. As well, one finds it difficult to imagine that 'good' times, especially economic, will return to the United Kingdom in the near future. Apart from caveats from the British political environment, a British prime minister opting for priorities and planning would find viable structures, ie a cabinet committee system and secretariats, already in place. In fact, these structures might operate more effectively than those in Canada. In the United Kingdom, countervaillance emerges from a reasonably well-developed system whereby the prime minister receives advice from four principal sources: the private office and the policy unit in No. 10, the Cabinet Office, and the Central Policy Review Staff. The advice emanating from these sources reflects the backgrounds and work circumstances of their personnel more than conflicting policy-sector views. In Canada, the proliferation of autonomous cabinet secretariats exacerbates the difficulty of integrating policy by institutionalizing sectoral views.

In both the United Kingdom and Canada, appointment of partisan personnel constitutes one of the greatest challenges confronting priorities-and-planning prime ministers. British prime ministers, unlike their Canadian counterparts, will not face a politicized mandarinate. Instead, they will attempt to take charge of a notoriously wilful permanent executive-bureaucratic community. British prime ministers will find little justification for sacking Whitehall mandarins on the grounds of incompetence. However, they must take care to resocialize their career officials in the private office and to use the policy unit and the Central Policy Review Staff to highlight government priorities. As well, they should continue and extend the recent practice that allows some ministers to hire partisan advisers capable of assisting in policy battles with permanent officials.

Canadian prime ministers who choose priorities and planning will have to take much more dramatic steps. First, they must fill the bureaucratic-intelligence and partisan-advice vacuums in the Prime Minister's Office with a relatively large policy unit reporting only to the prime minister and headed by a prominent party figure. Second, they must request all deputy ministers to submit their resignations. They will want to fire some and replace them with individuals whose views correspond to those of the government. They will want to shuffle most of the others into new departments so that each will have received a fresh remit and a lesson on who is in charge. Needless to say, the leaders of parties that could conceivably form governments will have thoroughly to acquaint themselves with the performance of incumbent deputies and scout the civil service, the private sector, and academe for possible replacements long before taking power.

Although it might suit other circumstances, the broker-politics style best fits strong administrations and majority governments in 'bad' times. Most presidents will find themselves more at home with the style. Assuming only gradual improvement of structures for collective decision-making, the style corresponds with the capacity of the us presidency for comprehensive programmatic commitments. As well, it relieves presidents of pressures toward stronger emphasis on making appointments on ideological grounds than the equally important task of representing key electoral constituencies normally allows. British and Canadian prime ministers can benefit from the style as well. Putting aside the common impulse in majority governments to overplan the mandate, the style provides for more careful stewardship of time and effort toward identifying and reversing conditions most associated with the nation's 'bad times' syndrome. Under such circumstances, prime ministers will probably make less use of machinery for collective decision-making. However, units that offer alternate advice to that provided by career-dominated cabinet secretariats might, in fact, become more active under broker politics. Bad times require that partisan sensitivity and creative imagination jolt bureaucratic inertia.

Chief executives who face good times but lack a strong electoral mandate and solid support in legislatures might try to follow the broker-politics style. However, they will find it difficult to keep on course. In the United States, the necessity of bolstering alliances with electoral constituencies will necessitate political appointments more attentive to relations between patron and client than to programmatic compatibility. A lack of congressional support will solidify appointees' fiefdoms by placing them in the centre of negotiations among special interests, career officials, and the legislators. Here efforts toward collective decision-making between departments become a potential executive-bureaucratic minefield. They might consume immense amounts of time while contributing little toward meshing administration policies. On the domestic side, the president would channel his efforts most productively in areas that promote his image as an even-handed provider and capable manager. With respect to the former role, he could attempt to set new standards concerning tax burdens and government benefits and to improve the effectiveness of budget control; concerning the latter, he could take steps toward alleviating public grievances about the inefficiency of the civil service and improving probity and prudence. In foreign affairs, he perhaps will find more latitude for creativity. He should watch, however, that international brush-fires do not distract him too much from his domestic strategy.

Many of the points made above apply to prime ministers heading minority governments during good times. Although collective decision-making will remain an essential element of the policy process, prime ministers should tone down considerably the use of such mechanisms for working out programmatic strategies. In fact, intensified centrifugal pressures in the cabinet will probably lead to the proliferation of ad hoc groups designed to solve specific conflicts. These will eclipse considerably the efforts of standing committees to co-ordinate policy sectors. As well, the circumstances of minority government suggest that prime ministers exercise caution in improving the partisan advisory system. This applies especially to Canadian prime ministers. They face a paradox: while they must take great strides in this direction in order to get control of the bureaucracy, the prevalent 'myth sphere' still holds that the permanent public service is non-political. However, they probably would remain within the bounds of perceived legitimacy simply by improving partisan advice in PMO, firing the deputy ministers most strongly associated with the previous government, and shuffling most of the others.

Weak administrations and governments in bad times usually call for survival politics at some stage. Since presidents do not have to maintain the confidence of Congress to remain in office, they can delay adoption of the style until preparation for the next election forces them to move into it gradually. In all systems, survival politics stretches the authority of chief executives to the point where they will have to violate conventions in some areas. For instance, chief executives following the style will probably use central agencies severely to circumscribe departmental authority and collective decision-making. As well, they will choose appointees more blatantly on the grounds of compatible policy stances and act more quickly to purge malcontents whenever dissension arises. The greatest error a chief executive can make is to employ the style when the circumstances do not warrant. Voters in all three countries still maintain a keen eye for 'imperial' styles.

SOME GUIDING PRINCIPLES FOR THE DEVELOPMENT OF CENTRAL AGENCIES

Here we start with some principles that apply to the most essential role of central agencies. This, of course, involves the setting of priorities and ensuring that substantive decisions adhere to these. At the beginning of an administration or government, the performance of these functions requires that chief executives share with their cabinets the responsibility for developing priorities and plans. The concentration of executive authority in their office does not exempt US presidents from this principle. If anything, they must work even harder to assure that their priorities and plans build upon workable points of consensus in the administration. During the course of US administrations or British and Canadian governments, collective decision-making again must come into play. It contributes to the executive-bureaucratic processes through efforts to keep the original consensus in sight, facilitate periodic adjustments as events require, and ensure that major positions and initiatives reflect priorities and plans. Once again, the United States cannot exempt itself from collective decision-making on the grounds of the pervasiveness of presidential authority. Too many conflicts arise between 'wretched' departments. The president can resolve only a fraction of these himself.

Even though instrumental reasons rather than constitutional convention undergird the utility of collective decision-making, presidents stand to benefit from the institutionalization of processes that permit secretaries to resolve between themselves as many disputes as possible.

Assuming that chief executives and cabinets adopt the suggested approach and develop units that can deflect some of the pressures toward centralization of authority, collective decision-making must be able to call upon secretariats. Such organizations help manage the caseload, distil advice to the chief executive and/or the cabinet, and monitor departments' adherence to decisions. Sufficient numbers of competent professionals should staff secretariats. To a degree, hierarchical organization must come into play to assure that sub-functions within secretariats become sufficiently delineated from one another. A policy-secretariat complex must strike a creative balance between public-service, professional, and partisan criteria for selection of staff. For instance, in the United Kingdom a public-service component lends detailed knowledge of bureaucratic minefields; professional expertise, as found in some Central Policy Review Staff members, contributes the specialized analytical skills necessary to assess the relative merits of departmental positions; and the presence of some advisers with partisan experience, as in No. 10, can keep the others thinking about the political and electoral consequences of various proposals.

We might want to retreat to agnosticism on how exactly to obtain the proper mix between these criteria. Some secretariats might be able to achieve an effective balance by taking on officials who as individuals possess a blend of the criteria. The National Security Council under Carter included some advisers with experience in government, widely recognized professional standing, and exposure to partisan politics. James Callaghan's policy unit, though not strictly speaking a secretariat, traded on its members' professional and partisan credentials. However, units within umbrella organizations might deliberately reflect different orientations. Here the Central Policy Review Staff, with its half-and-half mix of career officials and experts with political experience, achieves a productive internal countervaillance. Also, chief executives should watch very carefully the ecological balance provided by the organizations within which policy secretariats must operate. For instance, Canada's PMO runs so overwhelmingly as a switchboard for political affairs that it usually swamps resident policy advisers in 'fire-fighting.'

As for development and co-ordination of economic and fiscal policies, all of our countries have wisely separated policy and operational functions within this field. However, the US Treasury fulfils this requirement less well than the others by serving as a remote 'holding company' for several operational agencies. Although this arrangement maintains links to the 'sharp end' of policies, it adds to the clutter of a very large department and detracts from the clarity of its standing among central agencies.

An optimalist would argue that one department should house all key functions concerned with economic and fiscal policies. Such an arrangement would enable top advisers to settle, in house, issues arising from this extremely sensitive field. However, the optimalist view relies on two conditions rarely found in liberal democracies. An élitist political system would ensure acceptance of government economic policy with little effective dissent; the head of an omnibus economics department would maintain a direct and private advisory role regarding the economic policies that the chief executive adopts and/or puts before the cabinet. Among our countries, only the British system even remotely approximates these conditions. We must view HM Treasury's hegemony over economics and fiscal policy in this light.

Short even of a near-optimal situation, systems can do a great deal to improve the performance of central agencies involved with economic and fiscal policies. Here much depends upon the degree to which chief executives and/or cabinets choose to involve themselves in the field. In the United States, presidents' increasing interest has led to the proliferation of units in the Executive Office of the President that operate in the sector. In Canada, strains on the exclusivity of the minister of finance's relation to the prime minister have contributed to marked expansion of economics and fiscal policy units in both cabinet secretariats and operational departments.

The confusion of authority resulting from greater intervention by the chief executive and/or the cabinet in this field requires some institutional safeguards against disarray. One department should take a clear lead. Its head should chair the most critical committees and obtain clear designation as the chief executive's principal economic adviser. Here the US practice of simply designating the secretary of the treasury as the administration's economics 'spokesman' means precious little if he lacks special standing among competing agencies and preferential access to the president. As well, cabinet-level bodies attempting collective decision-making in this field should include only the most vital departments and agencies. Committees should operate with well-staffed and clearly delineated secretariats.

Turning to agencies involved in setting and applying policies concerning allocation and management of resources, units responsible for these policies, even the most vital, need not operate out of an omnibus economic department such as HM Treasury. So long as such a department maintains the lead in setting the fiscal framework, it does not have to guard jealously control of spending. Where the allocation function lies does not influence the effectiveness of expenditure review as much as the impact of policies designed to improve management. The latter rely in very large part on adequate demarcation of allocation and management from economic and fiscal policies. Management issues will simply float around in limbo if addressed in a department overwhelmingly concerned with economic and fiscal policies. They simply do not constitute a large enough portion of the budget, let alone a major segment of overall economic strategies. Keeping control over the fiscal framework in an omnibus department such as HM Treasury would ensure that the genuinely macro-elements of spending relate to the use of other economic instruments. Splitting off detailed expenditure review and brigading it with units responsible for management policy would give a context to the latter that it simply lacks when not directly connected to some specific part of expenditure review.

Creation of a department housing both allocation and management will fail unless two precautions are taken. First, the department must command respect within the executive-bureaucratic community. Its head must belong to the cabinet, it must maintain a relatively large complement of senior staff, and it must develop a departmental ethos. The latter condition requires that the department's staff consists for the most part of long-standing members rather than individuals on secondment from elsewhere in government. Even a recent internal study by HM Treasury recognized this point. It faults the department's generalists who serve stints in expenditure review divisions for lacking even fundamental training in financial management. Second, the agency must enforce its policies as much as possible through bilateral discussions with departments. However, it cannot afford to be impetuous. It must have received clear mandates through expenditure guidelines. If, as with the Public Expenditure Survey Committee in the United Kingdom, it can develop points of broad consensus with operational departments, this will contribute to its success. When bilateral discussions break down, the department should resort to the chief executive or the entire cabinet only in rare exceptions. Thus, committees of ministers should resolve most deadlocks. However, these should include some members with unquestioned standing in the cabinet.

Finally, regarding management policy (including effectiveness and efficiency and personnel), units in allocation and management departments handling these areas should have their own 'sign-off' power. Units responsible for allocation should not approve plans for departmental expenditure until those reviewing policies on management and personnel have assessed the performance of departments in these areas.

SOME FURTHER PRESCRIPTIONS FOR EACH COUNTRY

As the reader has probably already concluded, the various guiding principles for the operation of central agencies apply differently in the three countries. This section highlights this fact by focusing on how the principles relate to more specific issues arising from the structure and operation of central agencies in each system.

Jimmy Carter and Ronald Reagan both expressed a desire to accomplish a higher level of 'cabinet government.' Although Reagan's view of the concept follows much more than did Carter's the principle of collective decision-making, neither president appears fully to have understood the implications of the notion or effectively to have followed through by taking the steps necessary to institute it on the practical level. The very centrality of the theme to the stylistic plans for both administrations, along with Nixon's and Ford's practical efforts in the same direction, suggests, however, that the Americans have started out on an evolutionary process that might ultimately result in a much more conscious and concerted use of collective authority. Assuming that Americans will gradually adopt cabinet government more fully, in an instrumental sense, we may derive from this current study some relatively clear pointers about how best to proceed. Most obviously, cabinet committees must develop much sharper institutional forms. Initially, Reagan's creation of 'councils' appeared to satisfy our requirement much more than Carter's reluctance to delineate cabinet groups. As well, cabinet committees must be able to draw upon adequately staffed and functionally differentiated secretariats. Under Carter, various committees stemming from the National Secuity Council benefited from the relative effectiveness of the NSC staff. On the domestic side, Reagan's Policy Development Office, although better organized than Carter's Domestic Policy Staff, has erred on the side of leanness and inexperience in its complement.

This book has already stressed the degree to which more effective use of mechanisms for collective decision-making would improve development and integration of economic and fiscal policies in the United States. Here presidents should be careful to designate one of their top economic department heads as their principal economic adviser. The expectation in the West that the cabinet member responsible for the leading department in international economics enjoy hegemony in domestic economic policy lends special weight to the argument that the secretary of the treasury assume the pre-eminent role in the United States. Having taken that step, a president will find himself in a better position to force cabinet members involved in economic issues to settle among themselves a much higher proportion of disputes. On most matters, foreign nations would take Treasury's view as final. Currently, they too often wait to see whether the department's position unravels as advisers working out of the State Department, the Executive Office of the President, and the White House take directly to the president points they lost in exchanges with Treasury. Within the administration, the secretary, as the person with day-to-day responsibility for the largest share of economic instruments, would enjoy status in the cabinet more closely proportionate to his department's potential role. As well, he would follow through more completely on his ascribed responsibility by maintaining a much more direct relationship to the president.

Within the general field of allocation and management of resources, the evidence suggests once again that too many responsibilities focus upon the president. Specifically, budget review all too often generates so many brushfire disputes that the president finds that he must intervene much more than proper stewardship of his time would allow. In part, their immense authority within the executive branch, coupled with the extreme difficulty associated with getting budgets through Congress, forces presidents to involve themselves much more in expenditure details than would prime ministers. However, presidents can reduce the pressures bearing down on them. First, those, such as Carter, who have a weakness for details should be able to recognize the need for self-discipline regarding personal involvement in budget review sessions. Second, presidents should protect themselves from appeals by placing an authoritative checkpoint between departments and the Oval Office. The Office of Management and Budget, of course, partially fulfils this function. However, the president must assign to OMB a director with sufficient prestige and ability to convey to departments the administration's priorities in expenditure and its requirements vis-à-vis restraint and enforce these in all but the most exceptional cases. Of course, even chief secretaries, the British equivalents to OMB directors, sometimes fail to hold the line against departments' attempts to 'end-run' to a higher authority. In the United States, the lack of legitimacy of collective cabinet-level decision-making suggests that a British-style second defence, a star chamber, would fail.

The poor links between budget review and efforts within an administration to improve management of physical and human resources have raised perennial concerns in the United States. The continued absence of a suitable niche for management in OMB drives home the difficulties faced by officials concerned with effectiveness- and efficiency-oriented disciplines in a department that focuses overwhelmingly on control of expenditure. Authority over issues in the expenditure budget directly related to management would provide the most effective leverage possible to the 'M' function. By the same token, the Office of Personnel Management will never realize its potential until it obtains authority over expenditure items related to personnel. Many OMB budget examiners, of course, will argue that their ongoing relations with departments during the cycle of expenditure control put them in the best position to evaluate management and personnel issues. In so far as any budget examiner should keep a weather eye open for such matters, the point made by much of the 'B' side accurately reflects its contribution. However, the evidence from respondents on the 'M' side of OMB and from OPM suggests that, with rare exceptions, the 'B' side simply does not have the time and expertise to pursue management and personnel issues positively and imaginatively.

The material on the role orientations and backgrounds of US respondents suggests that a seemingly workable balance existed during the Carter administration among politicos, amphibians, and career officials. Of course, Carter should have taken greater pains to appoint older politicos and amphibians who had more experience in Washington and were more representative of areas of the United States other than the South and the eastern seaboard. He should also have chosen more Catholics. However, relatively little in the data suggests that the appointees and career officials were incompatible. Carter's efforts to bring together some appointive positions and the vast majority of 'supergrade' career positions under the Senior Executive Service at least advanced the notion that the two types of officials worked equally on policy issues. Unfortunately, the weakness of OPM has meant that SES has not operated as effectively as it might have. The Americans simply have not been able to bring departments into line in adopting system-wide norms for management of senior personnel.

Highly institutionalized cabinet committees and secretariats have spared the British prime minister many of the difficulties faced by US presidents. Ironically, the British enshroud the operation of this relatively effective system in a veil of secrecy. They argue, of course, that detailed public information about how the cabinet decides issues might provide too much intelligence to special interest groups about which ministers and officials they should concentrate their lobbying upon. However, the conventions of secrecy probably work to the benefit of some groups. Strategically placed segments of society certainly discover through the grapevine where best to concentrate their efforts toward turning the government around to their thinking on key issues. As well, secrecy helps British civil servants working in Cabinet Office secretariats or involved in interdepartmental discussions to continue to exert a strong influence on policy while maintaining their cherished anonymity. In Canada, publication of the cabinet committee structure since June 1979 has failed to expose the process to the predicted deluge of special pleading. As well, Canada's Privy Council Office still manages to process the cabinet's business effectively despite a dramatic relaxation of its secrecy rules, both for current and former officials, since 1975.

The British receive very high points for imagination in providing the prime minister and the cabinet with countervailing views. British optimalists might question this assertion. However, when compared with Canada's Prime Minister's Office, No. 10, especially through the private office and policy unit, assures that British prime ministers receive alternate advice that often challenges the conventional wisdom served up by the cabinet secretariats and departments. As well, notwithstanding frequent derision by British commentators, the Central Policy Review Staff has survived because both prime ministers and cabinets have found it useful to maintain a unit capable of putting sand in some, albeit too few for some, Whitehall machinations. Future prime ministers will probably want to maintain the practice of establishing a special unit of partisan policy analysts in No. 10. As well, they should ensure that CPRS remains functional: prime ministers should appoint heads with unquestioned eminence in British public life. However, the incumbents should not claim exceptionally strong links with Whitehall. In addition, prime ministers should preserve the sometimes violated convention whereby CPRS consists of equal proportions of career civil servants and outsiders.

Critiques of HM Treasury that blame it for the exceptionally poor performance of the British economy over the past decade have almost become set pieces of British political analysis. Yet so many of the nation's economic difficulties stem from industrial rot that one must ask whether the Treasury has not performed as well as can be expected. Certainly, the US Department of the Treasury and Canada's Department of Finance manifest a number of defects that suggest they would not hold up better than HM Treasury if faced with decaying economies.

The Treasury labours under one illusion that introduces some serious dysfunctions to the British central-agency system. It has over the years successfully fought off efforts to create a department that would house expenditure and management policy in a single organization operating independently of the principal economic department. The Treasury has maintained that it must exercise direct control over all economic instruments. Of course, this current study has favoured the position that expenditure control can run effectively out of an autonomous department so long as the principal economic department continues to set the fiscal framework. Brigading expenditure control in a separate agency provides an additional hurdle for departments that refuse to accept the constraints imposed by the fiscal framework.

In the fall of 1981, Sir Derek Rayner finally won his lengthy campaign to return to the Treasury direct control over expenditure for pay and complementing in the civil service. Earlier, this book argues, the British system had found a workable mid-point between Treasury dominance of the entire field of expenditure control and a separate department responsible for spending and management. Through its delegated authority over expenditure related to personnel and management, the Civil Service Department since 1968 gave added clout to ancillary functions such as recruitment, personnel management, government organization, and improvement of efficiency. Under reforms adopted by Margaret Thatcher, the ancillary functions now operate under the Management and Personnel Office which, in turn, forms part of the Cabinet Office. One would find it hard to think of a less satisfactory solution to the problem of co-ordinating policies on expenditure and management. The reform does not stop at severing the direct links between the ancillary functions and control of related expenditure. In addition, it shunts its functions to a central agency, the Cabinet Office, the permanent secretary of which (the secretary of the cabinet) will doubtlessly find little time for its concerns. The assignment of a second permanent secretary to run MPO suggests that the secretary of the cabinet's involvement in its concerns will be at one remove. However, the reforms do fit Thatcher's view of administration. Just as in her economic policy, she has set herself on a course that assumes that getting the macro right will bring everything else into line. Thus, control of expenditure on the civil service almost completely eclipses positive management and personnel policy as a government priority.

With respect to the quantitative data on the role orientations and backgrounds of British central agents, we found that they claimed relatively privileged pasts. As well, they manifested the most traditional views of their careers and interacted less frequently with outsiders. However, we would be hard pressed to say that they were non-responsive. Generally, they registered very strong orientations toward public service and very keen interests in the views of outsiders. The élitist nature of recruitment and career development in the senior ranks of the civil service, however, gives some pause for thought. Sociodemographic biases, especially links to public schools and Oxbridge, along with the near exclusiveness of the administration group within the civil service, build upon British élitism and turn it into a still heartier bureaucratic variant. A society such as Britain's, which denies many capable individuals a fair chance at becoming senior civil servants, does so at the cost of perpetuating and deepening cleavages within it. One can only note with alarm that some new universities that stress 'modern' and 'technological' programs have suffered disproportionately severely from cuts by the Thatcher government. Such actions will most certainly prolong and even exacerbate the difficulties faced by non-Oxbridge graduates in gaining positions in the administration group in the civil service.

Turning to Canada, we find the most institutionalized system of cabinet committees. As well, the most highly differentiated central agencies support ministers' efforts toward collective decision-making. Thus the Canadian arrangements come much closer than the others to fulfilling the canons for institutionalized executive leadership. The major difficulties with the Canadian system appear in the nature and organization of officials' support of the prime minister and the cabinet. The access to cabinet committees enjoyed by Canadian public servants far exceeds that of their opposite numbers in the United States and the United Kingdom. This fact has led to a blurring of the distinction between the role of ministers and that of officials which presents serious constitutional difficulties. Under current practice, public servants directly confront ministers on a footing that makes them virtual colleagues. Weak and junior ministers find themselves particularly disadvantaged vis-à-vis deputy ministers. These latter, in many cases, actually boast much stronger personal ties with both the prime minister and senior members of the cabinet. Most important, such officials continue to characterize their caste as mere servants of the Crown, while they often exert greater authority over the policies they administer than do those whom they theoretically serve.

Two tacks could remedy the current abuses. The system could revert to the British practice of strictly limiting official participation on cabinet committees and buttressing the non-partisan traditions of the civil service. Alternatively, Canada might abandon the view that its most senior officials remain one step removed from ministers and hence non-political. For a softening of the tradition of neutrality, the next prime minister would appoint to posts of deputy minister, and perhaps to posts of assistant deputy ministers, clearly identified partisan figures who would automatically submit their resignations at the end of the government's term. New premiers in the provinces of Manitoba and Saskatchewan recently broke with the non-partisan convention by replacing many deputy ministers who were permanent civil servants. Both premiers believed that the mandarinate had associated itself so strongly with the previous government that it could not serve them effectively.

At several points this book has faulted the Canadian system of central agencies for becoming excessively experimental. A compulsion toward rationalization has inflated the Privy Council Office to the point where it exceeds in size equivalent resources in the United States and Britain. The same tendency has resulted, during various stressful times, in the creation of five autonomous agencies serving essentially as secretariats to cabinet committees. In some circumstances, such organizations can strengthen collective decision-making. For instance, through the late 1960s and the 1970s the autonomy of the Treasury Board Secretariat greatly strengthened the role of its cabinet committee. However, a proliferation of such bodies – they now include the Federal-Provincial Relations Office, the Office of the Comptroller General, and the ministries of state for Economic and Regional Development and for Social Development – overly fragments support to the cabinet in the very process that attempts to integrate and co-ordinate its efforts.

Despite fragmentation in the cabinet's support system, the one explicitly political operation in the centre, the Prime Minister's Office, has yet to develop units that can play sustained independent roles in critical policy decisions. This fact puts Canada considerably behind the United Kingdom. Indeed, the next Canadian prime minister could profitably look to No. 10 as a model for how to monitor bureaucracy without relying so heavily on the Privy Council Office and how to institute a workable partisan policy unit. Conceivably, an office like CPRS, although housed directly under the prime minister, could fulfil both roles in a single unit headed by an eminent public figure.

Although the Canadian system of cabinet government has facilitated the process of setting and adhering to priorities, the meshing of these with economic policies has proved much more difficult. In macroeconomic policy, especially development of the fiscal framework and preparation of the annual budget, the Department of Finance has gradually succumbed to more vetting by the cabinet and the Privy Council Office. As well, the analytic capabilities of some operational departments and of the ministries of state for Economic and Regional Development and for Social Development rival those of Finance in some fields of economics. However, Finance still benefits from the prominence of its minister and the fact that he participates in all cabinet committees considering matters with substantial economic implications.

As for policies governing the allocation and management of human and physical resources, Canada's new system of expenditure envelopes has weakened considerably the comprehensive nature of expenditure control and the links between review of spending plans and management policies. Ironically, the system sought to provide a closer connection between the expenditure guidelines established for departments by the priorities and planning committee of the cabinet and the various programmatic commitments approved by its policy committees. In the mid-1970s, so the conventional wisdom goes, the Treasury Board had become ineffective in enforcing the guidelines. Established in 1979, the system of expenditure envelopes was intended to foster, within cabinet committees, communities of self-interest. Here ministers would be willing to recommend savings in their own departments if the 'new' money stayed within a policy sector broadly related to their departments' concerns. Yet three expenditure budgets based upon the system have failed significantly to reduce aggregate expenditure. Some aberrations point up particularly well that it does not accomplish what it set out to do. For instance, the Department of Industry, Trade and Commerce took on, after the 1980 election, a mandate to steer through the cabinet a new industrial strategy. In the course of deliberations in the relevant cabinet committee, then called 'economic development,' its chairman (a senator with the title 'minister of state') and its secretariat began to appropriate the task originally assigned to Industry, Trade and Commerce. Eventually, the prime minister struck an ad hoc committee on industrial strategy, chaired by the minister of finance, to settle the points of contention between Industry, Trade and Commerce and the Ministry of State for Economic Development (MSED). In the end, the latter won more points than the former. A MSED memo calling for $1 billion more in expenditure than originally proposed by Industry, Trade and Commerce resulted.

It seems almost inevitable that the Canadians will revert to the Treasury Board system for enforcing expenditure guidelines once abundant deviations from the game theory upon which the envelope system is based penetrate the collective consciousness of the players. After all, the Treasury Board takes root in statutory provisions dating as far back as 1869. If difficulties in expenditure control proper do not speed reassessment, we might expect that incongruities between spending and management policies will become more apparent. Currently the ministries of state control most of the former; the Treasury Board Secretariat finds itself largely relegated to the latter. In the event that the Treasury Board does resume its former role, it probably will do so with a more prestigious complement of ministers. One possibility comes to mind here. The chairmen of the major policy committees along with the president could constitute the board. Such a group would perform the dual function of representing the principal spending sectors and at the same time contributing very considerable clout to the difficult task of integrating and co-ordinating government-wide expenditure control. At this writing, Trudeau has taken a step in this direction by assigning responsibility for enforcement of mandatory wage-and-price controls in the public sector to a committee chaired by the president of the Treasury Board. Members include the finance minister, the Privy Council president, and the ministers of state for economic and regional development and for social development. The committee's jurisdiction extends to review of wage and price increases in private corporations under government regulation.

Finally, the operation of personnel management in Canada begs for extensive reform. Obviously, the findings in chapter 12 suggest that, at least among the senior ranks, Canadian officials lack clear orientations toward public service as a career. As well, the data suggest that poor practices in recruitment, training, and assignment make it unlikely that significant improvements are in the offing. The dispersion of authority over personnel policy contributes greatly to the current problems. With PCO, TBS, and the Public Service Commission frequently locked in 'turf' battles over policy, even the most obvious needs remain largely unattended. For instance, several studies during the 1970s strongly advocated intensified training for potential senior executives. However, officials continue to take on major responsibilities with little or no in-house training and developmental placement. It appears then that steps must be taken to reduce conflict in this field. First, PCO should divest itself of involvement in personnel policy except for specific appointments by order-in-council and the policies governing these. Second, the Treasury Board should reassert its statutory responsibility for setting government-wide personnel policy. Above all, it alone should exert influence over departments in efforts to get them to improve recruitment and training. Third, the Public Service Commission should retreat to its statutory task, namely assisting in the operational aspects of recruitment and training and in processing grievances and appeals.

This book has treated a number of issues concerning the relation between central agencies and executive leadership in the United States, the United Kingdom, and Canada. Granting that this concluding paragraph should be the one section of the book faithful to its claim of brevity, one can only underline once more the immense stress under which central agencies operate today. In some respects, the expansionary 1960s spawned the immense growth of these institutions over the last two decades. Although the seemingly intractable nature of today's problems and increasingly volatile electorates strain central agencies beyond their design, they have stood up reasonably well. However, the task at hand does not end with attempts to turn government under stress into the art of the possible. Today's chief executives must ensure that the next generation receives a legacy in which the principle of stewardship operates much more effectively. Sensitive and intelligent improvement of collective decision-making and central agencies will greatly advance this goal. I hope this book can make a small contribution to the never-ending task.

Appendixes

I METHODS: THE INTERVIEW DATA

Throughout, this book has relied heavily on interviews with 265 senior officials in American, British, and Canadian central agencies. This brief section describes the access that was achieved in each country, the bases for selection in each national segment, and the various procedures connected with verification of transcripts, choice of materials for use in the book, and preparation of files of quantitative data.

I first took on survey research of senior civil servants during a study of central agencies in Canada with my colleague George Szablowski. We decided to attempt interviews with all 102 senior officials in Canada's central agencies. We fell ten short of this goal. Persistence played a major role in our success. At one point, our granting agency would not clear our 'approved' funds. Our referees doubted that we would gain access and, therefore, insisted that we obtain official approval of the project. Efforts to receive written sanction proved unsuccessful and closed the catch-22.

We expected that in a system enamoured of the Whitehall tradition 'No' meant 'No.' As it turned out, the deputy minister of one of our departments had advocated our case strongly but had failed to convince his colleagues. One of his staff made it known to us that if we started calls in his department we would probably find officials willing to grant interviews. Two hours on the phone provided a full diary for the next two weeks. We now took a step we had held in reserve. We used various political contacts to represent our case with the other principals. The dam broke. The same bureaucratic discipline that had appeared to doom our project to failure now contributed to a success rate beyond all expectations.

Notwithstanding the ominous reaction of initial London contacts to my Whitehall project, I expected much the same scenario as in Ottawa: once I had established myself as a reputable scholar and demonstrated my intention to proceed, my gatekeepers would grant me access. I thought one tack suggested to me – letters from the heads of all Canadian central agencies to their opposite numbers in Whitehall – a bit extreme. The fact that all these endorsements produced only a faint glimmer of hope astounded me.

Eventually, two errors on Whitehall's part provided my opening. One permanent secretary chose to deal directly with me before he knew of efforts to keep me out; another, in a written response to his Canadian opposite number, overstated the co-operation his department would give. My protests concerning the overstatement (made known to me by a helpful secretary in Ottawa) produced peace offerings from all concerned. Yet I was still far from a satisfactory sample. Gradually, I enhanced the British segment to a respectable size by requesting interviews on the 'need to know' principle: 'In my interview with Bloggs-Wilson, she told me I would have to see Harkinson to round out the picture.' Even this approach ultimately met with the verdict that I had interviewed my limit. To leave nothing untried, I then contacted directly the remaining people I wanted to see. During the first hour of my calls, I made several appointments. By the second, secretaries were referring me back to my gatekeepers. Everyone who had granted an appointment called later with an excuse for turning me down.

The Whitehall story does not end on a sour note. The interviews I did receive, forty-one altogether, proved to be better than those in the United States and Canada. I gathered that such sessions were exceptional experiences for most of my respondents. They took them very seriously and did not pressure me with time limits. Apart from their weak numbers for purpose of statistical analysis, the British interviews produced a wealth of descriptive material that contributed greatly to the book. During my subsequent visits to London, former respondents have gone to great lengths in ample sessions designed to bring me up to date with recent developments.

When I arrived in Washington for the round of interviews there, I decided that I would avoid gatekeepers at all costs. Fortunately, the Brookings Institution took me on as a guest scholar. During a Democratic administration, an outsider could not ask for a better credential. The American Jesuit mafia also helped. Many respondents or their confidential assistants had graduated from one of our high schools or universities. I selected some 145 officials, in an effort to cover adequately all functions rather than work randomly; 132 of these actually gave me interviews. I staggered my contacts so that word that 'some Canadian at Brookings is conducting a study' would not flood Pennsylvania Avenue overnight. To my knowledge, officials granted interviews on their own, without consulting gatekeepers. In rare cases, the heads of units asked if I would mind seeing deputies to whom I had not written. Generally, career officials in the United States provided interviews as helpful as those of their British counterparts. However, most political appointees work under pressures far beyond those of other respondents in the three nations. Often I found them too tired and preoccupied to give first-rate interviews.

BASES OF SELECTION

As one might conclude from the preceding, terming the three national interview segments *samples* would stretch the reality. The Canadian interviews come close to being a population: 92 of 102 senior officials in central agencies in 1976. The Canadian segment is more than adequately representative with respect to both the various agencies involved and the levels of officials. Twelve per cent of respondents were from the Prime Minister's Office, 17 from the Privy Council Office, 5 from the Federal-Provincial Relations Office, 41 from the Treasury Board Secretariat, and 24 from the Department of Finance. Three per cent were at the level of deputy minister, 22 at the level of assistant deputy minister, 16 at the level of assistant secretary, and 49 at the level of director. Ten per cent of the Canadian respondents, mostly in PMO, filled senior positions not readily comparable to these grades in the civil service.

The efforts in Whitehall to control access led to my selecting respondents with a view to covering all key functions. Once I had convinced my gatekeepers that I should speak with someone within a functional area, I did try, however, to choose individuals at different levels. I worked to assure that I had a disproportionate number of neither high- nor low-level officials. Unfortunately, the Cabinet Office limited me more sharply than the other agencies. To achieve balance, I probably should have seen at least twice the number of officials there. In the end, 17 per cent of the British respondents came from No. 10, 10 from the Cabinet Office, 17 from the Central Policy Review Staff, 34 from HM Treasury, and 22 from the Civil Service Department. Ten per cent of the British group were at the level of permanent secretary, 17 at the level of deputy secretary, 27 at the level of under-secretary, and 44 at the level of assistant secretary. I interviewed one senior principal.

Having had the British experience with selection and being faced with the vast numbers involved in US central agencies, I decided to base choice of respondents there on similar grounds. In the White House, I tried to see each assistant to the president or his deputy. If further senior-level officials worked in a unit, I would see additional persons in proportion to its size. In both Treasury and the Office of Management and Budget, I tried to see all officials in the top layers down to assistant secretaries and associate directors inclusive. Below that, I tried to cover each deputate, either by seeing its head or a person in charge of a constituent office or branch. I followed much the same approach for the Office of Personnel Management. However, there I excluded many units that clearly did not play major policy roles. I chose, thus, 14 per cent of the US segment from the White House Office, 34 per cent from OMB, 22 per cent from elsewhere in the Executive Office of the President, 27 per cent from Treasury, and 9 per cent from OPM. These officials included 8 per cent who were assistants to the president or the deputy heads of agencies; 5 per cent who were deputy assistants to the president, under-secretaries, or executive associate directors; 21 per cent who were assistant secretaries in Treasury, associate directors in OMB, or their equivalents elsewhere; 34 per cent who were deputy assistant secretaries or associate directors or their equivalents; and 21 per cent who were office directors or branch chiefs or their equivalents. A further 11 per cent fell short of these levels but merited inclusion on functional grounds.

INTERVIEW DATA

The interviews, which averaged one and a half hours, provided a wealth of material for both the descriptive sections of this book and the quantitative comparisons found in part IV. With a few small modifications, I employed the interview schedule that formed the basis of the Canadian study and appears in Appendix I of *The Superbureaucrats*.[1] In the United Kingdom and the United States, tape-recordings of all of the sessions enabled us to make verbatim transcripts of each interview. Gail Lyons verified each transcript to assure that it was accurate in every detail.

Development of parts I–III of this book relied heavily on detailed outlines of material from each interview. In essence, this amounted to indexing. After going through all the transcripts, I developed lists of topics I wished to cover in various chapters. While writing, I drew upon the outlines to assure that I brought all contrasting views to bear on points that seemed to emerge quite naturally from the transcripts. It is important to stress my use of this procedure. It means essentially that various quotations of transcript material found in the text represent a significant school of thought among my respondents. The outlines of the transcripts enabled me to scan the materials to assure that my selection of quotations reflected the interviews in a balanced fashion.

Gail Lyons shouldered most of the responsibility for coding and analysing data from the interviews. However, George Szablowski – who had her working on similar data from his study of Swiss central agents – and I spent several sessions with Lyons developing the codebook. Graduate-student research assistants coded the data. Lyons checked their work for accuracy and consistency each day. She went to especially great lengths to assure that the research assistants employed the same criteria for their coding decisions. After completion of the coding, Lyons and Donald Naulls developed the SPSS data files upon which the analysis in part IV was based. Other scholars are welcome to use these at cost.

Level below cabinet	United States*
First	WH: chief of staff, assistant to the president OMB: deputy directors T: deputy secretary OPM: director
Second	WH: deputy assistant to the president OMB: executive associate director T: under-secretary OPM: deputy director
Third	WH: director OMB: associate director T: assistant secretary OPM: associate director
Fourth	WH: special assistant OMB: *deputy associate director, assistant director* T: deputy assistant secretary OPM: *assistant director*
Fifth	WH: adviser, senior staff, etc OMB: *branch chief* T: *office director* OPM: *deputy assistant director*

*WH = White House; OMB = Office of Management and Budget; T = Treasury; OPM = Office of Personnel Management; italics indicate career positions.

United Kingdom	Canada
secretary of the cabinet	clerk of the Privy Council and secretary
permanent secretary	to the cabinet
second permanent secretary	secretary of the Treasury Board
head	comptroller general
	deputy minister
	associate deputy minister
deputy secretary	deputy secretary
	assistant deputy minister
	deputy comptroller general
under-secretary	assistant secretary
	director general
	assistant comptroller general
assistant secretary	director
principal	group chief

Notes

CHAPTER ONE: EXECUTIVE LEADERSHIP AND
CENTRAL AGENCIES

1 Colin Campbell and George J. Szablowski *The Superbureaucrats: Structure and Behaviour in Central Agencies* (Toronto 1979)
2 See Thomas A. Hockin ed *Apex of Power: The Prime Minister and Political Leadership in Canada* 2nd ed (Toronto 1977) especially 308–43. Hugh Heclo and Aaron Wildavsky *The Private Government of Public Money: Community and Policy Inside British Politics* (Berkeley 1974) discuss the pitfalls involved in viewing the prime minister's job as presidential; see 367–8.
3 For a very helpful treatment of ministerial responsibility as applied to officials, see Kenneth Kernaghan 'Power, Parliament and Public Servants in Canada: Ministerial Responsibility Re-examined' in Harold D. Clarke, Colin Campbell, F.Q. Quo, and Arthur Goddard ed *Parliament, Policy and Representation* (Toronto 1980) 124–44.
4 Colin Campbell sj 'Political Leadership in Canada: Pierre Elliott Trudeau and the Ottawa Model' in Richard Rose and Ezra Suleiman ed *Presidents and Prime Ministers* (Washington 1980) 56–61
5 George J. Szablowski 'The Optimal Policy-Making System: Implications for the Canadian Political Process' and Laurent Dubozinskis 'Rational Policymaking: Policy, Politics, and Political Science' in Hockin ed *Apex of Power* 197–228
6 Richard E. Neustadt *Presidential Power: The Politics of Leadership with Reflections of Johnson and Nixon* (New York 1976) 23
7 Norman C. Thomas 'An Inquiry into Presidential and Parliamentary

Governments' in Clarke *et al* ed *Parliament, Policy and Representation* 294

8 Stephen J. Wayne *The Legislative Presidency* (New York 1978) 216

9 Richard E. Neustadt *Presidential Power: The Politics of Leadership from FDR to Carter* (New York 1980) 212–13

10 Thomas E. Cronin *The State of the Presidency* 2nd ed (Boston 1980) 13

11 Nelson W. Polsby 'Presidential Cabinet Making: Lessons for the Political System' in Steven A. Shull and Lance T. LeLoup ed *The Presidency: Studies in Policy Making* (Brunswick, Ohio, 1979) 83–94

12 Campbell 'Political Leadership'

13 Cronin *The State of the Presidency* 18

14 Ibid

15 Ibid 15

16 Polsby 'Cabinet Making' 83, 88–90

17 Stephen Hess *Organizing the Presidency* (Washington, DC, 1976), 20–4; John H. Kessel *The Domestic Presidency: Decision-Making in the White House* (N. Scituate, Mass, 1975) 9–10

18 Hess *Organizing the Presidency* 24

19 Kessel *The Domestic Presidency* 9–10

20 I.M. Destler 'National Security Advice to the President' in Shull and LeLoup ed *The Presidency* 115

21 William Keegan and R. Pennant-Rea *Who Runs the Economy?: Control and Influence in British Economic Policy* (London 1979)

22 Leon D. Epstein 'What Happened to the British Party Model?' *American Political Science Review* 74 (March 1980) 9–22; John E. Schwarz 'Exploring a New Role in Policy Making: The British House of Commons in the 1970's' ibid 23–7

23 *The Times* 21 May 1980

24 Richard Rose *The Problem of Party Government* (Harmondsworth 1976); Heclo and Wildavsky *The Private Government*

25 Rose *Problem* 412

26 Colin Campbell SJ and Harold D. Clarke 'Editors' Introduction: The Contemporary Canadian Legislative System' *Legislative Studies Quarterly* 3 (November 1978) 529–35

27 Neustadt *FDR to Carter* 212–13

28 Richard P. Nathan *The Plot That Failed: Nixon and The Administrative Presidency* (New York 1975), especially 14–15, 70, 82. See also Polsby 'Cabinet Making' 85.

29 Neustadt *FDR to Carter* 218

30 Destler 'National Security Advice' 115

31 Hess *Organizing the Presidency* 1

32 Ibid 1, 10; Richard Rose 'The President: A Chief But Not an Executive' *Presidential Studies Quarterly* 7 (Winter 1977) 6

33 Neustadt *Johnson and Nixon* 61; *FDR to Carter* 208–10

34 Hess *Organizing the Presidency* 10–11; Rose 'The President' 8–10

35 Polsby 'Cabinet Making' 91

36 Cronin *The State of the Presidency* 16

37 Neustadt *Johnson and Nixon* 7

38 Wayne *The Legislative Presidency* 32–49

39 Rose 'The President' 15; Peter Self *Administrative Theories and Politics: An Enquiry into the Structure and Processes of Modern Government* (London 1977) 121–5

40 James David Barber *The Presidential Character: Predicting Performance in the White House* 1st ed (Englewood Cliffs, NJ, 1972) 11–13

41 Barber *The Presidential Character* 2nd ed (Englewood Cliffs, NJ, 1977) 498

42 Neustadt *Johnson and Nixon* 30

43 Ibid 27

44 Ibid; Wayne *The Legislative Presidency* 205–6; Kessel *The Domestic Presidency* 113–14

45 I first discuss this framework in 'Political Leadership.' There I acknowledge my debt to Heclo and Wildavsky, to Stephen Hess, and Richard Rose, the latter especially in 'The President.'

CHAPTER TWO: THE AMERICAN PRESIDENCY

1 Richard P. Nathan *The Plot That Failed: Nixon and the Administrative Presidency* (New York 1975) 49–51

2 Bert A. Rockman 'Constants, Cycles, Trends, and Persona in Presidential Governance: Carter's Troubles Reviewed,' a paper delivered at the annual meeting of the American Political Science Association, 31 August–3 September 1979 30

3 Richard E. Neustadt *Presidential Power: The Politics of Leadership from FDR to Carter* (New York 1980) 218

4 Stephen J. Wayne *The Legislative Presidency* (New York 1978) 216

5 Ibid 201–10

6 Dom Bonafede 'A Turning Point' *National Journal* 11 (14 July 1979) 1170

7 Dom Bonafede 'Carter Turns on the Drama – But Can He Lead?' *National Journal* 11 (28 July 1979) 1237–8

8 Dick Kirschten 'No Matter What Jordan's Title, His Goal Is Carter's Re-election' *National Journal* 12 (14 June 1980) 976

9 Bonafede 'The Fallout from Camp David – Only Minor White House Changes' *National Journal* 11 (10 November 1979) 1895

10 Bonafede 'The Fallout' 1897

11 Kirschten 'No Matter' 976

12 This assessment relies heavily on in-depth treatments of related machinery during the Reagan administration available in various issues of the *National Journal* and subsequent personal interviews with officials.

13 G. Calvin Mackenzie 'Cabinet and Subcabinet Personnel Selection in Reagan's First Year: New Variations on Some Not-So-Old Themes' and Richard P. Nathan 'The President as a Manager,' both papers presented at the annual meeting of the American Political Science Association, New York, 2–5 September 1981

14 William Greider 'The Education of David Stockman' *Atlantic Monthly* (December 1981) 27–54

CHAPTER THREE: BRITISH CABINET GOVERNMENT

1 Brian Sedgemore *The Secret Constitution: An Analysis of the Political Establishment* (London 1980) 57–65

2 Joe Haines *The Politics of Power* (London 1977) 34

3 Peter Hennessy 'Whitehall Inquiry Fails to Trap "Mole"' *The Times* 23 September 1980

4 Sedgemore *The Secret Constitution* 82

5 Ibid

6 Richard E. Neustadt *Presidential Power: The Politics of Leadership with Reflections on Johnson and Nixon* (New York 1976) 23; Norman C. Thomas 'An Inquiry into Presidential and Parliamentary Governments' in Harold D. Clarke, Colin Campbell, F.Q. Quo, and Arthur Goddard ed *Parliament, Policy and Representation* (Toronto 1980) 294; Stephen J. Wayne *The Legislative Presidency* (New York 1978) 216; Richard Rose 'Government against Sub-Governments: A European Perspective on Washington' in Richard Rose and Ezra N. Suleiman ed *Presidents and Prime Ministers* (Washington 1980) 284–347

7 Peter Hennessy 'Committee Decided Callaghan Economic Policy' *The Times* 17 March 1980

8 Peter Hennessy 'Mr. Pym Still Has Time to Make the Nuclear Options Clear' *The Times*, 22 April 1980 and 'Cabinet's Atomic Minute Restored to File' *The Times*, 21 July 1980

9 'Falkland Islands: The Origins of a War' *Economist* 19 June 1982, 38

10 Sedgemore *The Secret Constitution* 114

11 William Keegan and R. Pennant-Rea *Who Runs the Economy?: Control and Influence in British Economic Policy* (London 1979) 159–72
12 Hugh Stephenson *Mrs. Thatcher's First Year* (London 1980) 93
13 Ibid 52

CHAPTER FOUR: CANADIAN CO-ORDINATIVE MACHINERY

1 Richard Gwyn *The Northern Magus: Pierre Elliott Trudeau and Canadians* (Toronto 1980) 300
2 Confidential memo, Prime Minister's Office, 29 November 1974
3 Jeffrey Simpson *Discipline of Power: The Conservative Interlude and the Liberal Restoration* (Toronto 1980) 127
4 R.J. Van Loon 'Kaleidoscope in Gray: The Policy Process in Ottawa' in M. Wittington and G. Williams ed *Canadian Politics in the 1980's: Introductory Readings* (Toronto 1981) 292–312
5 Gordon Robertson 'The Changing Role of the Privy Council Office' in Paul W. Fox ed *Canada: Politics* 4th ed (Toronto 1977) 384
6 Richard D. French *How Ottawa Decides* (Toronto 1980) 27–32
7 Report to Cabinet on Constitutional Discussions, summer 1980, and Outlook for the First Ministers Conference and Beyond [known as the 'Kirby memo'], prepared by officials involved in the constitutional negotiations, under the direction of FPRO and the Department of Justice, 30 August 1980 37
8 'Kirby memo' 51–2

CHAPTER FIVE: DIFFUSE MACHINERY

1 Recently Thomas J. Reese has provided a detailed assessment of this segment of Treasury in *The Politics of Taxation* (Westport, Conn, 1980).
2 Roger B. Porter provides a detailed examination of economic policy-making under Ford in *Presedential Decision Making: The Economic Policy Board* (New York 1980).

CHAPTER SIX: THE CONGLOMERATE

1 Hugh Heclo and Aaron Wildavsky *The Private Government of Public Money: Community and Policy inside British Politics* (Berkeley 1974) chap 3
2 Richard A. Chapman *Decision Making: A Case Study of the Decision to Raise the Bank Rate in September 1957* (London 1968)

3 William Keegan and R. Pennant-Rea *Who Runs the Economy?: Control and Influence in British Economic Policy* (London 1979) 210–11

CHAPTER SEVEN: THE INCREASINGLY CROWDED FIELD

1 P.M. Pitfield, Privy Council document 1978-3803 2–3
2 David A. Good provides the most thorough treatment of Finance's role concerning tax policy in *The Politics of Anticipation: Making Canadian Federal Tax Policy* (Ottawa 1980).
3 Richard Gwyn *The Northern Magus: Pierre Elliott Trudeau and Canadians* (Toronto 1980)

PART THREE: INTRODUCTION

1 Hugh Heclo and Aaron Wildavsky *The Private Government of Public Money: Community and Policy Inside British Politics* (Berkeley 1974) chapter 6
2 Richard Rose *Managing Presidential Objectives* (New York 1976)
3 Richard P. Nathan *The Plot That Failed: Nixon and the Administrative Presidency* (New York 1975)

CHAPTER EIGHT: REVIEW AND APPROVAL

1 Colin Campbell SJ 'The President's Advisory System under Carter: From Spokes in a Wheel to Wagons in a Circle,' a paper prepared for the annual meeting of the American Political Science Association, Washington, DC, 28–31 August 1980
2 Confidential correspondence
3 Leo Pliatzky, a former second permanent secretary responsible for public expenditure, offers a view of this sector's operations in the Treasury in his *Getting and Spending: Public Expenditure, Employment and Inflation* (Oxford 1982).
4 John (now Lord) Diamond and Joel Barnett, both former chief secretaries, have provided accounts of their roles in, respectively, *Public Expenditure in Practice* (London 1975) and *Inside the Treasury* (London 1982).
5 William Keegan and R. Pennant-Rea *Who Runs the Economy?: Control and Influence in British Economic Policy* (London 1979) 202
6 Ibid 205
7 Heclo and Wildavsky *The Private Government* chapter 5
8 Richard Rose and Guy Peters *Can Government Go Bankrupt?* (New York 1978)

9 *Report of the Royal Commission on Government Organization* abridged ed 1 (Ottawa 1962) 51–7
10 *Report of the Royal Commission on Government Organization* 55
11 *Revised Statutes of Canada 1970* chapter F-10, sec 5
12 G. Bruce Doern 'The Budgetary Process and the Policy Role of the Federal Bureaucracy' in Doern and Peter Aucoin ed *The Structures of Policy-Making in Canada* (Toronto 1971) 94–5
13 Colin Campbell and George J. Szablowski *The Superbureaucrats: Structure and Behaviour in Central Agencies* (Toronto 1979) 159
14 Aaron Wildavsky *The Politics of the Budgetary Process* (Boston 1964)
15 Sandford F. Borins outlines the system and its operations in 'Ottawa's Expenditure "Envelopes": Workable Rationality at Last?' in G. Bruce Doern ed *How Ottawa Spends Your Tax Dollars: National Policy and Economic Development* (Toronto 1982) 63–86. See Doern's 'Liberal Priorities 1982: The Limits of Scheming Virtuously' 1–36, in the same volume, for an assessment of the policy outputs produced under the new system.
16 R.J. Van Loon 'Kaleidoscope in Gray: The Policy Process in Ottawa' in *Canadian Politics in the 1980's: Introductory Readings* M. Wittington and G. Williams ed (Toronto 1981)
17 'Policy and Expenditure Management System,' discussion notes provided by the Privy Council Office, 1980
18 *Guide to the Policy and Expenditure Management System* (Hull, Quebec, 1980) 18
19 Ibid 19
20 Material concerning a visit to Washington, DC, of officials studying the US budgetary process in light of proposed reforms of expenditure planning in Canada, Department of Finance, January 1980
21 Sandford F. Borins 'The Theory and Practice of Envelope Budgeting,' Faculty of Administrative Studies, York University, Toronto, Ontario, January 1980
22 Douglas G. Hartle 'Some Notes on Recent Changes in the Federal Expenditure Budgetary Structure and Process,' Department of Economics, University of Toronto, 15 January 1980, 49
23 Ibid 48
24 'Policy and Expenditure' 2

CHAPTER NINE: IMPROVING EFFECTIVENESS

1 Richard Rose *Managing Presidential Objectives* (New York 1976) 2
2 Richard P. Nathan *The Plot That Failed: Nixon and the Administrative Presidency* (New York 1975)

3 Peter Szanton *Federal Reorganization: What Have We Learned?* (Chatham, NJ, 1981)

4 *Minutes of Evidence Taken before the Treasury and Civil Service Sub-Committee* 1980

5 Richard Rose *The Problem of Party Government* (New York 1976) 382

6 Ibid 386

7 Richard A. Chapman and J.R. Greenaway *The Dynamics of Administrative Reform* (London 1980) 188

8 Ibid 77

9 John Turner *Lloyd George's Secretariat* (Cambridge 1980)

10 Peter Hennessy 'Sir Derek Asked to Stay on in Cost-Cutting Role' *The Times* 3 March 1981

11 [Sir Derek Rayner] *Minutes of Evidence* Q 991

12 Peter Hennessy 'Efficiency the Goal for Improved Civil Service Department' *The Times* 13 February 1981

13 *The Future of the Civil Service Department; Government Observations on the First Report from the Treasury and Civil Service Committee* Session 1980–81, HC 54, 6

14 Harry Rogers 'Comments on Program Evaluation in the Federal Government,' notes for an address to the Conference on Methods and Forums for the Public Evaluation of Government Spending, Ottawa, 21 October 1978, 14

15 Frank Howard 'The Bureaucrats' *Ottawa Citizen* 22 April 1981

CHAPTER TEN: PERSONNEL MANAGEMENT

1 *U.S. Code and Administrative News* 95th Congress, 2nd session at 9801

2 Stephen J. Wayne *The Legislative Presidency* (New York 1978) 182–3, 186–8

3 Richard P. Nathan *The Plot That Failed: Nixon and the Administrative Presidency* (New York 1975) 49–51

4 Dick Kirschten 'You Say You Want a Sub-Cabinet Post? Clear It with Marty, Dick, Lyn and Fred' *National Journal* 13 (4 April 1981) 546–67

5 Hugh Heclo *A Government of Strangers: Executive Politics in Washington* (Washington 1977)

6 Peter Kellner and Lord Crowther-Hunt *The Civil Servants: An Inquiry into Britain's Ruling Class* (London 1980) 107

7 *Statement by HM Treasury on the 1982 Pay Claim by the Council of Civil Service Unions* for hearings by the Civil Service Arbitration Tribunal, commencing 19 April 1982, 4

8 Ibid 2
9 Ibid 21
10 Ibid 23
11 Richard A. Chapman and J.R. Greenaway *The Dynamics of Administrative Reform* (London 1980) 15
12 Ibid 40–1. The authors cite R.J. Moore 'The Abolition of Patronage in the Indian Civil Service and the Closing of Heileybury College' *Historical Journal* 7 (1964) 550.
13 *Report of the Committee on the Selection Procedure for the Recruitment of Administrative Trainees* Civil Service Commission, London 1979, 36–7
14 Ibid 39
15 Kellner and Crowther-Hunt *The Civil Servants* 132
16 *Report on the Selection Procedure* 21
17 *Guide to the Policy and Expenditure Management System* (Hull, Quebec, 1980) 17–18
18 Audrey D. Doerr *The Machinery of Government in Canada* (Toronto 1981) 60–8
19 *Final Report of the Royal Commission on Financial Management and Accountability* (Hull, Quebec, 1979) 118–26
20 Campbell and Szablowski *The Superbureaucrats: Structure and Behaviour in Central Agencies* (Toronto 1979) chapter 4
21 P.M. Pitfield 'Business Administration and Public Administration,' The James Gillies Alumni Lecture Series, York University, Toronto, 23 November 1977, 12, 13, and 16
22 Campbell and Szablowski *The Superbureaucrats* chapter 5
23 Nicole S. Morgan *No Where to Go?* (Montreal 1981)
24 Doerr *Machinery of Government* 46 and 63
25 Colin Campbell and George J. Szablowski *The Superbureaucrats* 225–30
26 The members were, in August 1980, Edgar Gallant, Jack Manion, Harry Rogers, Gordon Osbaldeston, Bruce Rawson, Michael Kirby, Marcel Masse, Blair Seaborn, and Paul Tellier.

PART FOUR: INTRODUCTION

1 Readers seeking extensive theoretical grounding for such distinctions between types of officials should consult the 'image' typology developed in Joel D. Aberbach, Robert D. Putnam, and Bert A. Rockman *Bureaucrats and Politicians in Western Democracies* (Cambridge, Mass, 1981) chapter 1.

CHAPTER ELEVEN: MODES OF OPERATING

1 Joel D. Aberbach, Robert D. Putnam, Bert A. Rockman *Bureaucrats and Politicians in Western Democracies* (Cambridge 1981) 224
2 Colin Campbell and George J. Szablowski *The Superbureaucrats: Structure and Behaviour in Central Agencies* (Toronto 1979) 58
3 Peter Hennessy 'Dispersing Some of the Fogs of Secrecy' *The Times* 10 February 1981
4 Colin Campbell and Ted Garrard 'Bureaucracy and Legislative Democracy in Canada, the UK, the US and Switzerland: From the Turtle Syndrome to Collegiality,' a paper delivered at the 1981 annual meeting of the American Political Science Association, New York, 3–6 September, 1–2
5 Robert Putnam 'The Political Attitudes of Senior Civil Servants in Western Europe: A Preliminary Report' *British Journal of Political Science* 3 (July 1973) 277
6 Norton C. Long 'Bureaucracy and Constitutionalism' *American Political Science Review* 46 (1952) 810
7 Kenneth J. Meier and Lloyd G. Nigro 'Representative Bureaucracy and Policy Preferences: A Study in the Attitudes of Federal Executives,' a paper delivered at the 1975 annual meeting of the American Political Science Association. Work cited by Lee Sigelman and William G. Vanderbok 'Legislators, Bureaucrats, and Canadian Democracy: The Long and the Short of It' *Canadian Journal of Political Science* 10 (September 1977) 623
8 Joel D. Aberbach and Bert A. Rockman 'The Overlapping Worlds of American Federal Executives and Congressmen' *British Journal of Political Science* 7 (January 1977) 23–47
9 Roger H. Davidson 'Breaking Up Those "Cozy Triangles": An Impossible Dream?' a paper prepared for the Symposium on Legislative Reform and Public Policy, University of Nebraska, Lincoln 1979; cited by Aberbach and Rockman 'The Overlapping Worlds' 43
10 Charles H. Sisson *The Spirit of British Administration* (London 1959) 112
11 James B. Christoph 'High Civil Servants and the Politics of Consensualism in Great Britain' in Mattei Dogan ed *The Mandarins of Western Europe: The Political Role of Top Civil Servants* (New York 1975) 28
12 Robert D. Putnam 'The Political Attitudes of Senior Civil Servants in Britain, Germany, and Italy' in Dogan ed *The Mandarins* 99
13 Christoph 'High Civil Servants' 32
14 Leon D. Epstein 'What Happened to the British Party Model? *American Political Science Review* 74 (March 1980) 9–22; and John E. Schwarz

'Exploring a New Role in Policy Making: The British House of Commons in the 1970s' *American Political Science Review* 74 (March 1980) 23–37

15 Christoph 'High Civil Servants' 29

16 John Porter *The Vertical Mosaic: An Analysis of Social Class and Power in Canada* (Toronto 1965)

17 Campbell and Szablowski *The Superbureaucrats* 157

18 Robert V. Presthus and William V. Monopoli 'Bureaucracy in the United States and Canada: Social, Attitudinal, and Behavioural Variables' in Robert Presthus ed *Cross-National Perspectives: United States and Canada* (Leiden 1977) 184–6

19 Colin Campbell and George J. Szablowski 'The Centre and the Periphery: Superbureaucrats' Relations with MPs and Senators' in Harold D. Clarke et al ed *Parliament, Policy and Representation* (Toronto 1980) 99

20 George B.H. Cruickshank et al 'The Tax Legislative Process' a report to the Honourable Jean Chrétien, minister of finance, from a committee of the Canadian Tax Foundation, November 1977

21 Colin Campbell *The Canadian Senate: A Lobby from within* (Toronto 1978)

22 Campbell and Szablowski 'The Centre' 201

CHAPTER TWELVE: ACCOUNTABILITY

1 Fuller discussions of accountability, especially as related to ministerial responsibility, appear in Kenneth Kernaghan 'Responsible Public Bureaucracy: A Rationale and a Framework for Analysis' *Canadian Public Administration* 16 (1973) especially 572, 598–9, and Kernaghan 'Power, Parliament and Public Servants in Canada: Ministerial Responsibility Re-examined' in Harold D. Clarke et al ed *Parliament, Policy and Representation* (Toronto 1980) 124–44.

2 Colin Campbell and George J. Szablowski *The Superbureaucrats: Structure and Behaviour in Central Agencies* (Toronto 1979) 187–90, and Joel D. Aberbach, Robert D. Putnam, and Bert A. Rockman *Bureaucrats and Politicians in Western Democracies* (Cambridge 1981) 203–4

3 Kernaghan 'Power, Parliament' 125

4 Richard Rose 'The President: A Chief But Not an Executive' *Presidential Studies Quarterly* 7 (Winter 1977) 5–20

5 Ezra N. Suleiman *Politics, Power and Bureaucracy: The Administrative Elite* (Princeton, NJ, 1974) 13 and chapter 8

6 Ibid 222–31

7 Robert D. Putnam 'Political Attitudes of Senior Civil Servants in Western Europe: A Preliminary Report' *British Journal of Political Science* 3 (July

1973) 257–8. The author cites Richard Rose 'The Variability of Party Government: A Theoretical and Empirical Critique' *Political Studies* 17 (December 1969) 413–45, and Michael Gordon 'Civil Servants, Politicians, and Parties: Shortcomings in the British Policy Process' *Comparative Politics* 4 (October 1971) 29–58.

8 Putnam 'Political Attitudes' 277
9 Joel D. Aberbach and Bert A. Rockman 'The Overlapping Worlds of American Federal Executives and Congressmen' *British Journal of Political Science* 7 (January 1977) 34
10 Max Weber in H.H. Gerth and C. Wright Mills trans and ed *From Max Weber: Essays in Sociology* (New York 1958) 90–1
11 Ibid 232
12 Richard A. Chapman and J.R. Greenaway *The Dynamics of Administrative Reform* (London 1980) 53, 62
13 James B. Christoph 'High Civil Servants and the Politics of Consensualism in Great Britain' in Mattei Dogan ed *The Mandarins of Western Europe: The Political Role of Top Civil Servants* (New York 1975) 32–6
14 Putnam 'Political Attitudes' 268, 279
15 Suleiman *Politics, Power and Bureaucracy* 117
16 Hugh Heclo *A Government of Strangers: Executive Politics in Washington* (Washington, DC, 1977)
17 John Porter *The Vertical Mosaic: An Analysis of Social Class and Power in Canada* (Toronto 1965) 436–7
18 P.J. Chartrand and K.L. Pond *A Study of Executive Career Paths in the Public Service of Canada* (Chicago 1970) 48–9
19 Ibid 70
20 P.M. Pitfield 'Business Adminstration and Public Administration,' unpublished paper, The James Gillies Lecture Series, York University, Toronto, 23 November 1977
21 Nicole S. Morgan *No Where to Go?* (Montreal 1981)
22 Suleiman *Politics, Power and Bureaucracy* 44, 64, 68.
23 Ibid 106
24 Putnam 'Political Attitudes' 268–9
25 David T. Stanley, Dean E. Mann, and Jameson W. Doig *Men Who Govern* (Washington, DC, 1967) 78–84
26 Aberbach and Rockman 'Overlapping Worlds' 26–8
27 Ibid 31
28 Ibid 30
29 Porter *The Vertical Mosaic* 433–44
30 Chartrand and Pond *Executive Career Paths* 32, 34. See also Porter *The Vertical Mosaic* 425–8.

31 Robert Presthus and William Monopoli 'Bureaucracy in the United States and Canada: Social, Attitudinal and Behavioural Variables' in Robert Presthus ed *Cross-National Perspectives: United States and Canada* (Leiden 1977) 177–9

APPENDIX I

1 Colin Campbell and George J. Szablowski *The Superbureaucrats: Structure and Behaviour in Central Agencies* (Toronto 1979)

Index

This index lists many topics under 'central agencies,' including areas of executive leadership dealing with expenditure and economic planning and personnel management. Numbers in parentheses indicate tables.